D1064870

WORKING DETROIT

WORKING DETROIT

The Making of a Union Town

DISCARDED

STEVE BABSON

With Ron Alpern, Dave Elsila, and John Revitte

ADAMA BOOKS

New York

HD
6519
D6
B33
1984

DISCARDED

Acknowledgments

Working Detroit was researched and written by Steve Babson, with research and editorial assistance from Ron Alpern, Dave Elsila, and John Revitte. The book is a project of Detroit Labor History Tours (DLHT), a non-profit group organized by the Michigan Chapter of Workers Education Local 189. DLHT is funded in part by the **Michigan Council for the Humanities** and the **Shiffman Foundation**. Inquiries concerning DLHT's slide shows, educational materials, and guided tours should be directed to Box 758, Detroit, MI 48231.

DLHT would like to thank the following people who helped produce *Working Detroit*.

Design:
Barbara Weinberg-Barefield, with **Steve Babson** and **Nancy Brigham**.
Typesetting and paste-up:
Bill Denney, Maria Catalfio, and **Karen Gatrell**,
with **Gary Grimshaw, Bill Parker, Leni Sinclair**, and **Sun Press**.
Research:
Jane Dobija, Florence Estes, and **Jim Jacobs**.
Maps:
Gary Grimshaw.

Readers of all or part of the manuscript:
Irving Bluestone, Ray Boryczka, Bill Bryce, Nancy Brigham, Milton Cantor,
Bob Dixon, Jane Dobija, Sidney Fine, Bernie Firestone, Miriam Frank,
Ernie Goodman, Jim Jacobs, Chris Johnson, Joan Kelley, Bob Kentor, Phil Korth,
Gerry Lazarowitz, Dan Luria, Norman McRae, Doris McLaughlin, Ron Means,
David Montgomery, Pam Nelson, Jim Obst, Oscar Paskal, Leon Potok,
Richard Thomas, Seth Widgerson and Bob Zieger.
*These readers are responsible for improving the book immeasurably,
but are not accountable for its final content.*

Copyright © 1984 by Adama Books
All rights reserved

No part of this publication may be reproduced, stored in a retrieval system, or transmitted in any form or by any means, electronic, mechanical, photocopying, recording or otherwise (brief quotations used in magazines or newspaper reviews excepted), without the prior permission of the publisher.

Library of Congress Cataloging in Publication Data
Babson, Steve.
  Working Detroit.
   1. Trade-unions—Michigan—Detroit—History.
2. Labor and laboring classes—Michigan—Detroit—History.
I. Title.
HD6519.D6B33 1984   331.88'09774'34   84-11019
ISBN 0-915361-01-9

Cover: Walter Reuther leads sitdown strikers out of Cadillac plant (site 35), January, 1937.

Adama Books
306 West 38 Street
New York, New York 10018

Song Credits

Page 78, *Union Maid*. Words and music by Woodie Guthrie, TRO © Copyright 1961 and 1963 Ludlow Music, Inc., N.Y., N.Y. Used by permission.

Page 120, *Minnie's in the Money* by Harry Warren and Leo Robin. © 1943 (Renewed), WB Music Corp. All rights reserved. Used by permission.

Photo Credits

Inset = (I), Top = (T), Middle = (M), Bottom = (B)

Photos courtesy of:
AFL–CIO, Metro Detroit: 66(I), 72(I), 113, 191.
Archives of Labor and Urban Affairs, Wayne State University: vii, 32, 33, 44(T), 45(M), 54, 63, 66, 76, 79, 82–83 (#4), 85(B), 87, 88, 88(I), 94, 98, 99, 110, 112, 114, 116, 116(I), 119, 120, 122, 123, 125, 127, 140, 143, 145(I), 147, 153, 188(I), 197.
Steve Babson: 190(I), 193, 210, 212, 213(I), 220, 225, 225(I).
Bentley Historical Library, University of Michigan: 55, 56, 137.
Burton Collection, Detroit Public Library: 3, 4, 4(I), 6, 6(I), 7, 8, 9(I), 10, 10(I), 11, 12, 13, 13(I), 14, 15, 16, 16(I), 19, 19(I), 23, 23(I), 26, 27, 28, 28(I), 34, 37, 38, 39(I), 41, 42(T&B), 44(B), 45(T&B), 46, 49(T), 51, 52, 53, 64(B), 95, 102, 157, 158, 159, 159(I), 161, 169, 170, 170(I), 171.
Corktown Citizens District Council: 3(I).
Detroit Fastfood Workers: 232.
Detroit Free Press: 75, 92(#1), 139, 199(T), 211.
Detroit Historical Museum: 5, 15, 17, 43, 47, 49(B).
Detroit News: Cover, 39, 57, 58, 61, 68, 72, 73, 77, 77(I), 78, 82–83(#1&2), 84, 85(T&M), 89(I), 90(I), 107(T), 109, 118, 121, 126, 145, 151, 162, 165, 165(I), 175, 194, 195, 199(B), 202, 216.
Detroit Public Schools: 196, 233.
Bob Dixon: 167, 174, 182, 198, 229.
GM Pontiac Motors and UAW Local 653: 231.
GM Truck and Coach Public Relations and UAW Public Relations: 229.
Robert Gumpert: 219, 227.
Henry Ford Museum, the Edison Institute: 22 (Neg. #0-4542), 30 (Neg. #455), 35 (Neg. #0-5167), 36 (T, Neg. #0-5100 & B, Neg. #D-1239).
Melvin Hite: 82–83(#5).
Hotel and Restaurant Employees Local 24: 205.
International Typographical Union Local 18: 190.
Russ Marshall: 222, 235.
Norm McRae: 106(T&M), 160.
Michigan Historical Division, State Archives: 1, 2, 9, 29, 30(I), 40, 47(I), 48, 60, 64(T&M), 70, 95, 115, 133, 152.
Michigan State University Library: 140(I).
National Automotive History Collection, Detroit Public Library: 18, 20–21(#1-4), 31, 62, 65, 69, 111, 148, 224, 224(I), 226.
Richard Oestreicher: 11(I).
Polonia Restaurant: 40(I).
Service Employees International Union Local 79: 228.
Teamster Local 285: 89, 135.
United Auto Workers: 71, 75(I), 80, 81, 82–83(#3), 86, 90(B), 91, 92–93(#2-3), 94(B), 95(I), 99(I), 101, 103, 104(I), 105, 105(I), 106(B), 107(B), 129, 129(I), 130, 130(I), 131, 132,(#1-4), 133(I), 134, 134(I), 136, 141, 141(I), 144, 149, 150, 155, 163, 164, 172, 179*, 180*, 181, 182(I), 183*, 184, 186(T&B), 187, 188(T), 192, 200*, 201, 203*, 204*, 207, 213, 223, 236-237.   *Photo by Earl Dotter.
United Press International/Bettman Archive: 185.
United Steel Workers District 29: 240.
Barbara Weinberg-Barefield: 164.
Dave Welsh: 208.
Jim West: 189, 209, 214, 215, 216(I), 217, 221, 241, back cover.
Wide World Photos: 104(T).
Jim Wilson: 156, 168, 176.
Walter Zukin: 59, 67.

TABLE OF CONTENTS

Prologue: (Nineteenth Century)

Part I:
Motor City (1899-1929)

Part II:
Union Town (1929-1941)

Part III:
War and Peace (1941-1960)

Part IV:
Black Detroit (1945-1975)

Part V:
New Workers, New Work
(1960-1979)

Part VI:
At the Crossroads

INTRODUCTION

Members of the CIO's United Retail, Wholesale, and Department Store Employees, 1942.

Just as workers have shaped the physical contours of our world, so have they shaped the history of our society. The story of their lives and their labor conveys, like a prism, a whole spectrum of themes and issues in American history.

This book focuses on the labor history of Detroit, a city whose people have produced an especially rich and varied spectrum of working-class life. Detroit's workers, known in the 1920s as one of the least unionized workforces in the country, became known the following decade for their leading role in the sit-down strikes and union organizing that transformed industrial America. Workers in the Motor City have since participated in the most violent racial confrontations of the twentieth century; but their unions have also been the seedbed of the modern civil rights movement. Having launched the automobile age and the moving assembly line in the first quarter of the twentieth century, Detroit's workers find themselves once again on the cutting edge of economic change, buffeted by multinational sourcing of production, foreign competition, and new technology.

Along the way, the pace of change in Detroit has always seemed a beat faster, the tenor of its social life a pitch higher, than elsewhere. Other cities have produced vital and progressive labor movements, but few have so often led the way in national collective bargaining as have Detroit's unions, particularly the United Auto Workers. Other cities have produced distinctive working-class cultures, but few have made their city's music the emblem of an entire generation, as Motown did. Organized crime, faction fights, and Red Scares have beset unions in many cities, but in Detroit these confrontations have occurred on a scale and with a rawness not usually found in other locales.

In exploring these varied themes in Detroit's history, *Working Detroit* cannot claim to present "the whole picture." An historical account is necessarily selective, and this book, like any other history, reflects contemporary concerns and predilections.

Fifty years ago, even twenty-five years ago, few historians concerned themselves at all with the lives and labor of working people. History was usually written from the vantage point of elite groups; working people, if recognized at all, were generally portrayed as part of the scenery. Thankfully, this is no longer the case, as movements for black civil rights and women's liberation, together with the anti-war movement of the 1960s, have encouraged a new generation of historians to focus on non-elites who make their own history.

Instead of a world made only by white, Protestant men, contemporary historians have revealed a past crowded with women, immigrants, and racial minorities. Instead of "the American people," they have found a society divided in many ways between workers and owners. And instead of a world governed primarily by consensus and shared goals, they have recovered a history in which people protested against injustice and inequality.

Working Detroit draws heavily on this recent scholarship. It also relies on more than 85 interviews with Detroit-area activists from the labor and civil rights movements. Combined with information culled from local research facilities, primarily the Detroit Public Library and the Walter Reuther Library at Wayne State University, the resulting book is part labor history, part social history, and part oral history.

It is hoped that such a perspective, encompassing workers as well as elites and conflict as well as consensus, makes history a better antidote for the collective amnesia of our age. History does not, as the old saying goes, simply repeat itself. But modern societies do grapple with recurring issues of freedom, justice, and security, and by examining the experience of preceding generations, we can understand how contemporary problems—instead of being "peculiar" and entirely unique—are distinctive episodes in a cycle of social change.

Detroit's current economic crisis, for example, is unprecedented in some respects, but in other ways recalls the severe depressions of the 1870s and 1930s. Today's revolution in robotics and computerized production methods, when compared with the inauguration of the moving assembly line in 1913, reveals different technical aspects but similar social consequences—dilution of some skills, transfer of others, and implementation of a new system of shop-floor control. Likewise, the fundamentally different experiences of black and immigrant workers also contain important parallels. Detroit's Black Christian Nationalist Church recalls something of the Polish National Catholic Church. The Dodge Revolutionary Union Movement of the 1960s recalls something of the Industrial Workers of the World in pre-World War I Detroit. The massive riot of 1967 and the Trolley Riot of 1891, while significantly different in the focus and intensity of violence, both tell us something about the volatile nature of grievances too long suppressed. Even the backlash against black and immigrant groups shares a common language: George Wallace's segregationist speeches in Michigan during the 1968 elections had much the same tenor as the anti-immigrant rhetoric of the American Protective Association eighty years before.

In these and many other historical episodes, there is much that has set workers apart from and, in many cases, against each other—black against white, skilled against unskilled, men against women, native-born against foreign-born. This diversity and fragmentation suggests to some observers that instead of a "working class," there are only "interest groups" in American society. Unlike Europe, social distinctions in America are supposedly so fluid that class categories have little relevance.

In *Working Detroit*, the many issues that divide workers are recalled as crucial features of their history. It is not assumed that all workers automatically have the same "real" interests, or that those who deviate from some idealized working-class perspective are harbingers of "false consciousness." Nevertheless, this book does describe a working class composed of those who sell their labor power to survive.

Individual workers do move up (and down) the social ladder, and salaried or high-wage workers do blend into a middle class of independent professionals and small-scale entrepreneurs. But higher income does not alter the subordinate status of workers in our present industrial society. No matter what their income, workers do not control the hiring and firing of others, they do not control the investments that make or break their jobs, and they do not control the product of their work. As a result, working people tend to see the world in different ways from the owners and managers of capital, whose position at the top of the social hierarchy gives them greater individual control over their economic lives.

This is not to deny that many workers have accepted the social hierarchy, have sought to escape the working class, and have defined themselves as racially, ethnically, occupationally, or sexually distinct from other workers. These are enduring features of working-class life, but so is the countervailing tendency to seek wider solidarities. In contrast to the competitive individualism celebrated by the dominant business culture, this tendency in working-class consciousness has, at various times and in varying degrees, defined workers' interests in more collective terms. It finds expression in the belief that workers can and should improve their lives together, not as competing individuals. At certain points in history, this cooperative ethic has also led workers to question the unequal distribution of power, wealth, and opportunity in our industrial society.

Working Detroit tells the story of how these contradictory tendencies in working-class life molded one city's history. The ways that workers see themselves and define their interests is understood as an evolutionary process, shaped by the changing nature of workplace relations, the surrounding context of social and political life, and the self-defining actions that workers have taken, collectively and individually, to advance their interests.

In Detroit, these actions produced a union movement of extraordinary breadth and militancy. Just as the city's employers commanded the largest and wealthiest corporations in the country, so did Detroit's unions, particularly the UAW, set the pace for the nation's labor movement. Few places in America boasted a more self-confident, combative working class than the Motor City. Times changed, however, and economic decline significantly eroded the city's industrial base. Today, many people lament the passing of this "old" Detroit, the once crowded city of fine homes and bustling factories, now partially decayed, partially abandoned.

But the human legacy survives. Detroiters still are, as Archbishop Edmund Szoka put it, "rather feisty as a group. They like to speak up and express their opinion. But that feistiness is a sign of their great strength, their great determination to stick it out, to weather the storm, to find solutions."

PROLOGUE

Stroh Brewery workers, circa 1890.

LABOR PAINS

When Henry Ford's grandfather, John Ford, arrived in Michigan in 1848, the bustling wilderness town of Detroit must have been a welcome contrast to the Ireland Ford had known. For John Ford's homeland, unlike Detroit, was a crisis-ridden land, full of death and despair.

Ireland's "troubles" stretched back at least as far as the 1650s, when English landlords took over most of the country's good farmland. Their land seizures forced the Catholic peasantry to crowd onto marginal plots barely large enough for one-room shacks. A small class of farmers (many, like the Fords, Protestants) did rent enough acreage from the landlords to produce wheat and beef for export to England, but the overwhelming majority of poverty-stricken families lived on a diet of potatoes and milk. High rents drove even tenant farmers to the verge of bankruptcy.

Ireland's poverty increased all the more in the 1800s when the English began evicting peasants from their small plots to make way for cattle and sheep grazing. In the mid-1840s, a deadly potato blight also destroyed the peasantry's last source of available food. Disaster followed: while English landlords continued exporting beef and wheat to England, the Irish starved. Since starving peasants could not pay their rents, mass evictions became commonplace.

"There is a very prevalent feeling among the landlord class," wrote Irish revolutionary John Mitchel in 1847, "that the people of Ireland ought not to be fed upon the grain produced in this country...and that it is desirable to get rid of a couple millions of them." The combined impact of the potato famine and evictions did just that. Between 1846 and 1851, of an estimated 8½ million Irish, one million died of starvation and disease and another million were forcibly removed from their plots of land.

"I am sick of Ireland," writer John O'Donovan lamented in 1848. "I would leave it exultingly, retire among the Backwoods of America...there to learn a rude but sturdy civilization that knows not slavery or hunger." As the Irish economy collapsed, even once prosperous Protestant households like the Ford's felt the same despair, the same longing for a "sturdy civilization." In 1847, the Ford family reportedly was evicted from its farm for non-payment of rent; with no land and no future in Ireland, John Ford and his 21-year-old son William (Henry's father) gathered the family together and set out for America.

The Fords were not alone in their trek to America's backwoods. In Germany, Scotland, England, and Scandinavia, millions of people abandoned their homelands in the same years. Their reasons for leaving were similar to, if less intense than, the reasons motivating the Irish: all across northern Europe, landlords were usurping peasant lands and consolidating huge estates to produce wheat, livestock, and wool for Europe's fast-growing cities. Rapid population growth in rural areas also forced much of the "surplus" population to abandon the countryside. And all the while, the expanding cotton factories of England were underselling the hand-loom weavers who made cloth in their village workshops.

Crop failures, economic depression, and revolutionary upheavals set millions more adrift in the 1840s. They moved from one rural area to the next, from rural areas to nearby cities, and from one country to its neighbor, always in search of employment, land, and food. Between 1845 and 1854, three million people left Europe altogether and set out for America.

"Go further west," one guidebook advised its emigrant readers. "Not until you reach Koshkonong [Wisconsin] will you find America." Thousands of these pioneer settlers "found America" in the wilderness of Michigan, and, as they poured into the region, Detroit grew by leaps and bounds—from barely 2,000 residents in 1830, to over 30,000 in 1855. Two of every three Detroiters in the latter year were foreign-born, most of them German, Irish, English, French, and Scottish.

They found Detroit a hard place to live. Clearing the towering, dense forests of eastern Michigan took a heavy toll in labor, and the town's primitive sanitation caused repeated outbreaks of disease. During one cholera epidemic in 1834, 7 percent of the town's population died in one month.

Michigan was nevertheless a "land of opportunity" for most immigrant settlers, a place where hard work and individual striving would be rewarded—or so one hoped. By 1850, thousands of immigrants like the Fords had managed to clear land and cultivate farms in the area around Detroit, while many others

Detroit's dockworkers, like those pictured above, needed strong arms and few skills. Since many of the Irish arriving in Detroit during the famine years had no industrial or craft training, many took jobs as dockworkers, as "section hands" building the state's railroads, or as unskilled workers in the growing number of factories and mills along the Detroit River.

Inset: A typical home in Corktown, the Irish settlement on the West Side named after Ireland's County Cork. (See map, page 26.)

Opposite page: The Michigan Central's railroad yards, where wheat, timber, and other raw materials from Michigan's interior were transferred to ships and local processing mills.

established their own workshops or stores in the fast-growing town.

Detroit had just entered the industrial age when John Ford and his family arrived in 1848.

Michigan's ample supply of lumber, copper, and iron ore provided the resources for this budding industrialism, with railroads and shipbuilding adding to the quickening pace of economic growth in the 1840s. These early industries were, however, quite small by today's standards: the city's single largest employer, the Michigan Central Railroad, employed only 200 men in its

machine shops on West Jefferson Avenue, while hardly a dozen of the city's lumber mills, machine shops, and metal foundries employed more than 30 workers. More typical was "Wesley's Cabinet Shop" on lower Woodward Avenue, employing only ten "hands" in 1848. At Eiling and Brewer's "Candle Factory" on Fort Street near Brush, just two workers produced 50,000 pounds of candles each year. Whether wood-worker, candlemaker, shoemaker, tailor, or saddlemaker, most of Detroit's skilled "artisans" worked with hand tools in 1850, many of them in their own homes or neighboring workshops. Some became "Master" workmen, taking on

Above: Stroh Brewery workers. Brewing beer was a distinctly German trade in Detroit, as elsewhere in the United States. By 1857, 15 of the city's 23 breweries (all of them small affairs by today's standards) were located in the German wards on Detroit's East Side.

Inset: the first large-scale Stroh brewery on Gratiot (site 1).

young apprentices and hiring a few "journeymen"—skilled workers who traveled from town to town in search of work. But Master workmen continued to labor alongside their handful of hired shophands.

Detroit's store owners did sell ready-made factory goods from the East to the thousands of pioneer settlers passing through the city. But many of these storekeepers also had workshops in their back rooms, where they and several journeymen turned out shoes, clothing, or furniture, much of it custom-made to suit a buyer's wishes. When these retail merchants expanded into wholesaling

and began distributing goods to stores in outlying towns, they either sub-contracted the added work to outside craftsmen, or hired more journeymen and increased their "in-house" production.

By 1850, George and Isaac Miller had turned their tobacco store on Woodward Avenue into a small factory, where between 20 and 30 workers bunched and cut tobacco leaves in the store's attic and basement. H.P. Baldwin's Boot and Shoe Store in the same neighborhood employed 20 journeymen shoemakers, each using his hand tools and all-around shoemaking skills to fill orders for Baldwin's wholesale and retail business.

Apprentice, journeyman, Master, and merchant: it was supposedly one big family, free from the class conflict that characterized Europe and the eastern United States. Like any family, disputes did periodically erupt—as in 1837, when high inflation followed by a temporary

business slump provoked the city's first strike. "Yesterday," the *Detroit Daily Advertiser* reported on April 4 of that year, "our streets were paraded by a large company of respectable looking journeymen carpenters carrying standards bearing this pithy couplet: 'Ten Hours A Day/Two Dollars For Pay.'"

This demonstration was exceptional in a town where journeymen and employers frequently united in educational organizations like the Detroit Mechanics' Society. Founded in 1818, the Society built a large meeting hall at Griswold and Lafayette streets in 1834, and maintained a library of 4,000 books for members drawn from dozens of trades and professions. The Detroit Typographical Society, formed in 1839, was also open to both print-shop owners and journeymen printers. In an era when many journeymen hoped to settle down and become Masters of their own print shop, a separate organization for journeymen made little sense. The Society applied itself to improving trade practices, providing sickness benefits, and furthering the "moral and social improvement of its members."

Nonetheless, Detroit's skilled workers were losing their independence. Instead of selling directly to customers for full value, workers frequently turned products over to a merchant, who paid a wage and often provided production materials. Cheap "ready-made" goods became common, and custom work slowly declined. Merchants also began to hire "two-thirders"—workers who had learned only part of the craft and who worked for less money, often in their own homes. Journeymen in an employer's workshop frequently had to compete with these underpaid subcontractors.

Conflict grew. "We agreed...to the lowest possible living prices for custom work," the Committee of Journeymen Tailors protested in the fall of 1851, "believing that, under the arrangement, [we] would have seats in the shops of [our] employers." Yet employers continued to have custom work done outside their shops, "for very little more than half the established bill of prices." In desperation, the tailors announced they would refuse to work until owners agreed to "get their custom work done on their premises and pay the established bill of prices."

Similar disputes between journeymen printers and their employers rapidly transformed the Detroit Typographical Society after 1850. Workers were particularly angered by the growing number of underpaid apprentices and two-thirders hired by management to replace fully qualified journeymen. In 1853, disgruntled printers expelled the larger employers from the Society and turned it into a union, affiliating their organization with the National Typographical Union (NTU).

When Detroit's Local 18 of the NTU announced its formation that year, the city's first permanent trade union was born.

Detroit recorded many other firsts in the 1850s. Railroad connections with Chicago and the East were completed; the Detroit and Lake Superior Copper Company built the world's largest copper smelter; and the city's shipbuilders launched Detroit's first large-scale floating dry docks. In 1853, George Russell's workshops on the East Side set another precedent by turning out 25 railroad cars—the first rolling stock built west of Albany.

The pace of growth and change quickened dramatically after the outbreak of the Civil War in 1861. Detroit's tanneries, lumber mills, foundries, and shipbuilders all expanded production to meet the demand for war material. Smaller companies merged and new companies formed: the Detroit Bridge and Iron Company, the Michigan Car Company (building railroad cars), and the Detroit Stove Works. In 1863, Detroit's machine shops began building marine steam engines; in 1864, the first Bessemer steel-making furnace in America was built in nearby Wyandotte.

The wilderness town John Ford first saw at mid-century had become an industrial city, with a highly diversified and booming economy. Detroit was the biggest shipbuilder on the Great Lakes, the biggest stove maker in the United States, and the biggest copper refiner in the world. The city's population swelled proportionally, reaching 80,000 by 1870 and 116,000 by 1880.

As Detroit grew, so did class segregation. Wealthy residents moved into ex-clusive new districts along Woodward, Cass, and West Fort streets. In large workplaces, day-to-day contact between workers and owners disappeared. Indeed, the entire scale of production was being fundamentally transformed. In 1856, a drugstore owner named Frederick Stearns began manufacturing prescription drugs in a one-room workshop with a single assistant; by 1881, Stearns' company was one of the nation's major drug manufacturers, with a multi-story factory employing 400 workers.

Stearns was only one of the "self-made men," as they called themselves, who built huge fortunes during Detroit's rapid industrialization. Hazen Pingree, a former leather cutter in a Massachusetts shoe factory, came to Detroit in 1865 with virtually no savings. Finding a job in H.P. Baldwin's small boot-and-shoe factory, he accumulated a modest bank account and, with a single partner, invested $1,360 in his own workshop the following year. At first, he employed eight workers; by 1886, he had 700 employees, and the entire process of shoemaking had changed from skilled hand work to semi-skilled machine production. Daniel Scotten's rise was equally meteoric: beginning with a small tobacco store purchased for $1,500 in

Detroit's Central Market, located in what is now Cadillac Square (site 2). Farmers, butchers, grocers and peddlers of all descriptions sold their wares in this publicly regulated market. "Not only goods but labor is here for sale," noted one observer in 1884. "Just as in Bible days, 'men are standing idle in the market place.' For the last 40 years, a woodsawyer, when wanted, might be found at the west end; at the east end, on Bates Street, white-washers and day-laborers are wont to congregate."

Land of the Half Free, Home of the Unequal

Our government is formed by, for the benefit of, and to be controlled by, the descendants of European nations.

Michigan Senate, 1842

When the state of Michigan was formed in 1837, its first Constitution abolished all legal protection for the owning or sale of slaves within its borders. That same Constitution, however, also granted voting and civil rights to white men only.

According to the prevailing racism of the day, whites regarded all non-white races as mentally inferior, morally lax, and generally incapable of democratic self-rule. Subordination was supposedly the "natural" condition of blacks, and in the South, slave owners guaranteed this outcome by making it a crime to teach black slaves to read or write.

In 1837, there were fewer than 700 blacks in the entire state and barely 150 in Detroit. Their numbers slowly grew as black mechanics and tradesmen from Virginia migrated to Detroit after 1840, and as field slaves fled north after 1850. Hoping to find a haven from the degrading slave system of the South, they found a society that recognized them in theory as "free men," but in practice barred them from virtually every public place and industry.

Blacks could not serve on Detroit's juries, could not enter the "front rooms" of hotels and restaurants, and could not find work or training in most trades. They were compelled to pay school taxes, but the public schools would not admit black children. Mar-

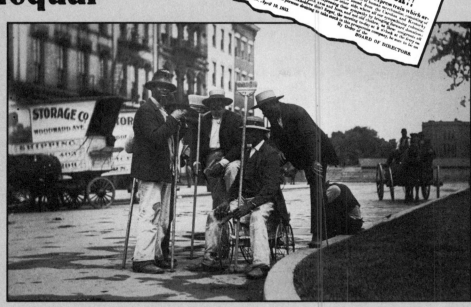

Above: Black street sweepers, Cadillac Square.

Inset: An 1853 notice announcing the safe arrival of 29 fugitive slaves in Canada.

riage between blacks and whites was legally prohibited, while customary practice and occasional violence restricted most black residents to a small area on the near East Side.

Ironically, it was the Irish—previously brutalized by the British—who enforced Detroit's racial caste system with a special vengeance. Many Irish feared that black laborers would take away the unskilled jobs they relied on, and economic competition fueled the race prejudice common to a nation where slavery was still practiced in the South. Resentment peaked in the Civil War year of 1863, when a predominantly Irish crowd, angered by the military draft and enraged by fabricated rape charges against a black tavernkeeper, rampaged through Detroit's black enclave, killing two

men and setting fire to 30 buildings.

This demoralizing turn of events could not turn back the 40-year campaign of Detroit's blacks to defeat slavery in the South and win political equality in Michigan. As early as 1833, a crowd of blacks from all over Michigan and western Ontario attacked Detroit's jail and freed two runaway slaves before the Sheriff could return them to Kentucky. Over the next 30 years, Detroit served as the major terminus on the Underground Railroad—the illegal network of hiding places and "safe houses," operated by blacks and sympathetic whites—that helped fugitive slaves escape to Canada.

"All history shows, and our experience proves," Detroit's Colored Vigilante Committee resolved in 1842, "that the Rights and Liberties of a peo-

---

1856, he became the city's largest tobacco manufacturer by 1875, with a huge three-story factory on West Fort Street producing two million pounds of tobacco annually.

The growth of such large-scale industry in Detroit did not produce the tightly-packed tenement-house squalor found in the industrial cities of Europe and the eastern United States. With cheap land available for expansion, Detroit's neighborhoods spread outward rather than upward. By 1880, the great majority of wage earners lived in small, single-family homes. One out of three Detroit families were buying or building their own frame houses, while the remainder rented.

For wage earners, working conditions and pay were also better in Detroit than in Europe and the eastern United States. The abundance of cheap farm land and the relative scarcity of labor on the western frontier forced employers to pay premium wages to attract workers. This wage gap was rapidly narrowing,

ple must be obtained by their own exertions.'' Acting on this principle, Detroit's black community organized a half-dozen petition drives, several court suits, and two unsuccessful referendum campaigns in 1850 and 1867 to win their voting rights. Finally, six years after President Lincoln's Emancipation Proclamation abolished slavery in the South, Michigan's white voters narrowly passed a Constitutional amendment in 1870 extending voting rights to non-white men.

Four years later, Michigan's male voters turned down a referendum proposal that would have further extended the ''suffrage'' (voting rights) to women. Many of those who demanded votes for women in this first of several unsuccessful referendums took their cue from the decades-long campaign to abolish slavery. Women who had learned to organize public meetings and demand human rights for blacks saw no reason why the same tactics and principles, embodied in Detroit's Women's Suffrage Association, should not win equal rights for women.

Their public campaign clashed head on with centuries of religious dogma. Christian churches (with the exception of the Quakers) had long prohibited women from speaking in meetings or becoming ministers, basing their outlook on the biblical teachings of St. Paul: ''Let the women learn in silence with all subjection....I suffer not a woman to teach, nor to usurp authority over a man, but to be in silence.''

Scientific opinion was equally contemptuous of the demand for equal rights. According to *Females and Their Diseases*, written by Dr. Charles Meigs in 1848, women had ''a head almost too small for intellect but just big enough for love.'' Based on such pseudo-scientific rationalizing, Michigan barred women from its universities until 1870 and denied them the vote throughout the nineteenth cen-

tury, allowing them only the limited right to vote in School-Board elections.

Many middle-class women found these restrictions on their political rights intolerable, but working-class women probably found the immediate issues of family survival far more pressing. Among newly arrived immigrant groups, the majority of men surveyed in the 1880s did not register to vote and, presumably, their wives and daughters were no less indifferent to the issue of suffrage.

Elite standards of family authority, characterized by an absolutely dominant husband and a submissive, frail, ''sensitive'' wife, also had little relevance in working-class families. Although women were expected to follow the lead of their fathers and

husbands, women in rural Europe and America did household and agricultural chores roughly parallel to the work of men. When husbands migrated to nearby districts to find temporary work, women ran the households and the farms; when such migrations eventually brought the entire family to a city like Detroit, women carried the full responsibility of household production if their husbands worked outside the home.

Women who also worked for wages generally saw their wage-earner status as temporary. For those with grievances in their work or life, they looked to the church, the ethnic association, or the union (if it admitted women) for support, not to politics or the Women's Suffrage Association.

D.M. Ferry Company, a national distributor of seeds, employed German women to cultivate its 300-acre seed bed on Grand River Avenue, circa 1870.

however, as the frontier moved steadily west and Detroit's factories grew larger and more numerous.

In the 1880s, when families spent at least 90¢ a day for the bare minimum of food and rent, Detroit's skilled tradesmen earned daily wages averaging $2.25 (machinists and printers) to $3.21 (iron puddlers). But these craftsmen were at

the top of the wage scale; unskilled laborers averaged only $1.33 a day, and half of all wage earners in the city made less than $1.50. Since a wide range of industries, from construction to railroad-car manufacturing, closed down during the winter months or slack season, most workers experienced prolonged unemployment every year. Under these condi-

tions, only 6 percent of the workers surveyed in Wayne County in 1884 could afford to even open a savings account.

Most workers lived on the borderline of poverty and minimal comfort, moving from one status to the other as they were laid off from one job and hired into the next. Once hired, work dominated their days. ''We go on duty at 5 o'clock

Until the invention of the Linotype machine in the 1880s, these skilled journeymen printers hand-set, letter-by-letter, Detroit's newspapers, periodicals, and books.

The title of "journeyman" had a literal meaning, for many workers "tramped" from city to city, joining the constant stream of tradesmen, settlers, and peddlers moving throughout the country. Their union traveling card insured that in towns with a union printing industry, they could count on a meal, a roof, and either assistance finding a job, or transportation to the next stop if work was scarce. The union's "tramp fund" thereby helped unemployed printers find work, and protected employed printers against the low-wage competition of desperate job seekers.

in the afternoon," one group of bakers said of their work schedule in 1884, "and usually get through about 8 or 9 o'clock the next morning...and on Saturdays not till 12 or even 1 o'clock." Their 15-hour workday was longer than average, but by the 1880s, most wage earners worked at least 10 hours a day, six days a week.

For factory workers, those 10 to 12 hours a day could be especially grueling. Craftsmen, working with hand tools, could set their own work pace, but in mechanized factory production, machines and supervisors drove the less-skilled workers at a constant rate of exertion. Carpenters in a seed-box factory "are compelled to keep up with the machines," one worker reported. "At night when they quit work, and come out into the fresh air, the men can be seen hawking and spitting, and they blow great quantities of black walnut dust from their nostrils." Older workers who could not maintain the pace were "turned out like old horses to search for a living."

Craftsmen in the shoe industry were also turned out as machines replaced many hand tools. "The world has come to such a pass with its ceaseless hum of industry," the Detroit *Free Press* reported in 1889, "that the shoemaker no longer makes the shoes of his generation.... His occupation is usurped by the big shoe factory, its cunning machinery, and its 700 workmen."

There were workwomen as well. Skilled men cut the shoe leather into the proper patterns, but hundreds of lower paid women operated the sewing machines that stitched the different parts together. For each sewer, "it is the same little stitch 'forever and a day,' " the *Free Press* reported, "...as all day long the iron wheels ring the monotonous song of the shoe."

Paying women, on the average, only 82¢ a day, factory employers who replaced men with women cut their labor costs in half. Hiring children at 50¢ a day, they saved still more. In 1884, the Director of Michigan's State Bureau of Labor Statistics found "children of 10 and upwards are frequently employed from sunrise to sundown" at the brickyards on Detroit's West Side. As men produced bricks "with the aid of machinery," women and children "set to work piling the bricks in rows, to the height of five feet.... Some of the children employed," the Director reported, "are not over seven."

Between 1860 and 1885, such scenes were all too common. In 1884, barely half the school-age children in the East Side's Third Ward actually attended school. The balance worked to supplement the income of their parents, usually as low-wage factory hands.

Detroit was prospering as it grew. But prosperity meant one thing to the "self-made" men who profited by it, and something else to artisans, factory workers, and unskilled laborers trying to scratch out a living.

Some of the former workers and shopkeepers who rose to positions of wealth preserved an enduring sympathy for the majority of working people who could not or would not claw their way to the top. But many of the "new rich" who built their fashionable homes along Woodward Avenue and West Fort Street nurtured a far less generous attitude—a belief their success signified Christian virtue, while the relative poverty of the majority was evidence of their "backwardness." Government should not help the poor, these businessmen concluded; the poor should help themselves—"like I did."

"Self-help" took on a different hue, however, when Detroit's carpenters, machinists, iron molders, and other craftsmen emulated the printers and formed unions in the decades after 1860. Employers bitterly denounced these early organizations as "criminal conspiracies" to deprive them of their profits, yet some craft unions survived and grew. Their strength was based on an important feature of the new industrial system: even as factory production came to dominate the economy and eliminate many old skills, this same process of industrialization also created new trades and new skilled workers that owners could not do without.

In Detroit's stove factories, for example, the owners managed the financing and marketing of the product, but had little direct control over the work process. Skilled iron molders organized the actual production of stoves on a contract or piece-work basis: they owned their own tools, and hired, trained, and directed their own unskilled helpers. In other industries, skilled machine builders, iron and steel workers, bricklayers, and other craftsmen exerted the same kind of control over their work.

So while some crafts were undermined by large-scale factory production—shoemaking and tailoring among them—other crafts were rising. Even in the declining trades, some skills were indispensable to production. While clothing manufacturers replaced the all-around skills of the journeyman tailor with specialized sewers and machine stitching, they still depended on the skilled patternmakers and cutters who shaped the pieces of fabric to be sewn.

The organizations these skilled workers formed were "craft unions," open only to members of their particular trade. Machinists and iron molders working in the same factory maintained separate unions, and the unskilled laborers in the plant did not belong to any organization. Given the extreme hostility of many employers to unions, only the hard-to-replace skilled tradesmen had enough bargaining leverage to defend their organizations. Few craft unions were eager, therefore, to admit unskilled helpers who would "dilute" the craft and undermine wages. An employer who hired such "green hands" to replace skilled journeymen typically provoked a strike and boycott against his business.

Yet even if Detroit's craftsmen made little room in their organizations for green hands, some went out of their way to aid the less skilled when they formed their own unions. The Sewing Women's Protective Association relied heavily on such support after demanding, in 1865, a new scale of wages for sewers in Detroit. "When a case of oppression of sewing women is made known," reported ships' carpenter Richard Trevellick, President of the newly formed Detroit Trades Assembly, "every trade is notified and the members all cease trading at the obnoxious establishment. Sentinels are placed around notifying people of the facts, and in every case the offender is brought to terms." Employing a tactic frequently used during strikes, the Detroit Trades Assembly also rented a hall and donated eight sewing machines to a cooperatively-owned workroom, allowing women sewers to support themselves during the boycotts. The fruits of the women's labor, noted one union newspaper, would go to them "instead of into the capacious pocket of the capitalist."

There were many craftsmen who wished to become, if not "capacious" capitalists, at least owners of a workshop that produced custom-made goods for specialty customers. The prospects for such individual enterprise,

however, were not as favorable as business advocates claimed. The number of small workshops in Detroit did grow steadily during boom years, but many of these were being opened by downwardly mobile cigarmakers, shoemakers, and

other skilled artisans competing with the factories that displaced them.

In the meantime, wage earners with no capital and nothing to sell but their brains and brawn doubled in number during the 1880s. Many of these were unskilled workers who could sometimes move up to semi-skilled jobs, but only one in ten—one in five among craftsmen—of those who stayed in Detroit could hope to escape wage-work and become white-collar professionals or businessmen. Starting a pharmaceutical business, for example, had been much easier in the 1850s, when Detroit was relatively small and not fully enmeshed in the national economy. It was another thing altogether when huge corporations like the Stearns Company were already on the scene, extending their control over a national economy tied together by railroads and telegraph lines.

Opportunities for advancement narrowed dramatically after 1873, when stagnation and decline in new railroad construction threw the national economy into a severe depression. Over-

Above: The Queen Bee Cigar Co. of Lansing, Michigan. Even after factory production came to Detroit, many cigar makers still worked in small-scale shops like this, hand-packing tobacco into the long cigar molds pictured here.

Inset: The Miller tobacco "factory" in the 1840s. Motive power for the cutting machinery in the basement was a blind horse walking on a treadmill.

Above: The entire workforce of the Michigan Stove Company in 1872.

Inset: Ten years later, the Company had expanded into this new factory on East Jefferson Avenue.

extended manufacturers who could not pay off their creditors and over-extended banks which could not pay off depositers triggered a wave of bankruptcies, layoffs, declining consumer demand, and more layoffs. Nationwide unemployment reached an estimated 20 percent by 1877, with another 40 percent of the labor force unable to find work for more than seven months of the year. As sales plummeted, companies lengthened the workday of their remaining employees and cut wages as much as 40 percent in an effort to protect their profits.

In 1877, when workers in dozens of cities demonstrated against the continuing wage cuts, panicked authorities responded by ordering police to arrest or shoot the protesting workers. In July, the violence peaked when federal troops and state militias across the nation mobilized to gun down striking railroad workers and their supporters in dozens of industries. In two weeks of pitched battles in the streets of Baltimore, Pittsburgh, Chicago, and other cities, over 100 workers were killed.

In Detroit, an unprecedented concentration of business and government power was mobilized against the striking workers of the Michigan Central Railroad. Three hundred reserve policemen were called out, additional "emergency volunteers" were recruited, and businessmen formed their own Protective Association to move against public demonstrations. There was no bloodshed—just sheer intimidation. By year's end, the combined impact of this employer repression and the continuing economic depression had destroyed all but a handful of Detroit's unions.

The bitter conflicts and hardships of 1877 reinforced a feeling among some wage earners that they were a separate and exploited class. Activists now called for "working class" organizations that could match the owners' growing economic and political power, and before the year was out, Detroit's German cigarmakers had formed a local chapter of the Workingman's Party of the United States. Their call for class solidarity appealed to Judson Grenell, a journeyman printer and the son of a Baptist preacher. For the first time, Grenell later recalled, he "saw an effort to explain the cause of poverty in the midst of plenty.... Wage workers, these Social Democrats insisted, were continually creating surplus wealth which became the property of the employing class.... The way to avoid this was to create a cooperative commonwealth with workingmen their own employers." Together with another journeyman printer, Joseph Labadie,

Grenell founded a weekly labor paper, *The Socialist*, to promote the same message among native-born workers.

"Absolute liberty is the thing to be contended for," the paper announced in an early issue. "Labor must control capital," and the surest path to that goal was "political victory.... The capture of Federal, state, and municipal governments by votes." In 1877, E.W. Simpson, President of the Carpenter's Union and a member of the Socialist Labor Party, fell far short of that goal when he garnered only 6 percent of the vote as the Workingman's candidate for Mayor. But three years later, a growing sentiment in favor of working-class politics carried Simpson to victory in his race for a City Council seat.

By then, Detroit's union movement was already rallying from the demoralizing effects of 1877. Though few realized it at the time, the recovery had begun in the fall of 1878 when a handful of representatives from Detroit's most hardpressed crafts—the shoemakers and cigarmakers—secretly formed the first local Assembly of the Knights of Labor, headed by Labadie.

"The Noble and Holy Order of the Knights of Labor," initially organized in Philadelphia, established itself in 1878 as the first truly national organization of working people in America. Founded by Uriah Stephens, a skilled garment cutter, mason, and former Baptist preacher, the organization combined all these elements into a unique whole—part union, part fraternal organization, part religious crusade. "The tabernacle—the dwelling place of God—is among men," said Stephens, and the Knights of Labor would therefore build upon "the immutable basis of the Fatherhood of God and the Brotherhood of Man." Reliance on such religious imagery was commonplace in the Knights. Jesus was a humble carpenter and God a builder of mountains: "He is not less because He worked," Richard Trevellick, a convert to the Knights, told his Detroit followers, "[and] neither are you."

Infused with this evangelical spirit, the Knights promised to replace the present "pauperization and hopeless degradation of the toiling masses" with a system that would "secure to the toilers a proper share of the wealth that they create." To that end, they not only favored restricting monopolies and corporations, but hoped also to "abolish the wage system" and replace it with an economy of worker-owned cooperatives; only then, the Knights declared, could workers together secure the full value of what they produced. By 1886, the Order had organized 700,000 workers nationwide, with membership open not only to skilled craftsmen, but also to unskilled laborers from "all branches of honorable toil...without respect to sex, creed, color, or nationality."

In Detroit, the Knights of Labor initially maintained a low profile, calling themselves the "Washington Literary Society" to confuse anti-union employers and protect members from immediate dismissal. As the economy picked up and unemployment fell, the Knights emerged from secrecy and, together with the Detroit Trades Council (successor to the Trades Assembly), grew from 1,500 members in 1880 to 13,000 by the end of 1886.

The 70 local Assemblies the Knights organized during the 1880s took every conceivable form. A few, including the original Pioneer Assembly, were mixed locals combining workers from dozens of trades. Most of the other Assemblies were craft organizations limited to a particular group of skilled workers. The biggest locals, however, were all industrial Assemblies combining both skilled and unskilled workers from a single workplace. The Garland Assembly, for example, united skilled iron molders and unskilled laborers from the Michigan Stove Works. Women shoe and cigar workers had their own local, the Florence Nightingale Assembly, and Detroit's German community organized seven different Assemblies for German workers.

Whatever their form, these diverse groups were drawn to the Knights for one overriding reason: the Knights provided a national and city-wide organization that could counter the power of large companies. When the Pingree and Smith shoe workers struck in 1885, the District Assembly of the Knights called on each local to buy stock in the strikers' cooperative shoe company, while the National organization helped organize a nationwide boycott of Pingree and Smith shoes. When the company's sales began to fall, Pingree and Smith finally capitulated in March, 1886.

The Knights extended the labor movement's reach into politics and culture as well as industrial organizing. In 1884, the movement's Independent Labor Party helped elect five state representatives from Detroit. By 1886, weekly labor newspapers were appearing in English and German, and singing societies, a workers' theater group, and

Above: In 1890, this Detroit store featured shoes from the worker-owned factory of the Knights of Labor— "Detroit Cooperative Shoes."

Inset: A lapel ribbon, circa 1886.

a debating forum—"The Dialectical Union"—were active. A cooperative barrel factory and an iron foundry were also organized in addition to a shoe co-op.

Detroit's labor movement even organized its own militia, the Detroit Rifles. "If trouble should come," reported the Detroit *Labor Leaf* in

Above: The Detroit Car Wheel foundry cast 46,000 railroad wheels in 1884.

December, 1885, just after the workers' militia received its first shipment of Winchester rifles, "the capitalists will use the regular army and militia to shoot down those who are not satisfied. It won't be so if the people are equally ready, like their forefathers of 1776."

Five months later, on May 1, 1886, the Knights launched a massive, nationwide strike to win the eight-hour workday at no reduction in pay. Over 6,000 workers responded to the strike call in Detroit, including metal workers, painters, lumber-mill workers, sailors, tannery workers, bricklayers, furniture makers, construction laborers, brewery workers, bakers, and foundry workers. Thousands of these strikers won reductions in hours, and thousands more—cigarmakers and stove workers among them—won a shorter workday through negotiation.

This unprecedented display of union power was followed in September by a record turnout for the city's Labor Day parade. The previous year, 3,000 had marched in the annual observance, which had no legal standing and was therefore held at night to avoid conflict with work schedules. Attendance had been limited by the rumored presence of employer-paid Pinkerton agents in the crowd—rumors that were apparently confirmed when a number of marchers were later fired. Labor Day was an entirely different affair in 1886. Buoyed by widespread support for the May strikes, the Knights and the Detroit Trades Council called for a daytime parade. An estimated 10,000 to 12,000 trade-union members downed their tools on September 6, closing most of the city's major factories in what amounted to a General Strike. Marshalled into 11 divisions by trade and organization, their procession stretched three miles along Jefferson Avenue as they marched to Miller's Gardens.

Among the prominent signs in the line of march, one banner in particular summarized the mood of the times: "Divided We Can Beg. United We Can Demand."

Unity, however, was easier to preach than achieve. Within weeks of the enormous Labor Day turnout, Detroit's labor movement split into bitterly antagonistic camps.

The very success of the movement sparked much of the initial quarreling. Moderate political leaders within the Independent Labor Party, seeing the potential for a greatly expanded labor vote, wanted to strengthen their existing alliances with politicians in the Democratic and Republican Parties. Radical leaders, on the other hand, believed the movement's sudden growth made coalition politics both unnecessary and unwise, since such alliances would dilute the Labor Party's impact. When Party leaders rejected the go-it-alone strategy, many radicals quit the organization.

In the meantime, the rapid membership growth of 1886 had brought a new generation of leaders into positions of power within the Knights. By 1887, 8 of the 15 Executive Board members of the Detroit organization were no longer working in the blue-collar occupations they had started out in: six had acquired full-time political appointments from Democratic Party administrations, one was a ship captain, and one was a hardware store clerk. Seeking to establish a respectable image for the Knights—and, critics charged, protect their political credentials as "peacemakers"—these leaders adopted a cautious approach that brought them into conflict with Detroit's more activist union leaders.

In 1887, iron molders went on strike to counter their employers' planned use of more half-trained and lower-wage "bucks," as the molders called them. The Knights' leadership called off the strike and forced the molders to accept a "peace treaty" favoring the companies. Many craft unionists resented such meddling by men who had no experience in their industry, and resentment grew all the more intense when the Knights' leadership, in Detroit and nationally, violated the organization's rules of internal democracy to silence their craft-union opponents.

Radical union leaders were equally displeased with the Knights' refusal to defend the Haymarket martyrs of 1886. These Chicago trade unionists and radicals were blamed for the fatal bomb attack on Chicago's police during the May strikes for the eight-hour day. Despite the fact that none of the accused were connected with the bombing (or were even at the scene), four of the men were sentenced to death and hung because their radical ideas allegedly inspired the unknown attacker. Seeking to preserve a respectable image and deflect the torrent of newspaper criticism directed at all unions, the Knights' top leaders applauded the executions.

Repudiated by both conservative craft-unionists and radical union activists, the Knights went into rapid decline in Michigan after 1886. By 1888, the Independent Labor Party had collapsed, and by 1892, the Knights had disappeared from Detroit.

As the Knights dwindled in size and prestige, craft unionists and radicals alike switched their allegiance to the newly formed American Federation of Labor (AFL). Organized in December, 1886, by opponents of the Knights of Labor, the AFL vowed it would respect the autonomy of craft unions and avoid political entanglements. Many of Detroit's leading union activists, hoping the AFL would restore the labor movement's momentum, jumped on the AFL bandwagon, bringing with them most of the Detroit Trades Council and many of the Knights' Detroit members. In 1887, Sam Goldwater, head of the Cigarmakers Union and a leader of the Socialist Labor Party, was elected President of the Detroit Trades Council. Two years later, Joseph Labadie, the radical printer and co-founder of the first Knights of Labor Assembly in Detroit, became the founding President of the Michigan AFL.

Nationally, however, the AFL was led by more cautious men. Sam Gompers and Adolf Strasser, the two cigarmakers from New York who founded the national organization, both believed in the need for strong unions and well-organized strike actions to defend workers' interests. But they rejected the centralized control the Knights had used to unify (or, as the AFL charged, abuse) the various trades. They also tended to ignore blacks, women, and unskilled workers. Neither were they inclined to question the "wage slavery" of industrial capitalism. "We have no ultimate ends," Strasser once declared. "We are fighting only for immediate objects—objects that can be realized in a few years.... We are practical men."

Many of the craft unionists who rallied to the AFL's banner also rejected the ambitious goals and the broader solidarity of the Knights. The tendency of these skilled workers to focus on craft distinctions and to exclude the growing number of less-skilled workers gradually became the dominant trend within the AFL, even as many socialists and radicals continued to hold leadership positions in some AFL unions. The strength of this craft ideology was rooted, in part, in the continuing paradox of the industrial revolution: mechanization led to the destruction of old crafts and may have generated an intense "class consciousness" among some workers, but it also bred a far narrower "job consciousness" among a new generation of craftsmen.

In the printing industry, for example, management was steadily dividing work into specialized functions, replacing the fully-trained printer with a new generation of workers who concentrated on particular tasks. Rather than pine after the "good old days," these new workers chose to break away from the original Typographical Union and form their own craft unions—the Pressmen in 1873; the Stereotypers (who made the printing plates) in 1885; and the Bookbinders in 1886. A similar process

Below: Shipbuilders in the Detroit Dry Dock Company's yards (site 3).

Inset: The Buhl Iron Works, 1881. Detroit's experience in casting metal parts, axles, and marine engine blocks later gave it the edge in producing automobiles.

occurred in other industries where new craft identities were emerging and old ones hardening: the Plumbers and Steamfitters split apart in 1889; skilled shoecutters broke away from the Shoeworkers Union in 1891; and Detroit's Machine Molders split from the regular Iron Molders during this same period.

These craft unions were capable of a stubborn militancy, particularly in defense of the work rules that preserved their skills against employer manipulation. Detroit's Machinists set standards that fixed the terms of apprenticeship for new workers, prohibited helpers from performing journeymen's work, and banned "piece-work" wages that pegged income to production speed. The city's cigarmakers meanwhile defended the practice that allowed one worker to read to the rest as a way of combating boredom.

Not all of the AFL's unions were nar-rowly defined craft organizations. Both the Brewery Workers and the United Mine Workers—originally formed as industrial unions within the Knights of Labor—switched to the AFL, but retained their commitment to the industry-wide organization of skilled and unskilled workers. Even craft workers in the AFL frequently went beyond the bounds of "job consciousness" when they joined workers from other trades in boycotts, sympathy strikes, and demon-

The Great Trolley Riot

However much Detroit's workers were divided on the job, they were united by at least one common enemy in the 1890s: the Detroit City Railway Company. In 1891, their unanimous loathing for this private monopoly sparked one of the most spectacular labor struggles in the city's history—a struggle so intense it moved liberal reformers and many former supporters of the Knights of Labor to launch a new political movement.

The privately-owned trolley-car system that catalyzed this social and political upheaval had managed, by 1891, to alienate both its customers and its employees. At a time when most big cities in America were switching to electric trolleys, the Railway Company continued to rely exclusively on the same plodding, horse-drawn trollies first used in 1863. With wages averaging only 18¢ an hour for men and 9¢ an hour for women, the streetcars charged a staggering 5¢ for each ride. For this exceedingly high fare, passengers were forced to endure the foul-smelling straw used to insulate the trolley's floor, the odor of horse manure, and the fumes from gas-fired heaters.

Streetcar workers felt especially abused. Paid for a 12-hour day, they were frequently kept at work for up to 18 hours to cover the morning and evening rush hours. When the hard-pressed car drivers formed an Employees Association and began pushing for a 10-hour day in April, 1891, the company fired 12 activists for

Above: Police escorting a trolley up Woodward Avenue.

Inset: A Detroit trolley, pictured at the intersection of Fort and Livernois Streets, about 1891.

"agitation and associating with men whom they knew were opposed to all corporations." Following a strike vote, picket lines were quickly organized—and just as quickly dispersed by city police, who escorted strikebreakers into the car barns. "The Backbone of the Strike Appears To Be Broken," the *Evening News* concluded.

But the real strike was only just beginning, for the popular resentment towards the Railway Company soon flared up in a massive outpouring of support for the car drivers. Thousands of Detroit workers abandoned their jobs in sympathy strikes and, by the second day of the walkout, huge crowds gathered at intersections to block

strations against anti-union employers.

But just as frequently, the tremendous diversity of working conditions divided workers and reinforced craft distinctions. As cigar molds replaced hand rolling in the city's cigar factories, the average wage of hand rollers declined from $1.76 a day in 1883 to less than $1.50 a day in 1889; in these same years, steamfitters' wages rose 40 percent. The Knights' slogan, "An Injury to One Is the Concern of All," had an enduring appeal among union activists, but in practice, steamfitters, electricians, machine molders, and other skilled workers looked upon their industrial environment in far more positive terms than the cigarmakers, shoemakers, and other declining crafts whose skill and pay were being eroded. Many of these skilled workers, in turn, saw little common ground between themselves and the unskilled laborers who did the digging, the hauling, and the carrying in every industry.

The gap between the skilled and the unskilled widened all the more when a new wave of European immigrants began filling the lowest-paid, least-skilled jobs in the city. After the mid-1880s, craftsmen and laborers not only saw the world from different occupational perspectives—more often than not, they also spoke different

Mayor Hazen Pingree driving an electric trolley in 1895, marking the opening of a new trolley line.

trollies driven by armed strikebreakers.

The strike verged on insurrection the following day as demonstrators built barricades across major streets, using lamp posts, trees, overturned streetcars—anything to block the trollies. Ironworkers ripped up two blocks of track in front of their shop and teamsters deliberately drove their wagons onto the rails to block oncoming trollies. Pitched battles between police and rock-throwing crowds raged at car platforms and intersections across the city. Toward evening, a cheering crowd of 5,000 men, women, and children rolled a captured streetcar down Woodward Avenue and dumped it in the river.

Panicked company officials pleaded with Mayor Hazen Pingree to "save the city" and call in the state militia. The Mayor refused. He recommended arbitration between the company and the union to end the strike, and warned

he was inclined to throw a few stones himself if the company refused a settlement too long. When the company capitulated that night, Pingree quickly gained national prominence as a "friend of the workingman."

It was a curious title for the man who not only had accumulated a fortune as the city's biggest shoe-factory owner, but had also fought the Knights of Labor in a bitter eleven-month strike in 1885–1886. Yet, the bruising conflict between the Railway Company and the city's workers had a transforming effect on Pingree. As a former factory worker and son of an itinerant cobbler, he was able to identify with wage laborers. As the Mayor and leading industrialist in the city, he now came to believe the greatest threat to social peace was the greed and callousness of private corporations, not unions. Together with a growing number of "Progressive" Repub-

licans, the Mayor concluded that workers needed "responsible" unions to defend their rights as wage earners, and "enlightened" government to defend their rights as consumers.

Pingree therefore championed municipal ownership of the trollies as the only means to improve service, a principle endorsed in 1894 by 80 percent of the population in an advisory referendum. (It took until 1922 for the city to win complete control.) In the meantime, the Mayor forced the private trolley companies to electrify their lines and lower fares to 3¢.

The Preston National Bank soon after dropped Pingree from its board of directors. Pingree, the bank president explained, was "antagonistic to corporate capital." The Mayor was unmoved: "This town needs somebody to tell the utilities crowd to kiss something else besides babies!" In 1895, the Pingree-sponsored municipal lighting plant replaced "the utility crowd's" overpriced street lighting operations, reducing costs from $132 per lamp to $83. The Mayor also forced the private gas utility to cut its rates in half. But after he won a campaign to end tax exemptions for shipbuilding companies and real-estate speculators, Pingree's shoe company could not secure loans from Detroit banks. As a final insult, he lost his family pew in the prestigious Woodward Avenue Baptist Church.

By the time he won election as Governor in 1897, Pingree had helped pioneer a major shift in municipal politics, establishing himself as one of the first big-city mayors to publicly ally himself with the working class and challenge big business. A generation of Progressives, both Republicans and Democrats, would follow in his footsteps.

WANTED, FOR SALE, TO RENT, ETC.

WANTED—HELP—FEMALE.

WANTED—GERMAN GIRL FOR HOUSEWORK; aged about 16 years. Apply 250 Randolph st. after 6 p. m.

WANTED—GIRL FOR GENERAL HOUSEWORK. 16 Howard.

WANTED—GIRL ABOUT 13 YEARS OF AGE TO help take care of baby; wages $1 per week. Apply 223 Fourth st.

WANTED—GERMAN GIRL FOR GENERAL HOUSE-work; one who can speak English. Apply 113 Elmwood ave.

WANTED—A WOMAN FOR THE LAUNDRY. HOWARD, 73 Congress st. west.

WANTED—ALL KINDS OF DOMESTIC HELP FOR city or country. Park Intelligence Office, 245 Woodward ave. Telephone 1565.

WANTED—FIRST-CLASS ORDER COOK, FEMALE. 50 Shelby st.

WANTED—IMMEDIATELY, GOOD, TRUSTY GIRL to learn dressmaking. Call at 22 Elizabeth st. west.

WANTED—A GOOD HOME AND $1 PER WEEK TO a good, trusty girl to assist in light housework. 688 Macomb st.

WANTED—DISH WASHER AT 157 JEFFERSON

WANTED—HELP—MALE.

WANTED—LADY AND GENTLEMEN, GUITAR and banjo players, to join musical society immediately. Address box G, No. 21, Free Press.

WANTED—ENGINEERS AND HOTEL COOKS AT British-American Employment Office, 49 Michigan ave.

WANTED—A MAN AND A GOOD STRONG BOY at 404 Twelfth st.

WANTED—HARNESS MAKER. WM. NEVISON, Northville. Mich.

WANTED—FIRST-CLASS BREAD AND CAKE baker; none but experienced man need apply. 53 High st. west.

WANTED—A GOOD, HONEST GERMAN BOY TO work in greenhouse; one that knows the work preferred. Call at greenhouses immediately, corner Third and Putnam aves. J. B. KEMPF, florist.

WANTED—A FIRST-CLASS WHITE BARBER. FRANKLIN HOUSE.

WANTED—FIRST-CLASS WHITE BARBER; GOOD job and good town to work in. Address JAKE SRIEGEL, Manchester, Mich.

WANTED—FIRST-CLASS WHITE BARBER AT Franklin House barber shop.

WANTED—DRUG CLERK; ONE WHO SPEAKS German preferred. 402 Center st., Bay City, Mich.

WANTED—BUSHELMAN IMMEDIATELY, AT HART, the English tailor's, 90 Woodward ave.

WANTED—A YOUNG MAN WHO HAS HAD SOME experience as stenographer and can work typewriter or caligraph; wages small for the present. Address box J, No. 3, Free Press.

WANTED—WHITE BARBER. 97 GRAND RIVER ave.

WANTED—PAINTERS AND JOINERS, CORNER of Third ave. and Joy st. S. J. MARTIN.

WANTED—DRUG CLERK; ONE WHO SPEAKS French preferred. Address box J, No. 8, Free Press.

WANTED—TO BOOKBINDERS—AN APPRENTICE two or three years at the

*Scanning the 1886 help-wanted ads from the **Detroit Free Press** could leave no doubt in the reader's mind what many of these employers were looking for: a worker who was white, Protestant, and, if not of British descent, then at least "A Good, Honest German."*

Inset: Detroit's 1899 Labor Day parade.

languages.

To the native-born Detroiters and the "old" immigrant groups already established in the city, the Poles, Italians, Hungarians, and Russians arriving in Detroit in the 1880s and 1890s often appeared as alien intruders, "artificially" transplanted to America, some claimed, by profit-hungry steamship lines and Papist conspirators. In fact, the new arrivals shared many of the same motives for migrating as their Irish, German, and British predecessors. The dramatic changes in agriculture and industry that drove these earlier immigrants out of northern Europe had simply spread to the east and south.

Russian, Austrian, and Italian landlords, like their English counterparts, were consolidating huge estates and usurping peasant lands. Like the Irish, the growing peasant populations in these countries were sub-dividing their tiny land holdings into ever smaller plots, and growing debts and rising rents pushed many families off the land. Factory-made goods also undermined village crafts, and religious persecution dogged both the Russian Jew and the Polish Catholic living in Russia's Orthodox Empire.

Many came to America and Detroit seeking work and freedom. They found much of the former and some of the latter. They also found a smouldering resentment among native-born and earlier immigrants, who feared the low-wage, "block-voting" newcomers would steal their jobs and capture political power.

"We are now simply the waste-house of Europe and the receptacle of its refuse and scum," the Detroit-based *Patriotic American* editorialized under a headline asking, in 1893, "Who Shall Rule?" As the official newspaper of the anti-immigrant American Protective Association (APA), the *Patriotic American* expressed the fear, common to many American Protestants, that the "Popish," "Un-Christian," and "semi-barbarous" multitudes "rushing en masse to...the United States" would destroy "the perfectly free, modern country that it is, or used to be, 40 or 50 years ago."

The solution was simple according to William Traynor, "Supreme President" of the APA, "Grand Master" of the Orange Lodge, and publisher of the *Patriotic American*. "The first step of the next Congress," he declared in 1894, "must be to close and seal our gates against the poverty and ignorance of Europe." Such anti-immigrant sentiment found a sizeable audience among Protestant workers in Detroit, where the APA had become a force in local politics by the early 1890s. In 1892, 80 Protestant members of the Street Railway Employees Association nearly split that union in half when their anti-Catholic caucus, the Patriotic Sons of America, began organizing a separate Protestant slate in union elections.

"Solidarity" between workers was still the byword of Detroit's labor movement, but in the 1890s, many workers defined such solidarity in terms of ethnicity and race, not in terms of class. A strike by Detroit's stonecutters in 1891 collapsed when the workers divided into competing groups of Italian, German, and British, each seeking a separate settlement with employers. That same year, "American" bricklayers refused to merge with a rival union of "foreigners...[who] take work away from us."

By the close of the nineteenth century, Detroit's workers were divided as never before. Skilled workers generally shunned the less skilled. Workers in rising trades often broke away from older crafts to form their own unions. Protestants sometimes excluded Catholics from their organizations, Christians often excluded Jews, and whites, with rare exceptions, barred blacks altogether. Poles fought the Irish for control of the city's Catholic diocese; the Irish fought the Germans for control of Detroit's Democratic Party; Italians fought Poles for jobs. Native-born Americans, it seemed, fought everyone.

The conditions of industrial growth and the efforts of union activists also produced a labor movement that sometimes transcended these differences, as in the 1886 eight-hour strikes and the 1891 streetcar riots. But more often than not, the labor movement splintered along the same lines of skill, religion, race, sex, and ethnicity that divided wage earners in the workplace and in the neighborhood.

All the while, as Detroit grew in size, as it generated a wide range of metal-working industries, and as it attracted skilled and unskilled workers from around the world, the groundwork was slowly being laid for the start of a new century and the appearance of a new age: the Age of the Automobile.

I: Motor City

Motor assembly at the Chalmers Motor Car Company, circa 1912.

Detroit On Wheels

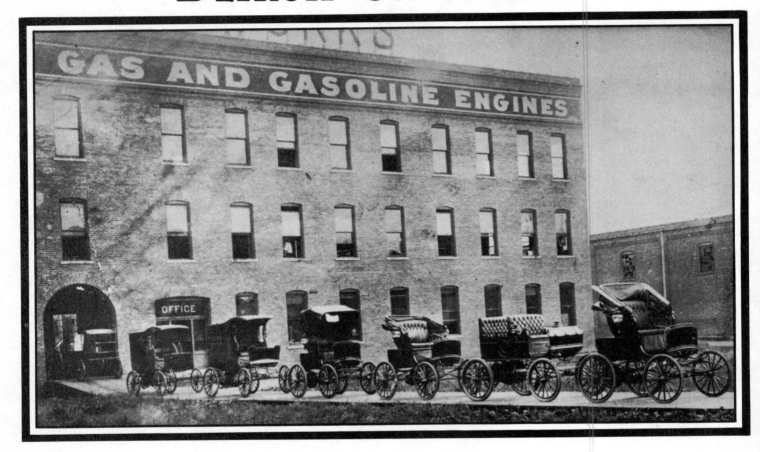

In 1899, just three years after an experimental "horseless carriage" sputtered and chugged its way down Detroit's streets, Ransom Olds opened the city's first automobile factory on East Jefferson Avenue, next to the Belle Isle Bridge. Producing one, sometimes even two cars a day, the new "Oldsmobile" plant launched Detroit into the Automotive Age.

For the hundreds of car builders who followed Olds, Detroit was an ideal place to manufacture automobiles. The city's strategic location on the Great Lakes provided easy access to iron ore from the Upper Peninsula and coal from Ohio, and Detroit's dominance in building marine engines gave it a head start in the production of internal combustion engines. Its numerous metal-working industries also provided a bountiful supply of skilled workers and engineers. Detroit's stove companies, brass and copper mills, shipyards, and railroad equipment manufacturers all employed thousands of molders, metal finishers, mechanics, and other tradesmen whose skills were easily transferable to the tooling and building of automobiles.

Equally important, Detroit's elite had the capital to bankroll the early auto companies. Fortunes made in Michigan timber and copper helped finance Olds, Buick, and Cadillac in their early years. Michigan railroad money bankrolled Packard, while the founders of Detroit Edison stood behind the first car-building venture of Henry Ford, the farmer/mechanic turned engineer.

These pioneer auto manufacturers soon established Detroit and the nearby cities of Pontiac, Flint, and Lansing as the leading centers of the new industry. By 1904, the fast-growing Oldsmobile Company produced 5,000 of the 22,000 cars built in the United States, and dozens of auto companies springing up in Detroit already employed 2,000 of the city's 60,000 factory workers.

These early auto workers were skilled mechanics, not assembly-line factory hands. Even the most rudimentary car they produced—complete with wooden carriage bodies and wire bicycle wheels—was regarded by contemporaries as a complex and exotic piece of machinery. Each car was built slowly and with a minimum of standardization. "In our first assembling," Henry Ford later remembered, "we simply started to put a car together at a spot on the floor and workmen brought to it parts as they were needed, in exactly the same way that one builds a house."

Skilled woodworkers and metal finishers constructed the bodies; skilled upholsterers stitched the leather seat covers; and skilled mechanics built the engines, machined the parts, and assembled the finished car. Unskilled shop hands fetched parts or did heavy work in the foundries where engine blocks and other components were cast. But even in the foundry many of the workers were skilled men who made the molds and poured the molten metal.

Skilled metal workers were the key to the auto industry's initial growth in Detroit. They were also the key to a sudden resurgence after 1901 in Detroit's labor movement—a resurgence that saw the number of union members in the city nearly double over the next three years. While Detroit was establishing itself as the nation's Motor City, it was also becoming, many employers feared, a Union Town.

Company managers bitterly resented this union upsurge, for the metal workers who led Detroit's labor movement fully believed that they, not the owners, knew best how to organize production in a socially progressive manner. In many cases, their unions did not try to bargain with employers (who were not inclined to negotiate in any case). Rather, union workers simply published a "price list" for certain tasks, insisted on specific rules for performing the jobs, and set maximum limits on how much work time and production they would perform each "stint," or day. If an employer did not abide by these rules, union tradesmen walked out of the plant and set up picket lines.

Where they could enforce their terms on employers, unions also insisted on a "Closed Shop"—a shop that hired only union members with full apprenticeship training in all facets of the trade. To union members, this arrangement seemed fair and sensible, since employers would otherwise hire half-trained "rate-busters" to speed up work and undermine both product quality and the craftsman's skill. The inevitable result of such "hoggish" speed up, argued union craftsmen, was falling wages, irregular employment, and a "debauched" workforce.

Skilled tradesmen could not always enforce their work rules, price lists, and Closed-Shop provisions on employers. But as the city's economy boomed after 1900, and as metal workers found their skills in growing demand, their unions took the initiative. In 1901, the Machinists Union struck for shorter hours, eventually forcing 28 metal-working shops to reduce the mandatory work day from ten hours to nine. That same year, the Amalgamated Iron, Steel, and Tin Workers Union forced two of the city's major employers, Detroit Spring and Steel and American Car and Foundry, to honor the union wage scale and grant 5 percent pay increases. The Iron Molders, after a six-month strike ending in June, 1902, forced the Buhl Malleable Iron works to grant authority to the union's Shop Committee to set wages on new work. Rejuvenated by these victories, Detroit's unions grew from a city-wide membership of 8,000 in 1901 to 14,000 in 1904.

Faced with these union gains, management spokesman John Whirl complained that employers "had no more real control than if they were in no way connected with the shop." Indeed,

Above: **Detroit Saturday Night**, the weekly newspaper of the Chamber of Commerce, made no reference to company spies in its idealized portrait of the Motor City. For daily newspapers like the **Evening News**, however, the seamy side of the Open-Shop campaign was headline news.

Opposite page: the 1899 Olds plant.

in some plants, they had great difficulty just introducing new machinery. In iron and brass foundries—where workers cast molten metal into parts for machinery, stoves, and automobiles—many employers were eager to install new semi-automatic molding machines, enabling them to turn out larger batches of standardized metal parts with less reliance on skilled labor. But in a Closed

Early Car Making

There were four basic production steps in building an automobile: 1) foundry work, 2) machining, 3) body work, and 4) assembly.

1) *The Cadillac foundry, 1906.*

To cast molten metal into automobile parts, a patternmaker first made a wooden model of the part. The skilled coremaker and molder then made a mold, packed it with sand (initially by hand, later by machine), and poured in the molten metal. In the past, their indispensable skills enabled these craftsmen to win union work rules in some foundries. After the Employers' Association launched its Open-Shop campaign, however, the foundry industry became predominantly non-union—"debauched" as some molders saw it, but "disciplined and reliable" in the words of the *Michigan Manufacturing and Financial Record.* Molders who could not accept the employers' discipline were replaced, the *Record* observed in 1910, as "their foreign helpers learned the trade and a considerable influx of iron molders of foreign birth came in."

Shop, union-enforced work rules regulated the introduction of such machinery, frustrating management's drive for more streamlined and profitable operations. In a Closed Shop, concluded Whirl, "the proprietors were merely the financial agents" for a production process controlled by union tradesmen. "It was for them [managers] to find out the cost of production as arranged by organized labor, and then make the selling price sufficient to leave them a profit."

To employers, such union "interference" was a burdensome restriction on their property rights and a significant barrier to growth. Entrepreneurs and managers saw themselves as the champions of economic rationality, and they did not want to concede or even share control over shopfloor operations with the blue-collar members of Detroit's craft unions. To counter union strength,

the city's industrialists therefore formed the Employers' Association of Detroit (EAD) in December, 1902, and began a long-term campaign to cripple the city's labor movement.

Between 1903 and 1907, companies repeatedly fired union employees and refused to renew Closed Shop agreements, provoking dozens of major strikes. An economic slump, beginning in 1904, gave the EAD a decided advantage. "The plan would be," according to Chester Culver, the EAD's Chief Counsel, "to declare an 'Open Shop' and replace the [union] crew with other workers from the unemployed people here in the city." Rather than allow unions to concentrate their efforts on individual employers, forcing each to accept a separate agreement, EAD member companies had organization spokesmen present a unified position to both the press and the labor movement.

The EAD strategy was very simple. It supplied a firm with strikebreakers and sought a court injunction against the union. This was a particularly easy matter in Michigan, where an 1898 court ruling defined most picketing as an illegal disruption of the peace. Under the inevitable court order, the police would break up picket lines and arrest union leaders.

To insure that unions, once driven from the workplace, would not stage a comeback, the EAD also established a city-wide Labor Bureau to recruit strikebreakers and screen out "troublemakers" from the workforce. After 1903, Detroit's employers frequently turned to this centralized employment agency for detailed records on each job applicant hired and each worker laid off by member companies. By 1906, the Labor Bureau had files on 40,000 people —nearly half of Detroit's workforce—

2) *The machine shop of the C.H. Blomstrom Company, maker of the "Queen" automobile, Detroit, 1905.*

The machinists pictured here produced finished engine blocks and other parts by grinding, drilling, and buffing the rough castings from the foundry. Belts attached to revolving overhead shafts powered the lathes, drill presses, and other machines crowded into the room. Each of these machinists could operate and repair most of the machines in the shop.

3) *Fisher Body, date unknown.*

Metal finishers used files, hammers, and other hand tools to smooth the seams in early car bodies.

4) *C.H. Blomstrom's chassis assembly department, 1905.*

Mechanics assembled the engine, transmission, and finished car at stationary work stations. Since many parts were cast and machined by dozens of outside contractors, the mechanic had to re-file and grind the ill-fitting components to produce a working machine. In assembly, therefore, only "the highest class of mechanics must be employed," *Machinery* magazine wrote in 1909.

---

and EAD spies planted in factories and unions made sure no "quarrelsome" or "insubordinate" workers slipped through the Labor Bureau's net.

Employers argued that screening was a necessary and morally justified defense against union "discrimination." For according to the EAD, the Closed Shop not only was bad for business, it was also "an injustice to those [workers] who have an ability to rise." The maverick "ratebuster" condemned by unions was, to the EAD, "the speedy and perfect workman" who "may be able to do twice the work in a given time that his benchmate can." Under the "false standard of equality" established by union work rules, "the good man," as the EAD termed him, "is kept down and the poor man kept up."

Fortified with this crusading spirit, Detroit's employers steadily wore down their union opponents. In 1907, the city's metal workers fought a series of bitter and violent strikes in a last-ditch effort to stem the anti-union tide. Their demonstrations failed to turn back Hungarian and other foreign-born strikebreakers the police escorted into the plants, and their picket lines were finally broken by court injunctions banning all "loitering" or "union patrolling" in the vicinity of the factories.

Less than 9 percent of Detroit's rapidly expanding workforce was unionized (15,000 out of 175,000) by 1911. Open-Shop employers were free to raise production quotas, lengthen the work day, and introduce new machinery without consulting union Shop Committees. Production speeds and output rose dramatically, but wages either crept up slowly or actually fell in Open-Shop plants. Union-supported apprenticeship programs collapsed in every industry but the building trades, replaced after 1913 by EAD's own management-controlled trade school.

The business climate was balmy indeed for Detroit's auto companies: a vast new market was opening up, capital was abundant, skilled and unskilled labor was available in ample supply, and the trade-union movement was demoralized and weakened. In this fertile soil, the city's economy grew rapidly, nurturing dozens of car and truck manufacturers. In 1910, 38 separate companies produced such forgotten models as the Faulkner-Blanchard "Gunboat Six," the "Huppmobile," and the Grabowsky "Power Wagon." In 1917, Detroit's car companies turned out one million automobiles and employed nearly 140,000 workers. By then, the city was attracting workers from all over North America — and beyond.

LABOR ROUTES

"Since 13 years old," Isaac Litwak later recalled, "I've dreamed of a free world." For Litwak, one of 15 million Europeans who emigrated to the United States between 1890 and 1914, his native Russia was a world of oppression. A Ukrainian Jew born in 1892, his entire childhood was shadowed by the anti-Semitic laws of the Czarist regime—laws which prohibited Jews from owning land, barred them from government employment, and forced them to live in specified areas of western and southern Russia. Frequent massacres of unarmed Jews by civilian and military rioters were routinely condoned and promoted by the Czar's government.

Isaac's boyhood dreams of a free world found their inspiration in the mass strikes and armed uprisings which nearly toppled the Czar in 1905. Before his twenty-first birthday, his dreams, socialist activities, and anti-Czarist organizing made him a political prisoner in Siberia. After his release from prison, he fled Russia to the United States, arriving in Detroit in 1913. Like thousands of other immigrants, Litwak found his first job in the city's booming auto industry, hiring on at the Ford Highland Park foundry.

Among his co-workers were many newly arrived Poles, Lithuanians, Hungarians, and Italians who had fled rural poverty, religious persecution, or

political oppression. Oppression, many found, was not easily left behind. In 1913, when Finnish and other foreign-born workers struck the Calumet, Michigan, copper mines over unsafe equipment, the official response was blunt and violent: the state government sent in the National Guard, the Sheriff deputized 1,700 men, and the company police killed two strikers. After their union was destroyed, many of the defeated miners set out for Detroit to join the city's already flourishing Finnish community.

Like immigrants from dozens of other European countries, they were drawn to the city by reports of plentiful work and high wages in the expanding auto industry. Relatives who had already established themselves in Detroit sent word to their families in Europe, and the glowing, sometimes exaggerated reports circulated from household to household. The city's employers also broadcast the message that Detroit was a place where jobs could be had for the asking. As early as August, 1907, Detroit's Board of Commerce asked immigration officials on New York's Ellis Island to steer foreign workers to the city. The Employers' Association of Detroit placed advertisements in nearly 200 newspapers across the country, encouraging both skilled workers and immigrant laborers to come to the Motor City.

Immigrant workers joined displaced farmers and unemployed harvest hands from the Midwest and South in search of work in the expanding industrial cities. Some of these rural migrants sought only seasonal work to supplement their farm income, but others hoped to find a permanent alternative to agricultural stagnation or rural isolation. Southern farm laborers were especially mobile after 1892, when the Boll Weevil first infested the cotton crop. By 1915, the dreaded insect had spread throughout the South, devastating entire regions and prompting many cotton farmers to switch to cattle grazing, soybeans and other less labor-intensive crops. Many of the displaced sharecroppers and harvest hands moved north.

For black migrants, the South had become especially inhospitable. Racist sentiment had been on the rise since the late 1880s, and over the next quarter century, blacks were stripped of their voting rights, segregated into inferior schools, and systematically terrorized by vigilante and mob violence. In 1915, the militantly racist Ku Klux Klan organization was revived in Georgia, promising a renewal of the lynch-law violence that claimed 100 black lives a year in the 1890s.

Black-owned newspapers like the *Chicago Defender* urged southern blacks to move north, where job opportunities were undeniably greater, even if race relations were hardly ideal. "To die from the bite of frost," the paper advised its southern readers, "is far more glorious than at the hands of a mob." When the outbreak of World War I closed off the supply of immigrant laborers, northern industries also sent labor agents into the South to bring out black workers. Detroit's black population suddenly mushroomed in response to all these trends, growing from less than 6,000 in 1910 to 41,000 by 1920. By the spring of 1920, upwards of 1,000 black migrants were arriving by train every week.

As workers from around the world streamed into the city, Detroit took on the characteristics of a gold-rush town, spreading outward and annexing neighboring land and towns at breakneck speed. From a city of 23 square miles at the turn of the century, Detroit expanded to 139 square miles by 1927. The flood of incoming workers swelled the city's population from less than 300,000 to over 1½ million in these same years, swamping old neighborhoods with newcomers who crowded into every available living space. Open fields and dirt roads on the edge of town gave way to hastily built row and tract houses. In some years, the Detroit Department of Buildings issued 21 permits for new buildings *every day*. "Families unable to

Below: Detroit's Ukrainian Workers' Theatrical Chorus, 1926.

Inset: Arbeiter (Workers') Hall on the near East Side, 1915. This German hall, with outdoor beer garden visible along the side, hosted everything from union meetings, to political campaigns, to dances. The Marx running for reelection as Mayor was Oscar Marx, a German businessman and Progressive Republican.

Opposite: Russian immigrants after arrival in Detroit's train station, 1917.

rent," the Detroit *Free Press* reported in the summer of 1913, "have purchased sites and lived on them in tents or shacks while their homes were being rushed to completion."

Like prospecting towns of the old West, Detroit was full of single men. Some never intended to stay: they planned to work several years, save money, and return to Europe or the South. Others hoped to bring wives and families to Detroit once they established themselves, while others regularly commuted back to their rural (usually Southern) homes between jobs.

By 1920, Detroit had 87,000 more men than women. Living in lodging houses and small hotels near the factories or on the city's lower East Side, these bone-weary workingmen relied on the city's numerous saloons for escape from the lonely grind of factory labor. Until 1916, when Michigan prohibited the sale of alcohol, Detroit boasted 1,600 licensed bars within its city limits, compared to just 310 established churches. Saloons were the poor man's social club and welfare agency, providing free lunches with a 5¢ glass of beer, postal services for transients, public toilets,

"Workingmen: Vote Your Ticket"

Jesus taught that the air and the sea and the sky and all the beauty and fullness thereof were for all the children of men . . . and that is what socialism teaches.

Eugene Debs

In the opening decades of the twentieth century, it appeared to many Americans that "the air and the sea and the sky" had been taken over by a small elite of wealthy "Robber Barons." John D. Rockefeller's Standard Oil Company controlled 85 percent of the nation's oil refineries and 90 percent of its oil pipelines, and the newly formed U.S. Steel Corporation owned over half the country's steel mills. Overall, the top 4 percent of American businesses controlled 57 percent of the nation's industrial production.

With this enormous economic power, corporations could often buy political power as well. Michigan was a prime example. While railroads owned 38 percent of the taxable property in the state, their lobbyists managed to limit the industry's taxes to less than 4 percent of the state's total levy.

Political democracy, many feared, could not survive if the wealthy were permitted to wield such power unchecked. Fueled by a growing sentiment for change, middle-class reformers in both the Republican and Democratic Parties therefore pushed for "Progressive" legislation to regulate corporations and reform the lopsided tax structure.

For some, however, reform was not enough. "Our present social and industrial system is insane," concluded Detroit Federation of Labor President William Baily. "Those who do the most useful and indispensable work receive the least by way of remuneration, while those who do the least, get the most." For Baily and a growing minority in the labor movement, the whole capitalist system was at fault. Inequality and poverty, they argued, could only be eliminated under a socialist system where "the means of production," as Baily put it, "shall be cooperatively owned and democratically managed."

The Socialist Party of America, formed in 1901, gave organized expression to such anti-capitalist convictions. Created by the merger of several smaller organizations, the Party's ranks swelled from 10,000 to nearly 120,000 members in 1912. In the Presidential elections that year, Eugene Debs garnered 900,000 votes as the Socialist Party candidate—a respectable showing compared to the 6.3 million ballots tallied by the victorious Woodrow Wilson, a Progressive Democrat. Socialists also did well on the local level, electing 79 mayors and 1,200 city and state officials.

No single "party line" encompassed the movement these elected officials represented. Most Socialists believed in a non-violent strategy of winning change through the ballot box, but a vocal minority argued that the ruling "capitalist class" would only bow to a General Strike or armed insurrection. Members from both wings of the Party looked to Karl Marx as their theoretical guide, but also quoted home-grown writers like Henry George. Christian Socialists invoked the oldest social critic of them all: "the social message of Jesus, which in an age of machine production means Socialism, and nothing else."

As Detroit entered the "age of machine production," the Socialist Party enlisted some 2,000 adherents, many of them immigrant workers organized into separate language federations for Poles, Russians, Finns, Germans, Hungarians, English-speaking workers, and a half-dozen other groups. To promote their vision of socialist democracy, members organized weekly Labor Forums, sold newspapers, and petitioned the state government for laws curbing anti-union court injunctions. Their outspoken defense of workers' rights also carried Socialists to leadership positions in many of the city's hard-pressed unions, including the Typographical Workers, the Brewers, and the Machinists.

newspapers, billiard tables, and companionship. Meeting rooms were open to political gatherings, trade unions, and weddings, and many saloons also took in boarders; many also doubled as brothels. Until the enactment of statewide prohibition, saloonkeepers sat on the city's election board, served as aldermen, and generally dominated Detroit's politics.

As immigrants continued to pour into the city, old ethnic and racial neighborhoods began to expand and shift. New immigrant "colonies" appeared, with many of these ethnic neighborhoods springing up around particular factories. The first Yugoslavs brought to Detroit by the American Car and Foundry Company settled on Russell and Ferry streets next to the plant. Hungarians working in

track gangs for the Michigan Central Railroad or as laborers in the Solvay Company's alkali plant on West Jefferson settled in the nearby town of Delray, soon to be annexed by Detroit. The new Ford plant in Highland Park attracted nearby colonies of Finns, Yugoslavs, Rumanians, and Lithuanians, while the Dodge Brothers' sprawling plant in Hamtramck drew new Polish immigrants

Presidential candidate Eugene Debs, former head of the American Railway Union, "whistle-stopping" from the back of his Red Special campaign train.

Socialism appealed to these workers as a doctrine of justice and reason. Their world was dominated by continual, sometimes chaotic change— change that was oppressive as often as it was liberating—and socialism promised to re-make this world according to more compassionate standards. In an age that celebrated the scientific innovations transforming industry, Socialists claimed their doctrine provided a "scientific" blueprint for humanizing industry and eliminating the anarchy of boom-bust business cycles.

Not all trade unionists, however, agreed that socialism was either desirable or practical. "The Trades Council [the city-wide union body] is dominated by a rabid socialism that ought to be stifled if we are going to be successful," W.H. Suit, President of the Car and Coach Painters' union, declared in 1904. "I don't want to be classed with this gang."

Neither did most voters. Despite the Party's success in winning leadership positions and support in the labor movement, Socialists never won a sig-

nificant following at Detroit's ballot box. The Party's poor showing stemmed, to some degree, from election laws which made many potential constituents ineligible to vote. One such law, the "Re-Registration" act of 1895, was specifically designed by its conservative sponsors to reduce the number of foreign-born voters in Detroit by 25 percent.

Yet even among the majority of workers eligible to vote, Eugene Debs only garnered 23,000 ballots in Michigan in 1912—about 4 percent of the total. Immigrant and migrant workers had cause to complain of the harsh conditions and long hours they found in many workplaces, but since they also found Detroit to be a freer place than the world they had left behind, they tended to shun revolutionary politics. Unlike their brethren in Europe and, to some degree, the southern United States, most Detroiters were free to vote (if they were men), free to form their own religious and fraternal societies, and usually free to dissent outside the workplace. The Socialist Party offered comraderie, a utopian vision, and dedicated union leaders, but except for workplace leadership, most workers relied on church, family, or saloon to salve the wounds of industrial labor.

When these Detroiters sought change at the ballot box, they turned to reform-minded politicians like Teddy Roosevelt, who carried the Motor City in 1912 as the presidential candidate of the Progressive Party. Six years later, the legacy of Hazen Pingree's Progressive Republicanism stirred Detroit's voters once again, when businessman James Couzens—a youthful participant in the 1891 streetcar riots—won the mayor's office on his pledge to municipalize the trolley system.

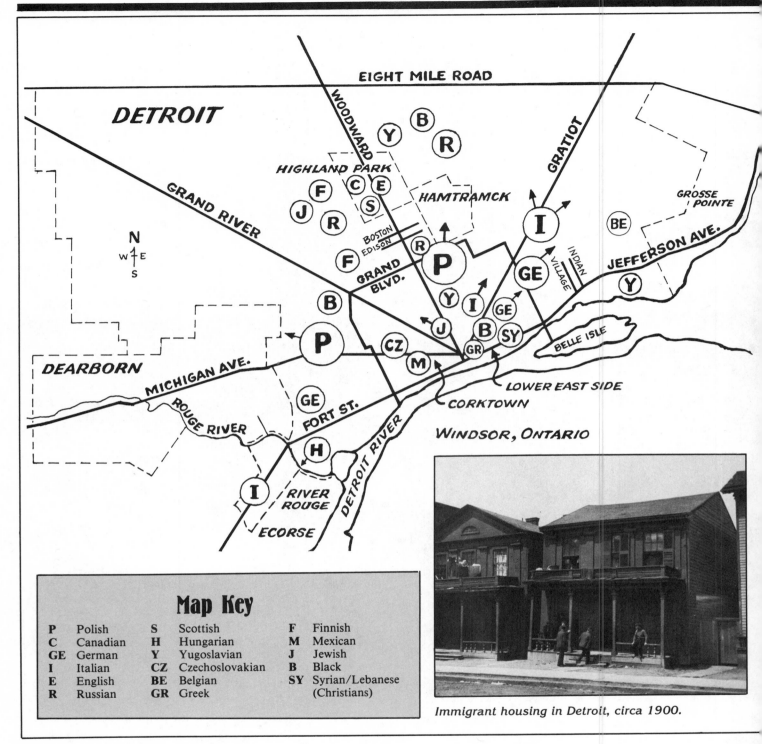

EIGHT MILE ROAD

DETROIT

WOODWARD

GRATIOT

HIGHLAND PARK

HAMTRAMCK

GROSSE POINTE

BOSTON EDISON

GRAND BLVD.

INDIAN VILLAGE

JEFFERSON AVE.

BELLE ISLE

GRAND RIVER

DEARBORN

MICHIGAN AVE.

ROUGE RIVER

FORT ST.

DETROIT RIVER

LOWER EAST SIDE

CORKTOWN

WINDSOR, ONTARIO

RIVER ROUGE

ECORSE

Map Key

P	Polish	**S**	Scottish	**F**	Finnish
C	Canadian	**H**	Hungarian	**M**	Mexican
GE	German	**Y**	Yugoslavian	**J**	Jewish
I	Italian	**CZ**	Czechoslovakian	**B**	Black
E	English	**BE**	Belgian	**SY**	Syrian/Lebanese
R	Russian	**GR**	Greek		(Christians)

Immigrant housing in Detroit, circa 1900.

north from the original Poletown.

For the impoverished and bewildered immigrant who spoke no English and often knew nothing of city life, these ethnic settlements served as a bridge to the new world. Recent arrivals from the old country might initially live in boarding houses run by and for their nationality group (the Finnish Coop Boarding House, for example) or get a home loan from an ethnic bank (the Croatian Building and Loan Association, among others). Ethnic churches, groceries, restaurants, and saloons also provided links with the Old World and a sense of solidarity in the New. National "Homes" were built to serve as community centers in each immigrant neighborhood, while mutual-aid societies provided sick benefits, insurance, and low-cost funerals.

Above all, ethnic ties often determined whether and where one worked. While many companies relied on the Employers' Association to provide workers during strikes and peak produc-tion periods, only a few companies bothered to set up centralized Personnel Offices to handle regular hiring. Even in large factories, hiring was often left to the individual foreman, who naturally favored his family, friends, and nationality group when it came to recommending new workers. As a result, entire departments in many plants often spoke a foreign language. From supervision on down, the pressroom might be Polish in one automobile factory, and predominantly Hungarian in another. Some na-

Mansion of A.L. Born, Secretary Treasurer of Oldberg Manufacturing, maker of auto mufflers, in suburban Bloomfield Hills.

Immigrant Detroit

Three of every four people in Detroit were immigrants or the children of immigrants in 1910. Poles, Germans, Italians, Russians, Austrians, and English-speaking peoples made up the city's leading ethnic groups, but counting them was no easy matter. In 1910, Poles were not counted at all. Because their nation had long been occupied by the neighboring empires of Russia, Austria, and Germany, census takers simply lumped them with the nationality groups of the conquering powers. Thus, at least half of the "Germans" counted were probably Poles. The government began tallying Detroit's largest ethnic group only when Poland became an independent nation after World War I.

Most of the city's population in 1910 lived south of Grand Boulevard — Hamtramck and Highland Park were still rural villages on Detroit's northern border, with only 5,000 residents between them. When the Dodge Brothers opened their plant in Hamtramck and Henry Ford began building factories in Highland Park and Dearborn, the city's population rapidly expanded into

these developing areas, blurring the boundaries of old ethnic neighborhoods. (The 1930 population figures in the accompanying table include these three fast-growing cities.) As the more established nationality groups moved outward, new groups of immigrants and Southern migrants took their place in the East Side slums around lower Gratiot. Detroit's wealthy residents moved outward as well, some to exclusive sections like Indian Village and the Boston Edison district, others as far as Grosse Pointe and Bloomfield Hills.

Some of these neighborhoods excluded Jews; most of Detroit's neighborhoods, rich or poor, barred blacks. The city's nationality groups, on the other hand, were frequently intermingled, with Russians, Lithuanians, and Rumanians living in and around Detroit's Poletown. The further each group moved away from the Detroit River, the more its members intermixed with the neighboring group. English-speaking immigrants were dispersed throughout the city, with a greater-than-average concentration in Highland Park. The city's outer wards were dominated by "native American" whites, and included the more prosperous descendants of the city's older ethnic groups as well as Appalachian hill people and former farmhands from midwestern states.

Major Groups in Detroit, 1910 & 1930

1910

		% of total
Total Population...	466,000	100%
Black..........	5,700	1%
Foreign-Born or Children of Foreign-Born....	345,000	74%
Polish......................		?
German.....................		29%
Canadian...................		16%
Russian....................		6%
Austrian...................		5%
Irish......................		4%
English....................		4%
Italian....................		2%
Hungarian..................		2%
Scottish...................		1%
Belgian....................		1%
(1% = about 4,700 people)		

1930

		% of total
Total Population...1,720,000		100%
Black..........	125,300	7%
Foreign-Born or Children of Foreign-Born....	1,018,000	59%
Polish.....................		13%
Canadian...................		11%
German....................		8%
Italian....................		4%
English....................		4%
Russian...................		3%
Scottish...................		2%
Irish......................		2%
Hungarian..................		1%
Yugoslavian................		1%
Czechoslovakian............		1%
Austrian...................		1%
Belgian....................		1%
Greek.....................		½%
Finnish....................		½%
Mexican...................		½%
Syrian/Lebanese............		½%
(1% = about 17,000 people)		

tionality groups were also associated with particular crafts: Italians dominated the tileworking industry, Germans predominated in brewing, and Scotsmen stood out in the tool-making operations of many auto plants.

When Detroit's workers formed unions, their trade organizations often bore the stamp of this ethnic segregation. There was a "German Branch #2," for example, of Detroit's Amalgamated Society of Carpenters in 1902, and a "Jewish Laundry Drivers Union" in the

1920s. While ethnic and religious ties bound many workers to their supervisor or foreman, ethnic solidarity could also embolden those who challenged Detroit's Open-Shop employers.

National and religious unity was a frequent rallying cry in the city's immigrant neighborhoods. But the call to solidarity was not always heeded. Yugoslavians, for example, were not a traditional ethnic group at all, but an

amalgam of Serbian, Croatian, and Slovenian peoples bound together in a new nation after World War I. Detroit's Yugoslav American Independent Club tried repeatedly to unite the three groups, but was undermined by the bitter conflicts between Serbs and Croats, the one Eastern Orthodox, the other Roman Catholic—and both intensely committed to separate national identities.

Divisions within Detroit's Jewish community were less embittered, but perhaps more confusing. Virtually every nationality group was represented, with German Jews usually living north of the downtown area and worshipping at the Reform Temple Beth El, while East-European and Russian Jews usually joined Orthodox temples in the heart of the lower East Side Jewish districts.

Even distinct nationality groups were fragmented by regional and political differences. Many northern Italians, coming from an urban and industrialized society, had little in common with local Sicilians, who came from the rural and clannish south. Detroit's Italian-language press was equally divided, with *La Tribuna* openly endorsing Italy's Fascist regime after Mussolini came to power in 1922, and *La Voce del Popolo* just as vigorously opposing the new regime.

Detroit's black community, in contrast, was relatively united behind the middle-class leadership of the Detroit Urban League, founded in 1916, and the National Association for the Advancement of Colored People (NAACP), which founded a Detroit chapter in 1912. Both organizations relied on black churches for support—principally the Second Baptist Church, a congregation with a large number of poor Southern migrants, and St. Matthews Protestant Episcopal Church, catering to a small number of established black businessmen and professionals. While the NAACP fought to break down discriminatory barriers, the League, under John Dancy, served as a multi-purpose social service agency, organizing vocational training, housing referrals, a baby clinic, recreation, and (with funding from the Employers' Association of Detroit) a job bank.

There was no comparable degree of unity in Detroit's Polish community. Polish nationalists who favored independence for their homeland from Russian, Austrian, and German domination frequently clashed with the conservative hierarchy of the Catholic Church, which more often favored accommodation. The resulting conflict impelled some American Poles to found the Polish National Church, whose four Detroit parishes rejected both the social-conservatism and the Latin ritual of Roman Catholicism, replacing the latter with a Polish liturgy. Pro-independence sentiment also inspired the formation of the Polish National Alliance, whose social insurance programs competed with those of the Polish Roman Catholic Union.

Nationalists and Catholics, in turn, often squabbled with the Poles in Detroit's Socialist Party, whose members formed five branches of their own sick and benefit society, the Polish Mutual Aid Association. While moderate and conservative groups centered their activities in the two Polish Homes (Dom Polski, sites 4 and 5) built shortly before World War I, Polish socialists centered their activities at the Peoples' Home (Dom Ludowy) on Harper Avenue at Joseph Campau. After the Russian revolution of 1917, even the socialists were split, with many pro-communist Poles eventually joining the Polish branch of the International Workers Order, located on Yemans Street in Hamtramck (site 6).

But whatever their political, social, and religious differences, the principle of group solidarity remained a compelling ideal for Detroit's foreign-born workers. National pride could sustain them in an alien and often unfriendly environment, even as it also separated them from native-born whites, blacks, and other foreign-born workers.

Above: Saint Albertus Church, facing St. Aubin Street (site 7). Built in 1884, St. Albertus was the first of Detroit's Polish churches. Together with neighboring Sweetest Heart of Mary (1889) and St. Josaphat (1890), St. Albertus marked the center of Detroit's expanding Poletown.

Inset: Downtown stores and workshops, Woodward Avenue and State Street, date unknown. Once the industrial and commercial hub of the city, the downtown's riverfront district declined in importance as new industries located their factories near Poletown and other outlying neighborhoods.

TOEING THE LINE

In the opening decades of the twentieth century, Detroit's social and industrial landscape was completely transformed. Tens of thousands of job-hungry workers from around the world poured into the city every year. The Employers' Association of Detroit drove many of the city's craft unions into near oblivion. Automobile sales were growing by leaps and bounds, led by the Ford Motor Company's annual sales of 11,000 Model Ts in 1909. The sum total of all these trends strongly influenced how managers ran their factories, particularly in the booming auto industry.

Cars had first been built at stationary work stations, with one or several skilled mechanics assembling the entire car piece by piece. Though these first custom-built models were too expensive for most working people, demand for automobiles grew dramatically among wealthier buyers, and car manufacturers began to search for production shortcuts to meet rising demand.

In the city's foundries, where molten brass, copper, and iron were cast into metal parts for auto manufacturers, the Open Shop campaign of 1903–1907 had eliminated union work rules and opened the way for increased mechanization of production. In car manufacturing itself, where unions had never won a significant foothold, the first innovations were primarily organizational, not mechanical. When Henry Ford streamlined operations at his plant on the corner of Piquette and Beaubien streets (site 9) in 1904–1905, he did so by dividing up certain assembly tasks into simple operations that less-skilled workers could perform. Under the new arrangement, these workers pushed huge bins of parts up and down the rows of stationary cars, with each work gang stopping to install a particular part—a fender, wheels, the dashboard—before moving to the next car.

Production efficiency in the final assembly of cars rose, but the soaring demand for Ford's Model T, introduced in 1908, rose even faster. Ford still had to rely on skilled mechanics to perform the complicated tasks in the Piquette plant—such as filing and fitting together the parts for transmissions and engines. These workers were not protected by union work rules, but their monopoly of mechanical skills and their crucial role in the production process enabled them to work at their own pace. Even the less-skilled assembly workers had some control over their work pace. As they pushed their bins from car to car, they could slow down to rest or to speak a word with their workmates. Beyond a

The Ford Highland Park assembly line (above) and body plant (inset) were both a far cry from the pre-assembly-line operations pictured on page 21.
Previous page: The "Crystal Palace," Ford's Highland Park plant.

certain point, supervisors simply could not force the men to adopt a faster gait or completely abandon their occasional socializing.

To gain greater control over the production process, Ford began to lay plans for a new plant in the rural village of Highland Park. It would be, he announced, the biggest automobile plant in the world, employing new production methods that would revolutionize the auto industry.

Ford was not alone in seeking ways to spur production and lower labor costs. Factory owners had been mechanizing and deskilling certain kinds of production for many years, but after 1900, the nation's larger corporations attempted to do so on a broader, more systematic basis. The principles of this new "scientific management" were most vigorously espoused by Frederick Taylor, a former steel mill supervisor who became, after 1903, the nation's leading consultant on

"productivity"—or worker output.

Like Ford, Taylor complained that in most workplaces—whether union or non-union—"the shop [is] really run by the workmen and not by the bosses. The workmen together carefully plan...just how fast each job should be done." Taylor's solution was simple: "All possible brainwork should be removed from the shop and centered in the planning or laying-out department." Management, in short, should redesign *every* job and divide it into dozens of simple, repetitive tasks performed by unskilled laborers or semi-skilled machine tenders. Skilled workers with their relatively high pay would no longer have to be tolerated in such large numbers. With deskilling, most craftsmen could be replaced, in Taylor's words, "by men of smaller attainments, who are therefore cheaper than those required under the old system."

When Taylor came to Detroit in 1909

and spoke to executives at Packard, Henry Ford was already planning to make his new Highland Park plant (dubbed the "Crystal Palace" because of its many windows) a model of "scientific management." Between 1910 and 1913, he put his ideas into practice by standardizing parts production and developing the auto industry's first moving assembly line (site 10). Where before, entire engines had been built by a single mechanic with a few helpers, now the engine blocks were pulled past a line of over 100 workers. Each worker performed a specialized task as the engine (or its parts) moved past: one would ream bearings, one every seven seconds, all day long; the next would file bearings, one every 14 seconds, all day long; and the next would put bearings on camshafts, one every 10 seconds, all day long.

With the mechanical assembly line setting the pace, workers could no longer choose their own work tempo, and average production time per engine was more than halved. In chassis production, the same division of labor and moving assembly line cut production time even further—from 14 hours per chassis, to just 93 minutes. It also allowed Ford to replace craftsmen with unskilled immigrant workers from Eastern and Southern Europe. Whereas one of every three Ford employees in 1910 had been a skilled worker, by 1917 the proportion of skilled craftsmen had fallen to one in five. Labor costs fell accordingly, and since there were still over 100 car companies competing for buyers, Ford was under pressure to pass some of these cost savings on to consumers. The Model T, which cost $850 in 1908 (as much as a Cadillac), cost only $290 by the early 1920s. As the price fell, sales skyrocketed—from 10,600 in all of 1909 to 16,000 *a month* by 1913.

By early 1914, however, it was apparent that Ford's spectacular innovations had one serious flaw: no one wanted to work for very long in the "Crystal Palace." Ford paid $2.25 for a nine-hour day, roughly the industry average. But assembly-line work was a hellish occupation, and workers unaccustomed to machine-paced labor cursed the line as a mechanical slave driver. Many felt the elimination of skill was personally degrading, and the modest pay and long trolley ride to Highland Park hardly seemed worthwhile when work was available elsewhere.

"The average worker," Ford claimed,

"wants a job in which he does not have...to think." Many workers apparently thought otherwise—they quit Ford in droves. To maintain a workforce of 14,000, Ford had to hire 52,000 workers during 1913, and each new employee required a costly breaking-in period. Organizers from the Industrial Workers of the World began directing their union message to disaffected Ford workers, and soon drew lunchtime crowds of 3,000 outside the Highland Park plant.

Drastic action was called for. On January 5, 1914, Ford therefore announced a profit-sharing plan that would double wages to nearly $5 a day. Civic leaders praised Ford's "generosity;" competitors cursed his "ruinous scheme," fearing their workers would demand the same; and people flocked to Detroit from all over the United States and Canada to reap the promised bonanza, scheduled to begin January 12.

Most were disappointed, for by January 12, Ford had hired only a fraction of the thousands who had applied. That morning, 10,000 angry jobseekers pressed against the plant gates in freezing weather, threatening to break into the factory. Plant guards inside the gates and city fire trucks parked outside together drenched the crowd with fire hoses, driving the people back and caking their clothes with ice. Infuriated, the crowd cut the city's fire hoses, attacked policemen, and broke hundreds of plant windows along Manchester before dispersing.

Despite this shaky start, Ford's gamble paid off. Absenteeism and turnover dropped, and productivity soared. "When we gave the $5 day," department head William Klan recalled, top management "called us in and said that since they [the workers] were getting twice the wages, they wanted twice as much work.... On the assembly line, we simply turned up the speed of the lines."

By 1920, competing car companies had followed Ford's lead, installing assembly lines and raising wages to roughly $5 a day. Undeniable benefits flowed from the rapid increase in worker productivity that followed. Mass production made once unaffordable goods like cars cheaper to produce, and therefore (with competition) cheaper to buy. Wages in the auto industry were also well above the national average, and big companies like Ford and General Motors provided savings and insurance plans for their workers. Even medium-sized companies encouraged workers to join factory-sponsored bands, glee clubs, orchestras, or sports leagues.

But autoworkers paid a high price for these "corporate welfare" plans and high wages. "You've got to work like hell at Ford's," a worker reported to one researcher in the mid-1920s. "From the time you become a number in the morning until the bell rings for quitting time you have to keep at it. You can't let up." The sheer, dulling monotony of this intensified work took a visible toll on each worker. Ford executives like Samuel Marquis reported as early as 1918 that "a good many men break down mentally and physically" under the strain of "continuous application to one line of work." Ford at least paid workers by the hour—most companies pegged wages to actual output, and continually lowered these "piece rates" and "Group Bonuses" to goad workers still further.

Whether hourly wage or piece rate, high wage or low, few autoworkers could count on collecting their paycheck all year long. By the 1920s, when many auto companies were redesigning car models every year, most factories would shut down in the late summer or early fall for retooling. These forced vacations *without* pay (only managers and owners got paid vacations) usually lasted six weeks. For some, the lay-off stretched into two or more months waiting for the new production season. And when rehiring finally began, there was no guarantee a worker would get his or her job back; it was usually up to the foreman, and he generally preferred younger men who could "get out production." Workers who could not get their old jobs back were often rehired as "beginners" at lower, starting wages.

Disabled workers were particularly vulnerable—and numerous. In 1916, the Ford Highland Park plant alone reported 192 severed fingers, 68,000 lacerations, 5,400 burns, and 2,600 puncture wounds. A safety campaign

"Nothing to Unlearn . . ."

Even with the coming of the assembly line, many jobs were still not tied directly to a moving conveyor. But the work was changing in these non-assembly departments as well. The Chalmers (now Chrysler) shop shown below sometime after 1910 had little in common with the machine shop shown on page 20. The women who machined parts on these simplified drill presses were only trained to perform a narrow range of tasks, repeated without variation all day long. A smaller number of skilled workers—the men pictured on the left —set up the machines and repaired them. H.L. Arnold, writing of Ford in 1916, concluded that the company "desires and prefers machine operators who have nothing to unlearn, who have no theories of correct surface speeds for metal finishing, and who will do what they are told, over and over again, from bell-time to bell-time."

reduced the carnage somewhat, but did little to stem the epidemic of industrial diseases caused by clouds of metal dust and sand, chemical fumes, lead poisoning, acid mist, and intense heat. Michigan's Workmen's Compensation Act, passed in 1912, provided only token support for the worker disabled by job-related accidents, and nothing at all for the victims of industrial disease. To survive, the disabled veterans of Detroit's industrial army had to rely on their families and the mutual aid societies of their particular nationality group.

D ay in and day out, the cars kept rolling off the line. Ten years after the inauguration of the $5 day, Ford's factories produced 7,000 Model Ts in *one day*. In the meantime, workers resisted the ant-like regimentation as

One Big Union

There has been for the past two months, and there is at this time, more restlessness, more aggression among the workmen in Detroit and elsewhere than there has been for several years past.

J.J. Whirl, Secretary, Employers' Association of Detroit, February, 1912.

To the Secretary of the Employers' Association of Detroit, there was special cause for alarm in 1912: the appearance, here and nationally, of the Industrial Workers of the World, or IWW.

Formed in 1905, this organization was entirely unlike the American Federation of Labor. The craft-dominated AFL sought primarily to protect the work rules of skilled tradesmen and win improved working conditions. The IWW, on the other hand, sought to make workers the eventual masters of industry—regulating capitalism was not enough. "This worn-out and corrupt system offers no promise of improvement and adaptation," the organization's founding manifesto brashly declared; reform "offers only a perpetual struggle for slight relief within wage slavery."

The "Wobblies," as they were called, advocated broad-based industry-wide unions that united workers of every craft, race, and nationality. Strikes under IWW direction would become General Strikes challenging the entire system. According to this scenario, the ballot-box strategies of the Socialist Party were as impotent as the craft conservatism of

I.W.W. organizer Matilda Rabinowitz under arrest by Detroit police in 1913.

most AFL unions. As the Wobblies saw it, only direct action on the job, not votes, would build the "Workers' Co-operative Republic" and finally "burst the shell of capitalist government."

There were others in the labor movement calling for broad-based unions that could unite workers of various skills and nationalities. Within the AFL, radical union leaders in the meat-packing, clothing, and railroad industries mobilized widespread support for industrial unionism after 1900, especially in Chicago and New York City. But the IWW's "mass strikes" took on a special, crusade-like quality, with charismatic leaders like "Big Bill" Haywood and Elizabeth Gurley Flynn rallying thousands of immigrant workers against "Capitalist Tyranny" and the craft-conscious "American Separation of Labor." With no strike

funds and only a handful of organizers, the IWW between 1909 and 1913 managed to lead huge strikes of immigrant steelworkers in Pennsylvania, of textile workers in Massachusetts, of silk workers in New Jersey, and of rubber workers in Ohio.

Workers who endorsed the IWW's militant leadership in these strikes did not necessarily accept the Wobblies' revolutionary politics. Between periods of peak mobilization, the majority of workers wanted to impose more equitable and stable rules on their employers, not wage a life-consuming struggle to overthrow capitalism. But the IWW, as a "revolutionary union," would not sign written contracts with employers—according to Wobbly leaders, such agreements were a dishonorable "truce with the enemy." As

best they could. Some took turns doing two jobs in short bursts so their neighbor on the line could sneak a smoke on the factory roof; some became "toilet loafers," and others—particularly the semi-skilled machine operators who fed parts to the assembly line—organized informal slowdowns and gave the cold shoulder to any "ratebuster" who broke ranks. Frank Marquart later recalled how two "speed kings" in his shop were treated: "No one spoke to them. Every time one went to the washroom, the belts on his machine were cut, the grinding wheel was smashed, his personal tools were damaged, the word 'Rat' was chalked on his machine..."

But organized union activity was difficult. It was also, according to the press, the government, and certainly the employers, "Un-American."

a result, the IWW found it difficult to establish on-going organizations after a strike ended and worker enthusiasm subsided.

Yet the Wobblies claimed they were the wave of the future, and Detroit's industrial leaders viewed their arrival in the city with foreboding. When IWW organizer Matilda Rabinowitz began drawing lunchtime crowds of 3,000 Ford workers, company officials promptly abolished outdoor lunch privileges and had Rabinowitz and four others arrested. More alarming to employers was the support the Wobblies won at Studebaker's #3 plant, located at the corner of West Jefferson and Clark (site 11). Resentment there had long simmered over the company's bi-monthly paychecks, which forced workers to stretch their modest pay over two weeks. On the morning of June 17, 1913, toolmaker Dale Schlosser, an advocate of the popular demand for weekly paychecks, was fired for an unexcused absence. When word of the sudden dismissal spread through the factory, Schlosser's co-workers in the tool room led the majority of the plant's 3,500 skilled and unskilled workers in a general walkout.

The first major autoworkers strike in Detroit had begun. By noon, thousands of men were milling in the streets outside the factory, joined by workers from the neighboring Timken Axle plant (site 12). Led by a worker carrying an American flag nailed to a pole, some 600 workers marched seven miles across town to Studebaker's #1 plant (located in the old Ford plant on Piquette and Beaubien, site 9). The strikers, separated from the factory by a hastily deployed squad of police, urged the lunch-time crowd of workers from Plant #1 to join the protest. "Now that we're out," shouted one iron-lunged speaker, "let's strike for the 8-hour day. We can get it. We can get the Cadillac and Packard [workers] too." Joined by some 200–300 supporters from Plant #1, the workers marched downtown to the Studebaker #5 plant on Franklin near St. Aubin (site 13). A similar effort to stop operations there generated scattered support, but failed to close the plant. The day ended with a rally featuring Polish, Yiddish, Russian, Slavic, German and English speakers, where the strikers elected the Wobblies official strike leaders.

Attempting to spread the walkout to the entire auto industry, on June 19, 2,000 strikers marched to the huge Packard plant on East Grand Boulevard (site 14). Circling the plant once, they were attacked by mounted police who charged into the crowd, singling out and clubbing down leaders as they fled through alleys and into houses.

With many IWW leaders now under arrest and the EAD supplying Studebaker with new workers, many strikers began to ask for their jobs back. The company had, in the meantime, made a partial concession to the unrest, agreeing to allow workers to draw 70 percent of their pay halfway through the two-week period. But the company refused to consider any demand for the 8-hour day or union recognition.

The IWW failed to win any lasting presence in the auto industry, but an important lesson had been learned: it was possible to unite skilled and unskilled autoworkers of diverse nationalities around militant trade unionism. Henry Ford, contemplating the labor instability in his Highland Park plant, no doubt took note. Within six months of the Studebaker strike, the $5 day was announced to prevent similar upheavals at the Crystal Palace.

MAKING AMERICANS

Even after the IWW's defeat in 1913, Detroit's industrialists looked upon the mass of immigrant workers in their city as an unpredictable genie—at once a highly profitable source of labor power, but also a volatile, alien force that could not always be controlled.

Radical politics and trade-union activity were only part of the problem. In the day-to-day operation of the factory, managers seeking to impose a military-style discipline generally found the rural backgrounds and varied nationalities of their workers far more troublesome. The recently arrived peasant from Europe and the farmhand from rural America were both used to hard work, but as raw recruits in Detroit's industrial army, these former agricultural workers often made poor factory hands. Most were accustomed to a varied rhythm of work that changed with the seasons: periods of intense labor during planting and harvesting, alternating with rounds of repair work, hunting, and household crafts in the winter—with each season punctuated by local festivals and religious holidays. People long accustomed to such rural ways often recoiled from the relentless and unvaried grind of factory labor. They resisted straight-jacket discipline, skipped work or came in late, and generally jumped from job to job in the booming auto industry.

Even "good" workers frequently stayed home to mark holidays traditionally observed by their ethnic or religious group. A Polish wedding celebration might last three or four days, leaving a bewildered management with depleted work crews. Ethnic rivalries could be equally disruptive when the clashing groups of foreign-born workers fought within plants. Heavy drinking also alarmed middle-class managers, who often saw alcoholism as a purely "foreign" import—caused by German beer, Italian wine, or Russian vodka.

The "foreign element" posed yet another problem. By 1914, Detroit's auto plants had become a Babel of languages. At Ford, foreign-born workers from 22 nationality groups made up over 70 percent of the workforce, and nearly half of these workers spoke no English at all. Work instructions required multiple translations, and safety signs in the plant had to be printed in at least eight languages.

For the city's "Captains of Industry," this all added up to an impossible state of affairs: an industrial workforce that could not understand work commands, resisted industrial discipline, and seemed to live entirely outside the norms of traditional American/Protestant culture. Industrialists and social service agencies therefore resolved to re-make Detroit's polyglot workforce into a uniform, disciplined mass of "good" citizens. They would Americanize the working class by extending "factory influence into the whole life of the workman," as Boyd Fisher, vice president of the Executive's Club of Detroit, put it in 1917. Echoing the solemn opinion of his fellow executives, Fisher declared that each businessman must become "a co-partner with the teacher, the minister, and the social worker in the business of reforming men."

Between 1910 and 1920, Detroit's business and community leaders were filled with the "reforming" zeal.

Even Americans, it turned out, had to be reformed if they were to meet management's approval, especially if they were Southern blacks. The Urban League's first director, Forrester Washington, was among those who disparaged the "loud, noisy type of Negroes unused to city ways that are flocking to Detroit." To educate the new arrivals in the ways of urban culture, the League published booklets outlining the "do's" and "don'ts" of proper behavior: don't be late for work; don't wear flashy clothes; don't use loud or vulgar language; don't wear overalls on Sunday; don't braid the children's hair in certain ways; and don't keep them out of school. The League carried this message directly to black workers in the factories, arranging noon-hour talks on good work habits by college men from the Young Negro Progressive Association.

Similar messages were directed at foreign-born workers in night-school classes sponsored by the Detroit Board of Commerce. Led by representatives from business, the Mayor's office, the YMCA, and the Employers' Association, the Board's "Americanization Committee" organized English-language courses in 25 public schools in immigrant neighborhoods, exposing some 4,000 workers each term to "Robert's Dramatic Method" of teaching English.

Nothing could compare, however, with the multi-faceted Americanization campaign of the Ford Motor Company. Henry Ford organized his own English School and required non-English speaking workers to take its 72-session course, during which the students learned not only English, but also how to properly brush their teeth, how to use a knife and fork, and how to get to work on time. Over 14,000 immigrants enrolled in Ford's School between 1914 and 1917 and no doubt learned valuable language skills—whether they wanted to or not. Unfortunately, they were also told in their civics textbook, the *Ford Guide*, that the "Yellow races...have been called half civilized, because they have not got ahead quite as well as white people." Black people, according to the

E PLURIBUS UNUM

"Commencement exercises were held in the largest hall in the city. On the stage was represented an immigrant ship. In front of it was a huge melting pot. Down the gangplank came the members of the class dressed in their national garbs...[they descended] into the Ford melting pot and disappeared. Then the teachers began to stir the contents of the pot with long ladles. Presently the pot began to boil over and out came the men dressed in their best American clothes and waving American flags."   S.S. Marquis, Ford Sociological Dept, 1916.

Opposite: McGraw School graduation, May, 1919.

Guide, "came from Africa where they lived like other animals in the jungle. White men brought them to America and made them civilized." Ford's "American" education even included racism.

To ensure compliance with its Americanization plan, the Employers' Association announced that only those who spoke English could get a job through its labor agency. To emphasize this point, Ford made a movie showing non-English speaking workers being turned away from an EAD employment line. The movie played in most Detroit theaters.

Ford even established a "Sociological Department," with 100 investigators visiting workers in off-hours to measure their home life against "American" standards. Those who passed muster were entitled to Ford's $5-a-day profit sharing plan; those who failed to "improve" themselves were dropped from the plan and frequently dismissed. Since Ford believed the only proper place for women was in the home, he excluded women workers from profit sharing (unless they were single and providing sole support for a dependent). If a man's wife worked outside the home, he too was ineligible for the $5-a-day plan. Additional ground for disqualification included gambling, drinking, taking in boarders, poor hygiene, or buying on credit. A list of 80 men taken off Ford's

"Honor Roll" in 1917 accounted for each worker's demotion in the same straight-laced terms: "Polish wedding, drunk," "selling real estate," "domestic trouble," "crap game while on duty." When Orthodox Greeks and Russians skipped work one day in January, 1914, to celebrate their traditional Christmas, Ford fired 1,000 of the missing worshippers.

All the while, Ford's Sociological investigators encouraged immigrant workers to leave their ethnic neighborhoods for "healthier" environments, thereby adding to the substantial pressures already undermining ethnic communities. Few nationality groups established permanent settlements during this period of chaotic, hothouse growth. New factories were always drawing workers to different parts of town, and new nationality groups and migrants crowded into the old immigrant districts. Some neighborhoods, especially on the lower East Side, changed character several times as Italian, black, German, and Jewish workers jostled for space. Ford's housing policies and high wages added to the perpetual upheaval: between 1914 and 1916, nearly 11,000 Ford workers moved to new homes.

As ethnic cohesion and identity were diluted, traditionalists fought a rear-guard battle to preserve their

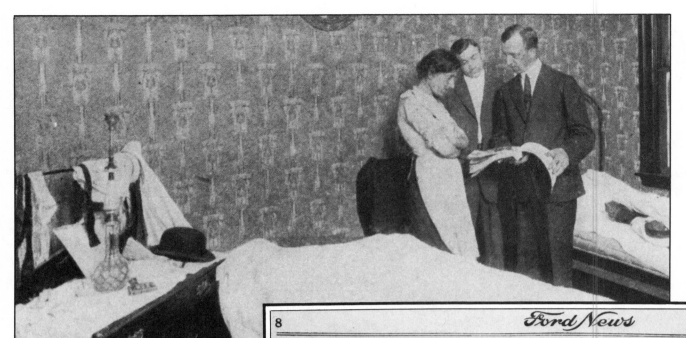

Employees should use plenty of soap and water in the home, and upon their children, bathing frequently . . . Notice that the most advanced people are the cleanest.

Helpful Hints & Advice to Employees,
Ford Motor Company, 1915.

language and culture. They faced formidable odds. Radio station WJLB might carry as many as 16 nationality programs a week in the 1920s, but a spin of the dial also brought "The General Motors Family Party," "The Palmolive Hour," and "The A&P Gypsies" into immigrant homes. Foreign-language newspapers still flourished in Detroit, but their pages also contained a growing amount of corporate advertising, much of it provided by the American Association of Foreign-Language Newspapers (AAFLN).

The AAFLN, founded by a consortium of corporations including Standard Oil and American Tobacco, was no friend of immigrant culture. The ads it funneled to money-starved foreign-language newspapers were designed to break down immigrant and rural values of thrift, community cohesion, and home-based production of food or clothes. The diversity and self-sufficiency of these immigrant cultures were the enemies of mass marketing, which stressed individual success, status anxiety, and conformity—whether you possessed a "Leisure Hour" electric washer

Top: *A Ford investigator explains the principles of American housekeeping to the wife of a Ford worker.*

Bottom: *An ad for the Ford company store, circa 1920.*

Henry Ford's Americanism, by promoting thrift and savings, differed from the stress on conspicuous consumption found in much corporate advertising. But like his Madison Avenue counterparts, Ford believed the foreign-born should conform to a single, "American" standard of dress, diet, speech, and hygiene, and his company store made all the ingredients of this American Way available at cut rate prices—"No profit added."

or had the foresight to neutralize the "Hidden Wells of Poison" in your mouth with Listerine.

"National advertising," declared AAFLN director Frances Alice Kellor, "is the great Americanizer." Indeed, "It is the answer to Bolshevism," she claimed in 1919, the year AAFLN channeled 5 percent of the nation's advertising to 700 foreign-language newspapers. The message of these ads, whether foreign- or English-language, newsprint or (in the 1920s) radio, was unmistakable: the consumer market was the democratic arena in America, where sensible shoppers could buy their way into elite status. While the ads were directed primarily to middle-class audiences, immigrants could hardly ignore the barrage of radio jingles, display ads, and billboard messages. "The boss?...There with th' pipe," a worker says in a 1920 ad for Edgeworth Tobacco. "Men at the top are apt to be pipe smokers. Ever noticed?"

Status was on sale at your local drugstore. You had only yourself to blame if you did not buy into it. America was, after all, the land of opportunity—for individuals, not for groups. Foreign-born adults might resist or ignore this corporate culture and cling to their customary ways, but with the exception of the Polish community (which supported nearly 30 parochial schools), most immigrant children went to public schools and learned an "Americanism" that stood in violent contrast with the traditional beliefs of some parents.

Most foreign-born adults sought to become more American in any case. Having come here because they rejected the poverty and oppression of the old world, immigrant workers hoped to build or buy their own home and establish a secure niche in their new homeland. Their ethnic pride was a protective response to both the anti-immigrant sentiment of native-born Americans, and the alien surroundings of a fast growing industrial city. As such, this ethnic consciousness was not opposed to Americanization, but to the sneering, belligerent "Americanism" of groups like the American Protective Association. While rejecting the cultural suicide demanded by such groups, Detroit's Poles could readily transfer their village loyalties to their adopted city; as early as 1908, immigrant newspapers like *Dziennik Polski* were, by popular demand, covering the Detroit Tigers in extensive detail.

The ethnic identity of Detroit's immigrant workforce was built upon,

A saloon in Detroit's Delray district, 1898.

Demon Drink

For many industrialists and middle-class reformers, the immigrant saloon was the greatest obstacle to "uplifting" and Americanizing Detroit's workers.

In nearby saloons, employers complained, "strikers and unemployed men congregate daily...pitching quoits [metal rings] to pass away the time while awaiting their evening controversy with strikebreakers." The *Detroit Journal* commended the City Council's 1907 action prohibiting new saloons near factories or in the neighborhoods of "well-to-do citizens," noting that saloons "defeat the efforts of altruistic employers to improve social conditions and raise the moral and physical standards of their employees."

Advocates of complete prohibition of alcohol grew in number as consumption of beer and other spirits rose dramatically after 1900. Temperance leaders called attention to the harmful effects of alcoholism and the corrupting influence of saloon owners on city politics. Even some trade unionists and socialists, fearing that heavy drink sapped the workers' will to resist, supported prohibition.

When a statewide ban on alcohol came to a vote in 1916, Detroiters rejected the measure at the polls. Rural voters, however, gave mandatory temperance the margin of victory, and three years later, nationwide Prohibition was enacted.

as well as in reaction to, America's dominant culture and institutions. The Americanization campaigns of Detroit's employers and advertisers, rather than obliterating this consciousness, contributed to an already complex mixture of identities, not quite "American" (as Henry Ford defined it), but also far removed from the peasant cultures of eastern and southern Europe.

This hybrid culture found expression in the very names Detroit's ethnic population chose for themselves. Because many employers wouldn't hire foreign-born workers into white-collar

jobs, some immigrants changed their names to improve their chances of escaping blue-collar work. Stephen Majewski was only one of many ambitious Poles who Americanized his name after arriving in Detroit, becoming "Stephen May." But when Poland gained its independence after World War I and Hamtramck became a separate city in 1922, a wave of national pride swept Detroit's Polish community, prompting some to readopt their Polish names.

Hamtramck's second Mayor was therefore known as "Stephen May Majewski" when inaugurated in 1926.

RED SCARE

On the evening of January 2, 1920, a dance was held at the former Schiller Hall on Gratiot and St. Aubin. Couples and families gathered around the dance floor or sat in the balcony of the old German hall, owned since 1918 by the Socialist Party of Michigan and renamed "House of the Masses." For nearly two years, the building (site 15) had served as a center for socialist, ethnic, and labor groups. That evening, at least five meetings were in progress on the building's upper floors, most of them focusing on the plight of 60 foreign-born radicals arrested in November, 1919, and now threatened with deportation.

At 9 p.m., the dance music was suddenly interrupted by heavy pounding on the building's front door. The sound of splintering wood immediately followed as several hundred city and state police, led by federal agents, burst into the hall. The small army quickly swarmed through the building, ordering the dancers and onlookers to keep their hands over their heads while officers battered down the meeting room doors on the upper floors. No reasons were given for the sudden attack. The 200 people in the hall were simply loaded into vans, driven to the Post Office, and herded into an impromptu prison on the fifth floor, where they joined 300 other bewildered, mostly foreign-born prisoners netted in smaller raids all across the city.

The police explained the next morning that those seized were "dangerous aliens" plotting to overthrow the government. Significantly, they held their educational meetings "in districts inhabited almost exclusively by foreigners." To protect the nation, the government planned to deport these Reds along with nearly 5,000 other "Bolsheviks" arrested that same night in 32 other American cities.

For the terrorized prisoners swept up in these "Palmer Raids" (led by A. Mitchell Palmer, U.S. Attorney General), the Bill of Rights was a dead letter: prisoners were denied any access to a lawyer during their interrogation, were never charged with a crime, and were never brought to trial before a jury. Immigration officials unilaterally determined that 600 of those arrested were politically "undesirable"—and they were promptly expelled from the country.

This was Americanization with a vengeance. Foreign-born workers who shed their old-world allegiances and adopted the government's version of "true Americanism" were officially welcome in the United States. But the rest—radicals, "enemy aliens," and those "hyphenated" ethnic-Americans who resisted assimilation—were subject to government surveillance, possible arrest, and even expulsion.

The events that gave rise to this coercive Americanism stretched back at least to April, 1917, when the United States entered World War I. Siding with the Allies (England, France, Russia, and Italy), the U.S. sent 1.2 million troops to fight the Central Powers (Germany and Austria-Hungary). A sizeable number of Americans opposed our entry into this European conflict, which had already raged for 2½ years and taken milllions of lives. German- and Austrian-Americans enthusiastically defended their respective "Fatherlands" against the Allies, while many Irish-Americans held back from a war effort that made the U.S. an ally of the hated British. Henry Ford, representing a deep strain of isolationism among native-born Protestants, initially blamed "war profiteers" for sparking the conflict—though he later agreed to build Navy patrol boats at his new Dearborn plant when the U.S. joined the fighting.

Radicals were especially opposed to the war. While the country's two major political parties and the national AFL all supported the government, the Socialist Party did not. It denounced the Declaration of War as a "crime against the people of the United States" and advocated draft resistance. In Detroit, the majority of local unions endorsed the war effort, but a significant minority condemned both the war and the national AFL's vigorous support of U.S. intervention. "If Mr. Gompers wishes to fight," declared the Detroit locals of the International Association of Machinists, "let him do so against [the capitalist] class, *not for it*. Long live...the fight against exploitation and oppression!" With both the Machinists and the Typographical Union in the anti-war camp, the Detroit Federation of Labor ended up giving only half-hearted support to the war effort. At one point, it actually endorsed a position condemning the draft law.

Many Americans shared these anti-war sentiments in 1917 and 1918, and their support gave the Socialist Party 20 to 40 percent of the vote in New York, Buffalo, Milwaukee, and Chicago. In Kalamazoo and Grand Rapids, Michigan, Socialists were elected commissioners and councilmen for the first time. But the majority of Americans supported the war, and after passage of the Espionage and Sedition Acts, anyone promoting "insubordination" or publicly opposing the war could be arrested and, if convicted, sentenced to a 20-year prison term.

P atriotic fever swept through many sectors of American society after the Declaration of War. German–Americans were a particular target because of the clumsy efforts of the German government and a few German-Americans to sabotage war production. "Patriotic" Americans rechristened the frankfurter a Hot Dog. Sauerkraut became coleslaw, and the hamburger became Salisbury steak. Public schools stopped teaching German, and many Lutheran churches, stunned by the mounting crusade against all things German, changed their liturgy to English.

"Enemy aliens," said auto manufacturer William Brush in 1918, referring to Detroit's German-Americans, "are not entitled to the slightest degree of respect from humanity." Decrying this "Enemy In Our Midst," Brush called for unusually violent measures. "The sooner we perfect plans for the total extermination of such monstrosities in human form," he declared in the *Detroit Motor News*, "the sooner will this country and the world find itself again at peace." To contain the alleged "alien threat," the Detroit branch of the newly-formed American Protective League, headed by former Police Commissioner Frank Groul, enrolled 4,000 volunteers to keep tabs on foreign-born workers and radicals in the city's factories.

Nationally, thousands of anti-war activists were jailed in 1917 and 1918, including Socialist Party presidential candidate Eugene Debs and the IWW's entire leadership. Socialist meetings were banned and anti-war newspapers, including the *Michigan Socialist*, were barred from using the U.S. Mail. Across the country, mobs of vigilantes attacked Socialists and ransacked local meeting halls.

When the war ended with an Allied victory in November, 1918, the focus of this patriotic reaction spread beyond the radical minority to include the AFL and all organized labor. Despite their pro-war stance, moderate labor leaders were now branded as "Bolsheviks." The AFL, it was pointed out, had called for higher taxes on wealth, had proposed continued government ownership of the railroads and telephone system (both temporarily nationalized during the war), and had advocated equal wages for men and women. For most conservatives, it was hard to distinguish between an organization endorsing these controversial (for the time) positions and the more revolutionary left.

The huge strike wave which broke out at the war's close fueled this anti-labor sentiment all the more. Led by a nation-wide walkout of 350,000 steelworkers, a record four million strikers downed tools that year in an effort to win union recognition and recover earnings lost through wartime inflation. State militias and federal troops violently suppressed many of the strikes, killing and woun-

Below: House of the Masses, formerly Schiller Hall (site 15).

Opposite page: War bond rally at Dodge Main.

NUARY 5, 1920.—TWENTY

SUNDAY RAIDS NET 280 REDS

House of The Masses Is Twice Visited by Police and Federal Officers.

NUMBER HELD IS NOW 800

Да здравствуеть россійская революція.

Русскій отдѣлъ №3 американской с. партіи

Да здра. свобод. русс.

ПРОЛИТАРІАТЬ ПРОЛИТАРІАТЪ

Above: *Members of the "Russian Division of the American Socialist Party," (as the large banner on the right proclaims), circa 1918. The smaller banner reads "Hail to the Russian revolution." In 1919, these pro-Soviet radicals, after being expelled from the Socialist Party, helped found the American Communist Party. The photo was found at the former Detroit Workmen's Co-Operative Restaurant (site 16).*

Inset: *Members of Michigan's 339th Regiment in North Russia, 1918. Fifteen thousand American soldiers, joined by British, French, and Japanese troops, intervened in the Russian revolution in an unsuccessful attempt to overthrow the new Soviet government. The Americans withdrew in 1920.*

sion, and publicly denounced the Socialist Party's strategy of gradual reform. The Party's leadership expelled the dissidents in one fell swoop in May, 1919. In September, the revolutionaries launched the Communist Party of the United States, confident that Soviet Communists were already building a "workers' democracy," and that American workers would soon follow their lead.

Events proved them wrong on both counts. In the meantime, both the labor movement and the Socialist Party rejected the Communists' revolutionary program. Conservatives, however, eagerly lumped the moderates and revolutionaries together. Business publications like the *Open Shop Review* declared that unionism "was the greatest crime left in the world," and was "nothing less than Bolshevism." Twenty states, including Michigan, passed "Criminal Syndicalist" laws outlawing advocacy of trade-union actions that violated existing statutes. Michigan's Jensen Law made it illegal to even carry a red flag in public.

In Detroit, anti-Red hysteria continued after the first Palmer Raid of January 2. On Sunday, January 4, the House of the Masses was raided again. The police, apparently disappointed by their small catch, entered a speakeasy below the hall, forced the occupants upstairs, and then hauled them off to the Post Office, where they joined the swelling crowd of prisoners (800 in all) jammed into the darkened corridors on the fifth floor. Twelve of these newly arrested men were released after showing their World War I discharge papers; a 15-year-old boy in knee trousers was also freed when officials finally decided he posed no immediate threat to the government.

In November, 1920, Eugene Debs—still a prisoner in the federal penitentiary in Atlanta—received 915,000 votes for President. It was the last hurrah for the Socialist Party, which went into a rapid decline in the early 1920s. The IWW was decimated by the wartime repression and played no significant role in the labor movement over the following decade. The AFL was also wounded by the anti-labor hysteria, and its member unions took a beating during the brief but severe depression of 1921. Between 1920 and 1924, the Federation's ranks plunged from 4 million to less than 3 million members, and for the remainder of the decade, the union movement remained on the defensive.

ding scores and arresting hundreds.

In Detroit, there was little bloodshed. But on May 1, as the *Detroit News* reported, "a dozen strikes, small clashes with police, and a big radical parade all marked the May Day demonstration of Detroit's radical workers." Protesting against long hours, piece-work wages, and the near doubling of prices since 1914, some 20,000 workers in dozens of industries reportedly took the day off. Thousands later crowded into Arena Gardens to hear Frank X. Martel, Business Agent of the Detroit AFL, introduce former Wobbly Arturo Giovannitti, a hero of the IWW's 1909–1913 strikes. The rally was filled with news that two ongoing walkouts at Ford parts suppliers, L.A. Young and Wadsworths Manufacturing, had flared into violence. After 500 strikers clashed with

police, a dozen men had been arrested. "Of the 12," the *News* reported, "10 are aliens."

The *Detroit Labor News*, official newspaper of the city's AFL unions, saw nothing alien in the May Day demonstrations taking place that year in Detroit and dozens of other major cities around the world. "Where man oppresses man and some live by the sweat of another's brow, the host of labor turned out in mighty demonstration. The significance of it is far reaching. A new world is in the making and Labor is to be the builder."

With popular uprisings toppling the Kings and Czars of Europe between 1917 and 1919, many American conservatives feared that a revolution would sweep over the United States. Many left-wing Socialists drew the same conclu-

WORLDS APART

In 1921, the federal government closed the door on unlimited immigration from eastern and southern Europe. "We do not want to be a dumping ground," explained General Leonard Wood, whose troops helped break the 1919 steel strike, "for radicals, agitators, and Reds who do not understand our ideals." With the Emergency Immigration Act, many native-born, Protestant Americans believed they had eliminated the root cause of worker unrest.

They had also eliminated a major source of low-wage labor for America's industries. The AFL, which supported immigrant restrictions for just this reason, hoped the Immigration Act would strengthen the bargaining power of union workers. Employers were determined, however, to avoid this potential consequence of a labor shortage, and during World War I they had

already discovered an alternative supply of "home-grown" labor—the thousands of Southern black workers migrating to the North.

For Charles Denby, a black farm-hand from Tennessee, the move North was both a search for work and a pilgrimage to freedom. To Denby and many others of his generation, Detroit loomed in the imagination as a land of "milk and honey and pearly gates.... We didn't want to believe in discrimination up North." But discrimination there was.

Detroit's employers needed black workers—but only to fill those jobs so stigmatized by low wages or harsh working conditions that native-born whites generally avoided the work. Without a ready labor force to fill such jobs, employers would have been forced to

upgrade wages or mechanize production. In the past, employing newly arrived immigrants had often been cheaper. Now blacks would fill the same role.

City agencies therefore hired more black men to dig ditches and haul garbage, and white families hired more black women as household servants. In the construction industry, black laborers did the heavy lifting and carrying. In the auto industry, they did the same in the super-heated foundries where engine blocks and other major parts were cast. Positions in the equally noxious and unpopular paint-spraying and wet-sanding departments of the auto industry also became known as "Negro jobs."

The thick clouds of soot and the sputtering, white-hot metals made foundry work particularly unpleasant. "The furnaces for melting the iron [were] so hot that within five minutes my clothes would stick with dirt and grease," recall-

Hastings Street

Since "white" Detroit was usually off-limits, black families had to concentrate in the lower East Side ghetto, an area characterized by the slum housing pictured above (a Monroe Street alley, circa 1930), and by the Hastings Street sub-culture pictured below (Hank's Kentucky Jazz Band, in a 1920s club featuring "Stroh's Temperance Beer").

Overcrowding and disease were rampant in this segregated district, where the Detroit Urban League found one group of 14 people living in a single attic. As thousands of black migrants squeezed into the area, "the pool rooms and gambling clubs," the League reported, "are beginning to charge for the privilege of sleeping on pool-room tables overnight." By 1916, the death rate among blacks in this tightly packed ghetto was double the city's average.

Yet Hastings Street and its surrounding area (site 19) had a life of its own. Jazz clubs, speakeasies, and hotels in "Paradise Valley" catered to a racially mixed (though predominantly black) trade, while neighboring institutions provided some of the services white Detroit denied: the "Colored" YMCA on St. Antoine, the all-black Neisner's department store on Hastings and Brewster, and the American Negro League's East Side baseball team, the Detroit Stars. Previous page: Calvary Baptist church during a 1927 baptism.

ed Denby, who hired on as a foundry worker at the Graham Paige automobile company. "There were only three or four...Polish. Their faces looked exactly like Negro faces. They were so matted and covered with oil and dust that no skin showed."

Black and white foundry workers suffered the same conditions, but unlike white foundry workers, Denby and his co-workers were rarely allowed to advance out of the auto industry's "job ghettoes." If they wanted cleaner jobs, only low-wage janitorial work was open to them. The skilled trades and better-paying assembly-line jobs were for "whites only."

The major exception was Henry Ford's huge plant in Dearborn, built along the River Rouge between 1917 and 1925 (site 17). Here, Ford hired nearly 10,000 black workers, with sizeable numbers scattered through assembly operations, skilled trades, and supervision. Ford, however, was no believer in racial equality. Like most white Americans, he believed his race was superior to the Negro, but unlike other employers, Ford also believed that "dominance is an obligation," requiring "the stronger [to] serve the weaker.... The Negro needs a job, and this it ought to be the desire of our industrial engineers to supply."

Yet even for Ford, the supply of jobs was limited when it came to blacks. River Rouge was the only plant his company integrated, and nearly half of Ford's black employees were still concentrated in the foundry. Ford also took special care to maintain "his" town of Dearborn as lily white; in 1930, the census counted only 43 black residents among the city's 50,000 inhabitants. Since race-mixing was not part of Ford's plan, his black employees either took the long trolley ride from Detroit or found a home in Inkster, the segregated town Ford helped develop to the west of Dearborn.

Ford's racism at least had its paternalistic benefits for blacks. Ford's son, Edsel, was a large contributor to the NAACP, and Ford Sr. subsidized several black churches, including St. Mathews (for whom he built a parish house). Prominent black ministers, in turn, became strong allies of the Ford Motor Company, screening their congregations for suitable job applicants to work at "Ford's."

F ew white employers sought such support in the black community, and fewer still made any serious effort to

THE DETROIT INDEPENDENT

Detroit's Only, and Michigan's Greatest Race Weekly Paper—Our Home Companion

VOL. 4, NO. 36.   DETROIT, MICHIGAN, FRIDAY, NOVEMBER 6, 1925.

WANT
Try them —
resu ts.
Phone Main 8161.

Clarence Darrow To Speak At Y. M.

Attorney Darrow and several of his associates, who are now defending Dr. O. H. Sweet, his wife, two brothers, and seven of his friends, on a charge of murder, while defending Dr. Sweet's home.

ATTY. JULIAN W. PERRY   ATTY. CHAS. H. MAHONEY   ATTY. CECIL R. ROWLETTE

ATTORNEY CLARENCE DARROW IN ACTIO

integrate their all-white operations. Segregated hiring, many claimed, was simply more efficient. According to the racial stereotypes of the day, blacks were believed to be less capable of performing skilled work and more able to tolerate extreme heat. The foundry was therefore alleged to "suit them best." Even when employers did not endorse such discriminatory stereotypes, they still claimed they could not integrate their plants because white workers refused to work next to blacks.

Many whites, in fact, saw the newly arrived and usually impoverished black worker as a dangerous competitor, willing to take any job for rock-bottom wages. Segregation minimized such competition by reserving the better jobs for whites; it also soothed the intense "Negrophobia" that plagued whites at all levels of society. One factory engineer (in a statement that perhaps said as much about his own feelings as those of his plant's employees) described how white Southerners would react to integrating their factory: "God Damn, I don't want that black S.O.B. to sit on

Home Sweet Home

In 1925, when a black physician named Ossian Sweet moved his family into a white neighborhood (site 20), a crowd of 400 angry whites stoned the house. In the melee that followed, Sweet's brother fired into the crowd with a shotgun, killing one man.

The NAACP hired Clarence Darrow to defend the Sweets in two murder trials. "If white men had shot and killed a black while protecting their homes against a mob of blacks," Darrow argued, "they would have been given medals." An all-white jury, presided over by Judge (and future Mayor) Frank Murphy, finally ruled the Sweets had acted in self defense.

my toilet seat. [Now] I've got to hang my coat alongside of his; I've got to handle the same tools as a nigger handled."

Such anti-black sentiments were deeply embedded in the culture of America—a society in which the enslavement of black people was still a living memory. There were white trade unionists, white radicals, and white reformers who rejected this prevailing racism, but there were many more whites who did not. For the vast majority, blacks were an alien threat. Individual Negroes could be tolerated and even befriended, but as a group, they had to be "kept in their place."

In practice, this meant white workers frequently refused to admit blacks into their unions as equals. Some, like the Amalgamated Association of Street Railway Employees, refused to integrate their ranks at all. Even when many white conductors and motormen quit during World War I to take better-paying jobs in war industry, the Amalgamated blocked any effort to fill the vacancies with black men.

Other unions admitted blacks, but then segregated them into separate "Colored" locals. Still others, like the Carpenters' Union, opened their ranks to a small number of black tradesmen—but then refused to have their white members work under black foremen. Since carpentry foremen were union members, this meant white tradesmen had some control over who their supervisors would be. "The guys complained—they weren't going to work for this black man," recalled Walter Ber-

Among the narrow range of jobs open to black Detroiters, two occupations frequently typecast as "Negro jobs" were domestic servant and foundryman.

tram, a white carpenter in the 1920s. "I was in the [union] meeting the night he got up on the floor and said he was forced out of his position because people were discriminating against him. . . . [The union] allowed him to work on the job, but not as foreman."

During the depression of 1921, Detroit's segregated unions paid a high price for such racially exclusive policies. Not surprisingly, black Detroiters had as little sympathy for whites-only unions as they had for segregationist employers. As a result, when white metal workers went on strike against the Timken Axle Company (site 12), the EAD-financed Urban League had little difficulty finding jobless blacks to act as strike-breakers.

That same year, the all-white dining room staff at the Detroit Athletic Club (site 18) discovered just how suddenly management could become "enlightened" on race matters. When the whites-only Waiters' Union struck the exclusive club to establish union work standards, management simply hired an all-black crew and reopened for business. For these black workers, strikebreaking was the only way they could enter such previously all-white jobs.

Entering a "whites-only" neighborhood or store became nearly as difficult during the 1920s, when 100,000 black migrants poured into Detroit. As the black population pressed outwards against nearby immigrant neighborhoods, a smouldering white resentment

flared up against these "uppity" Negroes competing for scarce housing. Few whites wanted blacks to move in as neighbors—such an event, as many saw it, could only mean a decline in neighborhood status and safety. A "color line" was therefore drawn around the black ghetto to contain, if not completely stop, the oncoming wave of black homeseekers.

The "Code of Ethics" of the realtors' association instructed salesmen to avoid selling homes to "members of any race or nationality. . .whose presence will be detrimental to property values." In all-white neighborhoods, "improvement associations" harassed and attacked black home buyers, while many hotels and restaurants refused to serve black customers. Some movie theaters in the city became whites-only, while others restricted black movie-goers to the balcony. Downtown department stores refused to hire blacks into sales positions; professional baseball teams barred black ballplayers; and dance halls discouraged interracial mixing by excluding blacks altogether or, like the Greystone Ballroom, admitting them only on Mondays.

Black resistance to such segregation was a frequent focus of white fears. "Plot To Rouse Negroes Barred," the *Detroit Free Press* announced in front-page headlines during the Palmer Raids: "Trouble Is Yet Feared Because of Subtle Propaganda For 'Race Equality.'" The Ford-owned *Dearborn Independent* had few equals, however, when it came to castigating those blacks who now demanded equality as a right, not a gift. The civil rights movement, Ford's paper declared in 1923, was simply, "The Jewish Attempt to Bolshevize the Negro."

For many rural-born whites in Detroit, such racial hate propaganda gave legitimacy to the militantly Protestant, "White Power" politics of the Ku Klux Klan. The KKK's membership soared in Detroit to 32,000 by 1924, paralleling an equally spectacular growth nationally. Since Michigan's Burns Law, passed in 1923, prohibited masked men from holding public meetings, the Detroit Klan rarely appeared in hooded uniform. But the KKK's burning cross appeared frequently—on Christmas eve of 1923, for example, when a crowd of 4,000 people burned an oil-soaked cross on the steps of the County Building.

Klan influence peaked in 1924 when Charles Bowles ran as the KKK's write-in candidate for Mayor. Bowles actually won the election by some 7,000 votes, but 17,000 of his write-in ballots were disqualified for misspellings, and John Smith became Mayor. The Detroit Klan soon went into decline, but its members and sympathizers continued to influence city politics, particularly through the police department's unprecedented violence against black citizens. Between January, 1925, and June, 1926, the police killed 25 blacks; in New York City, with a black population three times greater, police killed three black citizens during the same period.

Detroit's black ghetto was a world apart, separated from the rest of the city by a sustained and frequently violent race prejudice.

This racially polarized city was also a distinctly masculine world—literally so, since women were heavily outnumbered for the first 30 years of the twentieth century. The city was dominated by heavy industry, and during years of pell-mell growth in auto production, Detroit attracted thousands of single men. By 1920, there were 119 males to every 100 females, an imbalance surpassed only by Akron, Ohio, among the nation's 70 largest cities. Among blacks, the ratio was even more lopsided, with 137 men for every 100 women.

Outnumbered in the population, Detroit's women were a distinct minority in the workplace. They were only expected to seek paid work outside the home when they were young and single, or when their husbands' low wages meant two wage earners had to support the family. With the above-average wages in the auto industry and a prevailing ideology that viewed heavy industrial labor as "men's work," most women remained homebound. In 1920, fewer than one of every four females above the age of 10 worked outside the home, compared to more than one of every three in Boston and Washington, D.C., and slightly less than one in three in New York, Chicago, and Los Angeles.

More so than in any other major industrial city, working class women in Detroit worked full time on the non-wage, household tasks that held their families together. Marketing was a daily routine since "iceboxes" (cooled by block ice) were too small and inefficient to allow for storing food. Mill and factory pollution made cleaning a perpetual chore, and laundering by hand usually occupied several nights a week. Baking bread, cooking food, making and repairing clothes, ironing, washing dishes, childcare, overseeing boarders or

When women looked for wage work, industrial employers hired them as low-wage factory hands in places like the San Telmo Cigar Company (top, 1916), and the Jeffrey DeWitt Sparkplug Company (middle, 1913).

Below: Middle-class suffrage organizers were more visibly active in Detroit than women trade-union organizers. In 1918, their exertions culminated in a successful referendum campaign to win the vote for Michigan's women. Two years later, a federal amendment to the Constitution extended women's voting rights nationwide.

taking in outside sewing or laundry—all demanded seemingly endless labor.

The degree to which these household tasks monopolized a woman's life varied widely according to ethnicity. In Italian and Bulgarian homes, especially the Sicilian and Macedonian segments of these two groups, men were the unquestioned authority and usually the sole breadwinner among adult members of the family. First-generation wives in particular lived in relative isolation from the rest of the world, relying on the church

and the marketplace for their social contacts outside the home. The Macedonian societies, Tetovo and Boof, were for men only, as were most Italian societies and lodges; one exception, Figli d'Italia, admitted women but segregated them into separate lodges and meetings. Few Sicilian women and virtually no Macedonians worked outside the home, though younger, American-born Italians often rebelled against the isolation and sexual segregation imposed by their parents.

In Finnish and Hungarian families, on the other hand, women enjoyed con-

Children in Detroit's Johnston School practicing their future family and work roles in 1919.

siderably more freedom. Lois Rankin of Detroit's International Institute reported in the late 1920s that, "as in the home country, Magyar [Hungarian] women occupy a position of equality with men, and there is little subservience to be noted in their attitude." Hungarian and Finnish daughters were more often encouraged to continue their educations into high school and beyond, and in most cases, both groups opened their benevolent societies, sports clubs, and political groups to women and men.

These women were also more likely to seek wage work outside the home, but their options were little wider here than for women of any other nationality group. Typically, the city's industrial employers only hired women for light assembly and low-wage jobs: in the pharmaceutical plants of Parke Davis (site 36) and Stearns, in the cigar plants and candy factories on the East Side, and in the sewing rooms of downtown department stores and clothing shops. The auto industry was also a major employer of women workers, though the 12,000 women in Detroit's auto plants in 1930 represented only 6 percent of the industry's workforce. In the auto industry, most women were segregated into low-wage jobs as sewing machine operators in the upholstery departments, or punch-press and lathe hands in small-parts manufacturing.

To prepare their daughters for "something better" than these factory jobs, immigrant families often encouraged their teenage girls to enroll in business schools and learn typing, stenography, or bookkeeping. Clerical and sales jobs frequently paid less than factory work and were equally dead-end, but they were not as physically demanding and had more prestige. Teaching was also attractive, though the pay was low and the educational requirements were often more than immigrant families could afford.

Failing to find work in one of these white-collar occupations, women turned to the lowest-paid and least prestigious jobs available—as waitresses, hotel maids, or domestic servants. First generation immigrants and black women—whose families had the lowest incomes and the greatest need for a second adult wage earner—were especially prominent in these "service" sector jobs, particularly as domestics.

There was only one step lower on the occupational ladder: prostitution. It was a flourishing trade in a city with such a large number of unattached men and such a small number of job options for working-class women. After surveying women in some of the estimated 500 whorehouses in Detroit, the state factory inspectors' 1913 report found the "larger percentage of girls in disorderly houses coming from domestic, hotel and restaurant service." Two thirds of the women surveyed reported that non-support or desertion by their husbands drove them to their present straits.

Few of Detroit's working women joined the union movement, despite the low wages and often harsh working conditions that characterized their jobs. In some cases, they were never invited. Craft unions, always wary of half-trained "green hands" who worked for less and undermined union wages, often believed they could minimize competition from low-wage women workers by excluding them from the union. The Iron Molders went a step further by not only barring women from their membership, but also fining any member who taught a woman part of the molding trade. Such fines, the Molders hoped, would advance their goal of restricting "the further employment of women in union...foundries, and eventually the elimination of such labor in all foundries." For much the same reason, Detroit's Amalgamated Association of Street Railway Employees—the same union that barred black workers—was also "unalterably opposed," as it announced in 1918, "to the employment of women as either motormen or conductors."

Some unions did open their ranks to women as they became numerically prominent in certain industries, like cigar making and garment manufacturing. By 1911, the United Garment Workers' Union of Detroit had over a thousand women in its membership, more than half of them Poles and the balance mainly Germans, Italians, and French.

But in Detroit, because heavy industry was so dominant and "women's jobs" less numerous than in other cities, the trade union movement was relatively weak among women. In the same years women garment workers in New York were leading massive, bitter strikes to establish union working conditions, Detroit's United Garment Workers had organized only a small portion of a relatively small industry, and most of its members were concentrated in overall factories where employers had invited the union in. A union label was an asset in the overall market, since many construction workers and other tradesmen looked for the union label in work clothes.

When employers resisted the union, women workers (like their male counterparts) found it difficult to make organizational headway. In Open Shop Detroit, union organizing demanded continual struggle, and for most women workers, their family role usually took precedence over their workplace commitment. Characteristically, a female wage earner was either contributing sub-minimum wages to her parental family until she married, or supplementing her husband's wages until her next baby. In either case, working outside the home was supposed to be a temporary status—not the sort of life-choice that joining a union implied.

In this respect, boys and girls learned fundamentally different lessons about wage work. Boys frequently began as apprentices or helpers to men; they worked with adults and learned to define their "manliness" in terms of "standing up to the boss." Girls, on the other hand, entered workplaces where most if not all their co-workers were other girls and young women—the older women had married and left the job. "Standing up to the boss," far from confirming their expected adult roles, violated all the rules these romantically-inclined young women had learned about their male-dominated society.

Few women, especially in white-collar jobs, were eager to challenge those rules by joining a union. But even fewer women were eager to endure a lifetime of segregated, low-wage work with no prospect of promotion. Many young

girls therefore looked forward to becoming wives and mothers—roles which, for all the hard work, at least nurtured more self-esteem and personal authority than stitching upholstery for nine hours a day.

Perhaps because there were so many inhibitions to overcome, those women who did "stand up to the boss" frequently displayed an intense and high-spirited militancy. The voices of these rebels usually were not recorded by the press, but the testimony of several strikebreakers gives some sense of how women strikers at the Bernard Schwartz cigar plant treated "scabs" in 1921. "At night when I left [the factory], there would be about 50 to 100 pickets there," stated Mary Malczewski, a strikebreaker who testified for the company in court-injunction hearings. "They called me names every time we left the factory; the girls hollered after us 'rats,' 'dirty scabs,' 'dirty strikebreakers,' 'taking our bread away.' " The striking women —angered by wage cuts that lowered pay from $23 to $17 for every 1,000 cigars rolled—carried their battle into the

Below: Male cutters at Annis Furs were skilled employees who expected to work for most of their lives in the fur industry. Few if any of the younger women behind them were encouraged or trained to become cutters. Some might spend much of their lives as sewing-machine operators, but the majority hoped to escape the shop altogether and start their own families.

Inset: In 1901, women were only beginning to enter the clerical workforce at the Polk publishing company.

neighborhoods, picketing the homes of strikebreakers and calling out neighbors. "Mrs. Marchinkowski called my husband 'dirty scab' every time he was on the street," one strikebreaker testified.

The striking women eventually lost their battle. So too did the Women Conductors' Association, formed in 1918 to defend the jobs of 400 women hired under government order by the Detroit Urban Railway during World War I. At the war's close, the women launched a petition campaign and made formal appeals to Washington to protect their jobs. Neither strategy could overcome the opposition of the male union, the Amalgamated Association, and by 1920, only 50 women were left on the D.U.R.

Not every battle ended in defeat, however. When Boerth's restaurant chain fired two waitresses in April, 1918, and refused to raise the *weekly* wage of $7.50, the waitresses at all three restaurants launched a strike and boycott. After three weeks and four arrests, Boerth's capitulated. This victory, the *Detroit Labor News* noted hopefully, served "notice upon all employers... that henceforth their un-American attitudes...[would] be challenged by a militant and fighting organization."

THE SOARING TWENTIES

"A loyal Detroiter who scans the figures finds cause for the glorification of his city."
Polk's Directory, 1929

The figures Polk's cited were not for automobile production. As impressive as these were, the most visible source of pride for Detroit's civic boosters was the city's soaring skyline.

After 1910, new skyscrapers scaled upwards one after another in an unprecedented building boom, fueled by profits from the fast-growing auto industry. Overnight it seemed, Grand Circus Park (site 26) was surrounded by towering hotels and office buildings—the Statler, the Tuller, and the Whitney building, all completed in 1914. Five

years later, GM began construction of the world's largest office building on Grand Boulevard, sparking a renewed burst of construction that culminated in 1927–1928. In that two-year period alone, the city's builders completed the 46-story Penobscot Building; the New Union Trust Building and Cadillac Tower, both 40 stories; the 38-story David Stott Building; the 28-story Fisher Building; and the 19-story Bell Telephone Building. Investment in new construction totaled $200 million in 1927, 33 times more than the $6 million spent in 1900. "Detroit has crowded more than three-quarters of a century of achievement," Polk's enthused, "into a short space of two decades."

The twin cylinders of Detroit's spectacular economic boom in the

1920s—the auto and construction industries—could not have been more different. The auto industry was characterized by the mass production of identical goods: each car exactly like the one preceding and following it on the assembly line. The construction industry, on the other hand, was characterized by specialty production: each skyscraper different in innumerable ways from its neighbor. While small homes and building materials could be standardized and turned out on a near assembly-line basis, Detroit's skyscrapers were each "tailor made."

The two industries were also organized along radically different lines. In auto, three giant corporations, GM, Ford, and Chrysler, dominated the world market by the end of the 1920s.

Backed by enormous financial and marketing resources, these corporate giants spread the cost of building a factory over millions of cars, allowing them to undersell their small-fry competitors. But skyscrapers were not built in factories. They required dozens of specialty contractors whose "capital" usually consisted of a few cement mixers, some trucks, and perhaps a steam-driven power saw. Anywhere from 30 to 60 separate sub-contractors collaborated on a large building, each specializing in a particular trade and employing only a handful of workers.

Each workforce was distinctly different. In auto, the division of labor into simple tasks reduced the proportion of skilled workers in the labor force to less than 15 percent. By Henry Ford's estimate in the early 1920s, 85 percent of the jobs in his plants took only two weeks to learn, and 43 percent required only one day's training. The majority of construction workers, in contrast, were skilled tradesmen: carpenters, plumbers, electricians, plasterers, painters, and others able to apply their life-long craft to varying job specifications.

New building technologies and mechanization dramatically changed construction work, but innovation tended to eliminate *unskilled* jobs as often as skilled. Engine-driven hoists run by skilled engineers replaced the "hod-carriers" who previously carried bricks and mortar on their shoulders; steam shovels and trenching machines, run by skilled machine operators, likewise replaced unskilled hand shovellers. Even new techniques that undermined old skills usually created new crafts in their place. While the use of steel and reinforced concrete in tall buildings reduced the demand for stonemasons, this same innovation created a new demand for skilled iron and cement workers.

Craft unionism continued to flourish under these conditions, with many skilled tradesmen—particularly ironworkers, electricians, and sheet metal workers—winning union recognition and the Closed Shop during the boom years. Wages rose steadily: from 65¢ an hour for Detroit's unionized ironworkers in 1913, to $1.50 an hour by 1929. Several crafts were also able to maintain strict control over apprenticeship. Sheet metal workers required the future "mechanic" to go through three intermediate grades before qualifying as a full-fledged journeyman, with the union controlling job standards as well as testing.

Not all of Detroit's tradesmen prospered. Painters faced growing competition from the newly perfected spray gun, and carpenters saw much of their skilled work eliminated as contractors introduced factory-made window and door frames, or replaced wood altogether with metal. In 1920, the Associated Building Employers of Detroit began a new Open Shop campaign that quickly

Below: Detroit's building tradesmen, circa 1920.

Right: Building the Union Trust Building, 1928. "There were no safety practices then," recalled Clay Langston of the Associated General Contractors. "In those days production was king, labor was cheap, and unions were weak." Some tradesmen remember as many as one death a floor on tall buildings.

Opposite: Detroit and the just-completed Ambassador Bridge to Windsor, Ontario, 1930.

undermined older craft unions, particularly as employers hired non-union workers from Canada (called "nickel immigrants" after the 5¢ boat ride from Windsor). Seeking to stem the tide, the Carpenters Union in 1926 struck Vokes and Schaffer, a leading Open Shop contractor; union supporters intercepted Canadian carpenters at the Detroit River landing, and "stain bombs" were exploded on the woodwork at Vokes and Schaffer job sites. But to no avail. "By the time President Hoover got in, the Carpenters Union was pretty well shot," recalled Walter Bertram, an early member. "I had to drop out in the mid-1920s, because every job was an Open Shop job, and they kept paying less and less. The only jobs that were union were those that could be boycotted, like theaters or amusement parks."

Anxieties over changing technology and the spread of the Open Shop intensified the narrowly defined "job consciousness" of Detroit's skilled tradesmen. To protect themselves, each trade staked out its "job turf" and fought to protect it against poachers from other crafts. The Carpenters fought with virtually everyone, claiming that anything once made of wood always remained carpenters' work, even after it was replaced by iron or sheet metal. Detroit's Ironworkers were unconvinced. "'Mr. Carpenter,'" groused one Ironworker officer, "is hard to convince that iron was never wood at any stage." These "jurisdictional" disputes poisoned relations between workers, with one group of tradesmen frequently resorting to strike action to protest encroachment by a competing craft. Who should paint a radiator—the Plumbers or Painters Union? Who should build scaffolds—the Laborers, Carpenters, or Bricklayers? Who should control electric welding—the Electricians or Sheet Metal Workers?

In the rough-and-tumble of such infighting, bonds of solidarity took a beating. Workers so fundamentally divided by craft rarely even saw themselves as "construction workers"; they were bricklayers, "woodbutchers" (carpenters), or "tinknockers" (sheet-metal workers). The prevalence of small-scale family businesses meant many workers identified with their boss as readily as their fellow worker; some became contractors themselves, with a few even maintaining their union membership after they became small businessmen.

The skilled tradesman was often a man on the make, willing to wink at the occasional bribe some union leaders took from employers. Petty grafting was OK, many reasoned, so long as the union "Business Agent" did not steal dues money or flagrantly sell out the membership. "We had one of the crookedest BAs in the world," recalled Willard Sarrach, a sheet-metal worker. "But he was the most honest man in the world for us fellows. He built the union."

The construction industry was an idealized version of 19th century production: small-scale, competitive, and boasting a highly skilled workforce. Ironically, even as corporate-controlled mass production destroyed this form of economic life in most industries, the craft unionism of the building trades became the AFL's dominant form of organization in the 1920s. In this decade, while red scares and repression drove many industrial unionists into early retirement from the labor movement, the AFL's few industrial unions went into steep decline. Prohibition crippled the Brewery Workers, while mechanization and declining demand for coal undercut the Mine Workers. Only the construction crafts grew, even as the AFL's overall membership declined. Where building tradesmen made up 20 percent of the AFL's membership in 1920, they topped 30 percent in 1929.

These skilled workers saw the world through "hand-crafted" lenses, insisting that workers in mass-production industries divide themselves according to skill, even as skill levels were declining in most jobs. The results were disastrous in Detroit, where small groups of autoworkers could easily be isolated and replaced. "When we received a wage cut, my unit went on strike," recalled Joe Hattley, a woodworker in 1925 at GM's Fleetwood plant on West Fort Street (site 21). "But due to the setup under the old craft union, the metal finishers in the body shop, the painters, the trimmers and all the other units continued to work. Within three weeks time, we lost the strike and I was fired." Auto, like virtually all the other mass-production industries, remained non-union.

It was becoming clear to many that only an industrial organization combining all the workers in a factory could hope to match the power of a large corporation. But industrial unionism was easier to argue in theory than achieve in practice. Between 1914 and 1926, the socialist leadership of the Machinists Union pushed for an Amalgamated union combining all the metal-working crafts—Machinists, Blacksmiths, Boilermakers, and Sheet Metal Workers. But merger efforts fell through, and even the class-conscious Machinists got cold feet when it came to surrendering their members in railroad workshops—who logically belonged in an industrial union of railroad workers. (In 1926, the national union's socialist President, William Johnston, died and was replaced by more conservative leadership.)

In Detroit, only the Carriage, Wagon, and Automobile Workers Union attempted to organize auto workers on an industry-wide basis. Expelled from the AFL in 1918 for ignoring craft distinctions, the union's Detroit local grew to 30,000 members before losing a series of strikes and collapsing altogether in the brief depression of 1921. Revived at mid-decade by Communist leadership and rechristened the Auto Workers Union, the AWU by 1929 had little to show for its efforts beyond an ongoing network of factory newspapers, each distributed by clandestine committees of committed workers.

As the AWU discovered, even some autoworkers were a bit starstruck in the "soaring" twenties, particularly the small elite of skilled machinists, metal finishers, and tool makers. Many of these workers continued to see themselves as distinctly superior to the unskilled "riff raff" in the industry. "They wanted to build a fence around themselves," Nick DiGaetano recalled of the skilled metal finishers in his department at Chrysler–Jefferson (site 22). "The foundry men? 'Hell with them.' The assembly-line men? 'Hell with them. They have no trade,' they said. The polisher [metal finisher] was a big shot, like the molder, like the machinist, like the tool maker..."

"Big shots" like these seemed to have it made in the late 1920s. Henry Ford was retooling his plants to produce the new Model A, and toolmakers, machinists, millwrights, and electricians were in heavy demand to build and install some 15,000 new machines and retool 25,000 others. All the while, auto production climbed ever upwards, increasing by 170 percent between 1919 and 1929.

As the Soaring Twenties drew to a close, however, these skilled and prosperous tradesmen were heading for a fall. With little warning, the industry they worked in, the city they lived in, the nation they belonged to—all would soon be sliding into the terrible abyss of the Great Depression.

II: Union Town

Demonstration in downtown Detroit, circa 1930.

PARADISE LOST

Just as in Rome one goes to the Vatican and endeavors to see the Pope, . . . so in Detroit one goes to the Ford works and endeavors to see Henry Ford.

J.A. Spender, 1928

Spender was only one of many pilgrims who marveled at America's miracle growth in the 1920s, paced by Detroit's booming auto industry. Automobile production accelerated from less than one million a year in 1915 to 4½ million a year by 1929, boosting the number of registered cars on the road from 2½ million to a staggering 23 million. Entire new industries opened up with this boom in auto sales—road construction, suburban homebuilding, car servicing and repair, motels, resorts—and older industries grew apace. From the steel mills of Gary, Indiana, to the tire plants of Akron, Ohio, America's industrial heartland beat to the rhythm of Detroit's

assembly lines. By 1929, one of every six jobs in the U.S. was dependent on the production of automobiles.

Businessmen were lionized in the 1920s as the messiahs of this new Automobile Age. "The man who builds a factory builds a temple," said President Calvin Coolidge in one of his frequent pro-business sermons, and both he and President Warren Harding before him placed the federal government at the service of this corporate "priesthood." During their administrations, the wartime excess profits tax was abolished and income taxes for the wealthy were cut dramatically. Treasury Secretary Andrew Mellon, founder of Gulf Oil and Alcoa, authorized billions in tax refunds and abatements for corporations during the decade; Harding, Coolidge, and President Herbert Hoover meanwhile vetoed numerous farm-relief and social-service bills.

Administration of the law was equally one-sided. The Justice Department, far from opposing price-fixing conspiracies and other monopoly practices in busi-

ness, openly encouraged corporate mergers and industry-wide trade associations to reduce competition and stabilize profits at high levels. The Supreme Court similarly promoted business interests by voiding much of the Progressive legislation passed before 1920: the government, the Court ruled, could not place restrictions on the hiring of child labor, could not set minimum wage standards, and could not otherwise "interfere" with business operations. In 1921, the Supreme Court even declared peaceful union picketing unlawful. The very word "picket," according to the Court, suggested a "sinister" and "militant purpose" to deprive owners of their property rights.

Hugh Adams, in *An Australian Looks At America*, summed up the net effect of this pro-business mania: "America," he wrote in 1928, "is an employer's paradise."

Within a year of Adams' observation, it became painfully evident this corporate Heaven-On-Earth, far from being eternal, was headed toward its own Judgment Day.

The seeds of disaster were sown in the very years the economy grew most rapidly. Enormous wealth was created by the auto boom of the 1920s, and federal tax policies and anti-labor court rulings only served to concentrate these riches at the very top of society. In 1929, the richest 1 percent of the population took home 19 percent of the nation's disposable income, compared to 14 percent in 1921. During this period, production of goods and services also grew enormously, but mechanization and speed-up curtailed the number of wage earners who could buy the cascade of goods: manufacturing output climbed 91 percent between 1921 and 1929, while the total number of workers rose only 25 percent. Even with steady wage increases over the decade, the purchasing power of consumers lagged behind what they collectively produced as workers. By 1929, General Motors was selling cars by loaning customers money—an unheard-of practice before 1915.

With output threatening to race ahead of consumer demand, corporations were not eager to expand factory capacity at the same accelerating clip—not if they couldn't find enough customers to sell the added output at a profit. Many businessmen therefore began diverting their accumulated wealth into more speculative investments, like Florida real estate and the New York stock market. Even as manufacturing industries cut production in the spring and summer of 1929, wealthy speculators bid up stock prices to dizzying heights—well above the actual value of tangible corporate assets.

In the fall of 1929, the entire house of cards collapsed. Stock prices leveled off and then fell dramatically as panicked investors sold their over-valued paper assets. Speculators who had borrowed money to buy stocks on the upswing now could not repay loans once their stocks plunged in value. Overextended companies were awash in debts they could not pay.

By mid-1930, the nation's economy was sliding into a deep depression. Detroit, which led the economy into the boom years of the 1920s, now led the descent into the Great Depression of the 1930s. Unemployed workers scrimping to buy food and clothing certainly could not afford cars.

In March, 1929, the Ford Motor Company employed 128,000 people; in August, 1931, when Henry Ford closed his plants for retooling, the company's payroll fell to 37,000. As GM and Chrysler cut back their workforce, unemployment throughout Michigan multiplied at a terrifying clip, reaching an estimated 46 percent of the labor force by 1933.

As sales slumped, employers sought to preserve their profit margins by shortening the work day and cutting wages: the $5 day, raised to $6 and $7 for some autoworkers in the 1920s, dropped to $4 and $3 a day in some plants—and still less in many others. Michigan's autoworkers averaged only $700 to $1000 a year by 1932, a 50 percent cut from their 1929 average of $1600. Prices, meanwhile, dropped only 20 percent.

"There is nothing in the business situation to be disturbed about," Secretary of Commerce Robert Lamont declared at the onset of the crisis. Employment, he advised in February, 1930, "is picking up." Employment, however, did not pick up in February, or March, or any month of 1930. Local 25 of the Ironworkers Union counted 1,000

Above: Detroit, early 1930s.
Opposite page: A bread line at Detroit's Salvation Army.

members in 1929, working on dozens of major buildings; but now, with most construction suspended and work on the Ambassador Bridge completed, membership plummeted to 270. Building tradesmen and autoworkers, long accustomed to above average wages and relatively stable employment, found themselves cast adrift. Without unemployment insurance or federally funded welfare to cushion the blow of economic catastrophe, tens of thousands of unemployed workers exhausted their savings just to keep food on the table and shelter overhead. As the crisis deepened, families sold their furniture and dishes, pawned their jewelry and other valuables, and turned to neighbors and relatives for support. But individual measures proved increasingly futile. Hundreds, then thousands, of Detroiters were evicted from their homes for nonpayment of rent or mortgage, forcing entire families to live in tents, shacks, lean-tos, and garages. Public begging, burglaries, and Prohibition violations grew dramatically; at night, lines of hungry men began to form behind Detroit's big hotels, waiting for the garbage cans to be brought out.

Conditions in Detroit's black community were especially desperate. Traditionally excluded from many industries, black laborers and service workers suddenly found their options restricted all the more when heavy layoffs swept the city's foundries, hotels, and building contractors. With unemployment reportedly peaking at 80 percent in some neighborhoods, the whole fabric of black community life began to unravel. In Inkster, the sudden loss of tax revenue forced the town to close the schools and lay off the entire police force; the power company, unable to collect back bills, disconnected Inkster's electricity.

In the absence of state and federal programs to aid the unemployed, private agencies and mutual-aid societies were besieged by homeless and hungry people. The friars at the Capuchin Monastery (site 23) noticed a sharp increase in the number of men seeking food at their door in the fall of 1929. "The lines began to lengthen and kept on lengthening," recalled Father Herman Buss. "Six hundred, seven hundred people in the morning [and] noontime." To meet the escalating demand for emergency food, the friars organized a regular soupline that November, supplied by donated foodstuffs from bakers and farmers.

The following year, Detroit's Typographical Union voted to form its own unemployment fund for laid off printers, paying out $25 a week to families and $10 to single men. With regular dues from working printers, the union's fund was probably on sounder financial footing than organizations like the Hungarian Free Kitchen, the Jewish Emergency Relief Fund, and the Madonna Guild, each doing what it could to feed the unemployed with donated food and funds. Their slender resources were not nearly equal to the task, for many churches and ethnic organizations were themselves threatened with financial collapse. By the winter of 1930, four of six Italian-owned banks in the city were bankrupt; the Finnish Educational Association had lost control of its hall to creditors; and the Ukrainian Greek Church had closed both its parochial schools.

In March, 1930, the Communist Party's call for worldwide protests against unemployment brought 50,000 demonstrators and onlookers into downtown Detroit. They were not welcome. According to the *Detroit Times,* 3,000 police—including "horsemen, machine gunners, and plain clothesmen"—confronted the "Red Mob" in front of City Hall and along Woodward Avenue. When several demonstrators unveiled signs calling for "Work and

The Workmen's Hotel on Howard Street. "Make This Place Your Home."

Wages," the mounted police, "their clubs swinging and their horses stepping gingerly on their cork shoes," rode into the crowd, attacking demonstrators and bystanders alike. Twenty-two men and women were taken to the hospital.

Despite the huge and entirely unexpected turnout for the Communist-sponsored rally, government and business leaders continued to insist that unemployment was a passing problem. According to the *Detroit Free Press*, only a "double handful" of Communists had gathered downtown for the demonstration; the rest of the crowd had been "curiosity seekers," "gullible folk of limited mentality," and "immature boys and girls whose minds had been filled full of silly lies...." Unemployment, conservatives insisted, was the personal problem of each jobless worker—it was not a social issue. The jobless, it was claimed, were simply lazy and unmotivated, and government unemployment relief would only reward and perpetuate such "slothfulness."

Some conservatives saw the spreading misery of unemployment as a social good. According to President Hoover, "the passing adversity which has come upon us should deepen the spiritual life of the people;" prosperity, he claimed, was "just around the corner." Hoover's thoughts were echoed in Detroit by the Reverend Joseph Vance, pastor of the First Presbyterian Church: "Adversity is saving us," Vance preached, "from the fatty degeneration of sensual indulgence, giving us a new spiritual vision."

Others were even more hard-nosed. Professor E.G. Conklin of Princeton acknowledged that "some of the weaker...will naturally die under the stress of the times." But, he concluded, "the strong and hardy will survive and reproduce, and thus the human race will be strengthened." Conklin no doubt counted himself among the "strong and hardy." For him and conservative leaders in business and government, it was simply a matter of time before the economy "naturally" cleansed itself of bad debts, bankrupt companies, and "weak" workers; recovery would then follow automatically.

Since the system was supposedly self-correcting, the government was expected to do nothing to interfere with this allegedly natural process. Even collecting unemployment statistics could upset the fragile process of recovery. "One doesn't improve the condition of a sick man," Hoover's Secretary of Labor remarked in 1930, "by constantly telling him how sick he is." When Congress finally directed the Department of

Mayor Frank Murphy, second from right, and residents of the city-run Fisher Lodge for the unemployed.

A Labor-Union Mayor

"Mayor Murphy is a labor-union mayor in Open Shop Detroit," complained the business weekly *Detroit Saturday Night* in 1931. The city's New Deal mayor was, indeed, pro-union. He was not, however, anti-business. The grandson of Irish immigrants and the son of a prosperous lawyer, Frank Murphy invested heavily in the stock market before 1929, and thereafter cultivated close friendships with auto executives Walter Chrysler and Lawrence Fisher.

An "Independent Progressive," Murphy believed in private enterprise, but rejected the "ruthless and un-Christian individualism," as he called it, that characterized America's industrial order. A devout Catholic and an officer in both the Holy Name Society and the American Legion, Murphy also believed America would have to "substitute a socialistic sense for this individualistic sense" by regulating the corporate economy. "We have got to realize," he remarked while mayor, "that no one is secure until all are secure; that injustice to anyone is injustice to everyone."

Labor to count the actual number of unemployed, President Hoover refused to provide the funds for such a compilation.

Michigan's Republicans took an equally standpat attitude, with Governor Fred Green actually opposing a state unemployment commission in 1930 because it would unduly emphasize the problem. In Detroit's mayoralty election that fall, the leading conservative candidate, George Engel, promised only "a sound, level-headed and strong business administration." This was no time, he declared, for "fooling and experimenting" with social service schemes and "idealistic theories." Detroit's underfunded Department of Welfare, Engel argued, was already too expensive.

Engel's chief opponent, Recorders Court Judge Frank Murphy, had no qualms about idealistic experimenting. "I am for humanized government," Murphy announced, "a government that will touch the citizens in all their distress." Denouncing the "little group

Detroit's Radio Priest

To a national radio audience of 30 million listeners, Detroit's Father Charles Coughlin preached a weekly message of anger and frustration. "We are actors...in one of the most unique tragedies that has ever been chronicled," the Radio Priest from Royal Oak announced in a 1932 broadcast. "Abundance of foodstuffs, millions of virgin acres, banks loaded with money—alongside idle factories, long bread lines, millions of jobless, and growing discontent."

In the midst of this crisis, none of the "isms," according to Coughlin, offered salvation: communism because it was godless, "individualistic" capitalism because it was soulless, and socialism because it meant nationalized industry. Coughlin favored nationalization of only the banking industry, since an artificial "money famine" created by international bankers had, he claimed,

caused the Depression.

In the meantime, Coughlin backed Roosevelt in his campaign to unseat President Hoover in the 1932 elections—elections, the popular priest declared, offering a choice between "Roosevelt or Ruin."

---

of rich people downtown," Murphy portrayed himself as "the people's candidate," the champion of "the man and woman who is broke and hard pressed and hasn't a chance." With the enthusiastic backing of the Detroit Federation of Labor, the NAACP, and Detroit's major ethnic organizations, Murphy finished first in a field of four candidates—prompting spontaneous election-night celebrations in the streets around City Hall. Deploring the callousness of previous administrations, he promised a "new era in the Tabernacle [of government]."

Murphy quickly changed the scope and direction of government relief policies. To house the thousands of homeless men wandering the city's streets, the Mayor's Unemployment Committee (MUC) opened Emergency Lodges in empty factories donated by GM and Studebaker (site 9). The MUC also set up municipal feeding stations serving 14,000 daily, and distributed an additional 40,000 food baskets to hungry families over a two-year period. Like Mayor Hazen Pingree in the 1890s, Murphy promoted "thrift gardens" for the unemployed in vacant city lots, with 3,000 field gardeners using seed and equipment donated by the city. The city's Legal Aid Bureau forestalled hundreds of evictions and the Free Employment Bureau steered over 50,000 workers to the few available jobs (mostly temporary) in the city.

It was a new era for the city's unions as well. After publicly backing the unionization of municipal employees, Murphy pledged that future layoffs and rehiring of the city's blue-collar workers would no longer be guided by political favoritism, but strictly by length of service. The fear of sudden and arbitrary dismissal was thereby eliminated for workers with the most "seniority." The Mayor also discouraged low-wage contractors from bidding on city work, and honored union picket lines during a hotel strike—actions a grateful union movement acknowledged by naming Murphy honorary President of the Detroit Federation of Labor.

The Mayor's moderate brand of progressive reform won him the solid support of Detroit's working-class voters, who helped reelect him in 1931 by a 2–1 margin. Murphy's welfare and relief programs, however, did not appeal to most industrialists. The *Michigan Manufacturer and Financial Record* objected to the money "frittered away in doles" to "aliens" and "unacclimated Southern negroes." The Board of Commerce likewise attacked the "come one,

come all welfare policy of Detroit" that "attracted...derelicts from all parts of America."

By the end of 1931, such opposition, together with the continually worsening depression, had crippled Murphy's relief programs. One third of the city's taxpayers could not pay their bills in 1931–1932, and pro-business organizations like the Taxpayers' Protective Association openly threatened a general tax strike if Murphy did not reduce the city's levy. With unemployed Ford workers representing between 14 and 35 percent of Detroit's relief recipients, Murphy was further hamstrung by Ford's immunity from city taxes—most of the company's plants were in Dearborn and Highland Park.

Murphy was forced to turn to Detroit's banks to borrow funds, since appeals for state and federal aid fell on deaf ears. The banks charged more than interest: in return for the loans, they insisted Murphy first reduce welfare expenditures and cut the wages of 35,000 municipal workers. The Mayor denounced those "financial dictators," as he described them, who lacked even "a semblance of social responsibility." But he had little choice in the matter. By the end of 1932, only 7¢ of every tax dollar in Detroit went to the city's relief programs; 43¢ went to the banks, half of it in interest payments.

The city closed its Emergency Lodges in 1931, and the Welfare Department soon after cut its weekly food allotments to $1.90 per adult; thousands of needy recipients were denied any relief at all. After the Department of Public Works laid off 8,000 workers in 1931 and 1932, many streets went uncleaned and alleys became clogged with uncollected garbage.

Detroit finished the second full year of the Depression in sorry shape. With a third to a half of the city's workforce unable to find a job and relief aid cut to rations of bread and milk at several points, an estimated 150,000 people abandoned the city in 1931. Some had no particular destination in mind; like millions of vagabond Americans, they simply wandered from one shantytown to the next looking for work.

For the 10,000 Mexicans living in and around Detroit, there was ample reason to leave. The beet-sugar farmers and automakers who brought them north before 1929 were no longer hiring, and the city's Welfare Department was pressuring Mexicans on its relief rolls to return south. Most Mexicans saw little prospect of finding work again in Michigan, and the Mexican government, according to exaggerated newspaper accounts, promised free housing and land to returning workers. By 1932, three-quarters of the city's Mexican community had boarded trains for Juarez, Laredo, and other border towns.

Among the majority of Detroiters who could not or would not leave the city, some actually began to starve. How many were dying of hunger was a matter of dispute. A physician at the city's Receiving Hospital told the press in the fall of 1931 that four persons a day were brought to the hospital "too far gone from starvation for their lives to be saved." But since the final cause of death in such cases was pneumonia or some other complication, an official tabulation of death certificates gave no measure of starvation in Detroit.

It was obvious to everyone, however, that Detroit's unemployed were growing increasingly angry, resentful, and—when no options remained—lawless. Reports grew more frequent of people entering stores, ordering as much food

as they could carry, and leaving without paying. At night, hungry men looted grocery stores in some neighborhoods. "I was never personally involved in any of these expeditions," recalled Clayton Fountain, an unemployed autoworker, "but I knew some men who were, and nearly all my jobless acquaintances applauded the looting of stores." When money and food were scarce, Fountain and others foraged outside the town at night, stealing corn they later sold at 15¢ a dozen.

When the Welfare Department could no longer afford to subsidize the rent of impoverished workers, the number of evictions rose to 150 *a day* during the summer months, sparking small riots in some cases as tenants and neighbors battled police. Welfare supervisors who initially described the unemployed as "orderly and...brooding," were describing, in July and August, 1931, a "quickened irritability" among the 230,000 hard-pressed relief recipients in the city.

Some of these desperately poor people began to take up collective forms of pro-

test and self-help, primarily through the Unemployed Councils they formed in 1930 and 1931. Organized with leadership and support from members of the Communist Party, the Councils drew together some 1,500 neighborhood activists in a dozen different districts, including one Council for the Hastings–Ferry Street area, another centered along Woodward Avenue north of Grand Circus Park, and one large Council for the East Side. Significantly, the Councils brought black and white workers together on an unprecedented scale, particularly in the East Side districts where Italian, Jewish, and East-European families still lived in and near black neighborhoods.

Council members were not the only people in the city blocking evictions or bypassing disconnected gas and electric lines to restore service. "One day they were setting a family out in my block," recalled Dave Moore, a black teenager who had heard of the Unemployed Councils but had not yet joined. "And I just got together with a bunch of guys and said, 'let's put it back in.' We

An Unemployed Council demonstration in the winter of 1932, probably in Grand Circus Park (site 26).

Above: Hunger Marchers crossing the Fort Street bridge, March 7, 1932.
Inset: Teargas on Miller Road.

chased hell out of the bailiff across the old Brewster playground and we put the furniture back in." When Moore told a Bulgarian friend about the episode, his companion invited him to an unemployed rally on Ferry and Russell. "And that's how I got involved," Moore later recalled, "in the Unemployed Councils."

What Moore and others had "just decided to do," the Councils did more systematically. Joseph Billups, a black autoworker active in the Councils, remembered that once near Hastings

Street the Sheriff "went two blocks, just every house, setting it [furniture] out in the street. So we mobilized the people and...put the stuff back in. And we... [left] somebody there to take care of the sheriff if they came around."

Hungry workers of any nationality or race could turn to the Council's soup kitchens, where volunteers served food solicited from neighborhood merchants and farmers at Eastern Market. Unemployed Council rallies also pressured the Welfare Department to restore adequate levels of relief, with

many of the demonstrations held in a "free speech" zone designated by Mayor Murphy in Grand Circus Park.

At one such rally in the late winter of 1932, Detroit's Unemployed Councils targeted the Ford Motor Company for a major demonstration. On March 7, Council leaders announced, the unemployed would lead a Hunger March to the gates of Ford's Dearborn plant.

Many Detroiters, whatever their feelings about Communist participation in Council leadership, must have taken grim satisfaction in the choice of target. For by 1932, Henry Ford had lost much of the prestige and public support initially generated by his Model T car and $5-a-day profit sharing. Both the car and the profit sharing had fallen on hard times. Since Ford believed that farmers and "simple folk" like himself would always opt for the no-frills "Tin Lizzie," he stubbornly refused to update the Model T or join the trend toward annual styling changes. But as Chevrolet and Dodge began marketing moderately priced cars that were technically superior, more comfortable, and better looking, Ford's loyal following began to dwindle. By 1927, when he finally shut down his plants to retool for a new line of cars, Ford had lost his dominant position in the industry.

As competition intensified, Ford could not afford to pay workers twice as much as rival companies. "Profit sharing" was dropped after 1921, and Ford's weekly wages fell below the industry average by mid-decade. Several rounds of cost-cutting had all but eliminated the Sociological Department by 1925, and in its place, the company initiated increasingly repressive labor policies. Where one foreman had previously supervised 30 workers, by mid-decade there was one per 15 workers. A penitentiary-like atmosphere dominated the company's plants: workers were prohibited from talking, whistling, or even humming on the job. Sitting was also prohibited. "When we were not working," recalled Allen Nelson, "we *stood* at our benches. There wasn't a place to sit down, and if you sat, or even if you leaned against a machine, you were liable to be fired."

Other companies had similar rules, but no other company enforced them like Ford's "Service Department," headed by ex-prize fighter Harry Bennett. With an army of detectives, plant guards, and "spotters" recruited from Michigan's prisons and police departments, Bennett fashioned his Service Department into an instrument of terror inside the plants. A worker who took an extra minute at the end of his 15-minute lunch period, or talked back to his foreman, or attended a union meeting was likely to find himself thrown into the street by Service Department men—after first being "accidently" bruised around the head.

Ford still had some admirers in 1932, particularly among black community leaders who compared him favorably with other white employers. When Inkster's municipal government collapsed in 1931, Ford rescued the predominantly black town with a sizable subsidy—although he deducted the cost of his philanthropy from the paychecks of Inkster's Ford workers. The company also provided some former white employees in Dearborn with emergency loans and vacant land to grow vegetables.

But most of the thousands of workers Ford laid off between 1929 and 1931 were left to fend for themselves. Ford, like many employers, had little sympathy for the unemployed. "The average man won't really work unless he is caught and cannot get out of it," Ford argued in 1931. Ignoring the evidence of his own idled factories, he insisted there was "plenty of work to do, if people would do it."

The mass funeral march passing through Grand Circus Park.

For the 3,000–5,000 demonstrators assembled in West Detroit at Fort Street and Oakwood (site 24) on the winter morning of March 7, such callous remarks made Henry Ford a fitting target for protest. Unemployed Council leaders knew that Ford would not meet their demands for jobs, medical aid, and emergency relief for the unemployed. But they felt that marching on the huge Dearborn plant highlighted Ford's pivotal role in the crisis, and such a bold, symbolic action appealed to the high-spirited marchers assembling from Detroit, River Rouge, Ecorse, and other nearby towns.

Some may have expected a confrontation. The 69-year-old Ford, in his increasing isolation and paranoid state of mind, publicly claimed that a "Jewish conspiracy [of] bankers and radicals" was responsible for his troubles. Few marchers could have doubted that Ford's Service Department would treat such "aliens" harshly if given a chance. But the unarmed demonstrators, while determined to reach the plant's Gate 3 and deliver their protest petition, had no intention—as some sensationalist newspaper accounts later claimed—of storming the Service Department's stronghold.

No one was prepared, therefore, for the carnage that followed. After confronting and then bypassing a small contingent of Dearborn police at the city line, the protesters pressed up Miller Road, crossing Dix Avenue and approaching Gate 3 (site 25). As firemen prepared to douse the crowd with frigid

water, the police threw teargas. The crowd responded with rocks and pieces of coal from a nearby dump. Then suddenly, all hell broke loose. "Through [Gate 3's] openings," recalled Ray Pillsbury, a photographer for the *Detroit Mirror*, "policemen and guards leveled their guns and pulled the triggers. I would guess that hundreds of shots were fired into the mob. I saw their leaders drop, writhing with their wounds, and the mob dropped back, leaving their casualties on the road... [people] were pitching forward every few seconds and lying still."

When the smoke cleared, four men lay dead on Miller Road: Joe York, district organizer of the Young Communist League, Coleman Leny, Joe DeBlasio, and Joe Bussell. Between 50 and 60 unarmed demonstrators were wounded, some seriously. Among them, Curtis Williams, a 37-year-old black worker, later died.

No policeman or Ford Service Department official was ever brought to trial for this fatal assault on unarmed civilians. Instead, Dearborn and Detroit police immediately raided the headquarters of the Communist Party, the Auto Workers Union, several ethnic halls, and numerous private homes, arresting 60 suspected Communists and chaining two of the seriously wounded marchers to their beds in Detroit's Receiving Hospital.

Five days after the attack, a mass funeral march was held on Woodward from Ferry Street to Grand Circus Park, under a permit granted by Mayor Murphy. "As they came," recalled Josephine Gomon, Murphy's Executive Secretary, "they sang the Internationale. It was said that 60,000 people marched, and the volume of singing could be heard all over the city. It reverberated."

The Hunger March, in fact, reverberated across the country. Pro-business newspapers invoked the Red Menace and called for harsh measures against surviving demonstrators, though some eventually took a more sober view as the facts emerged. "Someone, it is now admitted, blundered in the handling of the Hunger Marchers," the Hearst-owned *Detroit Times* acknowledged on March 9. "The opposition offered by Dearborn police evidently changed an orderly demonstration into a riot, with death and bloodshed its toll."

The Detroit Federation of Labor, while disassociating itself from the marchers' Communist leaders, condemned the fatal violence of the Dearborn and company police in no uncertain terms. "When the businessmen of this community marched on city hall and demanded lower taxes...were they met with machine guns and tear gas?," the *Detroit Labor News* asked four days after the massacre. "Oh, what a different story when workers protest."

For Dave Moore, as for others, the Hunger March was "the turning point in my life.... The more I'd gotten involved in the Councils, the more I'd learned about the system.... [But] when I saw the blood flowing there on Miller Road, that was the point I became a radical. From that day on."

Support for Detroit's Unemployed Councils peaked that spring—but within a year, they had gone into a steep decline. Long-term organization among the unemployed proved extremely difficult, since few jobless workers cared to permanently define themselves in terms of their "failure" to find work. For some, the visible Communist presence in the Councils was also a problem, particularly as the Party attacked Mayor Murphy and other liberals as "Social Fascists." The majority of workers simply did not believe, as many Communist Party members did, that Frank Murphy's relief programs were only designed to undercut more radical solutions.

Murphy was still immensely popular in 1932, and most Detroiters agreed with the Mayor that Franklin Roosevelt, the Democratic Party's presidential candidate, would finally provide the needed federal support for Murphy's still-born relief programs. Buoyed by such hopes, Roosevelt swept the national elections in November, defeating Herbert Hoover by 23 million to 16 million votes. Norman Thomas, the Socialist Party's presidential candidate, garnered 900,000 ballots while the Communist candidate, William Z. Foster, polled only 100,000 votes.

With Roosevelt's election, many Americans saw reason for hope. Change was in the air, and the President-elect was promising new programs, new reforms, new policies—in sum, a New Deal.

Franklin Delano Roosevelt—"FDR"—seated on the right during a 1932 campaign visit to Detroit.

FALSE STARTS

In the winter of 1932–1933, there were still people making cars in Detroit. They were the lucky ones—or so it may have seemed to the 300,000 unemployed workers in the city.

Leon Pody, a metal finisher at Briggs Manufacturing, did not feel so lucky. "In 1928, we used to do eight sedan backs a day, and at that time, we received $1 an hour," explained Pody, whose job consisted of smoothing out welded seams in metal sedan bodies. After 1929 it had all gone downhill as Briggs, a medium-sized company building car bodies for Ford and Chrysler, mechanized the job and increased work loads. "Last spring," Pody testified during public hearings in 1933, "they sped us up to twenty sedan backs a day, [and] during the summer, up to

November, it had reached 32. . . . We were supposed to have a 52¢ basic rate, [but] they cut us back to 35¢ an hour."

Walter Briggs, vacationing in Florida, had little doubt his workers would accept these terms. After all, "they were lucky to have a job." If they did not want it, thousands of hungry workers wandering the streets would gladly take their place.

Briggs never finished his vacation. On January 23, 1933, 6,000 of his employees, led by the metal finishers, downed their tools and walked out of the factories. Their action sparked a strike wave of 15,000 body workers that paralyzed the city's auto industry.

The rebellion took everyone by surprise. The strikers had no savings to live on and no established union to direct their fight. And with nearly half the

city's workers unemployed, the companies would have no apparent difficulty recruiting strikebreakers. It seemed a hopeless struggle.

But for Leon Pody and many others, the deteriorating conditions in the body plants had become intolerable. Fear of starvation had kept many of them on the job for three years. But now they drew the line. Their grievances were numerous and deeply felt, speed-up and wage cuts among the most pressing. But underlying all their complaints were fundamental changes in the organization and status of their work.

In the 1920s, metal finishers used soldering irons, hammers, and hand files to smooth out body panels and seams. Skill played an important role in these

By the early 1930s, metal finishers were using motor-driven disc grinders instead of hand tools to smooth out welded body seams. Compare the operations in this Fisher Body plant (date unknown) with the turn-of-the-century methods pictured on page 21.

Previous page: Briggs strikers and State Police at the Highland Park plant (site 10) in the winter of 1933.

jobs, and metal finishers earned above-average wages. But towards the end of the decade, employers began to divide the work into less-skilled jobs, replacing the hand tools with power-driven disc sanders. Production speeds increased and wages fell. For the still-proud metal finisher, the new work arrangements were a step downward. "Our disc grinder threw a stream of lead particles in the face of our [work] partner," recalled John ("Little John") Anderson, a metal finisher at Briggs. "It was impossible to avoid it."

Mechanization and deskilling also transformed the work of interior trimmers. Previously, trimmers had sewn the upholstery into the car by hand, but in the 1920s much of their work was taken over by sewing-machine operators. Now, teams of trimmers simply installed pre-assembled upholstery. Mort Furay recalled how his father's craft was subdivided and deskilled: eventually, "a guy who had two thumbs," as he put it, "could snap headliners and seats into place." Many downwardly-mobile trimmers harbored a deep resentment over this dilution of their skills, and the fuse on their potentially explosive anger was lit when management cut wages and piece-work rates after 1929. With the inevitable bottlenecks and "dead time"

that occurred at the start of the 1933 production season, workers spent 14-hour days in some plants but barely cleared enough in piece-work wages for lunch and trolley fare.

When the companies announced yet another round of wage cuts in January, 1933, thousands of exasperated workers rebelled, shutting down all four Briggs plants in Detroit and Highland Park, as well as Motor Products, Murray Body, and Hudson Motors (sites 10 and 27–30). Since the Auto Workers Union (AWU) had just organized a successful walkout against wage cuts at Briggs' small tool and die-making plant, the striking workers from the big body plants chose AWU organizer Phil Raymond to lead their walkout. IWW organizers Frank Cedarvall and Leon Pody were also elected to the Briggs strike committee, which invited Norman Thomas, presidential candidate of the Socialist Party, to address the strikers.

Strike support came from many quarters. The Detroit Federation of Labor eventually endorsed the strike, and the Unemployed Councils frequently picketed the plants—their banners predicting that "The Unemployed Will Not Scab." Mayor Murphy gave passive support by denying the company's request for laborers from the city's

Employment Bureau. The Department of Street Railways also refused to provide specially-chartered trollies for transporting strike-breakers, and Murphy refused to allow the pro-company State Police (Briggs' Treasurer was chief advisor to the Governor) into Detroit.

This show of public support helped lead to quick settlements at Motor Products, Murray, and Hudson, with management at all three companies agreeing to rescind the wage cuts. But at Briggs, the strikers also demanded the company negotiate with their elected Shop Committee to iron out future disputes. Briggs' management, fearful the company might lose its Ford contract if it gave any such recognition to organized workers, refused to even discuss the issue.

Denouncing the strikers as communists, Walter Briggs returned from Florida and assembled an army of police to reopen his plants. He began with the Highland Park facility he had rented from Ford since 1928. Highland Park, after welcoming the 65 State Police sent by Democratic Governor William Comstock, sent 50 police officers to aid the company. Briggs also paid $4 a day to 130 men specially deputized by the County Sheriff—making the force a wholly-owned subsidiary of the company.

Picketing workers were driven from the plant gates and strikebreakers escorted in. Police arrested scores of strike supporters (Phil Raymond among them) for "agitating," selling papers without a permit, "criminal syndicalism," assault, immigration violations, and even "attempted cruelty to animals" —a police horse in this case.

To protect strikebreakers from harassment, the company housed them inside the factories. Barracks were installed in the Mack Avenue plant in Detroit for 500 men on the fourth floor and 300 women on the second. With strikebreakers trucked in and finished parts and car bodies trucked out under Detroit police escort, Briggs was able to revive production in both Detroit and Highland Park by early February.

The Strike Committee meanwhile splintered into warring factions, undermining any hope of sustaining the battle. Resenting the Communist-led AWU's leadership role, some non-Communist radicals joined with conservatives in a successful campaign to oust Phil Raymond as strike leader; the Unemployed Councils were also barred from the picket lines. In turn, the Communist Party's national leader, Earl Browder, alienated many potential supporters by publicly claiming the strike was a Communist-led rebellion. Since the overwhelming majority of strikers and shop-floor leaders were not Communists, Browder's exaggerated claim put Phil Raymond in a serious bind, for he had insisted he was leading the strike as a trade unionist, not a Communist Party organizer.

In March, the Briggs strike collapsed as hunger and despair drove the diminishing band of picketers back to work. Yet even in failure, the Briggs strike had a positive outcome: "This first 'depression strike'," as *Business Week* noted, "is the beginning of a process which establishes the limit of pay and hours and treatment that men will stand." It was, in fact, the stirring of a soon-to-be-born union movement.

That same March, Franklin Delano Roosevelt was inaugurated President. "This nation asks for action," Roosevelt declared as he took office. "We must act and act quickly."

Few doubted the need for urgency, for as F.D.R. entered the White House in 1933, the national economy had slumped to unimagined depths. A nationwide wave of layoffs, bankruptcies, and plant closings left a total of 13 million people—25 percent of the nation's workforce—unemployed. The country's banking system collapsed when Detroit's banks, unable to collect loans from bankrupt companies, announced they had lost their depositers' money and would close their doors. A chain reaction of panic withdrawals and nationwide bank failures followed. In Detroit and elsewhere, cash-starved cities were paying their workers with printed IOUs.

In this fear-laden atmosphere, Congress hurriedly enacted a dozen major "New Deal" reforms. There was something for everyone in this grab-bag of crisis politics: for the cities and the jobless, there were public-works projects and federal dollars to shore up sagging relief efforts; for farmers there were agricultural subsidies and crop controls; for reformers, there were new regulations barring the reckless banking practices of the 1920s; for drinkers, there was the repeal of Prohibition; for business, there was the National Industrial Recovery Act (NIRA), designed to promote business confidence and investment. Much like Republican policy in the 1920s, the NIRA encouraged trade associations to agree on industry-wide Codes of Conduct that eliminated "destructive competition," especially price and wage cutting. For workers, there was Section 7a of the NIRA establishing their right to "organize and bargain collectively through representatives of their own choosing"—a right not to be tampered with by the "interference, restraint, or coercion of employers."

Response to this impressive range of reforms was enthusiastic. Huge rallies and parades drummed up support for the NIRA's wage and hour standards, encouraging over two million employers to endorse the Codes and place a "Blue Eagle"—the symbol of NIRA compliance—on their products. In Detroit, 15,000 people paraded down Woodward in a hopeful "March of the Re-Employed," preceded by twenty ballet dancers in blue velvet costumes and six Blue Eagle flags. "Now it is the duty," speakers declared, "of all women to buy

The day the banks closed, February 14, 1933. The government-declared "Holiday," called to prevent panic-withdrawals from cash-starved banks, left Hamtramck depositers empty-handed.

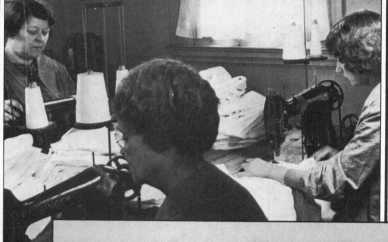

"It Paid Our Rent..."

For thousands of Detroiters, road-building programs (above, on Grand River), sewing rooms, and cultural projects ("Art Black's Federal Project Dance Orchestra") organized by the Works Progress Administration provided wages and a sense of hope. "The WPA brought us stability," recalled Wallace Christie, who spent 2½ years on road crews in Detroit. "It brought us through a rough time. I had a wife and two kids to support. It paid our rent, our food."

Together with other government programs like the Civilian Conservation Corps, the WPA not only produced thousands of jobs, but also valuable public improvements throughout Michigan, including hundreds of bridges, thousands of miles of roads, dozens of parks and recreation centers, and public art projects in post offices from blue-collar Hamtramck to suburban Birmingham.

from Blue Eagle stores."

A burst of adrenaline shot through the nation, raising the economy out of its nearly comatose state. But there was no full recovery. Through the remainder of 1933 and well into 1934, survival was still the paramount goal of most companies and most workers.

Survival wasn't easy for workers seeking positive change. Despite the promises of Section 7a, their right to organize proved illusory. As documented later by

Senate investigators, employers routinely fired or blacklisted union sympathizers, usually on the pretext of "shoddy work" or "insubordination." GM employed 14 detective agencies to spy on union supporters; Chrysler later admitted planting over 40 professional labor spies in its Detroit factories to infiltrate unions and obtain membership lists.

Most effective in nullifying Section 7a, however, were management-approved "Employee Associations" initiated and

bankrolled by many companies in 1933 and 1934. To attract support away from independent unions and AFL craft organizations, some employers—GM and Hudson among them—required membership in their company union to qualify for insurance benefits. At Great Lakes Steel in River Rouge and Ecorse (site 31), leaders of the company-financed "Employee Representation Plan" promised free beer and cut-rate hunting ammunition to participating steel workers.

"We bargained for clean windows and floors without grease," recalled Richard Frankensteen, a delegate to the company-sponsored "Works Council" at Dodge Main (site 32). "Things that were important, but meaningless in take-home pay. When it came to dollars and cents, we were powerless." Chrysler did not leave such matters to chance. Under terms established by the company, management representatives cast half the votes in Council meetings, and needed only a third to veto any proposal.

Unfortunately, the American Federation of Labor had no more clout than these company unions. Its craft organizations did not welcome the mass of unskilled and semi-skilled workers demanding aggressive leadership. Craft-union leaders had grown accustomed in the 1920s to running things their own way, and many feared that industrial unions would undermine their control. They insisted the AFL pursue a cautious, halfway policy: the Federation would organize autoworkers into all-encompassing "federal" locals, but only on a temporary, plant-by-plant basis. Once these catch-all local unions were established, the craft unions planned to take out the machinists, metal polishers, and other skilled workers, leaving the "federal" locals with only the least-skilled factory hands.

Militancy was not on the AFL's agenda. "I never voted for a strike in my life," boasted William Collins, the former street railway worker sent by the AFL to organize Detroit's autoworkers. "I have always opposed them." Since employers had made clear their intention to subvert Section 7a by organizing company-controlled unions, autoworkers might well have wondered how Collins intended to win recognition for bona-fide worker organizations. The answer came in March of 1934. Rather than challenge the companies with a strike—a challenge many rank and file members and leaders were calling for—the AFL would rely on President Roosevelt to determine if company-controlled unions violated Section 7a.

When Roosevelt unexpectedly sanctioned the company unions, the AFL's credibility was destroyed. "I remember that night being up in the Pengelly Building in Flint," recalled Leonard Woodcock, an AFL member at Borg Warner in Detroit, "and men simply tearing up their membership cards and throwing them on the floor.... There was a deep sense of betrayal which carried over in the adamancy against the AFL for years afterwards."

Detroit, circa 1933. To revive flagging sales, the Uptown Market, like many Depression-era retailers, advertised its willingness to accept the paper IOUs, or "scrip," some employers printed to pay their workers (center window). The Blue Eagle of the National Recovery Act (left window) signified compliance with government wage and price standards.

The Strawberry Strike

Autoworkers were not the only ones fighting long odds to win better working conditions. Workers in Detroit's grocery and produce warehouses had not suffered the same layoffs as autoworkers (hungry people bought food before they bought cars), but working conditions and pay had deteriorated rapidly after 1929. Dock workers at Kroger's Green Street warehouse (site 33) were on the job 12 hours a day in 1931, but were only paid for the time they spent loading and unloading shipments as they arrived. "We'd only get maybe five or six hours in actual pay," recalled Martin Haggerty, "and at 32¢ an hour that wasn't much."

"If you made $15 a week you got about $10 in scrip and $5 in cash," Bobby Holmes remembered. "You spent the scrip in their stores, where it was good." Like the auto companies, Kroger refused to give its workers any job guarantees. Warehousemen were simply expected to appear at the beginning of each shift to wait for work — and then frequently found the foreman giving jobs to friends and relatives.

Resentment among warehousemen came to a head in May, 1931. With a train load of Florida strawberries half unloaded, the night crew was taking its regular lunch break when the foreman suddenly laid off two men and replaced them with strangers. Led by a stocky 18-year-old named Jimmy Hoffa, most of the 175-man crew refused to continue work. The strawberries, meanwhile, began to spoil.

After several hours, management rehired the two laid-off workers and began negotiations with the warehousemen's independent union. The resulting one-year contract compelled Kroger to end all discriminatory hiring policies and to guarantee a half-day's pay for each man called into work.

The victory was short-lived. Kroger refused to renew the contract the next year, and eventually fired several of the "Strawberry Boys," including Hoffa. But this was only the beginning, both of an 11-year battle to organize Kroger and of Hoffa's tumultuous union career.

Blow for Blow

While employers and judges questioned the legality of the National Industrial Recovery Act, violence served as the final arbitrator of many strikes.

"At the slightest provocation," recalled toolmaker Bill Stevenson, a strike leader during the 1933 MESA walkout, "we were clubbed down unmercifully." The police, however, did not have a monopoly on violence. In late October, 3,000 striking toolmakers attacked eight different shops in Detroit, burning blueprints and tool diagrams as they drove from plant to plant. Their fast-moving motorcade stayed just a step ahead of the police, pictured above outside GM's Ternstedt plant (site 34).

Earlier that month, over 7,000 striking toolmakers marched through downtown Detroit to counter management claims they had returned to work (inset).

In the wake of this disaster, a new generation of independent unions began to fill the void left by the AFL.

The most militant of these newcomers had the tamest of names: the Mechanics Educational Society of America (MESA). "We don't meander with the NIRA," declared MESA leader Mathew Smith, an English socialist who immigrated to Detroit in the 1920s, "but fight any encroachment of the bosses by direct action in the plants." In fact, the name of this fire-breathing organization was intentionally misleading. "It was chosen to confuse the bosses," as Elizabeth McCracken, MESA's full-time secretary recalled later, "and many of them were under the impression the men in the shops were going to learn math."

MESA initially enrolled only the most highly trained autoworkers in the industry—the skilled "tool and die" makers. Tool and die makers were the ones called on to build the specialized parts for the cutting, stamping, and grinding machines the industry used to shape metal. Their skills were always in demand, particularly as companies began restyling their cars every year, and consequently, needed toolmakers to retool their factories.

In the Depression, employers had cut toolmaker wages as jobs grew scarcer, but the passage of the NIRA and its promise of economic revival gave these more assertive skilled tradesmen new hope. Having renounced the cautious, ineffectual leadership of the AFL, MESA's members brazenly challenged the entire industry in the fall of 1933, launching strikes to recover lost wages in the tool and die plants of Detroit, Pontiac, and Flint.

Their six-week battle won only modest gains in pay and working conditions, but MESA's David-against-Goliath stance attracted wide support. In 1934, the organization broadened its ranks to include less-skilled workers—closing a plant's tool and die operations had proven too difficult when strikebreakers could cross MESA picket lines along with production workers. Few unskilled workers actually joined, but many semi-skilled metalworkers did, and MESA's membership climbed to 35,000 by January, 1935.

That winter also saw the formation of the independent Automotive Industrial Workers Association (AIWA), centered at Dodge Main. Unlike MESA, the AIWA began as an all-inclusive industrial union—in part because the management-controlled Works Council at Dodge had originally been established as a plant-wide body. The worker delegates to the Council retained this feature of the company organization when they decided, in February, 1935, to organize an independent union. But it soon became evident this budding single-plant organization would have little leverage so long as competing companies remained unorganized. When worker delegates at Dodge proposed shortening the workday from nine hours to eight, management threatened to sub-contract part of their operations to low-cost suppliers like Briggs. If autoworkers were to improve their conditions, "the only way they could do so," as Richard Frankensteen later put it, "was to organize the competitors and force their wages up." Opening its ranks to as many autoworkers as it could reach in Detroit, the AIWA received the blessings of Father Coughlin and grew to 24,000 members.

With the AIWA's rapid growth, all the elements of a potentially powerful organization seemed to be at hand. All that was needed was unity: MESA's skilled tradesmen and militant leadership, combined with the AIWA's mass base among production workers, and the AFL's national resources, could then sweep aside the Open Shop.

Yet, however impressive the actual gains and future potential of Detroit's new unions, most autoworkers in Detroit and elsewhere were still unaffiliated and non-committal in 1935. The majority probably sympathized with the goals of MESA and the AIWA, and many were certainly prepared to join once the "final" battle to unionize the industry began. But a wait-and-see attitude prevailed in most plants, for as many workers saw it, Detroit's new unions were still no match for the determined opposition of Open Shop employers. So long as the companies controlled the plants and the police controlled the streets, striking workers simply could not prevent management from using strikebreakers to recommence production. Neither could Detroit's fledgling unions protect their members from company reprisals. Firings of union supporters were still common enough to make many autoworkers fearful of joining. Such fears were hardly diminished when the Supreme Court, in May, 1935, voided the entire National Industrial Recovery Act—including Section 7a.

This decision marked a crucial juncture for Detroit's struggling union movement. Having come so far, there

"You Milled Around Like Cattle..."

For workers like those pictured above, waiting to find jobs at Ford's Rouge plant in Dearborn, an overriding grievance in the Depression years was the rampant favoritism in hiring and firing. Job insecurity was especially prevalent in the auto industry, where companies routinely laid off production workers during retooling, and then hired whomever they pleased when production of new models began in the late fall.

"The bosses relatives came first," recalled Russell Leach, a production worker at Briggs. Then came the people who regularly catered to the foreman, "that is, cut his grass, painted his kitchen, repaired his garage.... [But] when you once reached the age of 40, you were no longer given any preference." Older men, most foremen reasoned, could not work as long or as fast as younger workers.

Younger women faced a different sort of discrimination. "We would all mill around at the gates," Ann Shafer remembered of her early years at Motor Products, "and the foreman would come and say, "I need you, you, and you...and the rest of you can go home.... You milled around

like cattle and hoped to catch the eye...and a lot of women put up with pinching and patting and other overtures in order to work."

The steel industry was no different. In hunting season, supervisors at Great Lakes Steel expected men returning from the woods to drop off a share of the kill. One worker in the Open Hearth department became so accustomed to such shakedowns he adopted the name "Boom-Boom"—while shooting ducks, the first "boom" was for the foreman, the second for himself.

Resentment over these varied forms of job begging and blackmail motivated many early union supporters. Charlie Westphal, a maintenance man at GM's Cadillac plant in Detroit (site 35), vividly recalled the day Cadillac workers were lined up for rehiring after a long layoff in 1933. "It was raining, a cold, real cold rain. They wouldn't even let us inside the gates, and we had a couple of thousand people out there in the rain. So we came down at the foot of Clark Street, and there was a bar there...and that's where we organized what we called the AF of L Independent Auto Workers."

was a real danger of losing momentum and succumbing to a demoralizing round of infighting between rival organizations. The "final battle" would have to be joined sooner rather than later, and victory would require new initiatives, new strategies, and new leaders.

THE TIDE TURNS

The prospects of a union breakthrough against Detroit's Open Shop seemed impossibly remote the morning of November 25, 1935.

Several thousand workers had gone on strike ten days earlier at the Motor Products Corporation, a manufacturer of automobile frames and body parts on the city's East Side (site 28). Demanding higher wages and removal of company-paid detectives from the plant, the strikers had initially won the backing of all the unions competing for members at Motor Products—MESA, AIWA, and the AFL's federal local.

But AFL support was grudging. Both AIWA and MESA were winning new members in the plant at the federal local's expense, and AFL leaders called

the AIWA-led strike "irresponsible" from the outset. It only took a company promise (never kept) of future union-representation elections to persuade AFL leaders to break ranks and lead their members back to work.

On November 25, the police escorted hundreds of AFL members and leaders past jeering picket lines on Mack Avenue. AIWA and MESA leaders called the AFL capitulation "the most disgraceful scene ever enacted in Detroit." The company called it the beginning of the end for the remaining strikers. They were right.

Detroit's union movement seemed as fragmented and weak as ever. But even as the AFL's strikebreakers crossed

MESA and AIWA picket lines that November morning, the elements of a unified and broad-based union movement were beginning to fall in place. That very month, the AFL's national leadership had split into two openly warring camps—a majority still committed to the Federation's traditional craft unionism, but a growing minority now committed to new forms of industry-wide organization.

The tremors that opened this rift in the AFL's leadership began shaking the organization in 1934. Strikes by dockworkers on the West Coast, truck drivers in Minneapolis, autoworkers in Toledo, and textile workers in New England and the South grew into passionate crusades after police gunfire killed 21 strikers in these four conflicts.

Rather than surrender to the fatal violence, tens of thousands of workers joined mass picket lines and general strikes, shutting down San Francisco, Minneapolis, and Toledo. Such tactics won at least partial victories in all but the textile strike.

This groundswell of militancy led to the final breach between craft-union leaders who repudiated the strikers, and industrial unionists who saw them as the wave of the future. In November, 1935, a half-dozen of these rebellious leaders formed the Committee For Industrial Organization (CIO) within the AFL. Their chief spokesman was John L. Lewis, President of the United Mine Workers.

Industrial unionism had finally found its voice. "Let him who will, be he economic tyrant or sordid mercenary," Lewis declared over NBC Radio in 1936, "pit his strength against this mighty upsurge of human sentiment now being crystallized in the hearts of 30 million workers.... He is a madman or a fool who believes that this river of human sentiment can be damned by the erection of arbitrary barriers of restraint." Lewis, in fact, knew better than most that anti-union employers would not surrender to mere "human sentiment." The CIO needed organizers: hundreds of organizers prepared to take on the biggest corporations in the world in a no-holds-barred campaign. To secure these leaders, Lewis turned to the militants he had expelled from his own union in the 1920s—John Brophy, Adolf Germer, Powers Hapgood—and veteran organizers like Rose Pesotta from the Ladies Garment Workers Union and Leo Krzycki from the Amalgamated Clothing Workers. Brookwood Labor College, founded in New York in the 1920s by A.J. Muste, also provided CIO unions with organizers, including Roy Reuther, Sophia Goodlavich, Merlin Bishop, and Frank Winn.

These men and women were Socialists, a fact the politically conservative Lewis (he'd endorsed Coolidge and Hoover in the 1920s) certainly was aware of. But he needed industrial organizers of proven ability, and, despite the fact that he barred Communists from his own union, he was also willing to work with radicals like Wyndham Mortimer, Bill McKie, and "Big" John Anderson, to build the CIO. "In a battle, I make arrows from any wood," Lewis responded when asked about his collaboration with Communists. "Who gets the bird?", he later added, "the hunter or the dog?" There was little doubt which role Lewis saw himself in.

The Communists, for their part, had stopped attacking their Socialist and liberal rivals as "Social Fascists." Such carping had isolated Party members from the labor movement at precisely the point when many workers were joining unions and fighting for recognition. To participate in this upsurge, the Party dissolved the Auto Workers Union late in December, 1934, and proposed a Popular Front with moderates and liberals. Individual Communists thereafter muted their radical politics and harnessed their considerable organizing skills to the CIO bandwagon.

The AFL's top leaders also compromised their views in an effort to salvage some control over events. Local leaders and members of the Federation's federal autoworker unions had long demanded their own national organization—coordinating the unionization of a large corporation's scattered operations was otherwise impossible. In August, 1935, the AFL grudgingly responded to this pressure by chartering the United Automobile Workers (UAW) as an international union within the AFL. But the Federation's cautious leaders initially muzzled the new organization by postponing elections and appointing conservative officers.

When delegates to the UAW's next convention, in April, 1936, finally won the right to elect their leaders, they settled on Homer Martin, a former Baptist minister and one-time autoworker from Kansas. The fledgling organization immediately allied itself with Lewis's Committee For Industrial Organization and invited the independent unions in the industry to join its ranks. MESA's two Detroit locals, led by fellow Scotsmen Bill Stevenson and "Big" John Anderson, split off from their parent organization and merged with the UAW in July. The AIWA and a third independent union, the Associated Automobile Workers of America, joined that same month.

The emergence of the UAW as a unified and democratic union gave a tremendous boost to organizing efforts in Detroit's auto industry. There were signs of new life in other sectors of Detroit's labor movement as well.

Below: During 1935 and 1936, production on this Hudson Motors assembly line climbed dramatically. Industry-wide output in each of these two years was higher than the annual production averages of the 1920s, though still only 80 percent of 1929's record-setting peak.

Opposite page: Cigar workers demonstrating in Detroit's Poletown.

Left: A Black Legion member in full dress.

Inset: Government investigators exposed and partially neutralized the employers' illegal spy networks.

The climate of fear among union supporters lifted in 1936, aided, in part, by public investigations into right-wing activity. The most spectacular of these began in May, 1936, with the arrest of 16 members of the "Black Legion" for murdering a young government worker. Subsequent arrests and trials uncovered 57 murders and attempted murders attributable to the vigilante group, formed in 1933 by "Male, White, Protestants." According to their oath, Legionnaires pledged themselves to "exterminate Anarchists, Communists, and the Roman [Catholic] hierarchy."

Most of the victims were trade unionists, radicals, and blacks. Many of the killers, on the other hand, were factory foremen and off-duty policemen—one prominent Legionnaire testified that at least 100 Detroit patrolmen were Black Legion members. With the highly publicized trials and convictions during 1936 and 1937, the black robed "death squad" collapsed.

Rebellious truck drivers in the AFL's Teamster Local 299, a small union of general freight drivers, ousted the local's corrupt leaders and began a recruiting drive with three new organizers—one of them Jimmy Hoffa, former Kroger warehouseman. Waiters and Waitresses Local 705 of the AFL's Hotel and Restaurant Workers also expanded its staff and began an organizing drive in the opening months of 1936.

While many workers opposed joining these unions, or, fearful of losing their jobs, chose to remain neutral, a growing number, particularly among the young, were eager to risk joining a militant movement for change. Their confidence was buoyed by a growing sense of common interests bonding workers together. That emerging "solidarity" had many long- and short-term causes. Americanization campaigns and steep declines in immigration after the 1921 Immigration Act had diluted the "alien" stigma that isolated many unskilled workers from the rest of the population. The city's workforce had also been sifted through a prolonged process of deskilling and mechanization that blurred the old hierarchy of industrial trades. Craft distinctions certainly had not disappeared, but they had become more fluid and unstable. The Depression narrowed the gap between skilled and unskilled still further, for floundering companies usually found more to cut from the above-average wage of their skilled craftsmen.

Indeed, the Depression had been a relentless leveler. Workers who had defined themselves in terms of their trade, their race, their nationality group, or their ambitions, had been merged, at least temporarily, into a single group: the unemployed. Racial and ethnic conflict might flare up as workers competed for jobs, but the very severity of the Great Depression indelibly stamped all its victims with a shared belief in the need for organization.

Unemployment had also partially merged the working worlds of men and women. The steep layoffs in Detroit's heavy industries idled many men whose wives and daughters still worked in service or retail trades. Unemployment among Michigan's wage-earning women was 30 percent lower in 1935 than among men, and in Detroit, the number of working women actually rose by 10,000 during the 1930s—even as the number of employed men fell 74,000. Since fewer couples could afford to get married, single women were also holding onto jobs longer. Three out of four wage earners were still men, but womens' wages, before and after marriage, had taken on an added importance within blue-collar households.

By 1936, these Depression experiences had transformed peoples' sense of the future. Story-book tales of upward mobility seemed a little ludicrous in the midst of widespread unemployment and poverty. In contrast to the wide-eyed individualism propagated in the 1920s, a shared sense of crisis and common misery gave many a feeling that their future depended on the fate of their whole plant, their neighborhood, their "fellow worker." Significantly, this collective future seemed to brighten during the year. For the first time since 1929, business seemed to be in a sustained recovery, with production of automobiles topping 3½ million—still well below the 1929 record of 4½ million, but a considerable improvement over the paltry 1 million cars produced in 1932.

Some may have welcomed this as a return to the "good old days," but more than a few now recalled that even in the best of times, they had always been treated like mere replacement parts for the machinery they tended. Workers expected a change for the better, and as the new production season began in the closing months of 1936, many grew confident they could win those changes sooner rather than later.

Their confidence was confirmed in the labor movement's unprecedented political gains. When the Supreme Court overturned the National Industrial Recovery Act in 1935, Congress quickly salvaged the worker rights guaranteed under Section 7a by enacting Senator Robert Wagner's "National Labor Rela-

Solidarnosc Detroit

The reason they responded to our education was their experience during the period of unemployment. That was a kind of school that they went through, that the only thing we had to do was to remind them of that experience. . . how helpless they were because they had no organization.

*Stanley Nowak
early UAW organizer*

In the first months of organizing, the UAW found its most enthusiastic supporters among foreign-born workers and their American-born sons and daughters. Organizers who could not secure commercial meeting space always counted on the Slovak Hall, the Dom Polski, or the International Workers Order to open their doors.

The UAW focused on Detroit's Polish workers. "I spoke twice a week on a Polish radio program in Polish," Stanley Nowak later recalled. "I wrote leaflets that were distributed on Sunday mornings in front of the Polish churches; I organized meetings in the Polish halls, and even some open-air meetings in parks and playgrounds." The weekly Polish-language newspaper *Glos Ludowy* (The Peoples' Voice) expanded its press run to 10,000 copies and devoted the bulk of its coverage to the CIO and UAW organizing drives.

Ethnic pride and class consciousness merged in organizations like "Polish Workers Local 187," one of the first UAW bodies formed in Hamtramck. Politics in this overwhelmingly Polish city were still dominated by the graft and corruption associated with its numerous saloons (three of Hamtramck's four mayors had been indicted while in office and two imprisoned). But in 1936, political debate shifted dramatically to the left with the appearance of the Peoples' League. In the April elections, League candidates ran on a platform favoring the CIO and opposing police interference in strikes.

Mary Zuk, League candidate and leader of the Housewives Committee Against the High Cost of Living, handily won election to the Hamtramck city council. When upwards of 10,000 workers sat down in the Dodge Hamtramck plant in the spring of 1937, it was Zuk who introduced the resolution that put Hamtramck officially on the side of the strikers.

Above: Passing food to the Midland Steel sitdowners.

Inset: John L. Lewis, founding President of the CIO.

tions Act." In November, 1936, politicians pledging to uphold this "Wagner Act" won sweeping victories over conservative and right-wing candidates, paced by President Roosevelt's landslide re-election. "If I worked for a wage," announced Frank Murphy, the former Mayor of Detroit who became, that November, the Governor-elect of Michigan, "I'd join my union."

On November 27, 1936—one year after the fiasco at Motor Products and just three weeks after Murphy's election—the first wave of a flood tide of worker unrest washed over Detroit's Open Shop. At 11:30 a.m., 1200 workers at Detroit's Midland Steel plant sat down and occupied their workplace (site 37). Following the example of Ohio's rubber workers, who had recently occupied the tire plants of Akron, the Midland strikers refused to budge until management met their key demands: recognition of the UAW as their sole

bargaining agent, and a 10¢-an-hour wage increase for all departments.

Their "sitdown strike" foreshadowed a dramatic shift in the balance of power between Detroit's employers and workers. In the past, management had always relied on the police to forcibly break through union picket lines and convoy strikebreakers into the plant; once inside, the strikebreakers could then be housed in makeshift dormitories and put to work on the machines left idle by strikers. But Midland's sitdowners had decisively turned the tables. Now they were on the inside, protecting their jobs and machines, while bewildered policemen trudged outside the plant in the snow and rain. When the Ford Motor Company sent Service Depart-

ment men to pick up the body frames Midland normally supplied, they were greeted by sitdowners who had barricaded the plant gates in anticipation of such a visit.

Equally important, morale among the sitdowners remained unusually high throughout the eight-day occupation. Instead of only periodic and often lonely picket duty, the sitdowners now lived together in a tightly knit, 24-hour strike community. The once alien and dingy plant became the scene of a continuous round of pinochle and poker, calisthenics, and even football, played in the plant yard. By the time the occupation ended, most of the sitdowners had also memorized the first verse and chorus of *Solidarity Forever:*

When the Union's inspiration through
* the workers' blood shall run,*
There can be no power greater any-
* where beneath the sun.*
Yet what force on earth is weaker
* than the feeble strength of one?*
But the Union makes us strong.
* Solidarity forever!*
* Solidarity forever!*
* Solidarity forever!*
For the union makes us strong.

The words were not mere rhetoric. In a city with a long and dismal record of racial conflict, the Midland sitdown stood out as an unprecedented example of racial unity. Scores of black and white workers participated jointly in the occupation, and Oscar Oden, a black assembler, was elected to the strike committee. Unity also prevailed between the Detroit AFL and the UAW–CIO, despite the fact that CIO unions had been expelled from the national AFL that same month. Frank Martel, the Detroit AFL's long-time President, endorsed the strike and exhorted the sitdowners to "Hold Fast To Your Guns." (Martel's figure of speech was potentially misleading, for the sitdowners had no firearms inside the plant.)

The 200 women workers who joined the sitdown on its first day were not, however, asked to "Hold Fast." Fearing a scandal if the women stayed overnight in the factory with the men, the UAW asked them to evacuate the plant—but the women did not return to their homes. Under the direction of Dorothy Kraus, they established a strike kitchen in the nearby Slovak Hall on Strong Avenue (site 38) and organized committees to visit and reassure the wives of men still occupying the plant.

When a shortage of body frames forced Chrysler and Ford to lay off 100,000 workers in early December, the pressure on Midland to settle finally grew irresistible. On December 4, the UAW's chief negotiators, Wyndham Mortimer and Richard Frankensteen, announced the terms of a tentative agreement: abolition of piecework wages as soon as possible; a 10¢-per-hour pay raise for all but the higher classifications; and recognition for the UAW's elected grievance committee.

For the first time in the city's history, a major auto company had been forced to come to terms with a union representing all its workers. The example was not lost on UAW organizers centered in Flint and Detroit's West Side.

Flint, less than 60 miles north of Detroit, was the homebase of General Motors, the auto industry's undisputed leader. If the UAW was to organize the industry, it would eventually have to win the allegiance of that city's 50,000 GM workers, concentrated in more than a dozen major engine, body, and assembly plants. Detroit's West Side was equally crucial. GM had three major factories on the West Side (sites 21, 34, and 35), and dozens of independent parts suppliers also produced everything from brakes to body trim for Ford's huge River Rouge plant in neighboring Dearborn.

Ranged against these corporate giants was the UAW's West Side Local 174. By all appearances, the companies had little to fear: when the local formed in September, 1936, it had only 78 members, a handful of organizers, and a treasury that frequently dipped below $10. With these meager resources, Local 174's President, a 29-year-old toolmaker named Walter Reuther, set out to organize the more than 150,000 auto-

workers in West Detroit and Dearborn.

The first target was the Kelsey-Hayes Wheel Company, a West-Side employer of 5,000 that made brakes for Ford. After UAW organizers Victor Reuther (Walter's brother), George Edwards, and Merlin Bishop hired on at the firm's McGraw Avenue plant (site 39), the UAW asked the company for a bargaining conference and began building its membership. The chief tactic was to call "quickie" strikes in one department after another. These brief sitdowns gave the union visibility, attracted new members, and put the company on notice that it could not fulfill its supply contract with Ford unless it improved working conditions and bargained with

Below: a sitdown ho-down inside the Kelsey-Hayes factory compound, December, 1936.

Unlike the Midland strikers, Local 174 did not evacuate the 80 women who joined the sitdown. The company immediately seized on their presence by circulating rumors of women held against their will and engaging in "immoral behavior." The UAW responded by inviting the police to interview the women and verify their voluntary participation. All 80 remained for the duration of the occupation—"with matrons provided to insure propriety," according to the **Detroit Labor News,** *"and stop any malicious gossip."*

Nest 79, Polish Falcons.

Two Halls, One Union

During the sitdown, Local 174 established its headquarters and strike kitchen in the nearby Polish Falcons hall on Junction Avenue (site 40). It was here the UAW also held its first mass meeting of Kelsey-Hayes workers the day before the sitdown.

Management had already sent out telegrams inviting workers to a meeting of its Kelsey-Hayes Employee Association, the company-sponsored union they tried to revive as a counter to the UAW. Coincidentally, the company meeting was to be

held at the Dom Polski Hall (site 4), just a few blocks down the street from the Falcons.

At 10 a.m. that morning, Local 174 held its own rally at the Falcons Hall. Afterwards, a crowd of several thousand UAW members marched to the Dom Polski Hall with their telegrams, took over the smaller meeting, and passed two resolutions: to abolish the Kelsey-Hayes Employee Association, and to support the UAW.

---

the union.

On December 10, 1936, Victor Reuther called one such strike in Department 49, where foremen were "riding herd" on the men and women in the hub and brake-drum section. "Twenty minutes before the shift was to end, I ran and pulled the main switch and shouted 'Strike! We've had enough of this speed-up!' The call for strike action spread through our whole department..., and we soon had an enormous gathering crowded around us." When Reuther explained to the company's personnel director that only his brother

could get the workers to return to their jobs, the production-conscious manager agreed to allow Walter inside the plant.

What happened next typified the brashness that became the UAW's trademark. Victor, speaking from atop a large crate, continued to "talk union" to a crowd of 500 workers until company officials returned with his brother. "I stepped off the box," Victor remembered, "and Walter stepped on and continued with the same speech. Danzig [the manager] grabbed his trouser leg: 'What the hell is this? You're supposed to tell them to go back

to work.'

'I can't tell them to do anything,' Walter replied, 'until I first get them organized.'"

The company, eager to meet its supply contract with Ford, feared that retaliating against the organizers would only provoke a more disruptive confrontation with the union. But the company also did not want to negotiate the issues of production speed and overtime pay that won the union such support. After several more quickie strikes brought these issues to the fore, company managers finally retaliated, barring the UAW negotiating committee from the plant and threatening to fire anyone who stayed on company premises after quitting time. Some 300 union supporters defied the company's ultimatum and, following the example of Midland Steel, barricaded themselves inside the plant.

Removing them proved to be more difficult than the company anticipated. In these opening episodes of Detroit's sitdown wave, no one had yet determined the legality of the sitdown tactic. The company claimed the occupiers were guilty of criminal trespass, but city and county officials refused to evict the peaceful protesters, particularly since the strikers had originally been invited onto company property as Kelsey-Hayes employees.

While public officials debated the point, the company tried to force the issue by infiltrating twelve professional strikebreakers into the McGraw Avenue complex. Entering on the fourth night of the occupation, their apparent goal was to provoke a violent incident as a pretext for calling in the police. But before the intruders could make their first move, UAW lookouts trapped the men in the plant's infirmary. "This was a Friday and there were a half-dozen union meetings in town," Sophia Goodlavich Reuther, Local 174's secretary, later wrote. "We called all the unions and asked them to come in a body to enforce the picket line. When they did, there were a few thousand strong yelling, 'Throw the scabs out, throw the scabs out!'" After a brief standoff, the thoroughly rattled strikebreakers finally surrendered, leaving the plant under police escort.

Five days later, with Ford threatening to find another brake supplier, Kelsey-Hayes signed a truce agreement and the plants were evacuated. As the sitdowners marched out the night before Christmas eve, 2,000 supporters and a union band helped them celebrate the new 75¢-an-hour minimum wage the company had agreed to for both men and women. In subsequent negotiations, Kelsey-Hayes also agreed to premium pay for overtime, seniority rules to protect job security, and a 20 percent reduction in the speed of the assembly line.

Hours after the strike's settlement, organizers Victor Reuther and Merlin Bishop left for Flint, where both played pivotal roles in the upcoming GM sitdown strike. That historic 44-day occupation, lasting from December 30, 1936 to February 11, 1937, riveted world attention on the UAW and elevated John L. Lewis to national prominence. When Governor Frank Murphy sent 3,000 National Guardsmen into Flint and deployed them between the sitdowners and the Flint police, GM abandoned all hope of forcibly evicting the strikers and eventually conceded victory to the UAW.

The world's largest corporation could be challenged and defeated by unarmed workers. The victory had an electrifying effect in Detroit. "Somebody would call

Below: National Guard troops march through Detroit on their way to Flint, January, 1937.

Inset: The Flint sitdowners.

the office," recalled Robert Kantor, an organizer for Local 174, "and say, 'Look, we are sitting down. Send us over some food.' " Local 174 grew at a rapid clip, with sitdowns at Cadillac and Fleetwood (sites 21 and 35) during the GM strike, and with sitdowns in dozens of smaller plants afterwards. Within ten days of the victory at Kelsey-Hayes, Local 174's membership had jumped to 3,000; by the end of 1937, it reached 35,000.

UNION MAIDS

In workplaces across the city, news of the UAW's Flint victory sparked excited debate.

"Little by little, we were getting information," recalled Estelle Gornie Cassily, a machine operator in one of Detroit's largest cigar factories. "And we figured, if they can do it, we can also do it.... So we decided on a certain day, a certain hour. And we sat down.... We got rid of the manager and took the factory over."

Estelle and her militant co-workers at General Cigar were not alone as they fortified their plant against possible counterattack. By February 20, little more than a week after the end of the Flint GM sitdown, 2,000 women cigar makers had occupied the five largest cigar plants in Detroit's Poletown (sites 41 and 42 survive). The longest and most bitterly fought sitdowns of the 1930s had begun.

The protesting women had accumulated a long list of grievances by 1937. Many plants had installed huge cigar-making machines, each tended by a team of four women—a feeder, a binder, a wrapper, and an inspector. "You can always tell the cigar workers that are feeders," one striker explained to the *Detroit News*, "because their faces are all marked from the tobacco dust. You don't stay pretty long if you work one of those machines."

You didn't stay healthy either. Humidifiers ran all day to preserve the tobacco, turning the multi-story plants into dank steam-houses that bred continual head and throat colds. "I worked from 7 o'clock in the morning until 6 o'clock in the evening," recalled Helen Piwkowski, a hand wrapper in one of the older plants. It was "hot.... And you couldn't open up the windows because you'd dry up the stock. We were just cooped up.... And don't forget, we ate where we worked, on the same benches."

And you didn't get rich. "The four operators on each machine are paid on a piecework basis, 84¢ each 1,000 cigars," the strike committee at General Cigar complained. "They average about $13 a week, with the pay of all four depending on the speed of the slowest workers on the team."

Because the AFL's Cigar Workers Union had abandoned organizing efforts in the Detroit industry, the predominantly Polish sitdowners sent a delegation to the UAW and asked for the help of Stanley Nowak, the Polish-speaking unionist they heard on the radio. The UAW, already spread thin by its own organizing efforts, initially refused to let Nowak go—but reportedly gave in when the 25 women threatened a sitdown in the office of Secretary-Treasurer George Addes.

Nowak immediately set to work establishing strike kitchens at the Polish Club and Dom Ludowy (Peoples' Home) to feed the striking women and their children. In each occupied plant, committees were set up to handle negotiations, entertainment, sanitation, and security. The companies initially made no moves to regain control of the plants, though an early meeting of strikers in the second-floor cafeteria of General Cigar was attacked "by a bunch of sluggers with clubs," Margaret Nowak remembered. Stanley Nowak and Councilwoman Mary Zuk only escaped by jumping out the window: "Mary landed in a policeman's arms; Stanley landed on the concrete and broke his ankle."

Two of the five occupied companies settled in early March, raising wages 20 percent and recognizing the Cigar Workers Union Local 155, newly revived (much to the UAW's relief) by AFL organizer William Kennedy. The 1,000 women who marched in the victory parade through Poletown and Hamtramck the night of March 5 believed the remaining companies would soon fall in line.

But a week of stalemate followed, then another, and life in the occupied factories settled into a siege-like routine for the remaining occupiers. The tedium was partly relieved by playing bridge, making signs for the frequent labor demonstrations in the city, and sewing or crocheting family clothes. In the General Cigar plant, one woman set up a beauty shop and gave lessons in hair styling. "Visiting hours at the plant end at 10:00 p.m.," the *Detroit News* reported, "and up until that hour the entrance hall is dotted with little groups of parents, sweethearts, husbands, and children."

"Some of the women had small children and they had to breast-feed them," Helen Piwkowski remembered. "Either the grandmother or the father would bring the child in the evening." For some women, arrangements like these put a terrible strain on their relations with husbands and families, and several marriages reportedly broke up during or immediately after the sitdowns.

Whatever the difficulties, the women were bolstered by the strong community backing they received. "They won the complete support of the whole neighborhood," according to Stanley Nowak. "Churches [and] priests supported it,

small businessmen supported it, Polish newspapers suported it, everyone was in sympathy with these women." A Citizens' Fact-Finding Committee, chaired by Judge Nicholas Gronowski, held neighborhood hearings for two weeks and delivered their findings—with a recommendation supporting the women—to Governor Murphy in mid-March.

By then, the women who had emulated the Flint sitdowners had generated their own imitators—in the very heart of Detroit's fashionable downtown.

Among the hundreds of shoppers crowding into Woolworth's downtown store (site 43) on Saturday, February 27, few would have guessed the young women and teenage girls behind the counters were about to seize their employer's store. Suddenly, without warning or fanfare, an organizer from the AFL's Waiters and Waitresses Union strode to the center of the main floor, blew a whistle, and shouted "Strike!" As whistle-blowing activists spread the pre-arranged signal through the building, 250 saleswomen

Above: Sitdowners inside the Mazer-Cressman cigar plant, February, 1937.
Inset: Pro-union demonstrators outside the Bernard Schwartz cigar factory.
Opposite: Sitdowners inside Woolworth's downtown store.

stepped back from their counters and folded their arms: the downtown's first sitdown had begun.

The 8-day occupation of Woolworth's flagship store followed many of the patterns established in Detroit's factory occupations—and added many new wrinkles peculiar to its own setting. Like their industrial counterparts, the Woolworth sitdowners evicted management and barricaded the doors when the company refused to bargain. But no one knew quite what to do with the 200 customers who decided to join the strike. "Patrons of the store seemed to enjoy the experience," the *Detroit Times* reported, "and only a few left [when] warned the doors were to be locked." Eventually, the strikers had to ask these good-natured allies to leave.

Like sitdowners in dozens of factories, the Woolworth occupiers established a galaxy of committees to sustain their struggle and build morale. For the mostly teenage girls cooped up in the darkened store, food and bedding committees were not enough—the romantically inclined youngsters on the Love Committee therefore established a booth where couples could spend five minutes during visiting hours. The Entertainment Committee was especially active, arranging sing-alongs, concerts, and speeches by special guests. "I was really thrilled when I heard what you cute kids had done," said Frances Comfort of the Detroit Federation of Teachers in one such appearance. "Some people say you're lawbreakers, but I'm here, a schoolteacher, proud to be among you."

Feature stories by Pathe News and *Life* magazine gave nationwide exposure to these novel aspects of white-collar militancy. But underlying the often superficial coverage were deeply felt grievances. The young women and girls at Woolworth's worked a 52-hour week, were paid 28¢ an hour, and barely cleared $14 after 6 days—about half the wage of many unskilled autoworkers.

Service workers in Detroit's stores, hotels, and restaurants fared even worse. The Depression had taken a savage toll on the city's hotels—6 of 20 major establishments were in bankrupt-cy court in 1937, and with the entire hotel industry slashing prices to secure business, cost-conscious managers were cutting wages to the bone. Hotel waiters were paid as little as $1 a day, waitresses 50¢ a day, and bellhops 10¢ a day, plus whatever tips individual workers could hustle or beg.

When the Woolworth workers—after seizing a second store at Woodward Avenue and Grand (site 44)—won union recognition and a 5¢-an-hour raise on March 6, their victory touched off a rapid-fire series of sitdowns among these underpaid hotel and restaurant workers. The Woolworth strike's catalytic effect was especially evident at the Barlum Hotel (site 45). Two days after the dime-store workers celebrated their victory in the Barlum's Lindbergh Room, the hotel's waitresses took the cue and called a sitdown strike. "The number of strikers and anti-strikers was about even," according to the *Detroit News*, but the union women were better organized, and after a "terrific uproar," the sitdowners in the hotel coffee shop forcefully subdued their opponents.

Hotel Statler sitdowners, 1937. "The union orchestra struck up some tango numbers," one newspaper reported during a sitdown at the Webster Hall hotel, "and young women with lace caps glided over the floor in the arms of men who wore tuxedoes with a numbered badge on the lapel."

There once was a union maid
Who never was afraid
Of the goons and the ginks
and the company finks
And the deputy sheriff who made the raid.
She'd go to the union hall
When a meeting it was called,
And when the company guards
came 'round
She always stood her ground.
Oh you can't scare me,
I'm stickin' to the union,
I'm stickin' to the union,
I'm stickin' to the union,
. . . 'til the day I die.
Union Maid, by Woody Guthrie©

"We Felt Our Strength..."

After we got together, we felt our strength. We felt that we were strong because we weren't individuals any longer. We were part of an organization.
"Bebe" Catherine Gelles

The sitdowns welded workers of diverse skills, nationalities, races and religions into a powerfully unified movement. To an unprecedented degree, the sitdowns also merged the goals and actions of women and men. Thousands of women were not only joining the labor movement, but many were occupying their workplaces with the same determination and militancy as male trade unionists. Housewives were also drawn into the fray—preparing meals in strike kitchens, canvassing local merchants for food, walking in picket lines, or speaking out on behalf of their husbands and children.

Not all the men approved of these new roles. "They weren't too anxious to have their wives participate," recalled Bebe Gelles, a former autoworker whose husband and sister-in-law both joined the Kelsey-Hayes sitdown. "But when the men needed us, when they was havin' all the trouble, they was glad to have their wives get out and help 'em."

Even so, many wives held back. Some rejected picketing and public speaking as improper roles for women. Others were afraid of picket-

The Women's Emergency Brigade and local Women's Auxiliary marching in front of the occupied Chrysler Jefferson Avenue plant (site 22) in March, 1937.

line violence, and still others, fearing their husbands might lose their jobs, hesitated to support the sitdowns at all.

To counter such fears and strengthen their strike-support activities, UAW members formed the Women's Emergency Brigade early in 1937, modeled after the organization formed in Flint during the GM sitdown. The Brigades, together with Women's Auxiliaries attached to each

local union, leafleted unorganized workers and helped smaller sitdowns maintain picket lines and food supplies. Members also visited the wives of men on strike, distributing food and clothing and "explaining to the women," as Rose Billups remembered, that union working conditions "bring happiness to the family.... The only way to get these things," Billups would conclude such peptalks, "is by joining."

Once the strike began, bartenders, elevator operators, boiler-tenders, and cooks all joined the shutdown. Three hours later, the five AFL craft unions jointly representing these workers met with the hotel's stunned managers, who granted 20-to-100 percent wage increases in return for a 30-day truce.

When "virtually all" (according to press accounts) of the Statler Hotel's workers sat down a week later, it was a far more deliberate and planned action. After organizers from five AFL craft unions entered the Statler (site 46) at 5 p.m. on March 15 and called the strike, the hotel's 400 employees immediately closed the dining rooms, kitchens, cocktail lounges, and elevators. While pro-union engineers dampened the

building's boilers, two hundred picketers from the Waiters and Waitresses Union took up their prearranged positions outside the hotel.

To prevent further sitdowns, the Hotel Association countered by announcing, at 4 a.m. the following morning, a "lock-out" of all employees in the downtown's major hotels. But before the buildings could be cleared, the Waiters and Waitresses Union led a bold invasion of the Book Cadillac Hotel (site 47). Led by organizer Floyd Loew, 60 union activists approached the hotel just before dawn, only to find the street entrances blocked by police. Only two patrolmen guarded the employees' entrance on the alley, "so we hollered 'Let's go,'" as Loew recollected the

event, "and rushed in and filled the alley so quick the other policemen couldn't get to what was happening." Pushing the patrolmen aside and entering the building, the union contingent—joined by waitresses and other employees still on duty—barricaded themselves inside the Esquire Room.

When Governor Frank Murphy arranged a truce the following evening, it was on terms highly favorable to these daring strikers: no reprisals against union members, full recognition of each AFL union as it signed up 51 percent of its craft, and arbitrated wage increases determined by a 3-person panel—with one panelist appointed by management, one by the unions, and one by Governor Murphy.

Labor's March

If lawless men can seize an office, a factory, or a home and hold it unmolested for hours and days, they can seize it and hold it for months and years; and revolution is here. . . .

**Detroit Saturday Night,
3/20/37**

"**R**evolution is here"—so it seemed to the worried editors of Detroit's leading business weekly in March, 1937. Although no homes were "seized," everything else seemed fair game in the winter and spring of that year.

The afternoon of Monday, March 8, was especially notable. At 1:30 p.m., a well-planned sitdown simultaneously swept all nine Chrysler factories in Detroit: Dodge Main, Plymouth Assembly, DeSoto, Dodge Forge, Dodge Truck, Amplex Engine, Chrysler Jefferson Avenue, Chrysler Kercheval Avenue, and Chrysler Highland Park (sites 22, 32, and 48–53). About 17,000 UAW supporters, joined by hundreds more in nearby plants of Hudson Motors (site 30), barricaded themselves inside Detroit's major automobile factories.

In the weeks immediately preceding and following this stunning escalation, the sitdown wave spread through virtually every industry in the city. Four

hotels, including two of the downtown's largest, were occupied. So were at least 15 major auto plants (including Chrysler) and 25 smaller parts plants; a dozen industrial laundries; three department stores and over a dozen shoe and clothing stores; all the city's major cigar plants; five trucking and garage companies; nine lumber yards; at least three printing plants; ten meat-packing plants, bakeries, and other food processors; warehouses, restaurants, coal yards, bottlers, and over a dozen miscellaneous manufacturers. In all, nearly 130 factories, offices, and stores were occupied and held for a few hours or up to six weeks. According to newspaper estimates, 35,000 workers joined these sitdowns and over 100,000 others walked picketlines outside the plants.

Even non-employees sat down. On March 11, 35 relief recipients occupied the Fort Street welfare office and demanded the removal of an unpopular supervisor—they were evicted the next morning. Three days later, 30 members of the Michigan National Guard sat down on the steps of the Ionia armory, demanding back pay for their strike duty in Flint—they were promptly paid.

As the sitdown wave rolled across the city, thousands of non-strikers were drawn into the movement. Store owners in working-class neighborhoods donated food and other provisions. The Salesmen's Union canvassed furniture stores to secure mattresses for the sit-downers. Unionized pharmacists at Sam's Cut Rate Department Store (site 54) filled prescriptions for sitdowners without charge, while the Detroit Federation of Musicians sent a small orchestra inside the Crowley Milner Department Store to play dance music for the occupiers. (Even the more commercial-minded got in on the act. "Let's Sit Down and Talk It Over," announced Jack's Clothing Store, "Yours For Union-Made Men's Wear.")

Sitdowns even spread to employers' offices and headquarters. On March 11, when Chrysler announced that sit-downers had "terminated their employment" and company lawyers were seeking a court injunction to clear the plants, strikers in the company's Highland Park trim plant retaliated by barring management from the corporate headquarters in front of the complex. With their factories and now their headquarters in the hands of rebellious workers, Chrysler's harried executives retreated downtown to the Buhl Building's 21st and 22nd floors. Squads of company guards and Detroit police were deployed in the building's lobby and alley to protect the company from further humiliation.

To union supporters, these events heralded a hopeful new beginning for the city's labor movement. To the Detroit Board of Commerce, they heralded something entirely different. "We have a right to feel upset," the Board editorialized in its weekly, *The Detroiter*, "when we feel the influence of acknowledged Communists—[like] Lewis, Brophy, and Martin...." Echoing the fears of *Detroit Saturday Night*, the Board wired the Governor on March 12 demanding "a militant program" to end the near-revolution. "Detroit's international civic reputation is endangered."

Above: Part of the crowd at Chrysler's Jefferson Avenue plant on March 8, 1937, shortly after 17,000 workers sat down in all nine of Chrysler's Detroit factories.

Opposite page: Dodge Main.

Temporarily Under New Management

By late afternoon, the streets around the occupied plants were filled with thousands of strikers, onlookers, and honking cars. "Jefferson Avenue," according to the *Detroit News*, "presented the gala aspect of a World Series crowd."

As UAW supporters celebrated, the union moved quickly to establish control around the plants. "Flying Squadrons" of roving picketers told bar owners in the immediate area of the factories to stop selling liquor and beer. "Few of them put up any argument," reported one Dodge leader. "Most contributed cigars and cigar-ettes for the strikers and said they didn't want to be responsible for any drunks causing trouble."

To trim the unmanageable cost of feeding 17,000 sitdowners, the UAW pared the occupying force in all nine plants to about 6,000. Union strike kitchens fed most of the occupiers, except at Dodge Main, where the UAW initially signed a contract with the Conant Factory Lunch Company, Chrysler's usual caterer. The 50 Conant workers had won their own sitdown 12 days before, joining the AFL's Waiters and Waitresses' Local 705.

No reasonable observer could support the Board's claim that Lewis, Brophy, and Martin were Communists—Lewis, in fact, was a long-time Republican who supported the Grand Old Party in every election but 1932 and 1936. Some of the secondary strike leaders were, indeed, Communists, but the great majority of sitdowners were not revolutionaries seeking to "Sovietize" America. Most saw themselves as loyal Americans seeking to enforce the law of the land and win rights illegally denied them by their employers. They wanted collective bargaining to humanize the corporate system and a "New Deal" to spread its benefits more equitably. Most had no intention of running the plants without capitalist management.

"We want to stand shoulder to shoulder with the management in the operation of the plants," declared UAW Vice President Ed Hall. "We do not mean that we want to run the plant, but we do demand recognition." Hall was neither a Socialist nor a Communist, and radicals active in the strike also recognized the limited aims of the sit-downers and endorsed the same modest goals.

Time To Occupy

"There is no doubt the sitdown is illegal," observed Governor Frank Murphy in March, 1937. "But laboring people justify the sitdown on the grounds that it is effective. They contend it is moral."

Many also found it a little monotonous. As negotiations dragged on for days and sometimes weeks, the occupiers filled the hours with [clockwise from the top] talk (Swifts & Co. meat packing), greeting press photographers (Goody Nuts Shop), playing cards (Dodge Main), watching fellow strikers perform skits (Farmcrest Baking), and, when all else failed, sleep (Dodge Main).

Autoworkers marched in the streets with American flags; Woolworth strikers reportedly sang "America" when their boss refused to negotiate. Even so, in the hands of sitdowners, these patriotic symbols conveyed very different meanings from those traditionally expressed at American Legion picnics. In practice, sitdowners and their supporters acted on principles of solidarity and group commitment that stood in sharp contrast with the ideology of individual upward mobility. Their goals were defined more often in terms of collective security and dignity. "We weren't for getting rich," recalled Bill Mileski, a sitdowner at Dodge Main, "because you never can get rich working. We wanted seniority, so the guy didn't have to be a kiss-ass to keep his job."

The fact that the Dodge plant he and thousands of others had seized belonged to investors in Grosse Pointe and New York City did not matter much to Mileski. "I felt that it didn't belong to nobody as far as I could see. It was just a place I had a job." When management agreed to treat workers fairly, they could have the factories back—but not a day sooner.

Mileski and his co-workers interpreted traditional ideas of patriotism in ways that conservatives found horrifying. Equally horrifying were the tactics these rebels employed: sitdowns, mass picket lines, barricades, Flying Squadrons, and Women's Emergency Brigades. For the strikers, justice was not simply a matter of law; it was a matter of power, and militant unionists discovered that the police, as UAW activist Paul Silver put

it, "never bothered us when we out-numbered them." His description of an early episode in the sitdown wave captures the flavor of this organized militancy. "When the police on horse-back tried to break the Briggs Meldrum strike," he recalled of an early confron-tation that winter, "when Emil [Mazey] led the sitdown there and you had to have outside support to get food to the sitdowners...the mounted police came in and rode them down. The next morn-ing, the Dodge workers [and] the Chev-rolet workers...moved on Meldrum,

and somebody handed us ball bearings, and they said 'when you get in the street, drop em'.... Then the mounted police came. And those horses just slid."

The rule of law was temporarily sus-pended, but the union placed blame for this breakdown directly on manage-ment. "The cause of the strike," the union announced in court hearings on the Chrysler injunction, "was the cor-poration's stubborn defiance of the ...Wagner Act, which requires that the organization representing the majority of employees of any company be the

bargaining agent of all employees of the company." The law was clear, said the union, and so was the UAW's majority. In the most recent election to the "Works Council" (Chrysler's company-controlled union) UAW candidates won 103 of the Council's 120 seats, after which they promptly resigned in favor of the UAW.

While acknowledging the UAW's overwhelming support, Chrysler refused to recognize the union as the *sole* bargaining agent for all its workers. Ig-noring the Wagner Act, the company announced it would now uphold the "minority rights" of craft unions and the Works Council by recognizing any and every union that claimed a following in its plants, no matter how small.

Chrysler apparently intended to deal with (or as the sitdowners saw it, favor) these negligible organizations as equals of the UAW.

"It was this very situation," the UAW reminded its members and the public, "which lost the Motor Products strike of 1935." Since Chrysler violated the Wagner Act requirements for majority rule and sole bargaining rights, UAW attorney Maurice Sugar argued that the court should deny the injunction request of such a blatant lawbreaker. Unions had been denied court protection for breaking the law in the past, and "if the doctrine is a good one, then it should work both ways."

As Sugar presented the union's case to a jammed courtroom, 5,000 demonstrators circled the County Courthouse and another 3,000 crowded the corridors outside the courtroom. Circuit Judge Allen Campbell had to order the courtroom windows shut when a 12-piece "Flying Squadron Band" on the courthouse steps launched into repeated verses of "Solidarity Forever" and "Hail, Hail the Gang's All Here."

Campbell soonafter ruled against the union. "Even if the Wagner Act is valid," the Judge declared on Monday, March 15, "it can hardly be contended that failure to abide by its terms gives the defendants the right to seize $50 million worth of property." The union had until 9:30 a.m., March 17, to vacate the plants. "There can be no compromise," the Judge warned, "between the rule of law and the rule of violent self-help."

March 3, 1937

The Detroit News

Plants Closed by Sit-Downs or Lockouts

Following are the business places where sit-down strikes or lockouts were in progress today:

Murray Corp. of America, 7700 Russell street.

Huyler's Concourse Restaurant, basement of Fisher Building.

Newton Packing Co. and Iowa Packing Co. 5075 Fourteenth avenue.

Zenith Carburetor Co. 696 Hart avenue.

Timken-Detroit Axle Co., 400 Clark avenue.

Ferro Stamping, Manufacturing Co. 1367 Franklin street.

F. W. Woolworth Stores at Woodward and Grand River avenues, and 6565 Woodward avenue.

United States Public Health Service, quarters in Insurance Exchange Building and old Daily Mirror Building occupied by women WPA workers.

Brown-McLaren Manufacturing Co., 5853 Fort street west.

Detroit City Ice & Fuel Co., 6247 Grand River avenue.

Michigan Malleable Iron Co., 7740 Gould avenue.

Thompson Products, Inc., 7881 Conant avenue.

Canada Dry Ginger Ale Inc., 4801 Bellevue avenue.

Mazer-Cressman Cigar Co., Inc., 5031 Grandy avenue.

Tegge-Jackman Cigar Co., 4771 Dubois street.

Bernard Schwartz Corp., 2180 Milwaukee avenue east.

Essex Cigar Co., 5247 Grandy avenue.

General Cigar Corp., 2682 Forest avenue east.

Swift & Co., packers, 3001 Michigan avenue.

American Lady Corset Co., 1060 Fort street west.

Webster-Eisenlohr, Inc., 5031 Grandy avenue.

Hand...

Stop the Presses!

Press coverage of the sitdowns was far more extensive than previous labor reporting. In 1933, the *Detroit Free Press* did not report on the Briggs strike until it was already lost. The sitdowns, in contrast, got front-page coverage.

As newspaper circulation climbed during the sitdown wave, publishers became especially eager to avoid embarrassing or disruptive conflicts with their own employees. The *News* settled a sitdown strike by 65 of its printing pressmen in a matter of hours, granting improved conditions and recognition to the Pressmen's Union after missing only three editions. The sitdown was one of the few that did not appear in the *News'* daily sitdown tally.

Newspaper truck drivers and mailers won recognition for their craft unions in the early spring without strikes, making the mechanical trades in Detroit's three dailies —the *News*, *Free Press*, and *Times*—completely union. The Newspaper Guild also succeeded in organizing white collar editorial workers at both the *Free Press* and the *Times*, but failed to organize the *News*—a task that would take 37 years.

The sitdowners disagreed, and by Wednesday morning, had made extensive preparations on behalf of "self-help." Barricades at the main gates were strengthened and fire hoses unravelled to repel the police. At Dodge, "we had bins of steel of the throwable size right across the front end of the Campau side, on the sixth floor," recalled Walter Duda, a sitdowner from the trim department. If attacked, "we were gonna drop it on 'em."

Massed in front of the gates were crowds estimated by police at 10,000 or more at both the Dodge and Jefferson Avenue plants. Signs were hung on the gates: "Give Us Liberty or Give Us Death," "Welcome Sheriff, We Are Here To Stay," and "Injunctions Won't Build Automobiles." At Dodge, "the picket line extended entirely around the plant," according to the *Detroit News*, "covering a distance of 1.9 miles as measured by a taxicab speedometer." At Jefferson, an improvised band of women and girls beating on tin pans led the huge picket line around the factory, singing the now favored tunes, "Solidarity Forever" and "Hail, Hail."

Had Governor Murphy sent the National Guard—and he refused to do so—the plants would only have been cleared with considerable bloodshed. The police, outnumbered and a little cowed, backed down. "They had 106 men in the Newton Packing plant," observed one Chrysler sitdowner, "and the Judge said to arrest them, but nothing happened. If they can't throw out 106 men, how can they throw us out."

The police apparently took such comments to heart, for they now began preparing in earnest to evict the sitdowners at Newton Packing. Sheriff Wilcox asked the court for permission to appoint 600 special deputies to evict the estimated 114 sitdowners, whose occupation of the plant on 14th Street near Warren Avenue was entering its fourth week. The company claimed (erroneously as it turned out) that the strikers had carried out their threat to turn off the refrigeration, jeopardizing $170,000 of frozen meat. In the meantime, owners of the Bernard Schwartz cigar plant also applied for an injunction against the 200 sitdowners marking their first full month in the Poletown factory.

The first major eviction, however, occurred unexpectedly at the Frank and Seder department store on Woodward Avenue (site 55), in the heart of the downtown commercial district. A dozen men had entered the store late on Wednesday, March 17—the day of the huge anti-injunction rallies at the Chrysler plants—and called a sitdown strike of the store's 550 employees. After ten hours, 300 police forced their way through the store's main entrance and drove the organizers from the building; the strike leaders, said police, were outsiders who forced a sitdown on unwilling clerks.

The next morning, the city requested warrants for the arrest of 11 men in connection with the Frank and Seder sitdown, charging them with "intimidation, coercion, and illegal seizure of property." The incident immediately took a grim turn when it was revealed that several of the so-called "professional sitdowners" had police records, ranging from prohibition violations to auto theft, and, in one case, conspiracy to kidnap.

Apparently, the turmoil and upheaval of the sitdown wave had shaken loose several bad apples. Some in the labor movement might argue that, with one or two exceptions, the crimes were minor—disturbing the peace and bouncing a check for $18 were hardly unusual events in the Depression. Others,

Top: Injunction day at Dodge Main on March 17, 1937.

Middle: Police evicting sitdowners from Newton Packing, March 20, 1937.

Bottom: Joint protest rally held by the CIO and Detroit AFL on March 23 in Cadillac Square.

however, saw an ominous threat to organized labor. "It was only after we more or less solidified our position," Floyd Loew of the Waiters and Waitresses Union recollected, "that the opportunists said, 'Hey, this is a good racket to get into'....I noticed first in the Crowley-Milner strike...faces that I would see at night over at the Cream of Michigan [a restaurant on 12th St.], some of the petty-hood hangouts." The union had taken elaborate precautions during the Crowley-Milner sitdown to protect the store's valuable merchandise, with upwards of 60 strikers patrolling entrances, elevators, and stairways to prevent burglary.

At Frank and Seder, there were no

Sitdowners marching out of Dodge Main after 17 days inside the plant.

reported thefts in the few hours the store was occupied, but Loew—whose union had nothing to do with the aborted sitdown—believed there were "definitely hoodlums" behind the ill-fated strike.

Frank Martel's official apology for the Frank and Seder sitdown was buried under headline accounts of "GANGSTERISM REVEALED!" The *Detroit News* was particularly agitated in its front page editorial of March 19: "A movement which purported in the beginning to be a protest of dissatisfied employees takes its place beside bootlegging, kidnapping, and gang crimes of all kinds." *Detroit Saturday Night* went a step further. Under a headline asking "Mr. Murphy—Where Are Your Troops?," the editors declared that "if government...refuses to forestall anarchy, there is only one recourse—the vigilantes."

The next day, 300 Detroit police stormed the Bernard Schwartz plant and fought a bitter, 15-minute battle with the 150 sitdowners still barricaded inside. With no injunction yet issued, Mayor Frank Couzens defended his surprise move by asserting that "outsiders" were participating in the sitdown, and that the plant's untended boiler was in danger of exploding. (The police subsequently acknowledged that no outsiders were found among the sitdowners, and that the plant's assistant boiler operator had actually joined the occupiers early in the strike.)

The police sledge-hammered their way through the plant's front door and were met by 30 women armed with heavy wooden cigar molds. Swinging their improvised clubs, the vastly outnumbered women retreated floor by floor to the roof, bruising several of the patrolmen who followed in pursuit. In the snowbound streets outside, 40 mounted police battled a crowd of 500 rock-throwing sympathizers, many of them UAW strikers from the nearby Bohn Aluminum and Dodge plants. When it was all over, the police allowed most of the sitdowners to go home, except for eight men and 30 women who were said to be particularly "irate, belligerent, and troublesome."

Across town, the 64 remaining sitdowners at Newton Packing—15 women and 49 heavily-bearded men—surrendered peacefully to the police. Downtown, police broke through the glass doors of a half dozen shoe stores on lower Woodward Avenue and evicted the striking members of the Retail Clerks Union.

The UAW immediately called for a demonstration in front of city hall to demand that Couzens and Police Commissioner Heinrich Pickert "cease raiding, slugging, and blackjacking strikers and innocent bystanders." When asked why the UAW cared about cigar workers, President Homer Martin replied that the union was "interested in these workers because they are workers and it does not matter to us what industry they are in. We consider these attacks a build-up for an attack on the automobile union sitdowns." Martin threatened a general strike if violent evictions continued.

Joined by the Wayne County AFL, the UAW's Merlin Bishop applied to the City Council for a permit to hold the demonstration on March 23. Councilman John Lodge declared the request an "outrage." "It isn't a request, it's a demand," the former mayor declared, "[and] I am sure no member of the Council will countenance such a thing." The Council dutifully voted to deny the permit. The union's position was equally emphatic: "We don't give a good whoop in hell about the permit," retorted Ed Hall. "We'll be there anyhow."

A last-minute compromise worked out by Bishop and Mayor Frank Couzens gave informal sanction for a rally in Cadillac Square, with the council finally giving its formal approval as thousands of demonstrators marched beneath its windows. Lodge's lone dissenting vote was nearly drowned out by the 50-piece UAW band.

Downtown stores closed at 3:30 that Tuesday as some 1,400 police deployed in and around Cadillac Square. By late afternoon, it was obvious the rally would reach mammoth proportions. Nearly 2,000 out-of-town marchers met in front of the Michigan Central Railroad Station and marched down Michigan Avenue to Cadillac Square. Streetcars jammed with workers lumbered along Gratiot, Woodward, and Jefferson Avenues toward downtown. Tens of thousands more marched five abreast behind UAW banners. "The Women's Auxiliary of the UAW," the *Detroit News* reported, "paraded in bright green overalls and green berets. Walter Reuther, UAW organizer, led both cheers and boos from atop a sound truck." By 5:30, Cadillac Square was filled with over 100,000 demonstrators.

During the rally, Leo Krzycki of the CIO was cheered loud and long when he called for a labor party to protect workers' rights. Frank Martel also got an enthusiastic reception when he promised the next election would bring "a police commissioner who puts human rights above property rights." In the meantime, Ed Hall vowed, "for every eviction there will be ten sitdowns."

Following the rally, passions quickly cooled on both sides. The police temporarily halted their raids on occupied workplaces, and the UAW—after securing the Governor's pledge to padlock the factories during negotiations—evacuated Chrysler's plants on March 25. The State Police immediately sealed the factories.

Two weeks later, John L. Lewis and Walter Chrysler signed an agreement: the UAW foreswore future sitdowns, while the company agreed to recognize the union and not "aid, promote, or finance any labor group...for the purpose of undermining the UAW." Both sides called it a victory.

LEADERS & RANKS

You'd be sitting in the office any March day of 1937 and the phone would ring. And the voice at the other end would say, 'My name is Mary Jones, and I'm a soda jerk at Liggett's. We've thrown the manager out and we've got the keys. What do we do now?'

Myra Komaroff Wolfgang,
Hotel and Restaurant Employees

The sitdown wave sweeping Detroit in the winter of 1937 transformed thousands of cautious union supporters into assertive militants. Previously unorganized workers like Mary Jones and her Liggett's co-workers were so enthused by the surrounding events that they spontaneously seized their workplace, demanded improved working conditions, and then thumbed through the phone book looking for a union. Such spontaneity was celebrated, then and for years afterwards, as the "Spirit of 1937."

The image only partly fit the reality, for in the earliest and biggest sitdowns, key groups and individuals planned much of what happened in advance. Sometimes, as at Kelsey-Hayes Wheel in December, 1936, a core of activists took the initiative in the belief their daring would activate a more hesitant majority. Three months later, when approximately 17,000 Chrysler workers took over nine factories in a single afternoon, the planning was so open and extensive that company officials knew in advance what was likely to happen—and knew also they would be powerless to stop it when it came.

The *Detroit News*, interviewing sitdowners in Dodge Main's trim department on March 9, the day after the sitdown began, reported a scene very different from Liggett's. "Shop stewards—there are nearly 1,000 of them in the plant—had spread the word that 1:30 p.m. was the time, they explained. All down the line went the warning [on March 8] after one of the Chief Stewards had received a telephone call from union officials, with the code phrase, 'My hand is up'.... 'Yea,' put in a youth in a leather jacket, 'and we showed 'em what a real sitdown looks like.... In two minutes, every man was sittin' down.'"

Underlying the Spirit of 1937 and the

Dodge workers, above and inset, often joined the union as part of their immediate work group.

Previous page: UAW organizer Richard Frankensteen addressing the men and women who occupied the Murray Body plant (site 29) in March, 1937.

Forging the Links . . .

On injunction day, March 17, the sitdowners pictured here paraded under signs identifying them by their departments (#82 and #102) in the huge factory.

Some of these groups grew out of informal social gatherings that predated the union. The "123 Club" in Dodge's Final Assembly, Department 123, "was just a good fellowship thing," according to one of its members. "Make the fellows feel that they're all one, you know, drinking together, gambling together, and having a good time." Other sub-groups that made up the union were more craft defined, like the Dingman's Welfare Club, organized by the skilled metal finishers at Dodge who removed imperfections from finished car bodies.

Some work groups were ethnic. "If you were Italian," recalled Charlie Westphal from Cadillac, "you worked in Department L32, machining. And of course, they helped get their friends in, and they all talked Italian."

In the weeks before the sitdowns, the union attracted some of these groups and repelled others. A neighborhood clique of young Poles centered in the Pressroom might join the union in a block, while a group of native-born Americans in the Inspection Department might identify with fellow Masons in supervision and resist the union.

Whatever the mixture, the moment of truth came when the union first challenged management in a decisive test of strength. Failure would reinforce fears of reprisal, while success would bring more groups and individuals into the union. Such a moment occurred at Dodge in October, 1936, when union pressure forced the company to reinstate UAW members it had fired or blacklisted. Following this initial victory, the Metal Finishers, headed by Frank Szymanski, voted to turn over their separate treasury of $500 to the united union body, joining ten other departmental groups in a unified Local 3 of the UAW.

spontaneity in many smaller sitdowns was this disciplined, organized assertion of union power.

By March of 1937, Dodge's 22,000 workers had produced a remarkably extensive leadership core, with roughly one steward for every twenty workers. This grass-roots leadership was the local-union's organizational foundation, the base upon which union organizers and local-union officers depended for unified action.

Yet the more prominent leaders—the local-union Presidents and Bargaining Committee members, the full-time organizers, the city-wide and national officers—generally came from different backgrounds than the rank-and-file members they represented and stewards they led.

First, a disproportionate number of top leaders were skilled workers. No matter what the industry, these trained and experienced workers possessed habits of self-assertion, planning, and overall knowledge of the work process that served them well as union leaders. In the auto industry, these leaders were the toolmakers who turned blueprints into new machines and fixtures, the skilled maintenance workers who repaired those machines, and the semi-skilled production workers who machined parts, put the finishing touches on metal car bodies, or installed interior trim and upholstery. These workers had an acute sense of their valuable and, to varying degrees, irreplaceable contribution to production, even when mechanization and deskilling partially eroded their skills.

The same was true in Detroit's service industries. The bulk of the sitdowners occupying the city's restaurants and hotels were lunch-counter waitresses, busboys, maids, bell-hops, and porters, but the organizers and leaders of the Hotel and Restaurant workers union were primarily cooks and waiters. Max Gazen, union organizer and strike cook for the Flint autoworkers, had been a chef for 13 years at the Detroit Athletic Club; Louis Koenig, the local's Secretary Treasurer, had been a waiter at the Stock Exchange Club in New York before coming to Detroit; Floyd Loew, the union's most effective organizer in 1936–37, was a former waiter at the Book-Cadillac, one of Detroit's leading hotels.

Significantly, Myra Komaroff, the most prominent woman in the leadership of the Hotel and Restaurant workers, was also one of the few organizers in that union who had gone to college, attending the Carnegie Institute in Pittsburgh for a year. A disproportionate number of UAW leaders had also spent some time in college, including the Reuther brothers, George Addes, and Richard Frankensteen.

Many of these leaders also came from families that had long identified with the labor movement. "I literally sucked this in with my mother's milk," recalled the Scottish toolmaker Bill Stevenson, an early leader of the UAW in Detroit, "because my father before me was interested in the labor movement." Teacher Mary Kaystead remembered her father, a life-long unionist, left no doubt whether she should sign up with the fledgling Teachers Union: "Better join them before you come home again," he ordered her one day. Kaystead joined and later became Executive Secretary of Local 231.

Such family backgrounds were not unusual among Detroit's union activists. When the Chrysler workers sat down in March, 1937, there were two Douglas Frasers active in the strike: Doug Senior, the Scottish electrician and Chairman of the UAW Shop Committee at DeSoto, and Doug Junior, the apprentice metal finisher—and future President of the UAW—who sat in at Dodge Main.

The Frasers' immigrant heritage was another common feature in the collective biography of the city's union organizers. Foreign-born workers and their American-born children outnumbered native Americans in the membership, as well as the leadership, of many Detroit unions. But while rank-and-file members more often looked to homelands in eastern and southern Europe, union leaders more often traced their origins to the German and English-speaking countries of the north.

Louis Koenig and Max Gazen, leaders of the Hotel and Restaurant union, came from Austria and Holland, respectively. The Reuther brothers, prominent in the UAW's West-Side organizing drives, were the sons of German immigrants. Bill McKie, head of the first union organizing campaign at Ford Rouge, and Dave Miller, leader of the sitdown at GM's West-Side Cadillac plant, were both Scotsmen and skilled tradesmen. Mat Smith, chief organizer of Detroit's first union of toolmakers, had been a machinist and union leader in England; Bobby Holmes, co-founder and first Secretary Treasurer of Teamster Local 337, had worked in England's coal mines before emigrating to Detroit via Canada.

...Links in the Chain

The sitdowns succeeded because of leaders like Isaac Litwak, pictured below during a Labor Day parade, and because of mass participation by previously unorganized groups, including the laundry workers (inset) occupying the Harper Hospital laundry in February, 1937.

Long before he became President of the Teamster Laundry Drivers' Local 285, Litwak had accumulated a lifetime of organizing experience. By his twenty-first birthday, he had already been imprisoned for political activity in his native Russia. After release, he emigrated to the United States in 1913 and worked at Ford before becoming, in 1920, a laundry worker. He helped form the Jewish Laundry Drivers union, forerunner of Teamster Local 285, representing drivers who collected and delivered linen to restaurants, diapers to homes, and work overalls to factories.

During the 1937 sitdowns, Litwak's drivers not only won union recognition for themselves, but helped the 800 "inside" workers—mostly women—who spontaneously occupied a dozen laundries in February. After the AFL chartered a new Laundry Workers' Local 129 to represent the inside workers, members of both unions sat down again in April and demanded 30 percent raises in minimum pay (to 35¢ an hour for inside workers), together with a reduction in the mandatory work week from 60 hours to 44 hours. Under Litwak's leadership, the drivers refused to settle until the owners also came to terms with the inside workers, whose less-skilled jobs would have been easier to fill with strikebreakers.

Having grown up in societies where Labor parties and trade unions had considerably more presence than in Open-Shop Detroit before 1937, these immigrant workers possessed a "sense of the possible" when it came to unions that many native Americans and East Europeans lacked. For British workers in particular, experience in Great Britain's industrial-union movement made them especially suited to leadership positions in Detroit's mass organizations.

There were many Italians, Poles, and Slavs who had industrial experience and also became union leaders in Detroit. But where eastern and southern Europeans predominated in leadership positions, they sometimes had to Americanize their ranks to avoid the stigma of "foreign" domination. In 1937, both the President and the Financial Secretary of the Steel Workers Organizing Committee at Great Lakes Steel were initially Bulgarians, but when the company attacked these leaders as "alien radicals," they decided to turn the Presidency over to "a tall, American-looking worker" (as one of the two later put it) named Bob Thompson.

In fact, many foreign-born union leaders were radicals, as were a significant number of native-born leaders. Socialism appealed to these labor radicals as both a secular morality and a vision of a non-exploitive future. Equally important, left-wing organizations helped sustain individual members and link them with other like-minded activists in Michigan's workplaces. The Proletarian Party included both Myra Komaroff of the Hotel and Restaurant Workers, and Emil Mazey, the UAW's leading organizer at Briggs. The Socialist Party included the Reuther brothers as well as Genora Dollinger, founder of the Women's Emergency Brigade in Flint. The Communist Party linked together dozens of activists in the giant Ford Rouge plant, from sheet-metal worker Bill McKie, to machinist Paul Boatin, a young Italian immigrant who joined the Party "because I saw the role they were playing. They were more active, more persistent, better disciplined."

For the many labor radicals who did not join a left-wing organization, their socialist perspective still sustained and deepened their personal commitment to the union movement. "I figured at first that labor unions might be a first step towards socialism," remembered Dobry Dobreff, a strip-mill worker and early union leader at Great Lakes Steel. Dobreff did not push his socialist beliefs on fellow steel workers, fearing he might alienate potential supporters. To make progress toward socialist goals, however, Dobreff saw a need for "a force from the bottom.... You've got to have a voice and the only way you have a voice is when you're organized."

The majority of union organizers were not radicals, particularly the grass-roots leaders the movement recruited during the 1936–37 organizing campaigns. Some of these activists had not even identified with the labor movement before 1936. "It wasn't until the sitdown strike at Bohn [Aluminum] that I became involved," remembered Catherine "Bebe" Gelles, "even though my husband was a union member. I was upset about the strike because we only had 35 cents and a half a ton of coal." Arriving at the union hall to "ask what was going on," she sat in on a membership meeting. "After listening to Walter Reuther I was 100 percent sold on the union and promptly joined the local Auxiliary." Over the next six months, Gelles became President of the District Council of UAW Auxiliaries and was arrested 13 times while leafleting Ford workers.

Gelles' commitment to the union grew well beyond the immediate circumstances of her husband's strike, but it was personal and familial ties that brought her to the UAW. The same was true for most union activists. "If I were going to raise a family," figured Otis Richards, a native of South Carolina who worked in the open hearth furnaces at Great Lakes Steel, "I better do something to make it a little better for them. Building for the future was the main thing... [because] it used to be when people retired, they went to the poor house, and even as a child that bothered me."

Richards became a union activist at Great Lakes, and eventually won election to union office. Unlike Dobreff the socialist, who saw the union as the first step in remaking society, Richards saw the same union as the best way to protect his family's future and his personal integrity. Yet Richards, no less than Dobreff, was building the same "force from the bottom," as Dobreff termed it, that would make Detroit a Union Town.

Union Town, Union Home

The sitdowns mobilized women as wives on behalf of striking family members, and as workers on behalf of themselves. In either role, they extended the labor movement's base into working class homes. When Detroit's unions revived the Labor Day parade in 1937 after a 21-year lapse, women marchers were far more prominent than in previous parades. (The march had been discontinued during World War I, and the subsequent years of union retreat discouraged its revival before 1937.)

Women's Auxiliary and Emergency Brigade members picketing GM headquarters (inset) and participating in Detroit's Labor Day parade (below).

HOLD THE FORT

By the early spring of 1937, the American labor movement seemed well on its way to organizing every wage earner in the country.

Nowhere had the movement made greater strides than in Detroit. In April alone, the UAW won formal recognition from Chrysler, Briggs, and Hudson Motors, bringing total membership to 245,000. After another sitdown at the Book-Cadillac Hotel, the AFL's craft unions won a signed agreement in mid-April covering 15 of Detroit's biggest hotels and upwards of 7,500 workers. The Cigarmakers counted 5,500 boxes of union-label cigars produced in Detroit the following month—up from the union's low point of only 150 per month in 1928. By June, the Detroit Federation of Labor claimed 17 new affiliated unions and 16,000 new members.

Nationally, over 480,000 workers went on sitdown strikes of one day or longer between September, 1936, and June, 1937. Hundreds of thousands more participated in short, "quickie" sitdowns, and 1½ million workers joined conventional "walkout" strikes. CIO unions like the Rubber Workers, the Electrical Workers, and the Packinghouse Workers grew almost as rapidly as the UAW, swelling national CIO membership to 3.7 million after just two years of existence. The fledgling organization had outstripped even the AFL, which gained 1 million new recruits and grew to 3.6 million.

Union growth seemed so irrepressible that United States Steel, long a pillar of the Open Shop, suddenly reversed itself and agreed in March to recognize the CIO's Steel Workers Organizing Committee. The company preferred to accept the union on peaceful terms before a disruptive and perhaps successful strike forced it to cave in under less favorable conditions. In Detroit, similar considerations paved the way for a formal agreement between the AFL's Building Trades Council and the city's General Contractors in large-building operations.

The workers' right to organize on the job for better conditions and pay had been won. The sitdown strikes had forced the issue on reluctant employers, and in April, 1937, the Supreme Court ratified the labor movement's achieve-

Forcing the Issue

Employers and police used force in the spring of 1937 to slow the CIO's momentum. At the Battle of the Overpass in May, UAW organizers Robert Kantor, Walter Reuther, Richard Frankensteen and J.J. Kennedy (left to right) took a severe beating from Ford Service Department men (entering on left, second frame).

The previous month, Detroit's police forcibly ended a 37-day sitdown strike at the Yale and Towne lock factory (preceding page). The *Detroit News* described a "brisk" half-hour battle as the air "filled with tear-gas bombs from the deputies, and lead weights, locks, rocks, and other small objects from the strikers."

A total of 79 women and 41 men were taken to jail, including UAW organizer George Edwards, Detroit's future City Council President and Police Commissioner. "The women,"

ment by finally declaring the Wagner Act constitutional. Having come so far, it seemed to many that nothing could stop the labor movement from conquering the remaining bastions of the Open Shop—chief among them, the Ford Motor Company.

Even with the momentum gained in the sitdowns, there was little doubt Ford would be a tough nut for the CIO to crack. For Henry Ford, Sr., defying the drift of events, chose to oppose both the Supreme Court and his son Edsel, who recommended a non-violent response to the UAW. "We'll never recognize the United Automobile Workers Union or any other union," Henry declared, following the Supreme Court decision. His defiance was more than verbal. As the National Labor Relations Board later described it, Ford launched "a far-reaching campaign of interference, restraint, and coercion"

that same spring—and the UAW was the target.

His weapon was the Ford Service Department, still headed by Harry Bennett. Since the 1932 Hunger March massacre, Bennett had assembled an even larger army of ex-policemen, prizefighters, former athletes, and bouncers, organized around a core of 800 present and former gangsters. Many of these underworld characters were recruited directly from prison. Republican Governor Frank Fitzgerald had appointed Bennett to the Michigan Prison Commission in 1935, and until Bennett's removal by Governor Frank Murphy in 1937, convicts were paroled to the Ford Motor Company at a rate of approximately five a week. Among the heavyweights who found their way into the Service Department were Angelo Caruso, former head of the Downriver Gang; "Legs" Laman, a kidnapper and rumrunner; and Eddie Cicotte, banned from baseball in the "Black Sox" scandal.

Inside the plant, Bennett had between 8,000 and 9,000 of the Rouge's 90,000 employees assisting the Service Department as spies and stool pigeons. Outside the Rouge, Bennett organized the "Knights of Dearborn," a vigilante and political organization headed by Ford foreman Sam Taylor, a former prizefighter expelled from the Molders Union for embezzling strike funds.

Under Bennett's increasingly harsh rule, "discipline" at Ford was meted out in blunt and violent terms. J.M. Waggoner, manager of the Ford Lincoln plant on West Warren (site 56), later remembered one of the many cases where rebellious trim workers were taken out of the factory by Service Department men and transferred to the Rouge assembly line for "toughening up." "I don't know what happened to them over there," Waggoner recalled, "but when they came back you wouldn't even know they were the same men. They had black eyes and pushed in noses.... They really dressed them down."

Fear of such violent punishment was

the *News* reported, "were the last to leave the plant. They came out bedraggled, weeping, screaming, and singing."

Their song, of course, was *Solidarity Forever*.

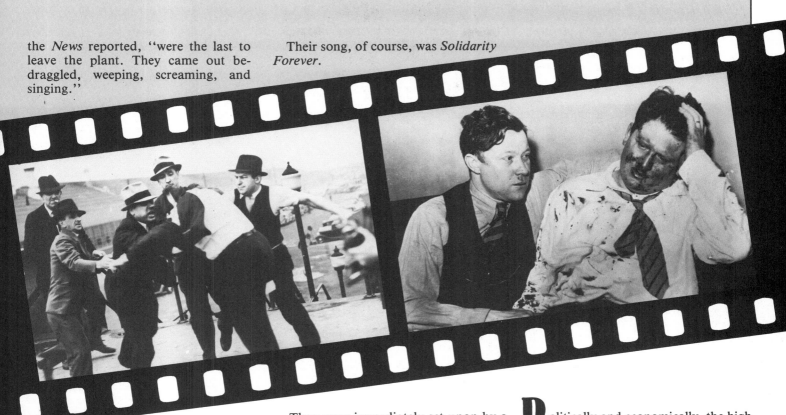

an effective lash for pushing Ford workers to the brink of nervous exhaustion. "No doubt about that!," Waggoner remembered. Even in Ford's luxury-car division, "you could go up to a man and say, 'Listen, instead of ten bodies today, I want twelve bodies today.' And you got them!" This reign of terror—in which workers were routinely fired for talking on the job or, in one case, for "smiling"—effectively drove the UAW underground inside the Rouge. When the union began a new organizing drive in the spring of 1937, it was virtually starting from scratch.

The afternoon of May 26, some 60 UAW members and officers set out from the union's Ford organizing office in Detroit to leaflet the Rouge plant two miles away. Most of the group, about 50 women, went by trolley, but Walter Reuther, Richard Frankensteen and several others went ahead with the sound truck to survey the scene at Gate 4, the plant's principal entrance (site 57). While waiting for the main group of leafleters, they walked onto the overpass across Miller Road and posed for photographers.

They were immediately set upon by a group of 35 Service Department men, led by Sam Taylor and Angelo Caruso. "The men picked me up," Reuther later remembered, "about eight different times and threw me down on my back on the concrete...kick[ing] me in the face, head, and other parts of my body.... Finally, they threw me down the stairs ...[and] drove me to the outside of the fence, about a block of slugging and beating and hurling me before them."

"When we arrived at Gate 4," recalled Bebe Gelles, head of Local 174's Women's Auxiliary, "we could see... Brother[s] Reuther and Frankensteen being severely beaten." When Gelles ran to pull three Service Department men off of a UAW man, "the three turned on me, knocking me to the ground and kicking me in the stomach, and then pushing me to the streetcar." Dozens of UAW members were treated for lacerations and multiple bruises. Richard Merriweather's back was broken and J.J. Kennedy was also hospitalized—his death four months later was blamed on the severe beating he received at this "Battle of the Overpass."

Remarkably, Harry Bennett insisted his Service Department played no role in the battle. When *Time* magazine ran a story and pictures contradicting Bennett's claim, the Ford Motor Company withdrew its advertising.

Politically and economically, the high tide of the spring sitdowns now began to ebb. The national economy fell into a demoralizing relapse after September, and the downturn was again steeper in Detroit than any other major city. In January, 1938, 200,000 of the UAW's 250,000 Detroit members were out of work, and the city's overall unemployment rate had soared to 41 percent.

No one could agree on the causes of the downturn. Businessmen blamed the New Deal and argued that sitdown strikes and corporate taxes had discouraged investment. New Dealers, in turn, blamed the monopoly control over investment wielded by large corporations, and pointed out that the richest 1 percent of all Americans still had a greater combined income than the bottom third of the population. Some argued that President Roosevelt had erred in cutting public works and jobs programs in 1937 by more than 25 percent in an effort to balance the budget. Citing the English economist John Maynard Keynes, these "Keynesians" called for a huge federal spending program to "prime the pump" of investment.

In Detroit, political debate in the fall of 1937 focused on whether the next mayor would favor the city's business elite or support the labor movement in the upcoming battle to organize Ford.

The UAW endorsed Patrick O'Brien, a well known liberal and former state Attorney General. O'Brien, together with the UAW's five City Council candidates

—Walter Reuther, Richard Frankensteen, Maurice Sugar, R.J. Thomas, and Tracy Doll—promised to end all evictions of sitdowners, to fire Police Com-

missioner Pickert, and to stop the blatant employment discrimination against blacks in city jobs. (In 1937, not a single fireman and only 40 of 3,000 policemen

Bloody Steel

The UAW's battle at the Ford Overpass was not an isolated event. The same day, 75,000 steelworkers began a nationwide strike against the "Little Steel" companies—including Bethlehem, Inland, and Republic—that refused to follow U.S. Steel's lead in recognizing the Steel Workers Organizing Committee (SWOC). The strike began with high hopes, but ended with bloodshed when company guards, police, and National Guardsmen

gunned down dozens of unarmed strikers, killing 18 people before the strike was over. Ten were killed in a single confrontation in South Chicago, when police fired without warning on a peaceful Memorial Day crowd.

In Monroe, Michigan, 35 miles southwest of Detroit, 400 "special police" hired by the city and armed by Republic Steel violently broke up SWOC picket lines outside Republic's Newton Steel Plant (below). Three

days later, thousands of CIO members demonstrated in support of SWOC at a nearby state park (bottom—Emil Mazey is holding Local 212's banner).

There was no strike for union recognition at Great Lakes Steel's downriver plants (site 31), but SWOC membership grew fast enough during the spring to alarm management. Expecting a confrontation, the company decided to begin buying tear gas and other munitions—a difficult task, since the Wayne County Gun Commission prohibited such purchases for use in labor disputes.

The company's Chief of Plant Police, Stanley Ferguson, was determined to circumvent the law. In June, he arranged to have the Mayor of River Rouge buy the munitions and secretly transfer them to the company. Such arrangements were apparently routine fare for Ferguson, a former Lieutenant in the State Police who developed close ties with Joe Tocco, a powerful local criminal. This particular scam, however, did not pan out. When County authorities seized the illegal carload of tear-gas bombs and launchers, Ferguson pled guilty to "Unlawful possession of tear gas."

were blacks.) Detroit's businessmen and Republicans countered by uniting around the candidacy of city clerk Richard Reading, who promised to prevent a "CIO takeover" of city hall.

Unfortunately, while the CIO eagerly backed the Labor Slate, the Detroit Federation of Labor (DFL) did not.

Through the 1920s, the DFL allied itself with the city's Republican Party —the "Party of Pingree," whose Progressive wing for many years supported moderate trade unionism. With the coming of the New Deal, most of the Progressives in the "Grand Old Party" abandoned the Republicans and endorsed Roosevelt. Some were literally thrown out of the Party in 1934, when the so-called "Better Element" physically ejected Frank Martel, President of the Detroit Federation of Labor, from the Wayne County Republican Convention. But even though they lined up with the New Deal, neither Martel nor the DFL were prepared to endorse a Labor Slate controlled by the CIO. The national conflict between the AFL and the Congress of Industrial Organizations (as the CIO would soon rechristen itself) had finally poisoned relations between the two organizations at the local level. The Detroit Federation of Labor, fearing a city hall friendly to the CIO might be hostile to the AFL, refused to endorse O'Brien or the UAW candidates.

The labor vote was therefore split. So too was Detroit's black community, as the pro-New Deal *Michigan Chronicle* lined up with O'Brien, and the more conservative *Tribune* actively campaigned for Reading.

Reading's backers drew attention to these fatal splits among labor and minority voters, while also tarring the CIO as "Communist dominated." Detroit's voters, exhausted and perhaps exasperated by the perpetual turmoil of the sitdown strikes, backed the conservative Reading by a wide margin: 261,000 votes to 154,000. The top UAW candidate, Maurice Sugar, came in 10th in a field of 18, one spot shy of election to the nine-person city council.

One of the few good things about the new mayor's tenure was that it was mercifully short. By 1940, Reading, the Superintendent of Police, and 80 patrolmen had all been indicted for selling jobs and skimming money from illegal gambling operations—a racket that boosted Reading's monthly income from $1,200 to upwards of $55,000.

In 1938, however, Reading was riding high, and Detroit's employers felt free to

Above: Small employers like the Geneva Lunch hoped to keep the Hotel and Restaurant workers' union at bay by advertising "union wages and hours," without union dues.

Inset: The "Reading Record" as Mayor included blatant union busting and rumored bribe-taking from illegal gambling interests. In 1939, Edward Jeffries, Jr., with the CIO's endorsement, handily defeated the Mayor. Shortly after losing office, Reading was convicted and imprisoned for grafting.

"Never Settle . . . For Anything Less Than a Closed Shop"

In the aftermath of the sitdowns, the Hotel and Restaurant workers found they could not consolidate all the gains of 1937. The traditionally high turnover among low-wage service workers made it possible for Woolworth managers to hire non-union women and successfully undermine the union's initial majority. Organizer Louis Koenig believed this taught the union a lesson: "Never settle a strike for anything less than a Closed Shop"—meaning, a workplace where management agreed to hire only union members from a union hiring hall.

launch a wage-cutting offensive against the UAW and other CIO unions. In February, the owners of Federal Screw (site 58) laid off half the plant's predominantly Polish- and Russian-American workforce and demanded the re-

Detroit housing inspectors making the rounds in 1938. The economic relapse of that year made it all the more likely that the tenants in these ancient buildings would remain trapped in their economic and racial ghetto.

black foundry workers. Amid charges that Reading's welfare department was directing relief recipients to hire-on as strikebreakers, the mayor provided upwards of 600 police to guard the strikebound plant.

In the inevitable violent confrontation that erupted on May 26, more than 70 people were seriously injured, including a dozen or more police and an unknown number of strikebreakers. "The police pursued unionists through fields and railroad yards," the *News* reported, "even...to union headquarters at 4720 Fort Street, nearly three-fourths of a mile away.... Mounted policemen galloped through the neighborhood and scout cars and foot patrolmen followed in formation."

Both unions in these two strikes survived their employers' attempt to break them. But the Steel Workers Organizing Committee (SWOC) at Great Lakes Steel (site 31) virtually collapsed when the company launched its counterattack. Supervisors browbeat and threatened union supporters, fired others, and gave some better jobs if they joined the company's Independent Union. The "Independent," revived in 1937 to counter SWOC's "foreign-born radicals," won only a small following. But the heavy layoffs in the 1937–38 recession amplified fears about job security, and SWOC's dues-paying membership at Great Lakes Steel fell from 1,200 to only 21.

There was worse to come as the reaction against the CIO gained steam. In the fall, the Congressional House Un-American Activities Committee (HUAC) opened hearings on an alleged "Communist conspiracy" operating in the 1937 sitdowns. Chaired by an anti-New Deal Democrat named Martin Dies, HUAC carefully orchestrated its Detroit hearings to provide a forum for conservatives anxious to unseat Governor Murphy in the upcoming elections. A string of anti-Murphy witnesses testified on the Governor's so-called "treasonable action" in refusing to suppress the Flint sitdown with armed force, while Republicans charged that Murphy was backed by "Soviet Agents" and would "Turn Michigan over to [the] Reds" if re-elected.

Detroit's voters overwhelmingly rejected the Dies Committee's smear campaign in the November election, with 59 percent voting for Murphy over former Governor Frank Fitzgerald. Rural and small-town voters, however, were aroused by the Republicans' shrill labor-baiting and gave Fitzgerald a 53–47 percent victory statewide.

maining workers (about 40 percent women) take 10–20 percent wage cuts. When the workers rejected the company demands and struck in early March, Reading ordered 400 policemen to escort 30 strikebreakers into the factory. Violent picket-line confrontations followed, as local residents and nonstriking workers from dozens of surrounding plants came to the aid of the Federal Screw picketers. Among the scores injured and arrested were Jimmy Hoffa and Percy Key. (Key, one of the few black participants in the 1937 Cadillac sitdown, was ridden down by mounted police and suffered a broken spine.)

The following month, Anaconda's American Brass subsidiary (site 59) announced a 10 percent wage cut for 700 members of the CIO's Mine, Mill, and Smelters Union. Protesting workers occupied the plant's power house and were evicted by police, and the company soon after imported Mexican laborers to replace the striking Polish-American and

A HOUSE DIVIDED

Everywhere, it seemed that employers were on the offensive in 1938, winning political victories in Detroit and Lansing, and forcing unions into violent strikes over their right to exist. And everywhere, unions seemed to be embroiled in bitter faction fights that weakened their defenses.

Almost overnight, unions had grown into mass movements, elevating dozens of new organizations and leaders into prominence and potential rivalry. Craft distinctions temporarily submerged in the sitdown wave now bobbed back to the surface, touching off fierce battles over union ''jurisdiction'' in scores of trades.

One of the more bitter struggles began in 1938 when Detroit's Teamsters, backed by the national AFL, launched a campaign to take brewery drivers away from the Brewery Workers Union. The internecine battling between these two AFL unions took an unexpected turn when the Brewery Workers counterattacked and began organizing campaigns at Pepsi and Coca-Cola, where some truck drivers complained the Teamsters had failed to adequately represent them. After unseating the Teamsters in a representation election at Coca-Cola, the Brewery Workers called a strike to win recognition at Dossin Foods, the Pepsi bottler. With drivers either honoring the Brewery Worker picket lines or staying home in fear, the Teamsters Union kept the company's plant going with stewards and union staff borrowed from other workplaces and locals. They all worked as unpaid labor. ''They ran the production lines, the bottling lines and everything else,'' according to Walter Schuler of Teamster Local 337. ''They loaded and unloaded the trucks and delivered the pop. Every business agent who worked for the Teamsters pulled a load of pop a day.''

After a year-long battle, during which hundreds of bat-wielding men frequently squared-off outside the plant, the Teamsters finally won this particular contest. Whatever the outcome, the labor movement was the ultimate loser as inter-union battles spread through Detroit's bakery, department-store, and hotel industries.

Dissension also grew within UAW ranks between 1937 and 1939, breeding an intense factionalism that nearly destroyed the union.

Problems appeared immediately after

the sitdown wave. The vagueness of the first contracts—usually only two pages long and limited to generalities—left ample room for abuse by foremen and plant managers who resisted the union. Workers were also impatient with the formal grievance procedure that rarely brought immediate results, and many simply "sat down" whenever protest seemed warranted. More often than not, these rank-and-file militants acted on the spur of the moment, without seeking the approval of top union leaders.

Yet rank-and-file members often could not agree on what they wanted. Some skilled workers favored restoration of the old wage differentials between themselves and less-skilled assembly-line workers, while assembly-line workers more often focused on production speed and working conditions as priority concerns. Some workers wanted plant-wide seniority to govern layoffs and protect the jobs of older workers; others wanted to enforce a 32-hour work week during recessions to keep people on the job—a principle 6,000 Plymouth workers struck for in 1938 at the Lynch Road plant (site 48). Workers in lower job classifications wanted promotional upgrading; workers in higher job classifications often resisted such "encroachments," particularly if the upgraded workers were black.

Whatever the grievance, everyone wanted action. But action was not always possible after the economy declined in the fall of 1937. With the union paralyzed by massive layoffs, thousands of demoralized autoworkers simply stopped paying dues or attending meetings.

In the midst of this shop-floor turmoil, UAW President Homer Martin touched off a bitter feud when he claimed that Communists were provoking the unauthorized "wildcat" sitdowns to undermine his authority. Since non-Communists as well as Communists were leading these workplace protests, Martin's assertion of "Red Subversion" served primarily as a headline-grabbing strategy to restore his credibility. The former preacher was widely perceived as an "unstable and erratic personality," in the words of Victor Reuther, with no stomach for militancy and little understanding of the industry he only briefly worked in. Twice during the 1937 GM and Chrysler sitdowns, John L. Lewis sent Martin on long speaking tours to keep him away from the sensitive negotiations.

Martin thereafter rolled like a loose cannon within the wallowing UAW. With little support in the membership, his efforts to silence opponents grew increasingly clumsy. He first tried to censor the local-union press, and then abolished many opposition newspapers altogether; after removing rebellious local leaders from office, he replaced them with his own appointees. By the fall of 1938, Martin had labeled virtually every opponent in the union a communist —including such officers as Richard Frankensteen and Ed Hall, neither of whom ventured further left than moderate New-Deal liberalism.

Martin finally overplayed his hand when, at Father Coughlin's invitation, he opened secret negotiations with Harry Bennett to establish a "sweetheart" union at Ford. When the UAW Executive Board learned of the President's unauthorized talks and demanded an accounting in January, 1939, Martin precipitously suspended 15 of the 24 Executive Board members. Two months later, he announced he was taking the UAW out of the CIO and back into the AFL; that same March, the suspended officers held a "UAW–CIO" convention in Cleveland to counter Martin's "UAW–AFL."

The pro-CIO coalition quickly won the support of the union's big locals and national leaders. The principal backers of the anti-Martin group, initially organized as a "Unity Caucus" in 1937, included the Socialists and Communists that Martin was trying to railroad out of the union. But as Martin recklessly broadened his attacks, neutrals like Secretary-Treasurer George Addes swung over to the Unity Caucus, followed by former Martin supporters like Frankensteen and R.J. Thomas. When

The top officers of the UAW in 1937, from left to right: Ed Hall, Wyndham Mortimer, Richard Frankensteen, George Addes, Homer Martin, R.J. Thomas, and Walter Welles (Walter Reuther is standing behind the group). Unity prevailed in the first flush of victory, but within a year, faction fighting pitted most of these officers against President Homer Martin. Just as, a half century before, the split between the AFL and the Knights of Labor undermined the gains of 1886, so it appeared to many that union infighting in 1938 and 1939 would destroy the gains of 1937.

Above: Roy Reuther during the 1939 GM tool and die strike, addressing autoworkers on Pontiac's Huron Street.

Inset: Pat Quinn, former foot-soldier in the Irish Republican Army, veteran of Ireland's independence war, and President of Dodge Local 3 during the 1939 "Slow Down" strike.

the UAW–CIO met in Cleveland, its delegates represented 370,000 members (90,000 dues-paying) compared to the 18,000 represented at Martin's rump AFL meeting.

To neutralize Martin's red-scare campaign, the UAW–CIO chose for its President the apolitical, tobacco-chewing "R.J." Thomas — a former Chrysler worker and union Vice President who supported Martin until 1939. The convention also reelected the left-leaning (but non-Communist) George Addes—a former worker in Auto-Lite's Toledo factories—as Secretary Treasurer. Walter Reuther, the former toolmaker and West Side UAW leader, was chosen to lead the union's key GM Department.

These men presided over a thoroughly democratized union, with new bylaws that sharply curtailed the authority of the President's office, strengthened the self-governing rights of locals, and transferred collective-bargaining authority to elected membership councils. Following the Cleveland convention, the UAW–CIO could justifiably boast it was the most democratic union in the country, with an aroused membership once again prepared to take on the still recalcitrant companies.

It was none too soon, for in 1939, GM, Briggs, and Chrysler effectively cancelled their collective-bargaining agreements. Announcing they could not determine which union—the UAW–CIO or UAW–AFL—was the legitimate bargaining agent, the companies simply ignored both.

At GM, neither union could rely on a production-worker strike to force the

The "Slow Down" is blood relative of the "Sit Down."
President K.T. Keller, Chrysler Corp., 1939

issue in the summer of 1939, for the company had already closed its assembly plants to retool for the 1940 models. (GM had begun to introduce its new models in the fall rather than the early spring.) But because the UAW–CIO had the support of GM's tool and die makers, CIO strategists led by Walter Reuther could still apply pressure on the company. In July, a strike of these pro-CIO toolmakers closed the 12 key plants where GM revamped its production machinery, threatening the company with lengthy delays in the introduction of its 1940 models. Four weeks later, the company threw in the towel. GM recognized the UAW–CIO as the sole bargaining agent in most of its plants, and agreed to abide by National Labor Relations Board elections the following spring. In the government-supervised balloting, the UAW–CIO defeated the UAW–AFL by a wide margin, winning heavy majorities in 40 of 44 plants.

Elections at Chrysler in September, 1939, were equally decisive. Of 44,000 voting in Chrysler's nine Detroit-area plants, 37,000 voted for the UAW–CIO, only 4,000 for the UAW-AFL, and 3,000 for no union.

Fortified by this mandate, the union called on Chrysler to end the speed-up campaign launched, according to the UAW, during the union's worst faction fighting. The company produced evidence that production speeds had actually fallen over this period; the union countered with its own figures, pointing out that even where speeds had fallen, the amount of production demanded from each worker had nevertheless increased. At the Plymouth plant, for example, management had cut wheel production per worker from 90 to 85 an hour—but, the union claimed, all the helpers had also been laid off. Fender production had been cut 6 percent while the number of workers had been cut 12 percent. At Dodge Main, the union claimed that new crankshafts weighed four pounds more than the old cranks, meaning each worker who lifted 125 shafts an hour was carrying an extra two tons per eight-hour shift.

The formal grievance procedure brought little satisfaction. Even by Chrysler's count, of 2,700 individual complaints about job conditions, seniority, and other issues, the company settled only 800 in the workers' favor. Since there was no agreed-upon referee to arbitrate the 1900 unresolved disputes, the workers resorted to direct action by establishing a network of in-plant leaders who challenged foremen at every turn.

At Dodge Main, the company claimed that 140 union Committeemen authorized to represent workers had been reinforced by 750 unauthorized "white-button" stewards—one for every 30 workers—who collected dues and organized repeated "slow downs." These shop-floor leaders, the company claimed, not only outnumbered the foremen and supervisors, but actually used the washrooms "as a command post from which to direct orders to employees."

On October 6, 1939, Chrysler declared it would not allow workers "to take into their own hands the running of the plants," and fired several stewards from

Dictates of Conscience

In our days, not only is wealth accumulated, but immense power and despotic economic domination are concentrated in the hands of a few, a natural result of limitless free competition. . . permit[ting] the survival of those who pay the least heed to the dictates of conscience.

Pope Pius XI,
Quadragesimo Anno

When Pius XI called, in 1931, for a spiritual crusade against the injustice and materialism of capitalism, American Catholics responded in diverse ways.

For Father Coughlin, the establishment of a just society required no fundamental change in capitalist industry. "Social justice cries aloud, not against industry," he proclaimed, "but... against the banker." The Depression, according to Coughlin, had one overriding cause: an artificial "money famine" created by Wall Street's "white-carnationed bankers."

By asserting that bankers were to blame for the Depression, Coughlin could propose deceptively simple solutions to complex problems. America's economy, he insisted, was basically sound—it was only necessary to remove the influence of "parasitic" bankers to restore prosperity. This reassuring perspective also gave Coughlin a ready scapegoat, for like his friend Henry Ford, he believed America's banks were controlled by an "International Jewish conspiracy."

When President Roosevelt rejected Coughlin's scheme to expand the money supply with silver, the radio priest formed his own National Union for Social Justice and backed William Lemke for President in 1936. Lemke attracted less than 2 percent of the vote (4 percent in Michigan), and the ill-fated third party soon after collapsed.

By the late 1930s, Coughlin's extremist views had taken him to the outer fringes of right-wing politics and trade unionism. Proclaiming that no true Catholic would join the "Communist-controlled" CIO, Coughlin formed the Workers Council For Social Justice in 1937 as a Christians-only alternative to militant trade unionism. To counter the "Jewish system of modern capitalism," as he termed it, he also called for a nationwide Christian Front: "A Christian Front which is not afraid of the word 'fascist'.... A Christian Front which will not fear to be called anti-Semitic" by its "communist opponents."

While Coughlin's radio broadcasts from Royal Oak attracted millions of listeners nationwide, few of Detroit's blue-collar Catholics endorsed his attacks on the New Deal. Fewer still identified with his choice of Benito Mussolini, Italy's fascist dictator, as "Man of the Week" in a 1938 edition of Coughlin's *Social Justice* magazine.

The lay members of the Catholic Worker Movement interpreted Pope Pius's words in a very different way. For them, the Papal encyclical was a call to voluntary poverty and militant identification with workers and the poor. "Ours was a long-range program," Dorothy Day later said of the movement she co-founded in New York during the Depression, "looking for the ownership by the workers of the means of production, the abolition of the assembly line, [and] the restoration of crafts."

The Catholic Worker Movement was not, however, a political movement. Day's long-range program was a distant utopia, an ideal that guided members in their day-to-day activities. Catholic Workers "gave" themselves to the poor "as you would to Christ himself," in the words of Justine Murphy. For the Detroit movement, founded by Lou Murphy in the fall of 1937, this took the form of a soupline feeding upwards of 800 a day and two communal shelters in Detroit's Corktown: St. Francis House for homeless men, and St. Martha's House (site 60) for women and children.

With labor contributed by the poor themselves and by students from the University of Detroit and Marygrove College (where Lou and Justine, respectively, both studied), the Movement's two Houses of Hospitality surthe Dodge Main body plant. More firings followed, eventually totaling 105, and workers began "job skipping" in retaliation—letting every second car pass by unfinished. Finally, the company closed Dodge Main altogether. The "lock-out" led to a strike when Dodge workers voted 10-1 to withhold their labor until management agreed to negotiate over production standards.

The strike reverberated throughout the Detroit community. Father Coughlin and the *Free Press* urged Dodge workers to end their "Communistic" and "Un-Christian" strike, while ACTU's Father Clancey, backed by Archbishop Mooney

and the *Michigan Catholic*, urged the strikers "to remain steadfast" until they won a new contract.

The UAW-AFL was also drawn back into the fray when Homer Martin made a special plea to the 1700 black workers employed at Dodge to return to work. Prominent leaders of Detroit's black community, led by the Reverend Horace White and Senator Charles Diggs, Sr., immediately denounced the move as a cynical effort "to invite physical violence and bloodshed" between white and black workers. Such a confrontation, the UAW-CIO declared, could only provide "an excuse to call the State

Troops and National Guard...to break our strike." When Hamtramck's city government refused to support the company's strikebreaking plan, Chrysler announced that only its Conant gate (on the Detroit side of the plant) would open for returning workers.

The expected violence did not occur—largely because black leaders like Diggs, White, Rev. Charles Hill, and Louis Martin of the *Michigan Chronicle* came out strongly in favor of the UAW-CIO. When 1,000 Detroit police escorted several hundred black workers through the Conant gate on November 27 and 28, 6,000 picketers let them pass without

Archbishop Mooney (right) opposed the anti-Semitic, anti-union views of Father Coughlin. He is pictured here with Michael Widman of the United Mine Workers, who helped lead the UAW organizing drive at Ford.

drew the Movement into the labor struggles of the 1930s. Such activism led, in 1938, to the formation of the Association of Catholic Trade Unionists (ACTU), headed in Detroit by Paul Weber of the Newspaper Guild.

With Archbishop Mooney's blessings, ACTU activists in the UAW like Paul St. Marie and the McCusker brothers began actively countering Coughlin's attacks on the CIO. ACTU, in their words, rejected both the "oppression of modern capitalism" and the "intrinsic wrongs" of Communism, steering a middle-of-the-road course that favored gradual reform. Through its newspaper, the *Michigan Labor Leader*, and through weekly discussions on WMBC's "Catholic Hour," ACTU broadcast its perspective to several thousand "Actists" in the Detroit area, many of them graduates of the labor schools established in over 30 parishes by ACTU's chaplain, Raymond Clancey.

"Actists" and Catholic Workers prayed together for justice and peace in weekly Holy Hours, where participants "asked for the help of God so they could be more effective working on the issues," as Father Clement Kern later put it. Yet despite its origins in the study-group meetings held at St. Francis House, ACTU's stress on fighting Communists in the CIO eventually set it apart from the Catholic Worker Movement, which avoided all such political in-fighting. According to Dorothy Day, ACTU "disagreed with our indiscriminate assistance in strikes where there was a strong Communist influence, and our loss of the opportunity to get our own men in positions ...to influence others."

vived on produce from a communal farm outside the city. Donated food from Koepplingers, Fred Sanders, Kraft Cheese, and various wealthy patrons also kept the houses and souplines going. "We'd go into the Women's City Club," recalled Marie Oreste, a Nazareth College graduate

who helped run St. Martha's House, "and there'd be a whole big cannister of rolls that people had left, or whatever, that they were donating to us."

Active participation in picket lines and strike kitchens, and distribution of their newspaper, the *Catholic Worker*,

provocation.

With only a fraction of the strike-breakers needed to recommence production, Chrysler had to capitulate. The company agreed to negotiate production standards, arbitrate unresolved grievances, and rehire all 105 men fired in early October. "Rank on the seniority list," the new contract also declared, "will not be affected by the race...of the employee."

The union was now firmly rooted in Chrysler and GM, and a new coalition between Detroit's black community and the UAW–CIO had borne its first fruit.

War in the Unity Caucus

Should the U.S risk war with Nazi Germany and Imperial Japan? This question dominated American politics in the late 1930s as those two dictatorial governments began to subdue and annex their neighbors in Europe and Asia.

A broad range of Americans, recalling the wasted sacrifices of World War I—"The War To End All Wars"—said no. As President Roosevelt moved towards a cautious alliance with England and China against the Berlin–Tokyo "Axis," New Deal supporters like John L. Lewis, head of the CIO, joined conservative Republicans in demanding the U.S. remain neutral.

Socialists and Communists in the UAW's Unity Caucus fell on opposite sides of this conflict in 1938. Socialists opposed military alliances as a first step towards war, while Communists supported any alliance that included the Soviet Union against Nazi Germany. Bitter quarrels over these issues inflamed factional disputes over who the Unity Caucus would support for union office, eventually splitting the Caucus down the middle. After 1938, Socialists and Communists in the UAW remained allied only until Martin was ousted. As their split became public, however, their positions on war and peace turned 180 degrees.

For years, Socialists in the labor movement had been abandoning their party and drifting into open support of New-Deal Democrats, particularly those who consistently backed social-welfare and labor-reform legislation. In the 1938 elections, most Socialists in the UAW were eager to support Michigan's Democratic Governor, Frank Murphy. Since more doctrinaire Socialists criticized their endorsement of such liberals, many labor socialists dropped out of the left-wing party. As war approached and the Nazis' anti-Jewish terror campaigns spread across Europe, more Socialists began to reject their Party's position and back FDR's war preparations.

The Communist Party, in the meantime, made an about-face on foreign policy. The abrupt shift followed events in the Soviet Union: finding no takers in the West for a military alliance against Germany, Moscow had signed a Non-Aggression Pact with the Nazis in August, 1939. The following month, the two powers invaded Poland and, under the terms of this "Hitler–Stalin" agreement, divided the country between themselves. American Communists were as surprised as anyone by this stunning reversal in Soviet policy, but most fell in line and defended Soviet actions as self-protective. President Roosevelt, they now declared, was a war monger.

Two years later, the Party line took another dramatic turn after the Nazis launched a surprise invasion of the Soviet Union in June, 1941. Overnight, American Communists became pro-FDR again, applauding the President's war preparations and calling for a military alliance with the Soviets against the Germans.

During the two-year period when Communists were attacking FDR, the Party's credibility in the labor movement took a severe beating. While some non-Communists continued to admire the zeal and organizing skills of individual Communists, the Party's knee-jerk endorsement of Soviet foreign policy baffled many in the UAW and other unions. For most, the Popular Front could not be re-established with the same conviction.

The Communists were not the only ones who paid a price for opposing FDR. John L. Lewis had endorsed the Republican "anti-war" candidate, Wendell Wilkie, in the 1940 presidential elections. When Roosevelt defeated Wilkie with 55 percent of the vote, Lewis resigned as head of the CIO, leaving the pro-FDR Philip Murray to take over.

As part of a nationwide preparation for war, the 210th Anti-Aircraft Regiment left Detroit for training at Fort Sheridan, Illinois, on March 4, 1941.

FORD, THE LAST MILE

The River Rouge plant has taken on many aspects of a community in which martial law has been declared, and in which a huge military organization. . . has been superimposed upon the regular civil authorities.

National Labor Relations Board

Henry Ford, the famed engineer of the Model T car and the moving assembly line, had become by 1940 an infamous patron of a private army. His reputation for violent anti-unionism led many observers to believe he might still defy the revived UAW–CIO.

Ford's Service Department had grown to 3,000 men, making it, according to *The New York Times*, the largest privately run secret-service force in the world. As Henry Ford, recovering from strokes in 1938 and 1941, retired from the firm's day-to-day management, Harry Bennett used the backing of this small army to become the de facto chief of the Ford Motor Company, eclipsing even Henry's oldest son, Edsel. The atmosphere of dread and apprehension that pervaded the Rouge plant thereafter permeated every level of the company. "The feeling of the average person towards Bennett was fear," reported Frank Riecks, a Ford manager. Fear took many forms on the shop floor— fear of informers, fear of physical punishment, fear of sudden dismissal. And these were not solely blue-collar fears. "This included supervision," Riecks recalled. "They felt that if they hit Bennett head on, they might be out of a job."

CIO organizers, on the other hand, were afraid that if they *did not* hit Bennett "head on," his company's lower wages and non-union working conditions would allow Ford to undersell GM and Chrysler. Such competitive pressure, union supporters feared, would eventually undermine the UAW's position throughout the industry.

Ford, the bastion of Detroit's Open Shop, had to be organized if the city's labor movement was to consolidate its gains. As it happened, all the elements for such an organizing campaign fell into place after 1939, notwithstanding the National Labor Relations Board's (NLRB) grim assessment of the Rouge plant.

If nothing else, workers were back at work in the dozens of machine shops, assembly plants, foundries, steel and

"Unionism, Not Fascism"

Above: UAW demonstrators are holding a sign picturing Henry Ford, Sr. with a swastika.

Inset: When 1,000 Ford–UAW members marched in the 1937 Labor Day parade, they all wore masks to conceal their identities.

Preceding page: State Police confront UAW picketers, April, 1941.

Many Americans saw reason to equate the elder Ford with Germany's Nazi regime, which gave wide distribution to Ford's anti-Jewish writings. In 1938, Hitler's government expressed its high regard for Ford by sending the German Vice Consul to Dearborn and presenting him with the Grand Cross of the German Eagle. After the ceremony, Ford assured reporters that accepting the medal did not "involve any sympathy on my part with Nazism." Ford's UAW opponents were not convinced.

If Ford was, in fact, pro-Fascist, he was not alone. *Detroit-Times* owner William Randolph Hearst, expressing only mild criticism of Nazi "excesses," advocated a German–U.S. alliance against "the onrushing hordes of Russian Communism," as the *Times* editorialized in 1939.

Hearst and Ford, like many employers, also saw a Red menace in the CIO, and Ford in particular instructed his managers to suppress this "alien" influence at all costs.

Union supporters were at risk even when they were far from the Rouge. "In 1939 when I was marching in the Labor Day parade," recalled Shelton Tappes, a young black worker in the Rouge foundry, "I had my Ford badge pinned to my lapel. And as I got to the Fox Theater, a man stepped out from the curb and took a good look at my badge.... The next day I found myself fired."

The National Labor Relations Act of 1935 prohibited the firing of workers solely for union membership, but Ford routinely ignored the law. In the fall of 1937, the Bill of Rights was also partially suspended in Dearborn when the company-controlled City Council banned all leafleting around the Rouge plant. Over 600 UAW leafleters were subsequently arrested in December and January for defying this denial of free speech.

rubber mills that made up the Rouge complex. During the 1937–38 recession, the Rouge's fulltime workforce had fallen from 87,000 to 11,000, and the UAW's dues-paying membership dropped accordingly—to a reported low of only 18 members at one point. By 1940, a modest economic recovery was underway in Detroit and nationally, spurred in part by the expanding production of military hardware. Ford's employment grew apace, even though Ford showed little interest in securing Pentagon contracts before 1940.

The government's role in regulating labor relations also expanded tremendously after April, 1937, when the Supreme Court ruled the National Labor Relations Act constitutional. Government officials were especially inclined to intervene in cases where conflict might disrupt military production, and Detroit was already becoming the nation's "Arsenal of Democracy." In 1939 and 1940, the NLRB established itself as the final arbitrator of interunion conflicts between the UAW–CIO and the UAW–AFL, conducting elections in scores of workplaces that established the UAW–CIO as the choice of Detroit's autoworkers.

Ford's lawyers, having made the preposterous claim their employer did not engage in interstate commerce, insisted that the company was exempt from federal labor law. The company thereafter concluded that NLRB rulings, including those ordering the company to reinstate union supporters it had illegally fired, were non-binding. Such blatant defiance of the law allowed Bennett to continue bullying UAW supporters, but a government-initiated suit was slowly closing in on Ford's "martial-law" rule.

So was the UAW–CIO, revitalized and emboldened by its strike victories in 1939 and its defeat of Homer Martin the same year. The factionalism that plagued the 1937–1938 organizing drive was now behind the union. To insure it stayed that way, UAW leaders agreed to put the Ford campaign under the direction of Michael Widman, an organizer loaned to the union by the United Mine Workers.

In 1940, Widman recruited 1,000 volunteers and a staff of 70 full-time organizers, including veteran Ford worker Bill McKie and young black activists Veal Clough and Shelton Tappes. Small neighborhood offices were opened far from the plants, and initial meetings were held in members' homes to reduce the likelihood of surveillance. Subcommittees were established for each of the major ethnic and racial groups represented at Ford. "We did the speaking on the Italian Hour," recalled Nick DiGaetano, a volunteer from Chrysler Local 7 who spoke frequently on radio broadcasts of the Italian Organizing Committee. Later, "we arranged meetings at Eastern High School and different halls in the Italian districts"—always tailed, he remembered, by "two of Bennett's racketeers."

It was, above all, the decade-long shift in the attitudes and politics of Detroit's black community that finally tipped the scales in favor of the union. By 1940–1941, a growing minority of

black workers and professionals believed the UAW–CIO, not Henry Ford, was the best friend of black people.

The emergence of this pro-CIO constituency marked a fundamental realignment. Until the early 1930s, Detroit's blacks had been nearly unanimous in their praise of Henry Ford and their distrust of unions. There were multiple reasons for this attitude. Many black autoworkers, to begin with, had been raised in Southern farm communities, where tradition and deference regulated much of daily life. Once in Detroit, these migrants faced a degree of racial segregation and discrimination that made them doubly dependent on the

city's conservative black leaders.

The small, relatively well-to-do black elite had little reason to trust the white labor movement. For men like Reverend William Peck of Bethel A.M.E. Church and Louis Blount of the Great Lakes Mutual Insurance Company, black capitalism was the only reliable means of self-help—and Henry Ford was the only reliable source of the jobs and wages making black business viable.

Black workers were also appreciative of Ford's more equitable hiring practices, and his highly publicized "rescue" of Inkster during the early-Depression years. Equally important, they had no more reason than their middle-class

Below: UAW appeals to black workers drew comparisons between union and non-union conditions in Detroit's auto industry. Hodges Mason, a local-union leader at Bohn Aluminum, here underlined the hourly wage increases at Briggs and Budd Wheel that ranged between 30 and 100 percent between 1936 and 1940.

Inset: The Negro Organizing Subcommittee for the Ford organizing campaign. Left to right: Joseph Billups, Walter Hardin, Chris Alston, Veal Clough, Clarence Bowman, Leon Bates, and John Conyers, Sr.

brethren to be immediately swayed by the UAW–CIO's formal commitment to integration.

"The whole thing about it," according to Joseph Billups, who became a UAW organizer, "was they had been, I call it gypped, so many times in joining the union.... They figured they would be used, used by white people and then kicked out." Positive action was required of the union, and the UAW's record, though better than any other Detroit union, was mixed. Black UAW activists like Sam Fanroy at Chrysler–Jefferson, Oscar Oden at Midland Steel, and Leonard Newman at Briggs had won elective office in their locals, but they remained isolated cases. At the same time, white workers at Chevrolet Gear and Axle had excluded black co-workers from a union-sponsored dance.

Black ministers were especially inclined to see the well-being of their congregation as dependent upon the good graces of the Ford Motor Company. Henry Ford gave financial support to many black churches, and his company routinely hired job applicants from favored congregations. Donald Marshall, the former policeman hired by Bennett to head Ford's "black" Service Department, underlined this close relationship by frequently appearing in these same churches as a guest speaker.

When black ministers occasionally deviated from the "Ford Gospel," Marshall turned the screws. The Reverend Horace White of the Plymouth Congregational Church, a well-known UAW supporter, found every pulpit on the

Violent confrontations on Miller Road during the 1941 strike pitted UAW picketers (top) against a much smaller force of predominantly black strikebreakers (middle). Black union supporters helped ease the racial tension by circling the plant in a sound car (bottom), urging the strikebreakers to leave the plant and side with the UAW.

West Side closed to him in 1938 when a neighborhood group invited him to deliver the annual Emancipation Day speech. The pro-union President of Howard University, Dr. Mordecai Johnson, was similarly barred from the Bethel A.M.E. Church after Marshall applied pressure on Reverend Peck.

Even the YMCA felt the weight of Marshall's influence. When the Conference of Negro Trade Unionists sought permission in 1940 to hold a public meeting at the all-black YMCA on St. Antoine Street, director Wilbur Woodson turned them down. "I'm in favor of unions," Woodson later remarked privately, "but I couldn't let them hold that meeting here. If I had, the next day Marshall would have been down here to know why. That would have meant I couldn't recommend any more men to Ford's. I've got to be an opportunist."

Woodson's logic made sense to an older generation of blacks who saw the Republican Party and the Booker T. Washington Trade Association as the traditional standard-bearers of black emancipation. That conservative generation still dominated Detroit's black elite in the mid-1930s—but they were rapidly losing their grip.

The younger blacks who now challenged this leadership were weaned on a far different political and social culture. They were more accustomed to industrial work, urban life, and trade unions, and a minority had even gained an intensive apprenticeship in direct-action politics through the Communist Party. "Every time a Negro would pick up a piece of Communist literature," Frank Marquart remembered, "he would always find something that pertained to the problems of Negroes." The Unemployed Councils, the League of Struggle For Negro Rights, and the campaign to prevent the execution of the Scottsboro Boys in Alabama appealed to young blacks impatient with the "go-slow" approach of the middle-class elite.

By 1936, winds of change were gusting through Detroit's black community. For the first time since Emancipation, black voters abandoned the Republican Party and cast their ballots in record numbers for New Deal Democrats, electing Charles Diggs, Sr., a prominent supporter of the CIO, to the Michigan Senate. The *Michigan Chronicle* was also founded by Louis Martin as a liberal counter to the black-owned Republican weekly, the *Detroit Tribune*. Both the national NAACP and Urban League endorsed the CIO, even as the Detroit chapters of both organizations continued to support the Open Shop.

When the Detroit chapter of the Negro National Congress (NNC) was founded in 1936, however, it had no qualms about industrial unionism. Indeed, the NNC was partly funded by the CIO, and made support of the UAW central to its program. (Among its early activists, the NNC counted a young man named Coleman Young—the city's future mayor.)

Ford, the Last Mile: Picketers at Gate 4 and pro-UAW women.

Over the next three years, black participation in Detroit's labor movement slowly grew. The AFL's Waiters and Waitresses Union opened its ranks to black workers in 1938, and in February of 1939 black maids at the Reid Hotel initiated a walkout to win a $15-a-week minimum wage. Five hundred black sanitation workers also signed union cards, making their public-employee local the largest all-black union in Michigan. Black progressives led by Diggs and White meanwhile established firm links with the UAW–CIO during the Dodge strike in the fall of 1939.

Two prominent black ministers, Reverend Malcolm Dade of St. Cyprian's Episcopal Church, and Reverend Charles Hill of the Hartford Avenue Baptist Church (site 62), also joined the UAW's Ford organizing campaign. At considerable risk, Hill endorsed the UAW–CIO and made his church available for union meetings. "If they met in a regular union hall," Hill explained, "then some of the spies from Ford would take their automobile license numbers and they lost their job. By holding it in a church, it would be difficult for them to prove that we were just discussing union matters."

Some in his congregation, however, would not risk worshipping in a pro-UAW church. "When I took a stand for the union," Hill remembered, "100 of them left." But for those who remained, and for a growing number of black workers throughout Detroit, the UAW's organizing campaign began to make some telling points.

Ford, the union acknowledged, did hire more black workers than any other employer. But the Service Department also abused them as roughly as white workers, and blacks at Ford were concentrated in the most dangerous and unhealthy jobs. Particularly for black foundrymen at Ford, the intense heat, thick clouds of soot, and repeated gas explosions all made death and lung disease far too common.

Black organizers like John Conyers Sr., Walter Hardin, Leon Bates, William Bowman, and Paul Kirk gave tangible evidence to Ford workers that the UAW was not a "Whites Only" union. The same message was conveyed by the integrated Women's Auxiliary as it helped sign up union supporters. "The Negro women . . . [each] used to bring in one member, two members," recalled Auxiliary-leader Rose Billups, "because

I promised that no one would know but myself. I used to go to the saloon, in the alleys, to meet the Negroes [who worked at Ford]. They gave me their dues, and I used to bring them to Mike Widman."

The pace of organization began to accelerate in the fall of 1940. In September, the small UAW-AFL com-

Clean Sweep

You worked on the assumption that this thing [the union] was going to come about and that it couldn't fail. . . . "Now, if they organize Fords [I told others], the whole country is going to go, and you might as well get in on this thing right from the start."

*Henry Hanson,
steelworker and union activist*

Hanson's prophecy exaggerated the national impact of the UAW's Ford campaign, but not its local impact at Great Lakes Steel. As the UAW organizing drive rolled towards victory in the spring of 1941, steel-union organizers in Great Lakes' strip mill began a strike in June that spread through the entire Ecorse complex (site 31).

Coming at a time when war-related business was improving and profits rising, the union's success in forcing a halt to operations brought management to a painful realization. "It was clear," recalled Joseph Jeffrey, then a rising executive in Great Lakes Steel, "that we just couldn't afford to have all that turmoil all the time." Stable and profitable production operations required stable and predictable labor relations. Collective bargaining seemed the only way to insure such stability, so the company agreed to recognize the CIO's Steel Workers Organizing Comitee (SWOC).

For some executives, recognizing SWOC was an unpleasant necessity. But for Jeffrey, who now took over the

company's newly-formed Labor Relations Department, the union was a potentially good thing—not simply because his family in Pennsylvania counted four generations of active membership in the United Mine Workers, but because a union contract could help Jeffrey and other young executives "modernize" Great Lakes Steel.

When the company's forerunner, Michigan Steel, began operations as a small, family-owned mill in 1922, its departments had been run along traditional lines. Superintendents, foremen, and even skilled workers hired their immediate subordinates—usually from their family and nationality group —and set pay scales as they pleased. Even after the company quadrupled in size, there was no company-wide hiring or management policy. Individual supervisors ruled their separate (and frequently antagonistic) "kingdoms" within Great Lakes Steel, giving many departments and occupations a distinctive religious, racial, or ethnic identity. Irish Catholics were concentrated in the open-hearth furnaces; English and Germans in the rolling mills; Scotsmen in the machine shops; and Poles in lower-level jobs throughout the company. While some departments were ethnically diverse, blacks were only hired at the Zug Island blast furnaces, where Italians otherwise predominated. All the chippers in the Ecorse mills were Greek.

In 1935, top management concluded that in-group favoritism was not worth the resentment it created among excluded workers. These self-contained kingdoms also cost the company

money, since skilled workers and foremen habitually padded production figures to improve their standing and income, and supervisors routinely submitted the inflated payroll claims of favored employees.

The company therefore began to dismantle these kingdoms. Top management first took control over hiring, transfers, and promotions, undermining the supervisors' control over jobs. When SWOC again began to attract a sizeable following in the mills after 1938, management extended the

mittee at Ford voted to dissolve and join the UAW–CIO. In October, Judge Lila Neuenfelt of Dearborn bucked the Ford political machine and declared the anti-leafleting ordinance unconstitutional. Hundreds of leafleters now regularly gathered at the plant gates to handbill workers and, every two weeks, pass out 50,000 copies of the UAW's *Ford Facts*.

Early the following year, Ford's bid on a $10 million defense contract to build trucks was rejected by the government because of the company's poor labor record. In February, 1941, an even heavier blow fell when the Supreme Court upheld the NLRB and ordered Ford to rehire the workers it had illegally fired.

As the banished union supporters re-entered the plants, the last veil of fear lifted. Ford workers now openly wore union buttons and plastered UAW stickers on their machines. "I was signing guys up at the rate of hundreds a day after that," recalled Percy Llewellyn, first president of the UAW Rouge local and one of the reinstated workers in the Motor Building. His superintendent, Al Smith, remembered the same sudden leap in the number of union supporters. "They just popped up all at once, started blooming all over the place; regular men, who had been working

These steelworkers, unhappy with the first contract negotiated at Great Lakes Steel, walked out on strike without union authorization in October, 1941. They hung an effigy of union official Orval Kincaid from a lamppost on Jefferson Avenue after he suspended some of the "wildcat" leaders from the union. Walter Reuther of the UAW and Gus Scholle of the Metro CIO intervened and arranged to have the suspended members reinstated; Kincaid was replaced shortly afterwards.

modernization campaign even further, establishing a seniority system to govern job security and promotions in a more even-handed way. Foremen, under orders to behave "as if" there was a union at Great Lakes Steel, were expected to take workers' grievances seriously, even if they did not always act on them. By 1940, there were noticeably fewer firings for union activity.

"The union is looking over our shoulder," one executive remembered the company telling its foremen,

"[and] we don't want to give them anything to shoot at." This new policy gave SWOC organizers considerably more freedom in the plants. The gradual breakup of the departmental kingdoms weakened the hold supervisors previously exercised over their work crews. And since foremen were now behaving "as if" there was a union, SWOC activists were able to claim—with good reason—that they were the union, not the company's nearly defunct Employee Representation Plan.

More and more workers looked to SWOC activists as people who could "get the job done" when it came to arguing grievances with foremen. When the autoworkers struck Ford in the spring of 1941, a majority of steelworkers concluded the time had come for SWOC to do the same at Great Lakes Steel.

Their confidence was rewarded when a June strike forced the company to recognize their union. For some, however, the first contract negotiated that summer and fall was a disappointment. Company executives like Joseph Jeffrey were prepared to accept the union as a potential ally in establishing standardized work relations in a giant corporation, but they refused to raise wages any higher than prevailing rates in competing companies.

Many SWOC recruits expected more, and SWOC organizers saw no reason to moderate their high expectations while the union fought for recognition. When the first contract brought less than many had hoped for, the dissidents temporarily shut down the mills in an unauthorized "wildcat" strike against both the company and the union.

Detroit was indeed a Union Town—but it was not at all clear what that meant in practice.

Government-supervised elections brought final victory for the UAW–CIO.

there for years."

Bennett's Servicemen redoubled their coercive tactics. Men were fired, beaten, demoted, or transferred in an effort to stem the tide. But Ford workers now had an acute sense of their collective power, and the rebounding economy dramatically reduced anxieties about job security. When Bennett fired several union stewards from the Rolling Mill in March, 3,000 workers sat down and won their reinstatement within an hour. Over the next two weeks, some 15,000 workers sat down in a dozen brief work stoppages.

The final explosion came on April 1. When Bennett fired eight men that night from the Rolling Mill, 1,500 workers sat down, sparking a general work stoppage that eventually paralyzed the entire complex. The UAW had hoped to win recognition at Ford through government-supervised elections, but Ford had refused to cooperate with the NLRB. With some 50,000 members now refusing to work, the die was cast for a general strike of Ford Rouge. It would not, however, be a sitdown. Because the Supreme Court had declared the tactic illegal in 1939, UAW leaders feared a sitdown might alienate public opinion and weaken government support. In addition, a sitdown would most certainly provoke a violent response from the Service Department. Some time before 1 a.m. on April 2, the union therefore called upon the strikers to march out of the Rouge.

"It was a thrilling moment," recalled UAW supporter John Fitzgerald, "a wonderful experience, to walk out along with all those men determined on one thing, through Gate 4, with Servicemen standing there looking at us and not daring to say a word. No supervisor, no officer of the Ford Motor Company, neither Harry Bennett, nor any Servicemen dared say us nay." Early that morning, union members set up picket lines and built barricades of automobiles and railroad ties across nearby highways. An estimated 10,000 picketers massed at strategic points, while another 1,000 waited in reserve at union headquarters.

With his Servicemen outnumbered, Bennett joined Dearborn Police Chief Carl Brooks, a former Ford detective, in calling upon both the President and the Governor to send troops. The plants, they announced, were being occupied by "7,000 to 8,000" sitdowners, led by "Communistic terrorists" whose single goal was to sabotage the nation's defense program. Government observers on the scene, however, noted that there was no sitdown and that Ford did virtually no defense work at the Rouge. Democratic Governor Murray Van Waggoner sent the State Police to Dearborn, but ordered them only to clear the barricades on Miller Road and replace the Dearborn police around the plant.

As Bennett's red scare fizzled, he set in motion a more credible threat: race riot.

The overwhelming majority of black workers joined the walkout on April 2—some enthusiastically, others with mixed or lukewarm feelings toward the UAW–CIO. Only about 1,500 to 2,000 stayed inside the plant as strikebreakers, most of them recently hired by Bennett, and a large number just arrived from the South. If these were Bennett's "sitdowners," he now decided to put them on their feet and send them out of the plant to attack the UAW's picket lines. A race riot might bring out the National Guard even if a bogus sitdown could not.

On April 2nd and 3rd, violent melees broke out on Miller Road between black strikebreakers under Bennett's orders, and the largely white picketers. Simultaneously, Homer Martin and Don Marshall went into the black community to address "back-to-work" rallies. The heightened racial tension, however, had unexpected results. Bennett's reckless tactics, by threatening a race war that black Detroiters could only lose, horrified many of the company's supporters. The Detroit Urban League dropped its vocal support of the company and fell silent, while the Detroit NAACP came out in favor of the UAW–CIO. Only the Interdenominational Ministers Alliance continued to support Ford.

On the picket lines, the Reverends White, Dade, and Hill encouraged black strikebreakers to abandon the plant, and after Michael Widman and Emil Mazey of the UAW assured their safety, over 1,000 came out between April 2 and 4. On April 3, tension was further reduced when Horace Sheffield and other union supporters in the NAACP's Youth Council circled the plant in a UAW sound car, directing appeals to the remaining strikebreakers to abandon Bennett's divisive tactics.

A week later, Ford finally capitulated and agreed to an NLRB election. It was now just a matter of time for the UAW–CIO, which had only a revived and discredited UAW–AFL to deal with in the upcoming May election. Editor Chris Alston directed numerous Negro Editions of *Ford Facts* at black workers in the weeks before the balloting, and a rally of 60,000 in Cadillac Square heard Paul Robeson, the celebrated singer and actor, endorse the CIO.

On May 21, 1941, the UAW–CIO won 70 percent of the vote, the UAW–AFL only 28 percent. Barely 2 percent voted for no union. Scarcely one century after the city's carpenters first organized for better wages and working conditions, Detroit had become a Union Town.

III: WAR & PEACE

Shift change at Ford Rouge.

FROM CLASS WAR TO WORLD WAR

Detroit, once the Open Shop capital of the United States, was now the nation's leading Union Town.

This momentous transformation meant different things to different people. To some union members, the long and bitterly fought organizing drives made the union the center of their lives, redefining their political and social outlook no less than their workplace attitudes. For these activists, the union was a rough-and-tumble working-class fraternity that would democratize the workplace and champion progressive causes.

For others, the union played a more modest role, taking its place alongside ethnic, church, and other neighborhood groups as an important pillar of stability in their lives. For them, the union meant a measure of security, higher wages, better working conditions, and a new sense of dignity on the job.

For still others, the union was a matter of indifference or active dislike. Seeing no link between their individual lot and the conditions they shared with their co-workers, they either believed themselves masters of their own fate or slaves to it; in either case, the union was irrelevant. For the especially ambitious, the union could even be a hindrance if its work rules and seniority list blocked their advancement.

Ambition, however, could also turn the union into a career opportunity. Those who shouldered the added responsibilities of union office usually did so because they cared—often passionately —about their organization and its goals.

But winning union office could also provide a vantage point of power and prestige for aspiring individuals, and inevitably, there were those who either saw their office as just "a better job" than factory work or as a means to special privileges.

Activists, militants, loyal members, dropouts, careerists: all played a role in shaping their union's character. And if it wasn't yet clear what that character would be in 1941, it soon became obvious that collective bargaining would dramatically change the role of union leadership.

To win recognition, union activists had waged a crusade-like struggle, beginning with a small band of believers and progressing through a series of widening confrontations. The atmosphere of these organizing campaigns had often been decidedly warlike: sometimes a guerrilla war of "quickie" strikes and slowdowns, and sometimes a trench war of sitdown strikes and walkouts, complete with fortified camps and battlefield strategies involving thousands of people.

Now, having fought management for the right to exist, unions would have to co-exist with these same managers. Militancy could light a fire under the company and strengthen the union's bargaining position, but uncontrolled militancy might also touch off a blaze that would jeopardize bargaining, forcing both sides into do-or-die battles for survival. Short of replacing capitalist enterprise with worker-controlled industries —and few trade unionists supported such fundamental change—collective bargaining required a certain degree of compromise with management.

At Ford Rouge, the union's new role emerged in dozens of small confrontations between managers and workers. In one such episode in the late spring of 1941, Sam Taylor—one of the company men who attacked Reuther and Frankensteen in 1937—was himself saved from a beating only by the union's timely intervention. "He was walking down through the foundry one day," recalled Shelton Tappes, President of Local 600's foundry division, "and [a chant] just, like a groundswell, went from worker to worker: 'Sam Taylor—throw him out.'" Tappes and two other union officers, while shielding Taylor and escorting him from the building, took most of the blows from the shovel-wielding foundrymen.

"The irony of the thing," Tappes later recalled, "was here's a guy that fought the union so hard, and the union had to protect him. Because we knew that if he was injured or killed...the UAW would have to take the blame." With Taylor safely removed from the building, the angry foundry workers settled for a symbolic reckoning: "they hung him in effigy, right there in the unit."

The union was an expression of worker discontent, but channeling that discontent towards specific goals often brought union leadership into conflict with some fraction of the membership. To win a compromise agreement with management on wage increases or improved vacations, union leaders might drop demands from a particular department that production quotas be lowered or working conditions improved. To hold the union to its principles, the leadership might also have to support black members demanding upgrading by

seniority into all-white departments—a move which frequently angered some whites.

The union leader was in the hot seat, particularly the local officer or working steward who faced members and company supervisors on a daily basis. It was hard for these local leaders to ignore management complaints that work stoppages over "minor" issues disrupted the complex, interdependent production process in a large factory, idling workers and expensive machinery in surrounding work areas. But it was harder still to ignore the heightened expectations of union members, many of them eager to resolve longstanding grievances and win new workplace rights. Militancy could not be turned on and off like a faucet, full-blast during organizational strikes and contract battles, and then bottled up and controlled once the collective-bar-

gaining agreement was signed.

But that was the trade-off that employers demanded. In return for the company's agreement to live by negotiated work rules, the union had to ensure that its own members also lived by the contract. Instead of relying on shop-floor confrontations to resolve disputes during the contract's term, both sides agreed to debate workers' gripes in a step-by-step grievance procedure. When disputes could not be peaceably settled by the grievance process, GM and the UAW agreed in 1940 to accept the ruling of a mutually agreed upon "umpire."

For most unions, the trial-and-error of collective bargaining had only just begun to work itself out when, on December 7, 1941, the Empire of Japan attacked Pearl Harbor, killing 2,300

UAW Local 351's President, Paul Silver (in sweater), with shop stewards and members.

Opposite page: Chrysler's Detroit Tank Arsenal.

Badge of Pride

"In Michigan we were very proud of the unions," remembered Margaret Wright, a welder in a bomb factory. A union button was a badge of pride for many workers, especially the shop stewards who spearheaded the union inside the plant.

The combativeness and pluck of these shop-floor leaders was also evident outside the plant. "Our shop steward used to drive me home," Wright remembered, "and a police car side-swiped our car one day. So he made the police car pull over to the side and the officer flashed his badge and said 'well, I'm the police.' And he [the steward] showed his shop-steward badge and said 'I'm a shop steward.' That shows you the kind of pride they had. He thought he had the same kind of authority that the police had."

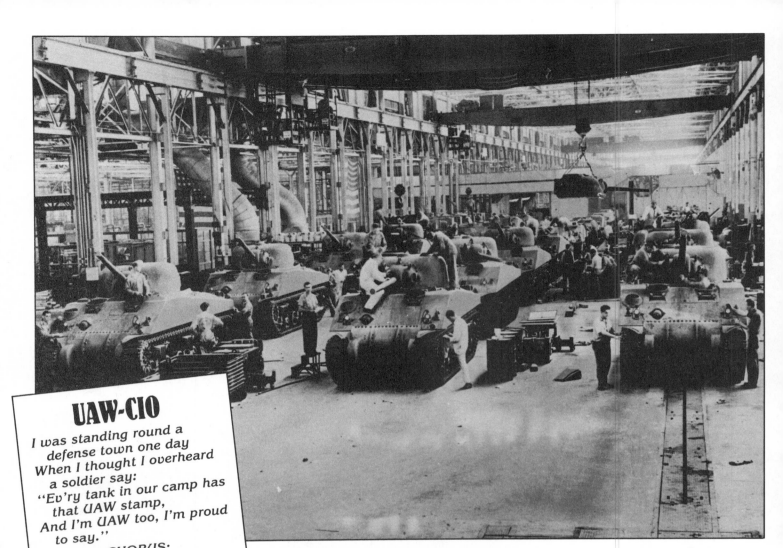

UAW-CIO

I was standing round a
defense town one day
When I thought I overheard
a soldier say:
"Ev'ry tank in our camp has
that UAW stamp,
And I'm UAW too, I'm proud
to say."
      CHORUS:
It's the UAW–CIO, makes
the army roll and go;
Turning out the jeeps and
trucks and airplanes ev'ry
day.
It's the UAW–CIO, makes
the army roll and go,
Puts wheels on the U.S.A.
There'll be a union label in
Berlin
When those union boys in
uniform march in;
And rolling in those ranks
there'll be UAW tanks;
Roll Hitler out and roll the
union in.

Using overhead cranes, workers in the Chrysler Tank Arsenal lower five-ton turrets onto Sherman tanks in January, 1943. The union celebrated its role in defense production in the song "UAW–CIO."

Americans and plunging the United States into World War II.

Within 48 hours, leaders of both the AFL and the CIO pledged their member unions to full support of the country's war effort. To clear the way for uninterrupted military production, they voluntarily took a no-strike pledge: in return, employers (with prodding from the government) agreed to accept the union as a "partner in production" for the duration of the war. The federal War Labor Board, made up of union, management, and government representatives, would replace collective bargaining as the final arbitrator of workplace disputes.

The rules of industrial conflict were thereby changed just as the curtain rose on industry-wide collective bargaining. As the wartime drama unfolded, the actors were changed as well, with nearly 30 percent of Detroit's male factory workers leaving the area after 1941, most of them to enter military service. In their place, some 400,000 new factory workers swelled the Detroit-area workforce. Most were newcomers from rural Michigan and the South. A considerable number were women workers, either entering the paid labor force for the first time, or transferring from low-wage clerical, factory, and service-industry jobs into better-paying war-industry work.

As new workers poured into the city to find jobs in war plants, Detroit began to burst at the seams. The proportion of available homes fell from an 8 percent vacancy rate to less than 1 percent, forcing thousands of migrant war-workers to squeeze into welfare shelters, empty storefronts, and temporary barracks. Housing was especially scarce in Detroit's suburban fringe, where huge war plants were rushed to completion: among them, the Hudson Naval Armory and Chrysler tank plant in Warren, and Ford's sprawling, mile-long assembly line for B–24 bombers in Willow Run (sites 63 through 65). Hundreds of thousands of war workers crowded into these semi-rural areas, overwhelming the meager supply of housing and social services.

The sudden in-migration quickly swamped Macomb County's partially-constructed sewer system, threatening Warren Township with an outbreak of typhoid fever. Similar conditions prevailed around the Willow Run bomber plant, where thousands of workers lived in tents, shacks, and trailers scattered along roadsides and next to open fields. In one case, investigators found 23 people living in a single house and garage, with additional workers squeezed into four trailers parked in the soggy back yard.

Many Detroiters did not welcome the 200,000 out-of-staters crowding into the metro area during the war, particularly the jobseekers arriving in busloads from the South. The housing shortage, made worse by occasional stipulations that "No Southerners" need apply for vacant homes, forced many Southern whites to live in government-built barracks like the 7,000-bed Willow Lodge in Ypsilanti—where "mountain dialects," according to one visitor in 1943, ran "heavy to the acre." The class and regional prejudices of established residents made life difficult for these frequently impoverished newcomers. "The children," reported one State Welfare official, referring to Ypsilanti's long-term residents, "hear their parents refer to the newcomers as 'hillbillies,' 'trash,' and the like. Soon they themselves catch this bitter resentment, [and]...juvenile gangs attack and beat up the children of the newcomers."

Southern blacks faced considerably greater obstacles finding either a home or a job. Discriminatory housing patterns were fixed in Detroit long before Pearl Harbor—one pre-war survey by the city's Housing Commission found 85 percent of all private housing closed to blacks, and half of the available dwellings substandard. Public housing was also segregated as a matter of policy, with the Brewster Projects designated for black occupancy, and the Parkside Homes restricted to whites (sites 66 and 67).

When war threatened in 1940 and America began gearing up for military production, job prospects for black Detroiters were equally segregated. As the self-proclaimed Arsenal of Democracy, the city's factories supplied war material for the fight against fascism. Yet democracy hardly prevailed inside the plants, where blacks were still confined to so-called "Negro jobs" in the foundries and janitorial departments.

Even with the growing demand for workers to run Detroit's expanding war industries, segregated hiring practices still restricted blacks to these low-status jobs. Some government officials recognized that complete military mobilization required utilization of every available labor resource; but it took a threatened protest march on Washington, D.C. by black leader A. Philip Randolph, head of the AFL's Brotherhood of Sleeping Car Porters, before President Roosevelt ordered all war contractors to integrate their plants in June, 1941. When Pearl Harbor put the country on a complete wartime basis, Detroit's rapidly expanding defense industries thereafter hired 75,000 black workers to alleviate the city's labor shortage—but not without considerable opposition from white workers.

The ugly truth," warned the Association of Catholic Trade Unionists in their Detroit paper, the *Wage Earner*, "is that there is a growing, subterranean race war going on in the city of Detroit which can have no other result than an explosion of violence, unless something is done to stop it."

When the *Wage Earner* made this prophetic comment in June, 1943, racial skirmishing had already been building for two years. Resistance to "race mixing" had always been strong among the city's whites, but wartime overcrowding together with the rapid increase in the city's black population (up 60,000 during the war years) heightened the racial tension. Equally important, most of the new workers entering Detroit's war plants had not gone through the unifying experience of the Depression-era organizing drives. For Southern whites in particular, the union movement's repeated calls for solidarity between the races seemed abstract and alien.

The minister's call to salvation was far more familiar, and the estimated 3,000 worker–preachers in Detroit's factories—some with makeshift pulpits in the plants—carried considerable weight among rural whites recently arrived in the city. For these unsettled migrants, storefront churches and basement tabernacles were havens of down-home religion and gospel singing. All too often, the God-fearing preacher was also

---

"The Plant Merely Dribbled Out Planes..."

During the war, this huge factory built over 8,000 B–24s. In its early operations, "the plant merely dribbled out planes," as the newspaper *PM* described it. "The men say the bugs could be easily eliminated," *PM* reported in 1943, "if there were some way of telling the engineers what is going on, but Ford doesn't believe in labor-management committees... [and] the workers don't think much of Ford efficiency. They contend that Ford over-emphasizes competition between shifts, and while they admit the virtues of competition, they say at Willow Run it defeats itself. They say, for example, that shifts will never start on jobs they can't finish that day, because if they do, the next shift will get the credit."

Ford's Willow Run bomber plant in suburban Ypsilanti.

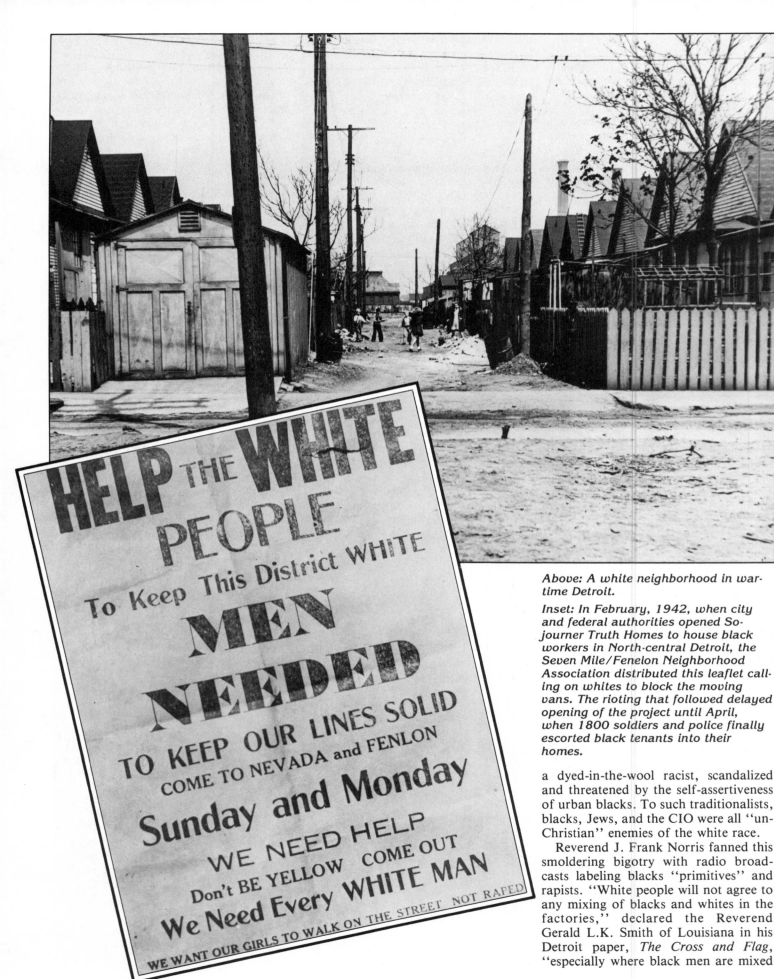

Above: A white neighborhood in wartime Detroit.

Inset: In February, 1942, when city and federal authorities opened Sojourner Truth Homes to house black workers in North-central Detroit, the Seven Mile/Fenelon Neighborhood Association distributed this leaflet calling on whites to block the moving vans. The rioting that followed delayed opening of the project until April, when 1800 soldiers and police finally escorted black tenants into their homes.

a dyed-in-the-wool racist, scandalized and threatened by the self-assertiveness of urban blacks. To such traditionalists, blacks, Jews, and the CIO were all "un-Christian" enemies of the white race.

Reverend J. Frank Norris fanned this smoldering bigotry with radio broadcasts labeling blacks "primitives" and rapists. "White people will not agree to any mixing of blacks and whites in the factories," declared the Reverend Gerald L.K. Smith of Louisiana in his Detroit paper, *The Cross and Flag*, "especially where black men are mixed with white women.'' Smith's demagoguery helped nurture a bumper crop of hate organizations: the Dixie Voters, the Southern Society, the Mothers of America, and the Ku Klux Klan.

Anti-black sentiments took increasingly lurid and preposterous forms. ''Blood runs out of their fingers,'' one white Packard worker said of black workers in his plant. ''If you handle the same machine, you'll get syphilis.'' Rumors circulated that younger blacks were secretly enrolled in a ''bump club,'' whose members intentionally jostled whites on crowded streets and trolley cars.

Not all white workers opposed integrating blacks into production departments and assembly-line jobs, and many CIO unions, particularly the UAW, actively supported the upgrading of black workers. But there were numerous opponents of such moves among whites of every ethnic background, and dozens of ''hate strikes'' sparked by these bigots flared throughout Detroit's war industries in 1942 and 1943. The conflict briefly spilled into the streets in February, 1942, when white crowds in North-central Detroit attacked black families moving into the federally funded Sojourner Truth housing project (site 68).

The Packard Motor Company was the scene of the largest and most intense of these wartime hate strikes. Packard's management was the most blatantly hostile towards upgrading black workers. The company's personnel director, C.E. Weiss, had long claimed responsibility for bringing the first ''load of niggers,'' as he called them, to work in Detroit during the first World War. Determined that they should stay in the foundry where he had put them, he only began transferring black workers into production jobs under extreme pressure from the federal government.

The first transfers began early in 1943, when three black women were moved into semi-skilled jobs in the huge plant on East Grand Boulevard (site 14). The new jobs were a boon for the women, who formerly could set their sights no higher than department stores paying $12 and less for a 48-hour week. At Packard, where production of aircraft engines and frames had replaced automobiles, they earned union wages of 85¢ an hour during training and upwards of $55 a week as lathe operators or grinders.

Previously, black women had only worked in janitorial jobs at Packard. White workers had accepted them as cleaning women, but when the first group of black females transferred from the training area into the plant on February 12, whites immediately resisted the move.

Trainees normally walked from the training area directly through the plant to their assigned positions. ''But when we got ready to go,'' June Tolan later remembered, ''we had to put on our hats and coats. And they marched us outside, two blocks down the street to the building where we were working.'' As they walked outside the factory, white workers yelled insults and catcalls out the windows. In one building, white women staged a two-hour work stoppage.

The local union, fearing the issue would inflame upcoming union elections in the plant, urged the black women to return to the training area until after the balloting. Two weeks later, after Norman Mathews—an electrician from Cornwall, England—was elected President of Local 190, the women returned to their new jobs.

White workers again sat down in protest. This time, according to John McDaniel, Chairman of Local 190's bargaining committee, ''the union leadership was pretty solid in its position that the whites and the colored were going to work based on seniority and equity of jobs.'' Union officers cajoled and argued with the striking workers; McDaniel even delivered one speech to a group of women who had retreated to the restroom, urging them to return to their machines and accept their black co-workers. Such persistence eventually paid off, and the hate strikes temporarily ended with June Tolan and four other black women working steadily at the grinders and lathes they had been trained to operate.

But the trouble at Packard was hardly over. In the spring of 1943, whites again struck over the upgrading of three black men to the aircraft assembly line. When the local union, its leadership now split over how fast to proceed, backed the company's decision to temporarily withdraw the men from the aircraft line, 2,000 of Packard's black foundry workers

Machining artillary shells in a bomb factory. Before World War II, employers had sometimes hired women to perform metal-working jobs like these, but never black women.

walked out to protest the union's vacillation.

The local hurriedly called a mass meeting on May 30 to discuss the problem, with UAW International President R.J. Thomas and Colonel George Strong of the Pentagon slated to address the members. When Thomas and Strong rose to the podium at the old Slovak Hall (site 38), they were both greeted by heckling and loud booing. The din grew louder as the UAW President defended the upgrading of black workers into previously all-white departments. "This problem has to be settled or it will wreck our union," Thomas declared above the noise. But even as he spoke, hundreds of members stalked out of the hall.

When the company finally returned the three black workers to the aircraft assembly line on June 3, 1943, 25,000 whites walked out of the Packard plant. They were encouraged, one government observer reported, by factory superintendents "who went through the plant telling workers they have no union, and that they might as well come back into the company union."

While thousands of white workers milled around the plant listening to anti-black speeches, Thomas and Local 190 President Mathews pleaded with the strikers to ignore the KKK's local leaders and return to work. Few paid them any heed, until Thomas and Colonel Strong declared that strike leaders would be fired. After 30 ringleaders were suspended on June 6, most of the whites returned to work. The aircraft assembly line had finally been integrated.

Less than three weeks later, the entire city erupted in violent and fatal rioting.

No one could later determine exactly when the fighting began on Belle Isle that Sunday of June 20, 1943. With temperatures well over 90 degrees, more than 100,000 Detroiters had crowded onto the city's major park, jostling for space and waiting in long lines to use the bath houses and canoes. The park police reported fights and minor racial confrontations throughout the day.

Towards evening, the brawls grew in scope and frequency. Racial fights broke out at the casino, the ferry dock, the playground, the bus stops, and on the narrow bridge leading to the shore. Several hundred white sailors from a nearby armory joined the growing melee. By 11 p.m., an estimated 5,000 people were battling on the bridge and nearby access roads.

Wildly embellished rumors swept across the city, inflaming members of both races. In the black neighborhoods east of Woodward Avenue, unfounded reports circulated that whites had killed a black woman and child and thrown them off the Belle Isle bridge. In the white neighborhoods west of Woodward, the same rumor was recast with the roles reversed: a black mob, it was claimed, had killed a white woman and baby and thrown them off the same bridge. While whites sought revenge by attacking black pedestrians on lower Woodward, blacks responded in kind by looting white-owned businesses along Hastings Street (site 19) and attacking white motorists.

With the police standing passively on the sidelines, the white crowd on Woodward became especially frenzied, stopping automobiles driven by blacks,

Lower Woodward during the 1943 riot. The white crowd is chasing a lone black man. Moments later, they overturned the car he had been forced to abandon (in front of bus) and set it afire.

beating their passengers, and burning the cars. Whites entered all-night movie theaters catering to second-shift workers and dragged black patrons into the street, where they and other victims yanked off passing trolleys were severely beaten.

While city and state officials debated the political consequences of calling in federal troops, the violence continued through the night and all of the following day, growing steadily more random, vicious, and lethal. Late Monday afternoon, four white teenagers shot an elderly black man because, as they later put it, they ''didn't have anything to do.... We didn't know him. He wasn't bothering us. But other people were fighting and killing and we felt like it too.''

With 100 fires burning out of control and riot activity reported across three-quarters of the city, the federal government finally sent 5,000 soldiers into Detroit—a full day after the fighting and killing had begun. The first contingent of 350 soldiers arrived in Cadillac Square, their bayonets fixed, just as 10,000 whites began to march towards nearby Hastings Street. Within three hours, the Army dispersed the crowds and clamped a tight curfew on the city.

Twenty-five blacks and nine whites were dead and 700 people of both races injured. The major cause of the racially lopsided death toll was Detroit's police. In contrast to their open tolerance of white rioters, the city's patrolmen had fired indiscriminately into buildings and crowds around Hastings Street, killing 17 of the 25 blacks who died in the rioting.

City officials commended the police and blamed the violence on the CIO and the NAACP. ''Negro hoodlums started it,'' said Mayor Edward Jeffries Jr., ''but the conduct of the Police Department, by and large, was magnificent.''

UAW President R.J. Thomas, on the other hand, vigorously denounced the police and called for a Grand Jury investigation of their discriminatory violence. He also made a spirited defense of the NAACP: ''It is a trouble-making organization, in the sense that unions are trouble makers for unfair employers, and in the same sense that those who believe in liberty are trouble-makers for Hitler.''

A campaign to replace Detroit's Police Commissioner quickly grew into a full-fledged challenge to Mayor Jeffries in the fall elections of 1943. Backed by the CIO, the Detroit Federation of Labor, and a thoroughly aroused black community, Frank Fitzgerald (no rela-

A wartime civil rights demonstration in Detroit's Cadillac Square.

War on Prejudice

The participation of white trade unionists in these rallies was a measure of how far the alliance between unions and civil rights organizations in the city had progressed. In the largest demonstration of this alliance, 10,000 UAW and NAACP members gathered in Cadillac Square in April, 1943, to protest racial discrimination in Detroit's war plants.

Whites who supported integration in the factories did so for many reasons. Some were pragmatic union supporters who recognized that without black–white unity, the union would splinter and collapse. Some were socialists and communists for whom class solidarity was a matter of

political principle and personal commitment.

Many were like Ernie Zipser, a drill machine operator at the Hudson Naval Armory. The American-born son of Hungarian Jews, Zipser described himself as ''more of a romantic'' than a radical. When many whites at Hudson refused to work next to blacks on the drill machines, Zipser stayed on the job. ''I wasn't about to leave that S.O.B. [machine], because I couldn't believe that we were fighting a war for democracy and the rights of people, and [when] a black man gets on the machine, everybody walks out. What kind of shit is that? It's hypocrisy.''

tion to the former Republican Governor) stunned the city's conservatives when he placed first in the non-partisan primary, topping Mayor Jeffries by nearly 40,000 votes. The final runoff between these two top vote getters pro-

mised to be a turning point in the long campaign to desegregate Detroit.

Jeffries mounted a campaign based squarely on appeals to white racism. ''Arrayed against me,'' he repeatedly claimed, ''are groups demanding mixed housing—the mingling of Negroes and whites in the same neighborhoods." The mayor's backers hammered away at this theme with scare-literature aimed exclusively at white voters: "FITZ-GERALD VICTORY MEANS STRATHMOOR AND COOLEY HIGH GET NEGRO FLOOD," blared one headline in a neighborhood newspaper.

Such race-baiting carried the day for Jeffries, who defeated Fitzgerald with 54 percent of the vote. Black Detroiters and the CIO could only take comfort in the reelection of city councilor George Ed-

"In the Money..."

Have you heard that
Minnie's in the money?
Take my word that Minnie's
in the money.
She hasn't got a guy who's
got a diamond mine,
But she's a welder on the
old assembly line
She's helping Uncle Sam to
keep his people free.
She's OK—hey, Minnie's in
the do-re-mi. ©

Benny Goodman,
wartime jazz hit

In November of 1943, 260,000 Detroit women were earning the "do-re-mi" of factory wages—six times more than the pre-war total of 44,000.

With the sudden need to maximize production, they were learning to operate cranes, welding torches, drill presses, riveting guns, and countless other industrial tools long associated with "men's work." For thousands of women, the possibilities opened up by this wartime experience seemed limitless, and the image and spirit of these "Rosie the Riveters" was prominently featured in popular culture during the war. "Just think of it," enthused one character in the 1943 novel *Willow Run,* "women doing just about everything the men do. Gee, imagine Willow Run someday—women running it—women building bombers!"

There were 15,000 women building bombers at Ford's Willow Run plant in 1943, more than one-third of the factory's peak workforce of 42,000. The plant could not have run without them, but women never came close to actually running this or any other war-industry factory. "The only place you had anyone in a supervisory capacity," recalled Dorothy Haener, a Willow

Run parts inspector, "was they had a woman who used to do a kind of policing job in the women's restrooms." Supervision and the highest-paying skilled trades—tool and die maker, electrician, etc.—still remained male preserves.

Women accustomed to low-wage service sector jobs were still only too happy to hire on as factory labor. "I couldn't wait to get up here and get in the bomber plant," one Willow Run worker remembered. "In Kentucky as a hotel waitress, I only made $2.40 a day. Here, I could make $10.85."

Employers, on the other hand, were not so eager to hire these women. They did so when government pressure and the wartime shortage of male factory workers left them no alternative, but many, like Henry Ford, still recoiled at the violation of man-as-breadwinner values these women workers represented. Their presence, Ford believed, could only lead to disruptive promiscuity in the plants—a danger he thought required separate lunch areas for men and women in his factories.

Ford, along with many male workers, saw women as temporary intruders into factory life, and most government officials were of the same mind. "When their men come home," Betty Allie of Michigan's Unemployment Commission predicted in 1943, "you will see women returning naturally to their homes. A woman's first interests are her home, her husband, and her children." To ensure that it stayed that way, General Motors, Great Lakes Steel, and other employers required women to sign agreements stating their employment in men's jobs was only for the duration of the war.

Even during this brief tenure, there was little official interest in accommodating women workers. Mothers with young children found only a handful

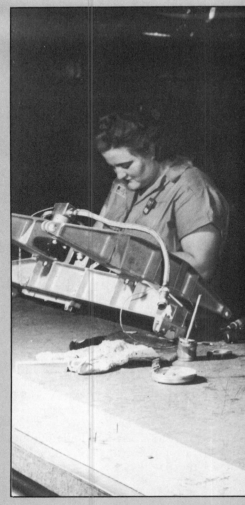

of employers with in-plant childcare, and the federal government's underfunded public programs had room for less than 10 percent of the estimated number of children in need. The vast majority of working mothers who could not find, afford, or trust such group childcare had to rely on relatives and friends to watch their kids.

The "double day" for women war workers went well beyond these childcare dilemmas, for even when their husbands were not at war, most men refused to share household work. Margaret Wright, a 20-year-old black woman, went from domestic work in a suburban household to welding in a Detroit-area bomb factory. "When your husband came home," she remembered, "he propped his feet up and opened a can of beer while you got dinner. When I got off from work, I

wards, the former UAW organizer and Housing Commissioner who represented liberal opinion on the City Council. It was otherwise a time of grim reassessment for the city's progressive unions and their allies in the black community. "The race riot and all that has gone before have made my people more anti-white than ever," commented Louis Martin in the black-owned *Michigan Chronicle*. "Even those willing to believe in the possibility of improving race relations have begun to have doubts—and worse, they have given up hope."

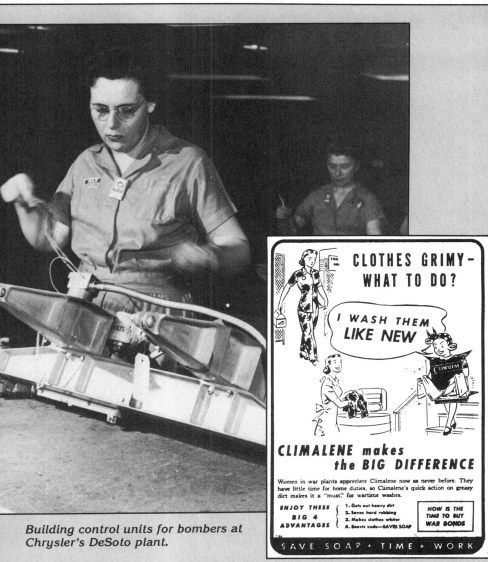

Building control units for bombers at Chrysler's DeSoto plant.

CLOTHES GRIMY— WHAT TO DO?

I WASH THEM LIKE NEW

CLIMALENE makes the BIG DIFFERENCE

Women in war plants appreciate Climalene now as never before. They have little time for home duties, so Climalene's quick action on greasy dirt makes it a "must" for wartime washes.

ENJOY THESE BIG 4 ADVANTAGES
1. Gets out heavy dirt
2. Saves hard rubbing
3. Makes clothes whiter
4. Boosts suds—SAVES SOAP

NOW IS THE TIME TO BUY WAR BONDS

SAVE SOAP • TIME • WORK

A wartime ad from the Detroit News.

had to wash, I had to iron, I had to clean house, I had to shop." When her husband refused to do even the occasional "man's job"—painting, emptying trash—Wright took her own earnings and her daughter and left to find work in California's warplane industry.

"It was very hard," Wright later recalled of her round-the-clock workpace, "to really participate in the union, but in Michigan they kind of kept us abreast of what was happening." There was, in fact, plenty happening in these war years. Not all of it was good for women wage-earners.

Employers who finally accepted the need and inevitability of women work-ing in war plants usually insisted that these women needed, wanted, and deserved no more than "women's wages" in return. In one of many cases challenged by the UAW, GM's Buick Division began production of aircraft engines in 1942 with men working as parts inspectors at $1.14 an hour. Several months later, the company replaced the male inspectors with women at $.79 an hour, claiming the jobs "always were women's jobs" and the more experienced men were only breaking in new work processes.

Experienced workers saw it differently. "Except that there is a division as to what's heavy and what's light," Irene Young, a veteran GM worker, explained to a 1942 UAW conference, "there's no difference in men and women's jobs. This is a carry-over from procedures they had years ago. Men got all the way from ten to twenty cents more on the same job." When the UAW brought the case to arbitration, the umpire forced GM to raise the women's wages to $1.04—still 10¢ an hour below men doing comparable work.

To counter these practices, the UAW established a Women's Bureau in 1944 and called for such wide-ranging reforms as equal pay for equal work, and establishment of community-run childcare, housing, and social-service centers near the plants. Since most women factory workers—86 percent of those surveyed by the UAW—wanted to stay in the paid labor force after the war, the union also called for equal seniority protection to ensure their job rights in the post-war economy.

In most cases, however, responsibility for implementing these policies was left with local unions. While some championed the rights of women workers, many were either indifferent or hostile. Some locals had already put women on separate seniority lists, preventing experienced women from protecting their jobs against less-senior men. Other locals condoned the actions of managers who purposefully transferred women to the few heavy jobs neither they nor many men could perform, after which the company could ignore seniority and replace women with men "who could get the job done."

The failure of many locals to challenge these practices caused considerable frustration among UAW women. "The policies of the UAW were always very good," remembered Millie Jeffrey, first head of the union's Women's Bureau. "Getting them implemented was another story."

HOMEFRONT

Detroit, where everybody has two sawbucks [ten dollar bills] to rub against each other. Detroit, the hottest town in America.

Daily Variety, October, 1943

The streetcars were jammed. Housing was scarce. The roads were choked with people struggling to and from work. Periodically, the city's volcanic race relations would erupt in hate strikes and street violence.

Still, most agreed the war-related economic boom was a hell of a lot better than a depression. The unemployed found jobs and the underpaid frequently found better jobs as unemployment fell below 1 percent by 1944. It was a seller's market for labor, and thousands took advantage of the situation, jumping from job to job when better wages beckoned.

Unlike the pointless drudgery of Depression-era factory labor, war work had a unifying purpose that boosted the morale of many workers. World War II, the CIO proclaimed, was a "peoples'

war of national liberation," and Detroit was the Arsenal of Democracy in this worldwide struggle. For those not swept up in this global vision of Freedom vs. Fascism, there was still the simple fact that American lives depended on the arms produced in Detroit and Michigan. "You knew what you were working for," said one war worker interviewed in Lansing—"to bring the boys back home."

There was also the pay, more than anyone could remember, despite a government-imposed ceiling on hourly wage rates. Prices also rose, and government rationing restricted the supply of war-related goods like gasoline and tires, meat and coffee. But even if inflation climbed faster than hourly wage rates, the long hours of overtime fattened pay checks and boosted real income (after inflation) more than 20 percent for Michigan's war workers.

"Hidden" inflation certainly took its toll. Clothing not only went up in price, but also declined in quality. Landlords frequently cashed in on the housing shortage by charging higher rents for apartments subdivided into smaller units.

Just the same, many war workers had money to spare for the first time in their lives. They could pay off mortgages, invest in savings bonds, buy meat "under the counter" at black-market prices, and go to all-night bowling alleys and movie theaters that catered to second-shift war workers. The war was a National Emergency; for many, it was also a taste of prosperity.

Prosperity had its price, however. Detroit's industrial workers averaged 48 hours a week on the job and perhaps a dozen hours more traveling to and from work. The six- and seven-day week was commonplace; a 70-hour week was not typical, but it was not unknown. Bone-weary workers and primitive safety standards also proved to be a deadly combination: in the first three years of the war, 53,000 workers died in work-place accidents in the United States, and 300,000 more were permanently disabled. The carnage in Michigan's work-places peaked in 1944 at a rate of nearly one death, five amputations, and 100 fractures, burns or other serious injuries *each day.*

Even so, war work had many advantages over the pre-war assembly line. Unlike cars, which were redesigned only once a year and then churned out at monotonously high volume, tanks, bombers, and heavy artillery were constantly being redesigned after relatively short production runs. The amount of retooling was enormous, and so was the demand for skilled workers. On the slow-moving assembly line in the Willow Run bomber plant, workers labored in teams, riveting and building whole sections of the plane, not just bolting together parts.

In aircraft engine plants, 25 percent of the labor force worked on drill presses, millers, and grinding machines, compared to only 6 percent operating such machine tools in pre-war automobile production. Skill levels were generally higher, and workers on these operator-controlled machines could regulate their

workpace more readily than assembly-line workers, particularly when the work was so new that production quotas had not been established.

The work, the wages, and the up-grading all made the war a boon for many workers. For owners and managers the war was also an unparalleled bonanza.

Since cost-plus defense contracts allowed management to tack a guaranteed profit on top of expenses, corporate profits naturally soared—from $9 billion before taxes in 1940, to $24 billion in 1944. Federal taxes reduced the windfall somewhat, but the government promised to rebate much of the tax after the war. In addition, the Pentagon financed the construction of scores of defense plants for private corporations; between 1940 and 1944, GM alone built $900 million of new factory capacity, almost all of it paid for by the government.

The logic behind this "welfare for the rich" was summed up by Secretary of War Henry Stimson: "If you are going to try and go to war in a capitalist country," Stimson confided to his wartime diary, "you have got to let business make money out of the process, or business won't work."

Business worked during the war, and the battered prestige of businessmen rose accordingly. After a decade of economic disaster and a bitter, unsuc-

cessful battle to defeat the CIO, corporate managers were now back in the saddle, coordinating vast new construction projects and shaping government policy. For many of these business leaders, the war was not only an opportunity to recover lost prestige, it was also a chance to recover control over the workplace. Some plant managers seized the opportunity with both hands, firing union activists, ignoring grievances, violating seniority, and forcing sudden changes in wage rates or production speed. "The company took advantage of the situation," recalled Norm Bully, a Buick worker in Flint. "The fact that we had pledged that we would not strike meant that when we went to negotiate for something, a mere 'no' was enough."

Clarence Boles, a U.S. War Production Board representative in Detroit, agreed. "The evidence is piling up," he wrote Washington in 1943, "that a determined effort is being made on the part of many manufacturers to create incidents which will 'needle' and provoke labor into unauthorized stoppages of work." Such incidents made it easier to fire militants.

Many workers did not need much needling. Despite patriotic appeals, the no-strike pledge, and the warnings of their own unions, they walked off the job in growing numbers all across the country. Over 2 million struck in 1944

Opposite page: A wartime rally at the Briggs aircraft plant.

Below: After Pearl Harbor, the same sound truck West Side Local 174 had used in pre-war organizing drives now broadcast the union's pledge to "Work and Fight for Victory."

alone—more than in the peak sitdown year of 1937. Michigan accounted for more than a quarter of the workers involved in these "wildcat" strikes, with most concentrated in the Detroit area.

The wartime labor shortage made Detroit's workers unusually bold, with only the threat of a draft notice serving to temper their militancy. Most workers were intensely patriotic, but the spectacle of wartime profiteering and flourishing black markets undermined appeals to patriotism. As American military success in 1944 assured ultimate victory, the need for wartime sacrifice also became less compelling. Emboldened by their steady employment and expanded job skills, war workers frequently took the offensive and challenged their equally aggressive managers over a wide range of issues, from smoking privileges to disciplinary firings. Violence against unpopular supervisors was not uncommon.

These unauthorized outbreaks of militancy put local union officers and stewards in a serious bind. Many feared the union risked losing the loyalty of its

members if it failed to support and direct these battles; still more feared they would lose their next union election if they could not settle grievances. But without the strike weapon, the union's only recourse when management stonewalled on grievances was to file a complaint with the federal War Labor Board (WLB)—where disputes took months to resolve, and management and government Board members often outvoted union representatives. The WLB, recalled Jess Ferrazza, President of UAW Local 212 at Briggs, "was sort of a box canyon. There was no way out of it because you could not get your grievance settled. The result was that our local union, Local 212, took the initiative in fighting the no-strike pledge."

With half the UAW's members participating in wildcat strikes, dissidents organized a Rank and File Caucus to oppose the no-strike pledge. "The public has been propagandized by an anti-union press," Ben Garrison of Ford Local 400 told UAW convention delegates in 1944. "In the face of this, Labor

has patriotically continued to sacrifice while the moneyed interests and large corporations have drawn tremendous surpluses." Only the strike weapon, Garrison concluded, could counter industry's "organized endeavor to smash the union movement."

The UAW's top leaders held their ground. So long as Americans were still dying in action, they argued, wartime strikes were demoralizing and unpatriotic. They were also a dangerous provocation in a political climate where conservative politicians were clamoring for ever more stringent controls on unions.

"The reactionary forces would like nothing better," predicted Norman Mathews, President of Packard Local 190, "than the rescinding of the no-strike pledge by the largest war-workers' union in America." Older labor leaders vividly recalled the anti-union backlash of 1917-1921, and many believed the CIO could be victimized in similar fashion if it challenged the government. Philip Murray, national leader of the

Ballot Box War

The same identical forces that had CIO members shot down on picket lines—those same people are today organized in a much better fashion to destroy us through the enactment of legislation.

Gus Sholle,
CIO Regional Director, 1944

The war was a time of rapid social change, but not a time of political reform. The nation's political agenda had shifted dramatically to the right, with the wartime emergency and appeals to national unity taking precedence over social reform. Discipline and efficiency were the virtues of the day, and neither left much room for potentially disruptive social experiments. Blacks and women did gain unprecedented access to previously segregated jobs in the war plants, but this was primarily because the wartime labor shortage made such upgrading "practical." Once inside the plants, these new recruits, along with other workers, were expected to behave like industrial soldiers. Obeying orders

was a patriotic duty.

In many cases, employers enforced that duty as a matter of law. Wages were not set by collective bargaining—rather, the federal government regulated and then froze wage rates. Unsettled grievances were also arbitrated by the government, acting through the War Labor Board. The War Manpower Commission could meanwhile freeze certain classifications of workers in their jobs, requiring them to secure government permits before they transferred to a new employer.

Many workers accepted these restrictions as necessary wartime measures. But many others did not, and as strikes increased during 1943, conservative politicians effectively mobilized public support for legislation to control and regulate unions. General George Marshall, Army Chief of Staff, called wartime strikes "the damndest crime ever committed against America," and Congress, acting with the same perspective in mind, enacted the Smith-Connally Act in 1943 to clamp down on such "treason."

Passed over FDR's veto, the law

gave the federal government the right to seize any "essential" factory or mine during a strike and order workers back on the job. Anyone who then promoted a strike in such federally-run plants was subject to imprisonment and a $5,000 fine. To foil efforts at repeal, the law also prohibited unions from contributing money to federal election campaigns.

Betrayed, as they saw it, by the government's increasingly harsh labor measures, Detroit's unions debated how best to respond to these political setbacks. Some activists pushed for a complete break with the Democrats as well as the Republicans. Even President Roosevelt, they pointed out, had only delayed the Smith-Connally Act because it was "too lenient"—the President wanted a Labor Draft that would place all workers under military discipline. The majority of delegates to Michigan's CIO Convention in 1943 were so embittered by this rightward drift that one week after passage of the Smith-Connally Act, they called upon the labor movement to "desist from the old-time habits of riding the bandwagon of outworn political parties.

Inside the plant: Buying war bonds was both a way to help the government finance the war effort, and a way of saving money when wartime rationing made many consumer goods scarce.

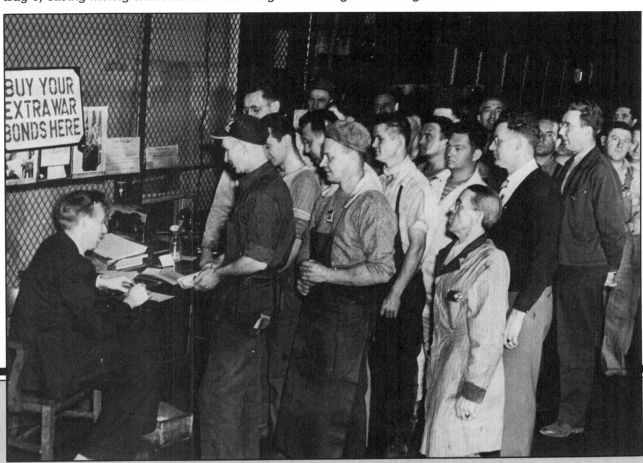

...We recommend heartily the creation of an independent labor party in our state.''

When the CIO's top leadership vetoed this initiative, some 400 trade union delegates defied their national leaders and met in Detroit the following year to form the Michigan Commonwealth Federation (MCF). Supported by prominent local-union leaders like Emil Mazey and Joe McCusker of the UAW, the MCF, modeling itself after the politically successful Canadian Commonwealth Federation, called for a pro-labor government and a mixed economy of ''public corporations, cooperative institutions, outright federal ownership, or private enterprise where it meets the requirements of public welfare.''

''When another depression comes,'' the new party announced, ''the common people will be able to turn to the MCF.'' Few voters, however, could even find the MCF on the ballot, since conflicts over whether to directly challenge the Democrats eventually pared the MCF slate to only six candidates.

The main thrust of union political action in Detroit was channeled through the CIO's Political Action Committee (PAC), formed in 1943-44 to register new voters and back Roosevelt's reelection bid. For most CIO leaders, FDR was still preferable —despite his faults—to the Republican alternative, New York Governor Thomas Dewey. A Labor Party, they reasoned, would divide the liberal vote and insure a disastrous defeat for the New Deal. To aid the faltering Democrats, PAC and its campaign committee, National Citizens PAC (funded by individual contributions to comply with the Smith-Connally Act), planned to mobilize CIO members and liberals in an all-out effort to defend the New Deal.

In Detroit, the UAW and Wayne County CIO made PAC a political action arm of tremendous breadth and potential. Every CIO local in the area provided a list of its members to the Wayne County PAC, which then checked the nearly 450,000 names against lists at the Board of Elections to see if each member was registered to vote. With grass-roots committees in 800 of Wayne County's 1032 precincts

and shop committees in every CIO workplace, PAC was able to register over 200,000 new voters in 1944. This unprecedented effort paid off spectacularly in the November elections: 43 of 53 PAC-endorsed candidates were victorious in Wayne County, and the huge majorities for Roosevelt in the Detroit area gave the President a winning margin of 22,000 votes out of 2 million cast statewide.

Whether Roosevelt's reelection would stem the rightward drift of American politics remained to be seen. But no one doubted that PAC had played a critical role in electing the President, and this marked a turning point in American politics. Some also hoped that it marked the beginnings of a newly independent labor presence on the political scene. ''I am not a Democrat and I am not a Republican,'' declared Tracy Doll, one of 16 CIO members elected to the Michigan legislature. Though he leaned towards the Democrats as the more responsive of the two major parties, ''I am strictly labor,'' Doll insisted. ''I vote for the interests of labor...for the interests of the people.''

CIO, expressed such fears when the UAW's Walter Reuther urged the CIO to withdraw its representatives from the War Labor Board. Withdrawing from the Board, Murray warned, would unleash a floodtide of militancy and "thrust into jeopardy the life of almost every [CIO] organization."

Reuther, placing himself between the contending factions at the UAW's 1944 convention, proposed the union continue the no-strike pledge in war industry and rescind it in the civilian sector. His compromise proposal was defeated. But so, too, was the resolution supporting the no-strike pledge—as was the resolution opposing it. Unable to agree on a unified position, the convention delegates called for a referendum on the issue among the union's one million members.

The results were surprising. At a time when the majority of UAW members were violating the no-strike pledge, a nearly 2-1 majority nevertheless voted to uphold the union's ban on strikes. Over two-thirds of the union's members did not even bother to mail in their ballots.

Many of these non-voters may have opposed the no-strike pledge, but their indifference to the whole referendum signified a far more disturbing development within the union. Barely seven years had gone by since the 1937 sitdowns, and only four years since the UAW's overwhelming victory at Ford; yet, in the brief span of 43 months, the war had opened a gulf so wide between the union and its members that two-thirds simply ignored the leadership *and* the Rank and File Caucus.

The membership, in fact, had changed dramatically. Thousands of union activists had left the plants and gone to war, and the new arrivals from the South and rural Michigan were not accustomed to unions. Most had no direct experience of how much workers had gained in the pre-war organizing drives. Unions had not done anything for *them* before 1941, and, as many saw it, not much since—except force them to pay dues and work in integrated factories.

The war had also changed the labor movement's leaders. Many had looked to the New Deal government in Washington as an ally—a frequently unreliable ally, but an ally nevertheless. During the war, however, the federal government had become a stern and often uncompromising taskmaster, regulating and then freezing wages, and forcing unions to abide by the bureaucratic strictures of the War Labor Board. The war, in short, created a dynamic in which union leaders often felt compelled to answer to Washington first, their members second.

The old terms of industrial conflict had changed for management as well.

Henry Ford, enfeebled by two strokes, had turned over control of the company to his security chief, Harry Bennett. Since Bennett's obvious incompetency and open grafting threatened to undermine the Ford Company's defense projects, the Pentagon discharged 26-year-old Henry Ford II from the Navy and sent him back to Detroit to counter Bennett's disruptive influence. In 1945, Henry II wrested control of the company from Bennett, thereby removing the UAW's long-standing nemesis from power. A team of ten executives from the Air Force's Office of Statistical Controls soonafter joined Ford Motors to help the younger Henry modernize the company; among them were two future Presidents of Ford Motors, Robert McNamara and Arjay Miller.

The year 1945 marked the end of another era. In April, with Nazi Germany weeks away from surrender and Japan nearly defeated, President Roosevelt died. Vice President Harry Truman, taking over the reins of government, promised to uphold the principles of New Deal liberalism in the post-war era.

Germany surrendered that May, Japan in August. Peace was at hand, and with it, hopes that America could leave behind the legacy of pre-war Depression—and fears that it might not.

Outside the plant: Chevrolet workers in Detroit at the start of a strike.

A New World

The bloodiest war in human history was over. At a cost of 50 million dead and millions more maimed, homeless, and uprooted, fascism had been defeated.

The world would never be the same. More important, few of the world's peoples wanted it the same. Economic depression, inequality, insecurity, oppression and discrimination: this was the pre-war world many people remembered. The war, with all its suffering and sacrifice, would be meaningless if it simply brought a return to such a discredited status quo.

With the surrender of Germany and Japan, popular movements for social change toppled pre-war elites throughout the world. In some places, change came peacefully, as in the British Labor Party's 1945 election victory; in other places, it came violently, as in the Chinese Communists' 1949 victory over General Chiang Kai Shek. National liberation movements against the colonial empires of Britain, Holland, and France led to the emergence of dozens of new countries, including India, Indonesia, and Viet Nam.

Many of Detroit's CIO activists and

union leaders were caught up in this post-war ferment of change and renewal. "Your sons, your husbands, your brothers and your sisters have fought and bled to preserve our American way of life," UAW Vice President Richard Frankensteen declared as World War II drew to a close. "Our boys are now coming back. Shall they come back to a city torn by hatred? Or shall we go to work and build a better city with opportunity for all to work at a decent wage, to live in decent homes, and to live in unity?" The answer, Frankensteen announced, could only be positive if a Labor Candidate like himself replaced Mayor Edward Jeffries in upcoming elections.

Backed by the CIO and the UAW, Frankensteen promised to rebuild the city and reverse 16 years of neglect. Detroit was undeniably in sorry shape. Many essential repairs and improvements had been postponed during the Depression, and the subsequent wartime overcrowding had accelerated the pace of urban decay. Under Frankensteen's promised administration, all this would change. By tapping into the city's portion of state sales-tax revenues, the new Mayor could modernize the trolley system, build new schools, clear slums, and help launch new public and private housing projects.

"If you will work and vote for the election of Richard T. Frankensteen," UAW Local 155 declared in its paper, *Common Sense,* "perhaps we can have a labor victory as well as our British fellow workers." In the August, 1945, Mayoral primary, Detroit's voters took the first step toward such a victory, giving Frankensteen 42 percent of the vote in a three-candidate race; Jeffries trailed with 34 percent and Wayne County Auditor Jim Friel followed with 18 percent. When Friel endorsed Frankensteen after the primary, the CIO candidate appeared to have the inside track in the campaign for the final runoff election.

Shortly before this stunning primary victory, the UAW announced it would also pursue a fundamentally new collective-bargaining strategy. In upcoming negotiations with the auto companies, union Vice President Walter Reuther revealed the UAW would demand a hefty chunk of the industry's wartime profits in higher wages—with no increase in auto prices.

The union's dramatic initiative was prompted by fear that the economy would slip into a new depression if corrective actions were not taken. Detroit's defense industries were already laying off thousands of workers as the war ended, and the purchasing power of those still on the job was being severely eroded by inflation and sharp cutbacks in overtime pay. Stable economic growth, the UAW argued, could only be insured by redistributing excess profits to workers. If prices stayed the same, the expanded blue-collar purchasing power would boost sales and spur business investment. "Increased production must be supported by increased consumption," Reuther insisted, "and increased consumption will be possible only through increased wages.... The economic facts of life," as Reuther saw

them, "prove that wages can be increased without increasing prices."

Reuther's claims received unusual support from officials in the federal government. The Commerce Department, headed by Henry Wallace, reported the auto industry could afford a 25 percent wage increase without raising prices and still remain profitable, once full-scale civilian production was restored. William Davis, Director of Economic Stabilization, believed the companies could afford 40–50 percent wage increases without price increases. But the key boost for Reuther's position came unexpectedly from President Truman, who declared the wartime wage freeze would only be lifted in cases where wage increases did not cause price increases. The UAW immediately announced it would ask GM for a 30 percent wage increase without any price increase. The union challenged GM to open its books to the public if it hoped to prove such a demand was unfeasible.

Detroit's industrial unions appeared to be on the verge of a momentous political and economic breakthrough. To many, Frankensteen's campaign seemed to be a Labor Party in embryo, and a CIO election victory in the nation's fourth largest city might therefore herald a complete realignment in American politics. Reuther's bargaining demands seemed no less daring, for the UAW was now challenging the unquestioned control over prices and profits normally monopolized by corporations.

Not everyone appreciated the boldness of these initiatives. "Walter Reuther is the most dangerous man in Detroit," complained auto executive George Romney, "because no one is more skillful in bringing about a revolution without appearing to disturb the existing forms of society." Publicly, GM charged that the UAW wished to see the company "relinquish its right to manage its business;" the corporations rejected the union's demands and offered only an 8 percent wage increase pending government approval of a matching price increase. Privately, GM negotiators chided Reuther for his ambitious strategy. "Why don't you get down to size," GM's Harry Coen demanded, "and let the labor statesmanship go to hell for awhile?"

Frankensteen was treated even more roughly. Mayor Jeffries and Detroit's three daily newspapers repeatedly warned of the dire consequences of a CIO election victory—including loss of jobs if nervous companies moved away. More ominously, right-wing groups and

anonymous supporters of the Mayor revived the race-baiting tactics of 1943. "White Neighborhoods In Peril" blared a typical headline in the *Home Gazette,* one of a string of neighborhood weeklies owned by conservative editor Floyd McGriff. A Frankensteen victory, McGriff's papers warned, would only multiply "the attempts of Communist-inspired Negroes to penetrate white residential areas." An extensive phone-calling campaign by "concerned property-owners" inflamed racial fears with warnings that a CIO victory would bring neighborhood integration and "destroy property values."

Nearly half a million Detroiters went to the polls on November 6. The results were a crippling blow for the CIO's political initiative. Backed by 2–1 majorities in the city's outlying wards, Jeffries won 56 percent of the overall vote. Frankensteen won heavily in the black, Polish, Italian, and Jewish wards closer to the river, but voter turnout in these pro-union strongholds was not enough to overcome the heavy middle-class vote for Jeffries on the Northwest and Northeast sides.

To many white-collar voters, racial integration was not the only thing to fear from a CIO Mayor. Worker discipline was also an issue, for the end of the war had unleashed a massive and chaotic strike wave over wages, overtime, disciplinary firings, and job downgradings to lower-paid civilian production. Nearly 85,000 Detroit-area workers were idled by these local strikes in September and October alone. Especially damaging to Frankensteen's campaign was a two-week strike by the CIO's Oil Workers Union at the Socony (Mobil Oil) refinery in suburban Trenton, Michigan. Beginning in mid-September, the strike quickly spread to major refineries throughout the eastern United States, causing acute fuel shortages in Detroit and elsewhere. Bus service was crippled, schools were closed, and thousands of angry motorists were forced to drive to Windsor, Canada, for gasoline. Many of Jeffries' supporters and undecided voters no doubt applauded President Truman's order directing the U.S. Navy to seize the refineries and break the strike.

In a desperate effort to distance himself from the negative press coverage generated by these and other strikes, Frankensteen denounced wildcat strikers in his union as a "mobocracy." The remark alienated many union members, and confirmed the belief held by Jeffries' supporters that Frankensteen could not manage his own union, much

Above: Union pickets during the General Motors strike.

Inset: The UAW's view of the postwar strike wave.

Preceding page: An Army veteran addresses GM strikers.

less a city.

On November 21, 1945 (three weeks after Frankensteen's defeat) the strike wave swelled dramatically when 225,000 UAW members, having voted by a 5–1 margin to strike GM, "hit the bricks" in a nationwide walkout against the giant automaker. Simultaneous walkouts by electrical workers, meatpackers, and steel workers raised the number of strikers nationwide to 1.6 million by the end of January, 1946. Throughout the year, coal miners, railroad workers, teachers, utility workers, municipal workers, and many others walked off the job, demanding hefty wage increases to compensate for wartime sacrifices and the ravages of inflation. All told, 4½ million people went on strike in 1946—the highest strike total in American history.

The federal government, relying on its wartime emergency powers, played a crucial role in deciding the outcome of these massive strikes. More often than not, the government weighed in on management's side. President Truman temporarily nationalized packinghouses, railroads, and coal mines in an effort to head off or forcibly end the walkouts. When striking railroad workers defied the government, Truman threatened to draft them and call in the army; when the coal miners refused the President's back-to-work order, the government fined their union $3.5 million.

Truman's role in the GM strike was more even-handed. After an emergency convention of UAW members rebuffed the President's initial request to return to work immediately, the President established a neutral fact-finding board to help arbitrate the strike. When the board declared, however, that GM's "ability to pay" should be considered in any settlement, the company immediately withdrew from the fact-finding hearings. Shortly afterwards, GM also rejected the board's finding that the company could afford a 19½¢ hourly wage increase (about 17.5 percent) without price increases.

The UAW accepted the board's proposal and found its public support greatly strengthened. A national committee that included both Mrs. Eleanor Roose-

UAW retirees at Belle Isle park, 1962.
Inset: Picketing during the 1949 strike for a pension plan at Ford.

velt and publisher Henry Luce (owner of *Time* and *Life* magazines) made a public appeal for contributions to the UAW's strike fund. Support poured in from numerous sources, including 300 Montana farmers who sent carloads of wheat to Detroit.

But while the government endorsed the principle of wage increases without price increases in the autoworkers' strike, it contradicted that same principle in the steel walkout. In that industry, the government assured the companies they could raise prices up to $5 a ton if they granted the United Steelworkers' Union an 18½¢-an-hour pay raise. The companies accepted the proposal, and by the end of February, several major strikes had been settled on the same pattern, with companies later raising prices to boost profits. Even the UAW's Ford and Chrysler workers (who had not gone on strike) voted to accept the pattern settlement.

Only the UAW's GM membership held out for 19½¢ and no price increases. Time was running out, however, for the many strikers who faced mortgage foreclosures and utility shut-off notices. Four months of picketing in the snow and rain had not significantly weakened Reuther's support among rank and file members. But without the full backing of the CIO or the government, it became increasingly clear the

UAW could not force GM to bargain over prices. Compelled to abandon Reuther's anti-inflation strategy, the union finally agreed on March 13, 1946, to settle the 113-day strike. Under the terms of the final settlement, GM agreed to boost wages 18¢-an-hour and provide additional benefits well above the company's initial offer, but without mention of prices.

The 1945–1946 strikes established an enduring pattern. On the one hand, the major unions proved they were strong enough to win substantial wage increases from unwilling employers. On the other hand, large corporations proved they were politically and economically strong enough to raise prices and more than recover the cost of higher wages.

Contrary to the UAW's predictions, this inflationary spiral did not choke off consumer demand and cause a new depression. Sales rose even when GM raised prices as much as $80 a car just two months after the 1946 strike settlement. Such price hikes did not deter millions of people from buying the things they either could not afford during the Depression years or could not find during the wartime scarcities—a new car, a house, appliances. Earnings saved from wartime employment primed the pump of this post-war spending spree, with government-insured mortgages and loans to war veterans giving the economy an added boost.

So even as corporations raised prices, their showrooms across the country were crowded with customers. Not surprisingly, corporate revenue grew by leaps and bounds. Over the first post-war decade, General Motors led the profit parade with an average $1.37 return *each year* on every $1.00 invested in automobile production.

It took more than just pent-up consumer demand to sustain such long-term profitability. It also took a complete reshuffling of worldwide trade, with the deck heavily stacked in favor of the United States. In this respect, World War II dealt America an enviable hand. Former trade rivals like Germany and Japan lay in ruins. Six years of total war had also virtually bankrupted the British empire. The U.S, alone among the world's major economic powers, emerged from the war with its industrial base intact and strengthened.

Equally important, American businessmen, unlike their demoralized and discredited counterparts abroad, had gained in prestige and confidence as the war progressed. In the post-war period, they aggressively expanded their operations worldwide, taking over markets previously controlled by the British, French, Germans, and Japanese. To sustain and expand booming export sales and foreign investments, the federal government pumped billions of dollars in foreign aid into the world economy —much of it earmarked for the purchase of American-made goods.

Between 1946 and 1955, the nation's annual production of goods and services increased by 40 percent (after inflation). Yet poverty and economic insecurity did not disappear. Brief downturns interrupted the boom in 1947, 1954, and 1958, with unemployment rising to nearly 7 percent nationally and 17 percent in Detroit during the last of these "recessions." Pockets of permanent high unemployment also remained in the urban ghettoes of the North and the rural uplands of Appalachia.

But most economists saw these problems as minor blemishes on an otherwise healthy economy. They assumed that continued economic growth would automatically eliminate poverty, while government spending on social services and arms production would stabilize the economy. Spurred by the growing Cold War with the Soviet Union and the shooting war in Korea, defense spending soon took the upper hand. By 1955,

military expenditures had increased 400 percent over 1947 levels, absorbing more than half of the federal budget.

Once again, Detroit was on the cutting edge of national prosperity. Automobile sales topped 5 million in 1949, breaking the 20-year-old record set in 1929. After a partial conversion to military production during the Korean war, the auto industry resumed its breakneck production pace in 1955, when sales crested at 8 million. Highway construction and suburban homebuilding grew apace in Detroit and nationally, creating millions of jobs and transforming the shape of urban America.

Detroit's workers were also transformed. Between 1945 and 1955, the city's industrial workers boosted their average wage to $98 a week, well above the $75-a-week national average for manufacturing, and 40 percent higher in real wages (after inflation) than their pay at war's end. The fact that the nation's wealthiest industry was concentrated in Detroit made hefty wage increases possible. Aggressive negotiating by the city's industrial unions, led by the UAW, made these wage increases happen. The UAW led the way in winning non-wage benefits as well, including company-financed pensions, medical and health plans, sick pay, life insurance, disability coverage, and paid vacations.

In the pre-union era, such benefits had been lavished on corporate executives and some white-collar professionals. Winning them for blue-collar workers represented something of a social revolution, but it was a revolution in slow motion, not a frontal assault on the status quo.

Typically, the union first "asked for the moon"—as the UAW did in demanding company-financed health insurance for its members and their families during the 1940's. And typically, the companies denounced such proposals as "socialistic meddling"—after which they would settle for a scaleddown version of the benefit. The union then built on this precedent.

During World War II, for example, the UAW, with federal support, forced employers to accept the principle of nonprofit health insurance for their workers. Initially, each worker paid the entire premium through a voluntary payroll deduction. Over the next 20 years, the union negotiated gradual improvements in the health plan, winning first partial payment by the companies, then full payment, then family-wide coverage, and finally, full coverage for retirees.

The battle for a guaranteed annual wage began in much the same manner. "It is more than a matter of economic justice to the wage earner," said Walter Reuther, then President of the UAW, at the opening of contract negotiations in 1955. Winning income guarantees for

UAW leaders during 1958 contract negotiations with Chrysler. The union's chief negotiators at the table included (left to right) Art Hughes, Assistant Director of the Chrysler Department, UAW President Walter Reuther, and presidential assistants Jack Conway (seated), Nat Weinberg, and Doug Fraser (also seated).

Post-war Detroit: While membership in ethnic organizations declined according to surveys conducted by the University of Michigan, membership in sports teams grew significantly.

"It was not, obviously, a guaranteed annual wage," Irving Bluestone, a top UAW negotiator, later acknowledged. "But it laid the basis for establishing guaranteed income," and over the next twelve years, the UAW won improvements that extended SUB to 52 weeks of coverage at 95 percent of take-home pay. The same strategy was followed for most of the benefits won by the union. "Invariably," as Bluestone put it, "Walter Reuther would talk about how, 'well, we laid the foundation, the principle is there. Now we've got to build on that and make it sweeter.' Which is essentially what we did, and what all unions do."

Changes in shop-floor relations were equally piecemeal, and equally far reaching.

In the pre-union era, managers and foremen had unquestioned authority to change job descriptions, speed up production, or fire workers. With the coming of the union, this arbitrary power was limited by negotiated work rules. Formal grievance procedures now regulated unionized workplaces. When a worker protested a company action, he or she brought the grievance to a union steward, who took up the dispute with the foreman or supervisor. If the grievance could not be resolved at this level, the union's chief steward or grievance committeeman would try to haggle out a mutually-agreeable settlement with the company's Labor Relations Department. If the dispute could not be resolved at this level, top negotiators from the union and the company took up the matter. After this final stage, an unresolved grievance either became an issue in future contract negotiations—and possibly a future strike—or the company and union agreed to hire a neutral arbitrator to decide the matter.

It was not a perfect system of justice. While a grievance worked its way from one stage to the next, the worker who was protesting, for example, an unjust firing remained unemployed, sometimes for many months—"guilty until proven innocent." Since the union paid at least part of the bill when outside arbitrators were hired, union officers also had to decide just how much justice they could afford before taking the case to arbitration.

Foremen and managers often subverted the process. "Some of them would say they'd follow the contract, but they wouldn't," recalled Joseph Jeffrey, head of the company's Labor Relations Department at Great Lakes Steel. "Their philosophy was, 'never say

autoworkers during seasonal layoffs was, in Reuther's words, "a matter of necessity to our nation, for freedom and unemployment cannot live together in democracy's house." The solution, he argued, was a guaranteed annual wage —in effect, a blue-collar salary.

"This is something that we will never, never do," replied Ford Vice President John Bugas, who countered with a company offer to help workers buy stock in

the corporation. Yet, with only hours to spare before the UAW's announced strike deadline, the company and the union managed to hammer out an acceptable compromise: a company-financed Supplemental Unemployment Benefit (SUB) fund. SUB, together with the state's regular unemployment compensation, guaranteed a laid-off worker at least 60 percent of normal take-home pay for 26 weeks of unemployment.

anything in favor of the workers.' So somebody would get fired, and we'd have a grievance in front of us. I'd ask the superintendent, 'why did you fire him?' 'Well,' he'd say, 'he wrecked his machine.' Then I'd find out it broke down because of poor maintenance. The worker had been complaining about it for years, but when it stopped, the boss blamed him.''

There were, however, bosses like Jeffrey who worked with and accepted the unions in their shop. Stable and productive work relations, they reasoned, required that conflict between the company and the union remain within tolerable bounds. To minimize workplace disruptions, some managers introduced their own collective-bargaining proposals to head off disputes. GM's Cost of Living Adjustment (COLA) was one such contract proposal, offered in 1948 by the company's President, Charles Wilson, to protect the purchasing power of wages against inflation. The UAW praised GM's initiative on COLA, calling it a partial vindication of the union's 1945-1946 strike objectives.

For working people in Detroit, it all added up to something unique. This was, above all, a city where 60 percent of the adult population in 1945 either belonged to a union or was related to someone who did—nearly double the national average of 31 percent. And however many complaints Detroiters had about their jobs or the frequent layoffs plaguing the auto industry, over 85 percent surveyed in 1951 still believed their city was an ''above average'' or ''very good'' place to work.

It certainly looked good to Bill Marshall in 1948 when he arrived in Detroit from the deep South. A member of the Amalgamated Transit Union, Marshall's local in Shreveport, Louisiana, had been on strike against Trailways for nearly a year. ''We lost that strike and I was blackballed,'' Marshall later remembered. ''When I came here, obviously, it was a desperation move. I had not worked in almost a year... [until] the union helped me secure employment at Greyhound in Detroit.... And they [Detroit Greyhound] didn't have that same attitude toward union people that we encountered in the South.'' There was union-management conflict, Marshall recalled, but his strike activity ''really wasn't a liability'' when it came to finding a job in Detroit's unionized transportation industry.

Marshall was only one of many

Above: Northland Shopping Center, in suburban Southfield, drew residents and businesses away from downtown Detroit, visible in upper right.

Inset: To project a pro-union message to its scattered members and the general public, the UAW formed radio station WDET–FM in 1948. The station promised in its opening statement that ''Instead of dismal repetition..., phony prize programs, [and] dishonest promotions of cereals, hair washes, and tooth pastes, WDET will broadcast decent music and intelligent discussions of community and national problems.'' Pictured here in 1952 are, right to left, Frank Marquart, Pat Sexton, Sam Fishman, and Art Valente, all local-union leaders in the UAW. The union later gave WDET to Wayne State University.

thousands of people attracted to Detroit by its national reputation as a ''Workingman's'' Town. Especially as southern blacks began the trek north, the city's population continued to grow, peaking at 1.9 million in 1953. Yet even as the new arrivals poured into town, thousands of white Detroiters were already exiting the city for the suburbs.

Many were simply following their jobs. World-War-II-era factories, built in Detroit's rural outskirts, had opened up new options for postwar development: employers could build sprawling, single-story factories on the cheap land available in Warren, Ypsilanti, Livonia, and Trenton, and workers could drive to these plants on highways (like I-94, west-

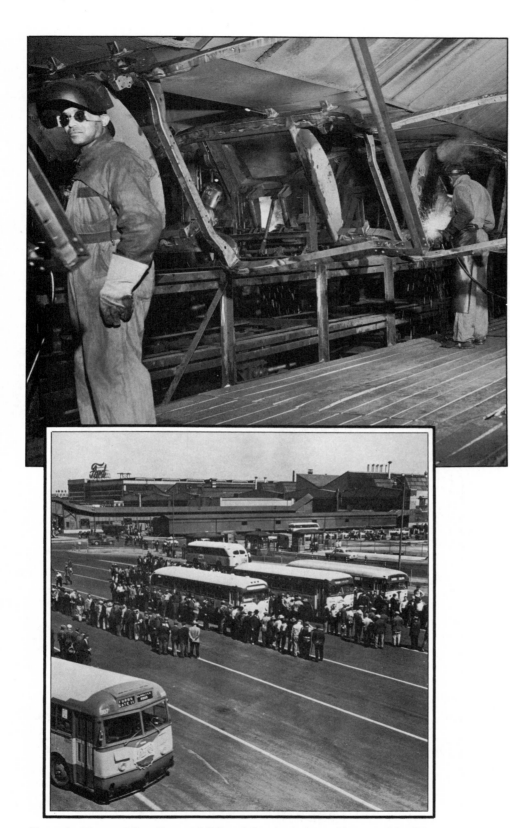

At work: The welding line at Midland Steel, maker of automobile frames. Inset: Shift change at Ford Rouge.

precedented concentration of stores was billed as America's first "regional" shopping center.

Contrary to the prevailing myth of a classless suburbia, the new communities springing up outside Detroit were not one-dimensional societies, each identical with its neighbor. Many, in fact, were extensions of the city's ethnic and religious neighborhoods. Italian- and German-Americans moved outward along Gratiot into Harper Woods and East Detroit; many of Hamtramck's Polish-Americans moved north into Warren and surrounding communities; and Detroit's Jewish community moved north and west from the Dexter-Davison-12th Street area into Southfield and Oak Park. These suburbs were not uniformly affluent. Towns like Warren, Lincoln Park, and Taylor were fast becoming blue-collar cities in their own right, with high levels of union membership and a corresponding tendency to vote for Democratic Party candidates. An economic slump meant layoffs in these towns. In wealthy Grosse Pointe to the east of Detroit and Bloomfield Hills on the far north, a slump meant lower dividends.

Nevertheless, these blue-collar suburbanites were no longer the same workers who had, in the pre-war era, occupied Dodge Main or barricaded Miller Road. There were, above all, fewer foreign-born workers among them. Immigration was legally restricted in the 1920s, discouraged by the Depression of the 1930s, and halted altogether by the warfare of the 1940s. In 1930, nearly two-thirds of greater Detroit's population was either foreign-born or the children of foreign-born parents; by the end of the 1950s, the proportion had declined to only one-fifth.

Many of Detroit's ethnic and communal organizations declined accordingly. Immigrant mutual-aid societies were replaced by the union-negotiated benefit plans and New-Deal programs that immigrant Detroiters had themselves fought for. Ethnic businesses—those that weathered the Depression—found it hard to survive in the postwar era, when corporate retailers moved into everything from fast-food restaurants to supermarkets. While metropolitan Detroit's economy was booming during much of the 1950s, the proportion of self-employed people in the labor force actually fell from 8 to 6 percent. The same trends that pulled shoppers towards the new suburban malls and supermarkets also pulled them away from many of the old ethnic stores and groceries.

bound to Willow Run) begun during the war. Between 1947 and 1955, Ford, Chrysler, and GM built 20 new factories in the Detroit area employing 70,000 workers—*none* were within the city limits. Homebuilding followed the same pattern. Of 260,000 new homes built in the metro area in the 1950s, nearly all were built in the suburbs. Symbolic of the massive population shift that generated this suburban construction boom was the Northland shopping mall, located north of the city on Eight Mile road (site 69). Begun in 1950, this un-

It was, indeed, a new world. Detroit's suburbanized working class had not become rich in the years since the Depression, but they were nevertheless prosperous compared to the 1930s. They had not become pro-business Republicans, but their political commitments rarely ventured beyond a mild reformism. They had not become complacent, but they were no longer as angry, as militant, or as willing to challenge the status quo. The status quo had changed, and most believed it had changed for the better.

The internal life of the industrial-union movement had also changed.

Where before, union members often lived in or near the same neighborhood as their factory and union hall, now a growing number were scattered throughout the metropolitan area, making the round trip to union meetings a matter of some inconvenience. Attendance usually peaked during union elections and annual contract negotiations. But as companies asked for (and unions agreed to) contracts that stretched over two- to three-year terms, such attendance peaks became less frequent.

The union's day-to-day presence inside the factory also changed. Corporations were growing in size, and as unions struggled to match their power, authority inevitably became more centralized on both sides of the bargaining table. In most companies, the Personnel Office had by now taken over the foreman's power to hire and fire, while many companies also curtailed the supervisor's authority to decide on grievances. And as the foreman's power declined, so too did the role of the union shop steward.

The shop steward, whether recognized by the company or not, had long been the union's rank-and-file leader, working alongside the members in the plant, collecting union dues, and bucking the foreman's rule. When internal faction fighting paralyzed the UAW's top leadership in the late-1930s and mid-1940s, stewards acted as all-around leaders for their immediate work group, handling grievances and disciplinary actions, calling quickie strikes if need be, and serving as informal counselors on everything from legal aid to unemployment insurance. "Uncertain conditions in the plants and chaos in the union [made] the steward the only adequately functioning representative of the workers," recalled B.J. Widick, a former steward at Chrysler's Jefferson Avenue plant.

By the 1950s, however, most stewards simply sent grievances along to an elected "Committeeman" or Chief Steward, who served as the full- or part-time grievance handler for as many as 1,000 workers. These officials, in turn, often got the company to settle the dispute according to precedents established earlier by an outside arbitrator or permanent grievance "umpire." The result, observed Walter Reuther, was that "the principles of interpretation established by umpire decisions have become a sort of common law.... Thousands of grievances are settled every year because the parties realize that the umpire has already ruled upon the question in dispute."

Between 1949 and 1955, UAW members at GM, Briggs, and other companies also voted by 8-to-1 majorities to make membership in the union and payment of dues a mandatory condition of employment. When employers agreed to implement such "Union-Shop" provisions, they usually agreed to automatically deduct the dues money from paychecks and turn it over to the union (as Ford had done since 1941). The steward's role as dues collector was thereby eliminated. At the same time, specialized union staff took over contract supervision, legal counselling, and social-service functions, further reducing—and in some cases eliminating—the steward's role.

Union members were often better served by these full-time staffers and elected officers. As the process of grievance handling and collective bargaining became more centralized, however, it became more remote from the average member. So long as the union negotiated better contracts and favorable grievance settlements, most members accepted this trend without complaint. But when grievances went unresolved or contracts failed to meet expectations, dissident members reviled their leaders as "porkchoppers" and claimed they had lost touch with rank-and-file interests.

Centralization of union authority and stabilization of collective bargaining undercut rank-and-file activism to some

At home: The "good life" of leisure-time living was the theme for this float in Detroit's 1949 Labor Day parade. The Institute of Laundering represented unionized employers.

extent, but did not eliminate union militancy. In the opening months of 1949, 200,000 autoworkers in Detroit and Flint launched wildcat strikes over speed-up that finally culminated in a three-week, union-sanctioned walkout at the Ford Rouge plant. The following year, the UAW struck Chrysler in a bitter, 104-day walkout to win fully-funded pensions. Detroit's steelworkers meanwhile joined five nationwide steel strikes between 1945 and 1959, the last a 116-day walkout to protect work standards and prevent crew-size reductions.

Between these contract battles, an ongoing skirmish over working conditions continued in many workplaces. While most unions agreed to prohibit strikes during the length of the contract, many reserved the right to strike over production-speed standards and health-and-safety issues. During the contract's term, the grievance procedure was supposed to resolve these and other issues without disruption. But sometimes, "proper channels" could not contain an aroused workforce.

"The company claimed I had 100 wildcat strikes in one year," recalled Charles Younglove, whose 1946 campaign for improved safety measures won him the local-union presidency at Great Lakes Steel. "I'll always say there were never wildcat strikes. There might have been 100 safety protests, though, where people said, 'hey, we're not going to work...until it [the job] is made safe.... Maybe that wasn't the way it should have been done, but how long do you wait on a possible permanent injury to correct a hazard?.... We shouldn't have to have a mangled body brought into some office and say, 'well, I told you it was unsafe.'"

But ongoing conflict did not prevent accommodation. Union and management representatives sat together on urban-planning committees and local boards of the United Way. Indeed, the United Way itself was launched in the early 1950s as a joint effort by Gus Scholle of the CIO, Walter Reuther of the UAW, and Henry Ford II. As a centralized charity umbrella endorsed by both the unions and the companies, the United Way eliminated the competitive and unregulated solicitations of dozens of private charities. Workers could contribute to many causes with a single gift.

All the while, union dues were collected by the companies. Between 1948 and 1964, GM alone "checked off" $203 million from workers' pay and turned it over to the UAW, relieving the union of the need to continually dun its members for unpaid dues. Having won the industry's recognition of a permanent union presence, the UAW gave the same recognition to management. In 1946, the union signed "company security" agreements at Ford and Chrysler acknowledging management's right to discipline or fire workers who led wildcat strikes.

It was a world of sharp contrasts for Detroit's industrial workers. At the end of every shift, thousands now returned to suburban homes. Their real income had steadily increased since the end of World War II, and many could afford "the good things" in life: a new car, a vacation, even a boat. These material rewards blurred the old class distinctions in dress and consumption. Workers who previously shopped at Sam's Cut-Rate Stores now ventured in-

to Hudson's Northland Center. Television, launched in 1948, continually reinforced this image of a classless world of upwardly mobile shoppers, each striving to get ahead. In this TV world, "Ozzie and Harriett" Nelson represented the dominant middle-class norm, comfortably housed in a suburban home, while Jackie Gleason in "The Honeymooners" lampooned the blue-collar working class, trapped in a one-room apartment.

Yet, when Detroit's workers returned to the plant at the beginning of each shift, they entered an entirely different world, a world seldom represented on TV. "Individual initiative," frequently extolled by politicians and the media, was virtually irrelevant. Regardless of individual goals, workers were pigeonholed into dull, repetitive jobs producing whatever products management sent down the line. A few might move into the skilled trades, lower supervision, or small business, but more often, a worker's ambition focused on the hope that his or her children would get an education and "make it" as a white-collar professional. In the meantime, the threat of future business slumps and layoffs hung over all but the most senior workers.

These enduring aspects of industrial labor continued to generate an underlying solidarity and commitment to job guarantees among factory workers, even as many of these same workers saw themselves stepping up to a new life of middle-class respectability off the job. Detroit's workers could therefore remain loyal, if not always active, union members—even as many also endorsed a new and prolonged Red Scare in the post-war decade.

Like the Knights of Labor 60 years before, the UAW established non-profit, worker- and consumer-owned coop stores as alternatives to corporate retailing. Without adequate financing or sales volume to make them competitive, most failed.

RED SCARE

"The people who support the New Deal this November," the conservative *Chicago Tribune* editorialized in 1944, "are supporting the Communists and building up the day when they plan the Red Terror sweeping down upon America."

In 1944, 25 million Americans ignored this kind of dire prophecy and reelected President Franklin Roosevelt to an unprecedented fourth term. Two years later, as predicted, fear was indeed beginning to sweep across America—a fear generated by the Right, however, and not by the Left.

Right-wing resentment against the New Deal had been smoldering for over a decade as government regulation of business, taxes on the rich, pro-labor legislation, sitdown strikes, social security, and demands for racial equality all followed one after another. Conservatives saw cause for alarm in all these breaks with tradition. America's wartime alliance with the Soviet Union, the presence of Communists and Socialists in the CIO, and the huge post-war strike wave only deepened their conviction the New Deal was the entering wedge of Soviet-style subversion in America.

In 1946, conservative opponents of

the New Deal finally turned the corner. With less than 40 percent of eligible voters casting ballots, the Republican Party captured control of Congress for the first time in 16 years. Conservative anti-Communists like Richard Nixon and Joseph McCarthy wasted little time mobilizing their new power against supporters of liberal reform.

The old Dies Committee, revived in 1945 as the House Un-American Activities Committee (HUAC), immediately began a decade-long investigation into the allegedly subversive activities of trade unionists, government employees, teachers, and Hollywood film makers. With bipartisan backing from conservative Democrats like John Rankin of Mississippi (a man who once declared slavery "the greatest blessing the Negro people ever had"), HUAC called over 3,000 witnesses to its hearings between 1945 and 1957. The Committee cited hundreds for "Contempt of Congress" when they refused to cooperate with the Red-Hunt.

Growing Soviet-American conflict and Communist victories in the Chinese civil war gave the Red Scare added urgency, since many conservatives saw the CIO and domestic radicalism as intimately linked with Moscow and Peking. As scattered cases of Soviet espionage were sensationalized by the press, publicity-conscious politicians spread the search for Red Agents across the country. If, as usually happened, none could be found, politicians stretched the definition of subversion to include progressive causes. "If someone insists there is discrimination against Negroes in this country," declared Albert Canwell, Chairman of Washington State's inquisition, "there is every reason to believe that person is a Communist."

As the political winds blew stronger from the right, President Truman and the majority of congressional Democrats trimmed their liberal sails and joined the conservative drift. Instead of defending or reinvigorating the New Deal, most Democrats abandoned their promised full-employment legislation and gutted price controls even as inflation soared. Faced with the 1945-1946 strikes, President Truman issued back-to-work orders and heavy fines against striking workers. When GM refused to cooperate with federal mediation efforts during these same strikes, Truman did nothing. One week after the GM strike ended, the President asked Congress for the authority to end future walkouts by drafting strikers into the armed forces.

Truman's proposed labor draft, the UAW declared, would "make peacetime strikes illegal and impose a fascist system of involuntary servitude on American workers." That spring, the union's Executive Board advised "that we work towards the eventual formation of a broad third party."

No such broad-based party was formed. Some left-liberals and New Dealers did launch the Progressive Party in 1948, with former Vice President and Commerce Secretary Henry Wallace as their Presidential candidate. Their efforts, however, were condemned by the UAW and most other unions, both because Wallace could not possibly win, and because Communists played a leading role in organizing his campaign. By 1948, the majority of AFL and CIO unions were also convinced that Truman, who had dropped his proposed labor draft, now deserved their support. Above all, the President had vetoed the Taft–Hartley Act.

Passed in 1947 by the newly-elected Republican Congress, the Taft–Hartley Act outlawed sympathy strikes, mass picketing, union hiring halls, and "secondary" boycotts against stores selling non-union goods. Under this measure, states could pass so-called "Right-to-Work" laws banning Union-Shop agreements. Before Taft-Hartley, if a majority of workers voted for a Union Shop—and if management agreed to such a provision—then all workers had to pay union dues as a condition of employment. But under

Above: Sensationalized reporting made the Red Scare front-page copy in the 1940s and 1950s.

Preceding page: In the 1950s, pickets at Detroit's Bushnell Congregational Church equated Communism with racial integration.

Hearings of the House Committee on Un-American Activities, held in Detroit, March, 1952.

Taft–Hartley, the anti-union minority could now refuse to pay, even though they received all the rights and benefits won by the union. (By 1954, 17 southern and western states had banned the Union Shop.) Taft–Hartley also required all union officers to take a non-Communist oath, and unions which failed to enforce the oath on their elected leaders automatically lost the protection of federal labor law.

When Congress overrode Truman's veto and passed Taft-Hartley, most unions rallied to the President's 1948 reelection campaign. The CIO mobilized thousands of its members to ring doorbells, register voters, and distribute literature, and the AFL's newly formed League For Political Education launched similar activities in Wayne County and nationally. Defying all odds, the labor movement's efforts made Truman victorious in November.

Throughout the election, the Red Scare continued unabated. To quiet his right-wing critics, Truman had already joined the hunt in 1947 by establishing a "Loyalty Oath" program. As the President and HUAC competed for headlines, the grounds for political suspicion grew broader still. Those who had supported the Spanish Republic in the 1930s against its pro-Nazi opponents were now labeled "premature anti-Fascists." Critics of General Chiang Kai Shek's corrupt and authoritarian regime in China were denounced as "Fifth Columnists" for the Chinese Communists. Branded as "subversives" for such politically tabooed beliefs, over 7,000 federal employees resigned or were fired between 1947 and 1952 as the result of Truman's Loyalty investigations.

In Michigan, the Red Scare generated an equally intense preoccupation with subversion—and subversion took on an equally broad meaning. In March, 1947, Governor Kim Sigler sounded the alarm by announcing that 15,000 Communists (seven times more than even the FBI estimated) were active in the state. Sigler even included the NAACP and the Detroit Council for Youth Services in his initial list of 20 "Communist-Front" groups.

The *Detroit News*, in a front-page series of articles entitled "Communist Plot Exposed," provided a daily diet of imagined scenarios for Communist subversion in Michigan. "As Petrograd Fell, So Detroit Can Fall," headlined one such scare story. "Blueprints Disclosed for Seizure of Detroit" warned another. The "blueprint," it turned out, was nothing more than a "what if" story about "foreign-born spies and... American-born traitor dupes" all working in an "iron-ruled Fifth Column disguised as the Communist Party of the United States." Readers were asked to

"Vision a City Paralyzed by Capture of Public Officials, Utilities, and Airports."

No evidence ever materialized, however, for such a plot. "So far," State Police Commissioner Donald Leonard publicly acknowledged in 1952, "we have never been able to prove that any person, even an admitted Communist, sought or advocated overthrow of the government.... Even our undercover agents who attended Communist meetings," Leonard admitted, "could get no such proof."

Proof or no proof, the imagined Red Menace provoked an ugly backlash in Detroit. The Book-Cadillac Hotel refused rooms to Communists and third-party politicians. The City Council banned the Communist Party newspaper, the *Daily Worker*, and warned over 100 ethnic halls and clubs they would lose their property-tax reduction if they rented space to "Communist-front" groups. Detroit's Police Chief, Harry Toy, issued hysterical warnings that "Soviet agents are coming into the U.S. disguised as Jewish rabbis."

The anti-Communist mania reached its peak when HUAC visited Detroit during the Korean war. Against the backdrop of American troops fighting the Chinese and North Korean Communists, a succession of spies and informers called by HUAC in February and March, 1952, named over 200 alleged Communists active in Detroit,

Above: During a key strike in the fall of 1954, the Square D Company denounced the United Electrical Workers (UE) as Communist dominated and called on police to protect 300 strikebreakers entering the plant. Though the left-leaning UE had previously been forced out of the CIO for refusing to purge alleged Communists from its leadership, local unions of the UAW–CIO, seeing the union-busting attack on UE as a precedent endangering them all, came to the beleaguered union's aid. That September, over a thousand UAW members massed at the company's gates to block the strikebreakers. After a series of violent confrontations, the strike was settled on compromise terms. A year later, Square D workers voted to switch from the UE to the UAW.

Inset: A leaflet calling for support of the Square D strikers.

many of them trade unionists. The names of the accused were immediately printed in the press, with predictable results: several were evicted from the city's public housing projects; a violinist for the Detroit Symphony who refused to cooperate with HUAC was expelled from the Musicians' Union and fired by the orchestra; teachers in Detroit's public schools and students at Wayne University were dismissed or suspended for alleged Communist ties.

The purges soon took a turn towards vigilantism. On March 3, sitdowns and walkouts by anti-Communist workers at Dodge Main and Chrysler's Mound Road engine plant forced several workers named by HUAC out of the

factories. Within a week of the HUAC hearings, the disturbances spread to a dozen plants, with 18 UAW members either fired by management or "run out" of their workplaces by angry coworkers.

The UAW, while condemning Communists in the union and barring them from elected office, opposed the "runouts" and filed grievances to restore discharged workers to their jobs. "We have no alternative under the union rules and the United States Constitution," said Zygunt Mizejeski, President of UAW Local 410 at Midland Steel. The real target in these Red Scares, the UAW argued, was not the handful of alleged Communist trade unionists named by Governor Sigler and HUAC, but the union movement itself.

There was ample evidence for the UAW's claim. In 1952, the National Industrial Conference Board explicitly advised managers that "even if you don't have a trained saboteur [in the workplace], industrial security can... help you rid your plant of agitators who

create labor unrest." HUAC was eager to help, providing data on over 60,000 people to inquiring employers between 1949 and 1959. At Ford, "industrial security" and the Red Scare were merged in the person of John Bugas, former director of the FBI's Detroit Bureau and, after World War II, head of Ford's Labor Relations department.

Backed by this combination of government authority, corporate power, and public hysteria, the Red Scare overwhelmed individual workers and entire unions.

The United Public Workers (UPW) was the Red Scare's principal victim in Detroit. This CIO-affiliated union had drawn the attention of news editors and city officials for at least two reasons. In 1946, workers in the city's Department of Public Works voted to keep the UPW as their collective-bargaining agent, defeating the AFL's bid to win recognition for its public-employee union. The following year, after passage of the

Taft-Hartley Act, the local UPW's top officers also refused to sign the non-Communist oaths favored by their federal and municipal employers.

In the supercharged atmosphere of the Red Scare, the daily press leapt on the UPW. What was, in fact, a left-liberal union with a handful of Communists in its ranks and leadership became, in the eyes of the media, a hotbed of treason. Even a UPW demonstration for higher wages, said the *Detroit News*, was actually a "Commie 'rehearsal'...aimed at familiarizing Commies themselves and their dupes with parts they will play on 'Take Over Day.'"

In 1950, the city's Loyalty Commission launched a frontal attack on the union by charging Thomas Coleman, a 50-year-old garbage collector, with disloyalty. Coleman's background hardly seemed subversive. A 32nd-degree Mason, the President of the NAACP's Romulus chapter, and the co-founder of the first black American Legion Post in Michigan, Coleman also had a son fighting in Korea. Yet, with no proof that Coleman had even contemplated illegal activity, the Loyalty Commission suspended him from his job. Coleman was unfit for employment, the Commissioners ruled, primarily because he had supported the Progressive Party in 1948.

Though Coleman was later reinstated, his union could not survive the drumbeat of constant accusation. Members either quit the union or were absorbed by AFL rivals, and by 1955, Detroit's UPW had been destroyed.

Communists in the labor movement would have had a tough time surviving the Red Scare even if their Party had been able to fall back on a mass base of support. By 1946, however, this was no longer even conceivable. Unlike its European counterparts, the Communist Party of the United States had only a small following in the industrial working class.

Ten years before, the Party had committed itself to a Popular Front with non-Communists in the hope of gaining a broader base among supporters of the New Deal. Communist membership grew slowly among workers as well as intellectuals, but many of these new adherents owed their primary loyalty to the New Deal or the new industrial unions of the CIO, not the Party. Individual Communists usually downplayed their Party membership, and while many won support as reformers and popular trade-union leaders, the Communist Party, as an organization, won little lasting support among workers.

Whatever following the Party could claim was also undermined by its erratic policy changes. Too often, these sudden shifts seemed motivated by a primary allegiance to the Soviet Union, as American Communists continually recast their Party line to conform to Soviet initiatives. Between 1939 and 1941, such parroting of Soviet foreign policy had American Communists first supporting, then opposing, and then once again supporting a military alliance against Nazi Germany. When the U.S. later entered World War II as an ally of the Soviets, the C.P. dropped its militant line and became a zealous supporter of any measure that maximized war production—with little apparent regard for the unequal sacrifices demanded of American workers. Ironically, this sometimes put the Communists in the CIO on the right wing of the American labor movement.

In Detroit, even the most patriotic UAW members could not match the Communist Party's war boosters, who

Above: Members registering to vote in union elections at UAW Local 900, Ford Lincoln, in 1947.

Inset: Walter Reuther and supporters celebrate his election as UAW President at the union's 1946 convention.

advocated incentive-pay plans to spur arms production for the American and Soviet armies. Most union activists opposed incentive pay as a speed-up scheme, under which management gave workers only a fraction of the income gained from higher production. As a result, the Communists' incentive-pay proposal was derisively shouted down by UAW and CIO convention delegates in 1943, and Communist-backed candidates for union office were defeated in Detroit's Chrysler and Packard plants.

After the war, the Communist Party shifted once again to a policy of trade union militancy. Its prestige among union activists, however, had been irreparably damaged by its wartime speed-up drive. Unlike European Communists, the American Party had no heroic legacy of underground resistance to fascism to fall back on. Post-war prosperity undermined the Party's renewed call for anti-capitalist politics, and the continuing decline of ethnic consciousness and associations eroded the Party's base among the foreign born. The Party's support for Stalin's authoritarian rule alienated some workers, particularly after Stalin installed a pro-Soviet regime in Poland. Nationalist sentiment in Detroit's enormous Polish-American community thereafter fueled the already intense anti-Communism ignited by the Red Scare.

Communists in the UAW were especially hard-pressed. In this case, they faced an opposition that was not hampered by the pro-business, "sell-out" image that characterized many anti-Communists.

Walter Reuther's anti-Communist caucus within the UAW, while often described as the right wing of the union, was actually a broad coalition of socialists, liberals, and members of the Association of Catholic Trade Unionists. Opposing this Reuther Caucus was a group led by George Addes, the union's popular Secretary Treasurer. Most of his followers were, like Addes himself, non-Communist, but the Addes Caucus did rely (with some misgivings) on Communist-Party backing in its frequent tussles with the Reuther coalition.

The factional fighting between these two groups, as it came to dominate the internal life of the UAW between 1944 and 1947, often centered on issues that had little to do with Communism or anti-Communism. Much of the infighting over staff appointments and leadership positions was shaped instead by long-standing personal ties and local issues. "You get in a factional fight," recalled Doug Fraser, a former member of the Addes Caucus, "and sometimes you wonder what the hell the differences are. It becomes personalities and loyalty.... That happened to me. With Dick Leonard, I left the Reuther Caucus because we thought we were getting the short end.... It wasn't philosophical or ideological or anything like that."

Underlying these personal battles, however, was the issue of Communist Party involvement in the union. For some members of the Reuther Caucus, this question of "Communist infiltration" was primarily a rhetorical weapon for defeating factional rivals: by charging that left-leaning opponents were "agents of Moscow," they could easily gain notoriety and a certain degree of support. But for many others in the Reuther Caucus, Communist activity in the union was a matter of legitimate concern. In the eyes of these Reutherites, Communists sought only to use the union as a weapon on behalf of Soviet and Communist Party initiatives.

The Addes Caucus responded by tarring its opponents as reactionary sellouts. Reuther, his opponents claimed in one rhetorical flourish, was simply "The Bosses' Boy," doing the bidding of anti-union employers by splitting the UAW. Such characterizations carried little weight among those who recalled the Addes Caucus' wartime record of shop-floor conservatism. Reuther, they recalled, had advocated greater militancy —not less—between 1944 and 1946. As Nat Ganley, a leading Communist in the UAW, later acknowledged, Reuther's wartime opposition to incentive pay had "won him a strong rank-and-file support within the UAW." The added prestige of leading the post-war GM strike made it possible for Reuther "to ride in as the great hero on the white horse," as Ganley put it, "leading the crusade of the downtrodden masses, which he did and did very successfully."

Reuther's militancy and high-profile leadership proved decisive. Less than two weeks after the end of the 1945-1946 GM strike, he won the UAW Presidency by defeating the pro-Addes incumbent, R.J. Thomas, in a closely fought convention battle. Over the next two years, Reuther's caucus consolidated its hold on the union, winning a series of elections that drove the Addes Caucus and its supporters from all but a handful of leadership positions.

Popular support for the Red hunt varied widely during and after these faction fights inside the UAW. In most cases, only a small minority of people participated in the violent "runouts" of Communist and other left-wing workers from Detroit's factories. A far larger proportion, however, endorsed the Red Scare at the polls. Detroit's voters, for example, supported the 1949 proposal for a municipal Loyalty Commission 264,000 to 78,000. But Red-baiting wasn't always successful. When Carl Stellato, President of UAW Local 600 at Ford Rouge, attempted to dismiss five local officers for refusing to sign non-Communist oaths, the membership reelected all five to their posts in 1951. Stellato, an anti-Communist and former Reuther supporter, abandoned the purge and later attacked Reuther for raising dues. In 1952, shortly after the HUAC hearings in Detroit, Reuther removed Stellato from office for failing to dismiss the five dissidents. When elections were held for new officers, Local 600's members reelected Stellato by a wide margin.

Within five years of this incident, the Red Scare was losing public support. U.S.-Soviet relations were improving, and right-wingers like Senator Joseph McCarthy, by accusing even President Eisenhower of "coddling Communists," finally alienated many conservatives. The Communist Party had also shriveled to a fraction of its former size as thousands of disillusioned members dropped out or were driven into political retirement by government repression. From its peak of roughly 80,000 members in the early 1940s, the Party's ranks had thinned to no more than 10,000 in 1957.

By then, the search for subversives had already scarred the labor movement. In 1949-1950, the CIO expelled eleven unions (including the UPW) whose officers refused to purge elected Communists from their leadership positions. Government prosecutions and membership raiding by other unions subsequently destroyed most of these maverick organizations. Thousands of trade unionists—Communists and non-Communists alike—were denied their civil liberties, fired from their jobs, or driven into early retirement because of their unpopular beliefs. In Detroit, the police Red Squad began collecting political files that eventually included 110,000 "suspected" subversives. Most had done little more than attend political meetings, sign a petition, or walk a picket line.

Thirty years after the Palmer Raids, dissent was once again "Un-American."

WAGE-EARNING WOMEN

Oh how I longed for a little money of my own! Just enough to meet a friend for lunch occasionally without having to appeal to Charley. But, alas, Charley was right. I had never earned a dollar in my life. . . . "You're a mother [said Charley]. That's your job. You don't have to earn money, too." It was all so beautifully simple! "Yes, boss," I murmured obediently, frankly relieved.

"The Sandwich Maker,"
Ladies Home Journal, *April, 1959*

These were, supposedly, the "real," deep-down longings of every woman in the 1950s: to quit her job if she had one, renounce career plans if she had any, and devote her every waking moment to children, home, and husband. There was no other "natural" activity for a woman to pursue.

Gone were the Rosie the Riveter images of women factory workers that prevailed during World War II. Gone also were the strong-willed and venturesome women featured in the film and magazine fiction of the previous decades. In 1939, the majority of heroines who appeared in publications like *Ladies Home Journal* were career

women; twenty years later, when writer Betty Friedan surveyed the fiction in these same magazines, she found only one heroine in 100 who even had a job.

The end of the war marked the turning point in this shifting image of American women. The preceding fifteen years of Depression and World War had put a tremendous strain on traditional family roles: perpetual uncertainty about the future discouraged early marriages and large families; mass unemployment hit men's occupations harder than women's; and wartime production drew women by the millions into previously all-male factory occupations.

For men who felt threatened by these multiple violations of traditional roles, the post-war economic boom buoyed their conviction they should now be the sole breadwinner. For women anxious to start a family, this same economic boom was occasion for a post-war "baby boom." And for many working-class couples, "the wife at home" became a mark of distinction, a measure of progress towards middle-class standards of security and childrearing.

An unrelenting barrage of advertisements, movies, TV shows, and magazine stories celebrated the virtues of these traditional family roles. Politics was "Really a Man's World" as one 1949 story reminded women. "Have Babies While You're Young," advised another. Women could hope for nothing better than "Careers At Home." "Should I Stop Work When We Marry?" asked the anguished heroine in one story. Of course, said doctors, psychologists, and many husbands. Otherwise, the working wife not only "wasted" the job a male breadwinner might need, but also violated her

femininity. "I Denied My Sex," one maverick heroine confessed in a 1954 *True Romance* story.

Despite the intensive campaign to shutter women inside their homes, a steadily growing proportion of women joined the paid labor force. In 1950, just five years after the post-war layoffs in the city's war industries, 29 percent of Detroit-area females 14 years or older worked for wages outside the home, slightly higher than the proportion of women wage earners in 1940. By the end of the 1950s, the proportion of women earning wages had climbed to 33 percent.

Many of these women worked in service-sector jobs and professions that paralleled their homemaker role as custodians to men and children. They were nurses, secretaries, hotel maids, housekeepers, waitresses, teachers, and laundry workers. They worked when they were young and single, when their

children had grown up and left home, or when they were divorced, widowed, or separated from husbands.

During the childrearing years, however, work outside the home was supposed to stop. Only the "bad" mother, it was argued, would "abandon" her children to become a wage earner.

Some working women rejected the burden of guilt these middle-class norms imposed. "I didn't feel bad, I felt mad," recalled Wanita Allen, a young black woman who hired into Ford's River Rouge foundry during World War II. Like most women war workers, she was laid off in 1945. And like many women who worked to support themselves and their families, Allen—a divorcee with a young daughter—jumped at the chance to rehire into Ford when post-war production of cars began.

"I felt mad because I knew they were lying.... You'd hardly ever find anybody [who was working] that would just neglect their children." She had little choice but to work in any case. It was either find a job, go on welfare, or "throw" herself on the mercies of the first available man. Ford, moreover, paid high wages. "After a taste of a decent job," recalled Allen, a former domestic servant, "to go back to housework [was] just almost impossible."

Sometimes, working in an all-male factory environment could be nearly as difficult. After Lavina Beber, mother of five, hired into Dodge Main in 1951, management put her in the previously all-male radiator department, where she worked as an assembler. Initially, as she remembered it, "the fellahs wouldn't even as much as say hello to me." But Beber found that women could hold their own in the plant and win the respect of their male co-workers. "I learned to build that radiator from the frame on up, and I'd go over and I'd tell the fellahs, 'hey, go take a smoke break.' And then on their breaks, they would come over and help me.... We worked together."

Most men and women, however, did not work together in Detroit's auto plants. As in the pre-war years, the majority of the 44,000 Detroit-area women working in the auto industry in 1950 labored in segregated departments off the main assembly line—in "female ghettoes" as Edie Van Horn described the electrical wiring room and the upholstery-sewing departments at Dodge Main. "We were paid less on comparable work than other jobs in the plant," remembered Van Horn, Chief

An unemployment office on East Jefferson Avenue in August of 1945—the month World War II ended. The women crowding into this office for benefits were among the 200,000 in the Detroit area who saw their wartime factory jobs eliminated in the closing months of the war. During 1945, women were cut from factory payrolls at twice the rate of men.

Preceding page: Women upholsterers at DeSoto, circa 1950.

Steward for 16 years after hiring into the wire room in 1946. "And we were on separate seniority lists. The whole struggle to wipe out separate seniority lists, we went through that in the wire room."

It was a slow, piecemeal struggle. In the late 1940s, women on sex-segregated jobs had seniority rights only for their particular job classification, so when the company periodically cut back production, women threatened with layoff had no way of "bumping" into the jobs of less-senior men. But by the mid-1950s, Dodge Local 3 had successfully pressured the company to widen bumping rights, moving first to department-wide, then to plant-wide, and finally to division-wide seniority.

In 1958, when Chrysler closed the electrical-wiring room at Dodge and transferred production to non-union contractors, the 1,000 women in that department had the right to bump, according to seniority, into jobs anywhere in the plant. Even so, the company sought to prevent such wholesale transfers by encouraging the women to sign voluntary layoff slips and wait until "jobs they could do" opened up. "We

Below: Picketing in Detroit during the 1947 phone strike.

Inset: At the time of the walkout, there were some 8,000 Detroit-area women working for the phone company.

knew that meant they'd never get back in," remembered Van Horn. "So the union fought that and...more than half [of the wire-room women] were able to transfer into the pressed steel department, the motor line, and final assembly, where women had never worked in large numbers before."

For most of these blue-collar women, the union was a welcome source of protection and support against the harsh conditions prevailing in Detroit's factories. For women in white-collar clerical and service jobs, on the other

hand, such pro-union sentiments were slow to develop.

At Michigan Bell, unions had little legitimacy before 1940. "The company had indoctrinated us," union activist Helen Berthelot later said of herself and the thousands of other women working for the phone company. " 'Nice girls' didn't belong to unions. We were afraid of them."

Working conditions were characterized by low wages and harsh supervision —operators could not talk to their co-workers, slouch in their chairs, or use anything but stock phrases in responding to customers. Despite this, women

Picketing during Michigan's first teacher strike—East Detroit, 1947.

operators balked at joining either the AFL or the CIO in the 1930s. After the Wagner Act forced Ma Bell to discontinue its company-controlled union in 1937, Detroit's phone workers wanted only to affiliate with the independent National Federation of Telephone Workers (NFTW).

Berthelot, a former officer in the company-sponsored union, later recollected a ten-year evolution from the passive lobbying of the NFTW to the active militancy of the union she helped build in Michigan. "Little by little, we began to realize that we were not getting the amount of money that we should be getting...and management wouldn't listen to us. Other unions were having contract negotiations. They were getting increases and we weren't."

In 1947, the mettle of these budding trade unionists was tested in a massive, nation-wide strike of phone workers. Some clerical workers and operators crossed the NFTW's picket lines in Michigan, but most women stuck with the union through 44 days of mass picketing, confrontations with the police, and company firings of 33 Michigan women—all eventually reinstated by union pressure.

"That is what built the union," Berthelot remembered. "We didn't get much of a wage increase, and we didn't get half the things we asked for, but we proved that we could go on strike, we could stay out on strike, we could

negotiate." Within two years, the NFTW would merge with the CIO's Telephone Workers' Organizing Committee and rechristen itself the Communications Workers of America (CWA).

Not every strike ended in victory, and not every working woman joined a union. Among those who did, few became leaders. Some who held back were the "nice girls" Helen Berthelot had once been herself. Others, "by the time they became active in the union, they were married and had children," she recalled. Since Michigan Bell did not provide maternity leave or childcare facilities, working mothers often dropped out of their jobs and the union simultaneously. Fran Smith, the most prominent exception to this rule, had time to serve as a local-union president in Detroit and a member of CWA's national Executive Board in Washington primarily because her husband—also a CWA activist—took a large share of the responsibility for raising their two daughters.

Most wives could not count on such support from their husbands. When these women re-entered the paid labor force, they had to take jobs they could easily leave and take up again between babies. Restaurants, offices, stores, hospitals, and wealthy households all relied on this constant turnover of underpaid women, and unions found it difficult to organize the small-scale

workplaces where many of these women worked.

In the winter of 1946–1947, a seven-week strike of 1,000 women and men in Detroit's biggest restaurant chains did win pay raises and higher minimum-wage levels. But the non-union "drive-in" restaurants opening in Detroit's outskirts paid their cooks and waitresses less than half the 60¢-an-hour the Hotel and Restaurant union had won in Detroit's downtown eateries.

Organizing the drive-ins proved to be more than the union movement could handle. When "carhops" and kitchen workers at Richard's Drive In, Greenfield and 8 Mile (site 70), struck for wage increases and union recognition in the summer of 1951, management had little trouble finding strikebreakers to replace them. When waitress-union leader Myra (Komaroff) Wolfgang surrounded the drive-in with upwards of 50 picketers, Richard's opened its windows to young "hot-rodders" and toughs it had previously turned away. When fights broke out on the picket line, the company won a court order limiting the number of pickets to 15.

The strike ended after five months when a Circuit Judge declared all picketing at the site illegal and jailed four union organizers for contempt of court. Among those sentenced to jail terms of 15 to 30 days were organizer Max Gazen, a former strike-kitchen chef during the UAW's 1937 sitdowns, and Pearl Craig, a carhop, mother of a four-year-old child, and picket-line captain for the fast-food workers. After the Richard's strike collapsed, all but a handful of the fast-food restaurants in Detroit remained non-union.

The more than 20,000 women working in Detroit-area schools in the 1950s also had no union contract. School Boards could hold teacher salaries well below blue-collar wages, could distribute promotions to favored friends, and could cram upwards of 50 students into each classroom. Effective opposition to these practices came only from the American Federation of Teachers. The Detroit Federation was not yet strong enough to win formal recognition or collective-bargaining rights, but it could mobilize a growing number of teachers to apply pressure on the city's School Board. Their first major success came in 1947, when a majority of the school system's 7,000 teachers voted their intention to strike over salaries. Stunned by the appearance of this budding trade unionism among white-collar professionals, the Board promptly granted long-awaited raises.

That same year in suburban East Detroit, teachers actually carried through on their strike threat when the School Board refused to bargain. After a three-week walkout, the city capitulated and agreed to raise salaries by $400 a year. To cap their victory in this first public-school strike in Michigan's history, the triumphant teachers successfully campaigned in the next election to replace two anti-union school-board members with union-endorsed candidates. Community support at the polls and on the picket lines didn't surprise union President Kathryn Rothenberger. "Most of [the town's] parents work in factories in Detroit. They know we've got to have money to live. The Board is just trying to protect the industries out here from higher taxes."

But what East Detroit's teachers won on the picket lines, they eventually lost in the state capitol. Following the successful strike, Michigan's legislature passed the Hutchinson Act, outlawing future public-employee strikes and requiring the immediate firing of any union supporter who honored a picket line. There were no provisions in the Act requiring public employers to negotiate with unions—or to even acknowledge their existence.

By law, by custom, and occasionally by force, women who worked for wages were expected to shun and avoid the labor movement. Working outside the home was either supposed to be a brief sojourn for single girls, or a way of temporarily supplementing the husband's earnings. Many male trade unionists also accepted these confining stereotypes, and concluded that women workers were "impossible" to organize. For all these reasons, only 9 percent of the Detroit-area women surveyed by the University of Michigan in 1959 belonged to a union. Among men, 47 percent identified themselves as union members.

The numbers would have been still more lopsided if it had not been for the crusading zeal of a few women trade unionists. For this activist minority, unions were a calling. "I was not a cog or a robot," remembered UAW Chief Steward Pat Sexton, who worked at Dodge Main for 3½ years on the upholstery trim line. "On the contrary, I had a purpose, a very human one at that." Mary Ellen Riordan, President of the Detroit Federation of Teachers at a time when the union had little legal backing, remembered finding that same sense of purpose in the Papal Encyclicals she studied at Marygrove College. "Rerum

Light assembly and inspection was the job "ghetto" where women factory workers most often were concentrated.

Novarum in particular talked about the dignity of people, the rights of human beings to the fruits of their own labor.... That impressed me just tremendously."

For Phoebe Nowaczewski, a mother of three and the first woman gear cutter trained at Chrysler, union activism sprang from down-to-earth considerations. "I got active because I figured, well, I have to work for a living, and I better start finding out what my rights are. So I started attending the union meetings.... I just sat in the back with my little ones." In Detroit's union halls, she was one of the few working mothers sitting anywhere. It did not take long for her to move to the front of the hall. In 1952, the 3800 men at Chrysler's gear and axle factory voted Nowaczewski—one of only 33 women working in the plant—onto UAW Local 961's Executive Board.

A local-union officer in one plant, a Chief Steward in another, a strike leader in a suburban school district, a union organizer in the phone company. Small beginnings. Yet these union women, as UAW activist Olga Madar observed years later, "were the first women's libbers in [post-war] Michigan."

TALE OF TWO UNIONS

Detroit in the post-war era was a union town. But it was also a town of two fundamentally different unions: the International Brotherhood of Teamsters and the United Auto Workers.

At the head of each were men who, on the surface, seemed to have much in common. Jimmy Hoffa, head of the Teamsters, and Walter Reuther, President of the UAW, both came from small-town rural backgrounds—Hoffa from Brazil, Indiana, and Reuther from Wheeling, West Virginia. Their childhood homes were both in coal-mining districts, and Hoffa's father, who died when Jimmy was seven, was a coal miner; Reuther's father was a beer-wagon driver.

In Detroit, both men played crucial roles in the rise of their respective unions. Both also displayed a singular militancy, with scars to prove it. Each had been severely beaten by police or company thugs during the tumultuous organizing drives of the 1930s, and both had bounced back, giving as much as they got until their unions prevailed.

Neither man smoked. Neither drank. Both immersed themselves in the organizational life of their unions, and their political skills won them a loyal, if not always unanimous following. In the opinion of many neutral observers, when it came to the tactical maneuvering of collective bargaining, each stood head and shoulders above the men they faced on the opposite side of the bargaining table.

As it happened, both Hoffa and Reuther also became intense anti-Communists.

But there were fundamental differences between them. Reuther and his brothers, Victor and Roy, were raised in the Socialist tradition of their father's Brewery Workers Union. Even as they joined the anti-Communist crusade in the post-war era, they continued to espouse a unique brand of "social unionism" that made the UAW a national symbol of progressive reform.

There was considerably less of this social activism in Hoffa's brand of bread-and-butter unionism. As head of both the Teamsters' Central States Drivers' Council and Detroit's Local 299, he played a crucial role in expelling left-wing leaders in 1941. He thereafter pursued a dual career as labor leader and businessman, a combination he saw no need to apologize for. "I find nothing wrong with a labor leader having a business," he told government investigators, even "in the same industry that that union has organized." It was, he claimed, the American Way.

Of the many social and political issues that set Reuther and Hoffa apart, none was more telling than their categorically different reactions to organized crime. While Reuther publicly and emphatically opposed the mob, Hoffa just as certainly worked with it.

In Detroit, organized crime was not an issue that Reuther, Hoffa, or any other trade-union leader could ignore. Indeed, the city was notorious for the pervasive influence and power of its gangs, whose profits in gambling and illegal booze grew to enormous proportions during Prohibition. Because of its easy access to Canada, where alcohol was legal, Detroit became a national port-of-entry for bootleg liquor between 1920 and 1933. After Prohibition's repeal, the city's gangs continued to ply the waters between Windsor and Detroit, smuggling people as well as narcotics across this hard-to-patrol border.

Such lucrative trade could hardly escape the notice of public officials. But rather than oppose the heavy trafficking in illegal goods, many politicians became willing partners in the city's crime syndicate—a fact brought out in stunning detail in 1941, when former mayor Richard Reading, Sheriff Wilcox, and Police Superintendent Fromm were convicted of taking bribes from gambling racketeers.

Many of the city's businessmen were also linked with the mob, none more so than Harry Bennett, the dominant executive in the Ford Motor Company between 1932 and 1945. Bennett's Service Department employed hundreds of gangsters as anti-union enforcers, many of them paroled directly from prison to the Ford payroll. Anthony D'Anna, a known mobster allied with the Licavoli gang, held the contract to haul away cars from the Ford Rouge plant. Chester LaMarr of the infamous Black Hand held a part interest in the food-catering concessions at the Rouge; both he and D'Anna also owned Ford dealerships.

Wherever there was money for the taking, gangsters inevitably sought a piece of the action. From their lucrative base in illegal rackets, many mobsters branched out into legitimate business, often beginning in trades closely

Detroit police attacking demonstrators in the early 1930s. Opposite page: A Michigan trucker, circa 1930.

"Only One Way to Survive"

"The police would beat your brains in for even talking union," Jimmy Hoffa later remembered. Employers "hired thugs who were out to get us. Brother, your life was in your hands every day. There was only one way to survive—fight back."

This was a world where politicians and police officials took bribes from illegal gambling rings, and where employers like Ford, Briggs, and Michigan Stove hired gangsters to terrorize union activists. Hoffa was not alone in concluding that legal and ethical norms counted less than raw power. He therefore felt justified employing whatever means he thought necessary to make the Teamsters, and himself, a force which people *had* to deal with.

associated with the transportation and consumption of bootleg liquor—including trucking, hotels, and restaurants. Control over trucking, in turn, made it possible to extort money from dozens of industries where small businessmen depended on motor freight. The repeal of Prohibition, by eliminating the market for bootleg liquor, forced Detroit's mobs still deeper into the economy in search of new "investment" opportunities. With the rise of Detroit's labor movement after 1937, many found what they were looking for in the profitable trade of union racketeering.

By taking control of a union, enterprising gangsters could embezzle dues, steal merchandise from the inside, sell "labor peace" to employers, and pad the union's payroll with gang members and relatives. In-plant gambling operations could be dramatically expanded. As a Committeeman or local officer, a

gang member could collect bets while he moved around the plant on union business. The same end could sometimes be achieved through a union official who wasn't a gang member. In return for contributions to his or her next union-election campaign, the officer could help place a gang-member in the maintenance department, providing him with the needed cover to move around the factory—collecting numbers slips, baseball and football bets, and horse wagers.

More often than not, company officials looked the other way. "If management knows that a gambling syndicate put up the campaign dough that elected 'Joe Dice' as UAW Building Chairman," reported one UAW investigator, "to management, all that was Okay—hunky dory." Even if they privately frowned on racketeering, managers knew full well "that the whole set-up of gambler plus union officer... would not get too nasty with management about shop grievances or speed-ups.''

Few of these ''Joe Dice'' rose very high in the UAW. A lot of autoworkers gambled on the job, but few were willing to tolerate an overly cozy relationship between their local union leadership and management. One notorious petty hood and gambling operator, Carl Bolton, did win election during World War II as Vice President of Ford Local 400, centered in the company's revitalized Highland Park plant. But in 1947 the local's Reuther Caucus dropped Bolton from their slate and forced him from office. When Bolton attempted a comeback the following year, he finished near the bottom of a 15-candidate list, polling only 360 votes in the entire plant.

It was a different matter in the Teamsters Union.

For one thing, truck drivers, unlike autoworkers, did not work together as a compact group. Long-distance drivers in particular were scattered along hundreds of miles of highway, allowing their union officers greater latitude in how they served—or abused—the membership.

Some over-the-road drivers also owned their own trucks, and a few eventually set up their own businesses, buying or leasing additional rigs and hiring a handful of drivers. Compared to the auto industry, class lines in a small-scale, competitive industry like trucking were more fluid and harder to define, and many drivers saw nothing wrong with a union leader dabbling in a little private enterprise on the side—just so he delivered on wages and benefits during negotiations.

A clever operator, backed by sufficient muscle, could sometimes exploit such wide-open standards of conduct and turn a Teamster local into a private racket. One such operator was William Bufalino, President of Teamster Local 985. Bufalino never worked a day as a jukebox service man before becoming President of the Teamsters' ''jukebox local.'' ''Before I was in the union,'' he later admitted to Congressional investigators, ''I was on the employers' side,'' working as both director and lawyer for Detroit's Wurlitzer distributor. Backed by mob money and supported by Hoffa, Bufalino went directly from the company's board room to the Presidency of Local 985 in 1947. Bar owners who did not do business with mob-owned jukebox companies thereafter found a Local 985 picket line blocking beer deliveries to their establishment. Holdouts were frequently bombed.

Hoffa was also adept at using his union position to further his private business deals. In 1949, he and fellow Teamster official Bert Brennan formed Test Fleet Incorporated, a truck-leasing company registered under their wives' names. Initially, they had no trucks to lease and no customers to rent them. But as head of Michigan's Teamsters, Hoffa solved both problems by intervening directly in a strike of owner-drivers against Commercial Carriers, a car-hauling firm with a terminal in Flint.

Gang leader Anthony D'Anna (right) giving testimony at the Kefauver Crime Committee's 1951 Detroit hearings on his business connections with the Ford Motor Company.

Fickle Friend

Union pickets from the AFL's Hotel and Restaurant workers, pictured here during a coffee break, counted on Teamster support during their 1946–1947 strike to raise cafeteria wages in Detroit from $24 to $27 a week. So long as the Teamsters refused to cross the waitresses' picket lines, cafeteria owners could not secure table linen, food, or bottled drinks. The strike appeared doomed, therefore, when Hoffa denounced the strikers' demands as "silly" and ordered his drivers to cross the picket lines. His sudden turnaround had two

probable motives: retaliation against Detroit-AFL leader Frank Martel, who had cancelled the charter of the Teamsters' gangster-ridden "jukebox" local, and possible collection of a payoff from the restaurant owners, who had hired former Teamster official and Hoffa-confidant John Curran as their "labor relations" counsel. After the Teamsters' bakery and laundry drivers defied Hoffa's order and refused to cross the picket lines, the restaurant owners gave in and met the strikers' demands.

DETROIT TIMES

Only Detroit Newspaper with All Three Major News Services—INS, AP and UP

2   Detroit 31, Mich., Wednesday, Jan. 22, 1947   5 Cents

Teamsters Bolt Strike in Restaurants

By ED BRAND

The powerful AFL Teamsters Union, backbone of the restaurant strike, has bolted the walkout and is ready to

The strike began when the company decided to replace the driver-owned trailers with its own rigs; the strike ended when Hoffa ordered the drivers to return to work on the company-owned trucks. Commercial Carriers subsequently rewarded the Teamster boss by loaning Test Fleet $50,000 and leasing its rigs from the Hoffa-owned company.

Similar deals followed in real estate, resort properties, race horses, and trucking companies. When Hoffa negotiated retirement plans, the pension funds set aside under joint union-management administration were sometimes loaned to mob-owned businesses, often with little or no collateral.

Many Teamster locals resisted such encroachments by organized crime. "I

belong to the old school of trade unionism," Isaac Litwak, founder and President of Teamster Local 285, once remarked. "I didn't make a profession out of it. I believed in working people.... We had a tough fight to keep the Mafia and the Purple Gangsters from taking over the union," he recalled. In the 1930s, when the laundry drivers represented by his local were first organized, "there was a price on my head. I had to sleep in different hotels to keep from getting killed." Despite the pervasive organized-crime presence in the laundry industry and two violent assaults on Litwak, the drivers' local remained clean.

In Hoffa's home Local 299, there were also drivers who challenged his

rule. In 1941, the CIO's Motor Transport and Allied Workers Union began to attract dissident support from Teamster carhaulers, sparking a violent raiding war between the two rival organizations. To protect their base, Teamster leaders cancelled all local elections. "If a notice were placed for an election," R.J. Bennett, a local official, acknowledged in private correspondence to national Teamster President Dan Tobin, "it would be a wide-open opportunity for some of our disgruntled members to cause us no end of trouble with this particular branch of the CIO."

But cancelling elections did not prevent the CIO from attracting dissident Teamsters. "The CIO had tougher guys than any of us expected," according to Dave Johnson, a Business Agent in Hoffa's Local 299. In the fall of 1941, CIO Flying Squadrons began to gain the upper hand in violent street confrontations with their Teamster opponents. "So," Johnson recalled, "Jimmy went to see Santo Perrone."

By Johnson's account, Hoffa enlisted Perrone—a gang leader who sold his strikebreaking "services" to employers —for the added muscle he needed to intimidate the CIO. Hoffa's negotiation of a sizeable wage increase for Teamster drivers also persuaded many dissidents to return to the fold, and by the end of the year, a bloodied CIO had abandoned its raiding campaign on Local 299.

Santo Perrone was no stranger to Walter Reuther and the UAW. But he was certainly no friend.

Perrone began his strikebreaking career in 1934 when, as a foundry worker at the Detroit–Michigan Stove Works on East Jefferson Avenue, he organized goon squads to help management break a strike. John Fry, President of Michigan Stove, rewarded Perrone by

Above: Jimmy Hoffa testifying before government investigators.
Right: Walter Reuther, arm in sling, recuperating from gunshot wounds in 1948.

Adversity made both men all the more popular with their rank-and-file constituencies. Reuther nearly lost his life in an assassination attempt by unknown gunmen. Hoffa, throughout his career, was subjected to continual investigations by state and federal authorities—some justified by his shady dealings, others amounting to little more than legal harassment. The rally-round-the-flag loyalty generated in both unions by these events was amplified by Hoffa's and Reuther's success in negotiating wage and benefit improvements for their memberships.

Changing the Guard

In the autumn of 1950, Michigan's Old Guard Democrats had little doubt they were witnessing a revolution.

"I have just watched Socialism take over the Democratic Party by Communist processes," announced Teamster attorney George Fitzgerald, referring to the Party's tumultuous Wayne County District Conventions. Delegate Nellie Riley was equally alarmed: "Socialists," she publicly warned, "are in complete charge of the Democratic Party machinery."

Rhetorical charges of left-wing subversion came naturally enough to conservatives like Fitzgerald and Riley. Yet exaggerations aside, most observers in 1950 agreed the state Democratic Party would never be the same again. In a bitter struggle for party control, the Old Guard had lost out to a new generation of leaders, and the most visible partners in the new ruling coalition were the Michigan CIO and its largest member union, the UAW.

This transformation of the Michigan Democratic Party was, in many respects, the mirror image of an equally decisive change in the state's Republican Party.

The longstanding Republican leader in Wayne County, AFL attorney Edward Barnard, had held onto power through the 1930s despite the desertion of AFL members to the New Deal Democrats. In 1940, Barnard was finally ousted by the "better element" Republicans, financed and led by Ford executives Harry Bennett and John Gillespie. That same year, one of the state's largest Chevrolet dealers, Arthur Summerfield, led an equally decisive take-over in the Genesee County Republican organization, centered in Flint.

As a result of these parallel events, the auto companies—which had only passively funded Republican candidates in the past—now actively controlled the Party's statewide organiza-

tion. Automobile dealers paid into a centralized campaign fund, with each expected to contribute in proportion to his sales volume. Money was supposed to come from the contributors' personal funds, but at least seven dealers were fined under the Federal Corrupt Practices Act for illegally taking the money from corporate cash. Their investment paid off handsomely. By 1942, Michigan's Republicans had captured the governorship and both U.S Senate seats.

The Democratic Party's Old Guard, led by conservative politicians from Detroit's Irish, Greek, and Italian communities, offered no effective counter to this Republican sweep. The CIO therefore resolved to take matters into its own hands by removing the Old Guard from power. "We are not accepting the Democratic Party in Michigan as it now is," explained the *CIO News* in March, 1948. "Our purpose in going into it is to line up with

setting him up in the trucking business and giving him generous contracts to haul metal scrap away from the plant. Perrone, in turn, was expected to keep Michigan Stove non-union.

His strongarm tactics thereafter kept the labor movement at bay. Only twice did union drives, both organized by the UAW, gain a foothold at Michigan Stove—and on both occasions, only because Perrone had been arrested for bootlegging and firearms violations. When he returned from jail in 1939 and 1944, beatings, bribes, and window smashings followed in short order, driving the UAW from the plant.

Michigan Stove's President, John Fry, was an influential man. In his dual role as Deputy Police Commissioner, he secured the parole which returned Perrone to Michigan Stove in 1939. As a close friend of Dean Robinson, President of Briggs Manufacturing, Fry also arranged in April, 1945, for Perrone's son-in-law, Carl Renda, to take over the scrap-hauling contract at the main Briggs plant on Mack Avenue (site 27a). Renda simply sub-contracted the work to the previous scrap-hauler, pocketing between $50,000 and $100,000 a year for

its liberal elements and remold the Party into a progressive force."

In alliance with reform Democrats and the Detroit Federation of Labor, the CIO's Political Action Committee encouraged hundreds of shop stewards to run for precinct office in the Party's District Conventions. They swamped the Old Guard's scattered candidates and gave the liberal coalition two-thirds of the delegates at the statewide convention in 1948. The new Democrats promptly endorsed a platform committed to taxing corporate profits, protecting civil rights, expanding public housing, and improving workmen's compensation beneifts. On this New Deal platform, former Detroit lawyer G. Mennen Williams won his first of six terms as Michigan's Governor.

The Old Guard was not content, however, to surrender control of the Party. Led by the Teamsters, they counterattacked in 1950 with hundreds of precinct candidates running on forged nomination petitions. Both the

Courts and the County Election Board claimed they had no power to invalidate the forged petitions, even those with names of voters who had died or left town years before. CIO organizers therefore took matters into their own hands, forming squads of "bouncers" to bar the fraudulent candidates from the Party's District Conventions. George Fitzgerald complained bitterly of "storm troopers guarding the doors and the Chairman presiding with a baseball bat," but when the Teamster candidates were invited to defend their nomination petitions, only a handful bothered. At the state convention that followed, nearly 500 of the 1200 delegates were CIO members.

Following this decisive battle, the Teamsters and the CIO moved in opposite political directions. On the national level, Hoffa led his union into a longterm alliance with the Republican Party—a move many Teamster locals in Michigan later repudiated by rejoining the Democrats. The CIO, in the

meantime, helped the revived Democratic Party capture every executive office in the state by 1954.

This Party was not, as many Republicans claimed, a Labor Party in disguise. CIO leaders like Gus Scholle, Roy Reuther, and Helen Berthelot were prominently involved in the Party, but the top leadership positions were held by a wealthy Ann Arbor businessman, Neil Staebler, and the heir to a shaving-cream fortune, Governor G. Mennen "Soapy" Williams. Democratic voting strength, however, was distinctly working class. Even when the Republicans, led by Presidential candidate Dwight Eisenhower, swept the national elections of 1952 with 55 percent of the vote, 73 percent of autoworkers polled in Detroit supported Adlai Stevenson, the Democratic Party's candidate; 85 percent voted Williams into a third term. Among black and Polish–American autoworkers, Party support was even higher, with more than 90 percent backing Democratic candidates.

his "services." "While it is not proved by judicially admissible evidence," the Crime Committee of the U.S. Senate concluded in 1951, "the inference is inescapable that what Renda, the entirely unequipped college student, was being paid for was the services of his father-in-law, the muscle-man, Santo Perrone."

Judicially admissible or not, the evidence bore the stamp of Perrone's handiwork. In the 14 months immediately following the Company's new contract with Renda, four officers of UAW Local 212 in the Briggs plant were savagely beaten. One, Genora Dollinger, was attacked by assailants who broke into her house and brutally clubbed her in the face as she lay in bed.

Ken Morris was attacked in 1946 after returning home from work and parking his automobile. "I was winding up the car window," he later remembered, "and someone came up behind me and blackjacked me, cracking open my skull. I remember being carried in a stretcher ...and my wife crying and saying to a policeman she had just come to Detroit as my bride.... The policeman advised her, 'Little girl, you better go back to Nebraska. This is a rough war.' "

It was a war the UAW would eventually win. Far from collapsing, Local 212 elected Morris its President the following year. But even as Local 212 parried these attacks, unknown gunmen set their sights on the union's top leaders. On April 20, 1948, a shotgun blast ripped through the window of Walter Reuther's Detroit home, catching Reuther at point-blank range and nearly severing his right arm. Thirteen months later, a second shotgun attack caught Victor Reuther in his home, tearing open his chest and destroying his right eye.

The police never solved these near-fatal assaults on the Reuthers and the officers of Local 212. Many UAW leaders felt they knew why. "We believe that law enforcement agencies were not really interested in solving these crimes," Emil Mazey, Secretary Treasurer of the UAW, later testified in government hearings. "They were paid off by the organized rackets."

Mazey's claims were not without evidence. The police did manage to "lose" the lead pipe and hat found at the scene of Ken Morris's beating, and the principal detective investigating the shooting of Victor Reuther, Albert DeLamielleure, was later convicted of owning an illegal interest in the Perrone gang's hangout on East Jefferson Avenue. The police "disciplined" the officer by cutting his annual pay $355.

The Perrone connection in all these assaults was apparently proven in 1953 when gang member Joseph Ritchie, in sworn testimony taken by Wayne County's Prosecuting Attorney, said he and two other Perrone henchmen shot the Reuthers. Unfortunately, Ritchie escaped from the Statler Hotel where police were holding him, fled to Canada, and recanted his testimony. The police made no effort to extradite him.

The Reuthers survived their war with organized crime. Jimmy Hoffa, in his dealings with the mob, did not fare so well. In 1975, after serving four years in prison for jury tampering and defrauding the union's pension funds, Hoffa was kidnapped and murdered by the Tony Provenzano mob of New Jersey. By most accounts, Hoffa was killed because he planned to turn against Provenzano and the other gangsters he helped entrench in the Teamsters.

Hoffa's union had long since become an outcast in the labor movement. In 1957, the very year that Hoffa became national President of the Teamsters, the newly reunited AFL and CIO expelled the gangster-ridden union from their ranks.

Mob influence in the AFL, centered primarily in the Teamsters and the east-coast Longshoremen's union, had been a major stumbling block in the Federation's post-war efforts to reunite with the CIO. The first step towards merger had been taken in 1953 when the two organizations signed a no-raiding pact. But CIO leaders needed assurance that a merged AFL–CIO would not include the mob influence evident in several of the AFL's major unions.

AFL President George Meany, by expelling the east-coast Longshoremen in 1953, removed at least one such barrier to merger. The CIO (headed by Walter Reuther after the death of Phil Murray in 1952) had already expelled eleven left-wing unions from its ranks, reassuring the AFL's conservative leaders on that score. Since most AFL affiliates had long since abandoned opposition to industrial unionism, merger negotiations proceeded on the national level without major difficulty, culminating in the formation of a united AFL–CIO in December, 1955. State bodies of the AFL and CIO were given two years to merge their local operations.

The new organization's most pressing task was deciding what to do about the Teamsters, particularly after the U.S. Senate began investigating the union's criminal ties in 1957. The AFL–CIO's

Ethical Practices Committee ordered member unions to give the Senate's McClellan Committee their full cooperation, but Hoffa's predecessor, Teamster President Dave Beck, took the Fifth Amendment 140 times. Hoffa was arrested during the hearings for allegedly bribing a federal attorney. Indictments immediately followed charging him with perjury and illegally wiretapping his Business Agents' phones.

"The International Brotherhood of Teamsters," the AFL–CIO sadly announced in the fall of 1957, "has been and continues to be dominated or substantially influenced by corrupt influences." Hoffa in particular had "associated with, sponsored, and promoted the interests of notorious racketeers." That December, the AFL–CIO's national convention delegates voted five to one to expel Hoffa's union.

Unable to block the expulsion on the national level, Hoffa managed to delay the verdict in Michigan, where the Teamster-dominated AFL refused to merge with the Michigan CIO. AFL–CIO President Meany finally broke the logjam in February, 1958, dissolving the Michigan AFL and chartering the newly organized Michigan AFL–CIO.

Twenty-two years after the AFL expelled John L. Lewis and the fledgling CIO, the labor movement had been reunited. The product of that reunion, the Michigan AFL–CIO, was now an undeniable force in the state's economy and society, possessing financial, political, and membership resources unimaginable a quarter century before. Much had been gained since 1936.

Yet much had also been lost. Even with the expulsion of the Teamsters, the labor movement's image nationally and in Michigan had been irreparably damaged by the spectacle of labor racketeering. Even acknowledging that the overwhelming majority of union leaders and staff were honest and devoted, it was also apparent that upscale salaries and expense accounts were moving some top leaders into an income bracket and life style that blunted the movement's crusading zeal.

This growing complacency was especially evident when it came to race relations. Even though the AFL–CIO represented the most racially integrated organizations in America, it was apparent that integration had only gone so far in most unions. Discrimination prevailed in most workplaces, and with it, the living and working conditions of black Americans were growing relatively worse, not better.

IV: Black Detroit

Detroit, 1963.

Crossing The Color Line

Detroit had long been a beacon of opportunity for the migrant workers of Europe and North America. It was no different for the thousands of black Americans migrating to the Motor City in the 1940s and 1950s.

Among them was Robert Spearman, a young carpenter from Monticello, Georgia. When he left behind the poverty and racism of his hometown in 1943, there was little doubt which route he would take to a better life. "I was making about 15 cents an hour [in Monticello]," Spearman recalled, "and I knew I could do better than that in the North. When I got here," he remembered of his first years in Detroit, "I made ten times that."

In 1955, Willie Stamps made the same trek north from his home near Jackson, Mississippi. The 15-year-old Stamps already felt, as he later put it, "a need to explore, to getting some answers to

why...we were living in a situation where I saw double standards." When his questioning ended in confrontation with Mississippi school authorities, his family decided to send him north. "My father sat me down and said, 'for what you want to do and how you want to live, you're not going to be able to do it here.' So I took off." After joining relatives in Detroit, Stamps graduated from high school the following year.

Spearman and Stamps were among the three million southern blacks who migrated north between 1940 and 1960. They left behind a region where mechanization of agriculture was undermining black employment, and where segregation was stifling black initiative. The North, in contrast, seemed to promise everything the South lacked—jobs, decent pay, hope for a better life. As thousands of these migrants made their way to Detroit, the city's black population swelled from 150,000 to nearly

500,000.

"The only thing I came for was a dream," recalled Barbara Henningberg, an underpaid domestic servant from Atlanta. "That's all people were looking for."

Henningberg's family found "a little piece" of that dream in Detroit. But they also found a city where blacks were still barred from all but a handful of neighborhoods. They found a city where established political leaders were determined to preserve the "color line" between the races. And they found a city where liberal, pro-CIO candidates had failed to unseat that political establishment in the elections of 1937, 1943, and 1945.

Now, in the middle and late 1940s, thousands of newly arrived black migrants squeezed into Detroit's segregated neighborhoods, filling the dilapidated ghetto homes to the bursting point. Acute overcrowding in these already depressed areas caused a steady decline in living conditions. And that deterioration, as it reached crisis proportions, sparked yet another confrontation between the city's political establishment and CIO unions. The outcome of this political battle would shape the future of Detroit and its labor movement for years to come.

The focal point of controversy was the city's worst slum district, the lower East Side. For nearly a century, the homes and shacks in this area immediately east of the downtown had provided the first available homes for Germans, Poles, Russian Jews, Italians, and southern blacks arriving in Detroit. As the gateway to the city for each successive group, it came closest to being a melting pot of races and ethnic cultures, with each new group pressing in upon the previous arrivals, hastening the migration of the older, more established groups to outlying neighborhoods.

After 1917, however, the East Side gateway swung partially closed. Most of the city's new arrivals were black migrants from the South, and many whites in surrounding neighborhoods sought, for the next 30 years, to contain these newcomers within the East Side's "black areas."

Living conditions in the tightly compressed lower East Side had never been comfortable, particularly in the Black Bottom district closest to downtown (site 71). But during and after World War II, as thousands of impoverished jobseekers from the South crowded into its rickety wooden structures, the area deteriorated all the more rapidly. Over half the buildings had been built before 1900, and since many had no indoor plumbing, the residents had to rely on some 3,500 outdoor latrines, all little more than a stone's throw from the downtown business center. By 1945, only 8 percent of Black Bottom's residents lived in their own homes; 92 percent were renters, and 90 percent were black.

The city's political establishment, backed by private investors and downtown employers, agreed with the city's reform organizations, public-housing advocates, and CIO unions that Black Bottom's aging structures had to be torn down. But they agreed on little else.

Real-estate developers and downtown businesses wanted urban renewal, but they did not want the New-Deal formula of replacing slum housing with public housing. Businessmen wanted to encourage higher income residents to live near the downtown's department stores, restaurants, and clothiers, and public-housing tenants were not the sort of clientele they had in mind. Under the "Detroit Plan" proposed by business interests in 1946, the city would buy up and demolish the slum property in Black Bottom—but rather than build public housing, the vacant land would be sold at well below cost to private real-estate developers. The Detroit Plan's backers predicted that, with taxpayers subsidizing 75 percent of the expenses for clearing the site, developers could profitably build low- and moderate-cost housing without the "socialistic" involvement of the Public Housing Department. But how much of this new housing would go to former residents was not clearly spelled out when the city began condemning slum property in 1947 and 1948.

These initial moves were therefore opposed by the Wayne County CIO, taxpayer groups, and prominent members of the City Council, all of whom condemned the Detroit Plan as a self-serving scheme to bilk taxpayers and subsidize the profits of private developers. Rather than squelch public housing, the Detroit Housing Commission submitted an alternative proposal for building 12 new public projects, 4 in slum areas like Black Bottom, and 8 others on vacant lots in outlying neighborhoods. By dispersing public housing across Detroit, the Commission's plan promised to counter the concentration and segregation of the poor in the inner city.

During the next three years, the legal and political battle over Black Bottom simmered. In 1949, City Council President (and one-time UAW organizer) George Edwards ran for Mayor against former Burroughs executive Albert Cobo, a chief architect of the Detroit Plan during his tenure as City Treasurer. Backed by the Wayne County CIO, Edwards charged that Cobo's recent investment in a new business venture, the Cobo Realty Company, gave ample grounds for questioning the overall motives behind the Detroit Plan. "Is this the reason," he asked in his campaign literature, "why Cobo opposes a federal Housing Program?"

A majority of Detroit's voters were more concerned that Edwards, as a liberal promoter of public housing, would be a liberal promoter of racial integration. White homeowners, including many CIO members, voted heavily for Cobo on election day, particularly in the outlying wards on the Northeast and Northwest sides where Cobo defeated Edwards by 96,000 votes—accounting for 90 percent of his winning margin city wide. The CIO candidate won heavily in the lower East Side wards, and nowhere else.

For the fourth time since 1937, a CIO candidate for Mayor had challenged the city's established political structure and lost. And for the third time in a row, the

Slum backyard with outdoor latrine on Clinton Street, Detroit's lower East Side.

The Herman Gardens public housing project on Detroit's West Side was one of several rushed to completion during World War II. New Deal planners hoped to improve and expand the city's public housing program after the war, but funding was redirected to favor private real-estate developers.

issue of racial integration undercut CIO voting strength.

This string of defeats in Detroit's Mayoralty elections contrasted sharply with the outcome of state and national elections, in which Detroit's workers voted heavily for CIO-backed candidates. "We are not as bad off in any other election as in this one as far as issues are concerned," observed one CIO campaigner after the Edwards defeat. "The state issues and national issues"—unemployment insurance, workmen's compensation, full employment—"are tied up more in the shop." It was a different matter during municipal campaigns, when issues of housing, neighborhood integration, and police conduct dominated political debate. "They told me the union is OK in the shop," another Edwards campaigner said of the pro-Cobo union stewards in his plant, "but when they buy a home, they forget about it.... As long as they think their property is going down, it is different."

The political support these white workers gave Cobo and the Detroit Plan was legally buttressed three years later, when Michigan's Supreme Court ruled that cities could sell land to private developers at subsidized rates. Following this ruling, the Wayne County Circuit Court dismissed the CIO's legal challenge of the Detroit Plan. With this go-ahead, Cobo's bulldozers demolished 700 buildings in the heart of Black Bottom, displacing nearly 2,000 black families in the process.

But when the city invited bids on the cleared land in 1953, no buyers stepped forward. Private developers considered the site too expensive for low- and moderate-cost housing, and too close to black neighborhoods to attract upper-income whites. For the next five years, the land lay vacant and unused, earning the dubious title of Ragweed Acres. Finally, a non-profit corporation launched by the UAW and backed by corporate donations built the first housing in this "Lafayette Park" project. When the first apartments opened in 1958, rents were four to ten times higher than what the original residents of the area had paid.

After the bulldozing of Black Bottom, the same pattern was repeated throughout the aging core area of the city. New highways, new industrial parks, and new medical centers followed in rapid succession, with most projects built on land previously occupied by low- and moderately priced housing. Urban renewal, under Cobo, became little more than "Negro removal." Detroit's expanding black population had to double-up in the remaining slum areas or push into nearby neighborhoods.

When Andrea Ford's family drove from Florida to Detroit in 1955, the only affordable shelter they could find was her grandmother's apartment on Leland Street, immediately north of Ragweed Acres. Five relatives and two boarders already lived in the six-room flat. "With our arrival," Ford later recalled, "the total number of occupants reached 13. But somehow, room was made for us. At night, every couch in the house was used as a bed, and cots were set up in the living room."

Many of those living outside the lower East Side fared little better, especially the black families living near Eight Mile Road in "temporary" shelters built for war workers. "We lived in a Quonset Hut," remembered Luther Campbell. "One hut, two families. There was just a cardboard wall separating the two. You could hear the people crunching their bread next door."

Such extreme overcrowding could not be bottled up inside the "black areas" of the city. Something had to give, and ironically, the very color line that whites hoped Cobo would preserve with his anti-public-housing policies, was breached instead by the Mayor's demolition crews. As Cobo's bulldozers pushed poorer blacks into surrounding black neighborhoods, higher-income blacks, in turn, pushed into nearby white areas.

For these black homebuyers, it was not an easy migration. "First you had to find a house that whites would let you buy," recalled Quintus Greene, a black realtor. "Then you had to finance it without the help of white bankers. Then sometimes you'd have to figure out how to protect a house after you'd moved in."

Despite assaults, window breakings, and cross burnings by white neighbors, the relentless pressure of Detroit's growing black population gradually broke down the barriers surrounding all-white neighborhoods. Many of Detroit's whites, unable to stem the black migration and unwilling to live with black neighbors, fled to the suburbs and redrew the color line at the city's borders.

As early as 1948, Dearborn's Mayor Orville Hubbard ran for reelection on a platform accusing the Hancock Insurance Company of "conspiring" to integrate the city. Hancock's planned rental housing project, Hubbard argued, would inevitably bring low-income blacks into Dearborn, which then had fewer than 50 non-white residents in a population of 50,000. Urged by handbills to "Keep the Negroes Out of Dearborn," voters defeated the Hancock plan in an advisory referendum and reelected Hubbard by a wide margin.

Other suburbs followed Dearborn's lead, excluding low-income apartment houses through carefully drawn zoning restrictions. Where these failed to keep out black homebuyers, violence was often the last resort. As late as 1967, an inter-racial couple moving into suburban Warren had their home showered with rocks and garbage by neighboring whites. (The 1980 Census counted only 297 blacks among Warren's 161,000 residents.)

Grosse Pointe's method for excluding "undesirables" focused nearly as much attention on foreign-born whites and their descendants as on blacks. Under a screening system exposed in 1960, realtors routinely hired private detectives to investigate prospective homebuyers and determine whether they were "swarthy" or spoke with a foreign accent. The racial, religious, and occupational background of each buyer was investigated, with the aim, realtors explained, of "preserving neighborhood values" and excluding "cliquish or clannish groups unlikely to absorb local customs." Prospective homebuyers were then graded by an elaborate "point system." To win the broker's recommendation, Jewish homebuyers needed a rating of 85 points or better to overcome the anti-Semitic "neighborhood values" of Grosse Pointe. Italians had to score 65 and Poles 50. Blacks and Orientals were barred altogether. In 1967, when the Interfaith Committee for Open Housing was organized in Grosse Pointe—with the wife of a UAW officer as President—only two black families (not counting live-in servants) were known to live in the five Grosse Pointe communities.

The segregation of these and other suburban neighborhoods meant, in turn, the segregation of many suburban workplaces. Of 2,400 employees at GM's Fisher Body plant in Livonia, there were

Below: Lafayette Park under construction.

Inset: Left to right, U.S. Senator (and former member of the Steamfitters Union) Pat McNamara, Governor G. Mennen Williams, UAW President Walter Reuther, and L.M. Weir, head of the Carpenters Union District Council, at the 1956 groundbreaking for Lafayette Park's first apartment building. When private real estate developers proved unwilling to back new construction in the urban renewal area, the labor movement helped form a non-profit corporation to build cooperative housing.

Drivers block a bus during a transit strike. While united in this job action, most of the workers pictured here would afterwards return to racially segregated neighborhoods.

only 20 black workers in the early 1960s. Only six blacks could be found among the 4,000 workers at GM's Technical Center in Warren. In the aging Detroit plants of Briggs and Chrysler, on the other hand, black workers made up 15–20 percent of the workforce.

Detroit was becoming a black city, and its union movement, like everything else in town, reflected this momentous shift in contrasting and sometimes contradictory ways.

At the Briggs plant on Mack Avenue (site 27), blacks and whites worked together in virtually every department after World War II—but at lunch or shift break, the whites-only bars and restaurants around the plant enforced a rigid segregation.

At nearby Hudson Motors, blacks and whites picketed together in November, 1948, to protest management's disciplinary action against a black woman—but at the local union's Halloween dance the previous month, black members were denied entry when a local-union officer called the police to "keep the niggers out."

The UAW officially condemned such segregated social events, and prohibited any local from participating in the whites-only American Bowling Congress. But even when local unions sponsored integrated teams, Detroit's Bowling Proprietors' Association barred blacks from most of the city's alleys.

"We believe it is necessary," announced Olga Madar, head of the UAW Recreation Department, "for some group to take the lead in conducting democratic bowling competition." In January, 1948, the union therefore launched its own International Bowling Championships, to be held at Herbert Fenton's Dexter Recreation Center.

Some UAW locals also took aggressive measures to extend equal rights beyond the plant gates. "We cannot effectively unite our members inside the plant," the Fair Employment Practices Committee of Briggs Local 212 declared during 1947, "and permit bigoted, narrow-minded, cockroach businessmen to flagrantly practice discrimination right outside the plant." Integrated committees of union activists visited restaurants near the factory, requesting and, where necessary, demanding service for black members. Where owners refused, the local first condemned the holdouts in its newspaper, and then brought court suits against several for violating the Michigan Civil Rights law.

Occasionally, a symbolic gesture could bring the races together. When black workers in Dodge Local 3 complained in 1945 that the annual dance featured only polka music for Polish members, the UAW's Consultant on Minority Affairs, George Crockett, suggested an unusual solution. "I called in the local leadership," Crockett later recalled, "and I told them, 'Get a larger hall, hire two bands, one at one end

playing polkas, and alternate the music. See how it works.' Well they did, and they had the best dance they'd ever had."

Usually it was not so easy. At Great Lakes Steel in Ecorse (site 31), the first black upgraded to crane operator in 1944 was greeted by a wildcat "hate strike" of white workers. In 1952, when Frank Levand won promotion to switchman in the previously all-white transportation department, white workers wildcatted again.

Only a relative handful of whites participated in this second walkout, thanks to the persistent efforts of United Steel Workers Local 1299. In the intervening eight years, the union had hammered away at the color line in the plant, pushing for integrated locker rooms and non-discriminatory upgrading into all departments. When Charles Younglove won the local-union Presidency after World War II, his slate also included Mike Brown, the first black elected full-time grievance man in Local 1299—with most of his votes coming from white workers.

In steel, auto, and dozens of other industries, winning white support for desegregation took years of determined, sometimes solitary organizing. In the late 1940s, Olga Zenchuk, Secretary Treasurer of Detroit's United Packinghouse Workers, began a one-woman picket of segregated restaurants near one meat-packing plant. Only three other whites, as she recollected, joined the protest. "I made up the slogans: 'They (blacks) Fought In The War But They Can't Eat Here,' and black people would join the picket line.

"But most of the whites would say to me, 'You're not going to get elected anymore because of what you did there.' And I said, 'Well, that's OK.... I think this is the right thing, that blacks and whites should be able to go into this restaurant.'

"And I kept getting elected, regardless, by a pretty good majority."

By the early 1950s, most factory workers saw workplace integration as either morally right or just plain inevitable. In either case, whites usually accepted black co-workers in the plant. Residential integration, however, was another matter. "Negroes shouldn't be held down," said one white Detroiter polled in 1951. "They should have equal opportunities and...as we become better educated we will have less prejudice. And we should have less. But I don't want to live next to them. Isn't that funny, after all I've said?"

Such attitudes were not uncommon. Of 600 Detroit-area residents interviewed that same year, 56 percent of the whites polled called for racially segregated neighborhoods, but only 2 percent expressed a desire for workplace segregation. The leading role taken by Detroit's unions in desegregating the city's factories alienated some white members, but most continued to back the union movement: of those polled in 1951, only 10 percent gave unions a negative rating, while 42 percent described them as "very good"—a ratio that climbed to 53 percent among blacks.

Yet however great the strides made on behalf of workplace integration, an enormous gulf still separated the races in many industries, particularly those with craft unions or no unions at all. In the city's downtown office buildings, black janitors cleaned the floors and emptied the trash, while managerial positions remained whites-only preserves. Black laborers did the heavy lifting and carrying on construction sites, but the skilled electricians and plumbers remained (with a handful of exceptions) all whites. Black workers labored in the sweltering heat of Detroit's industrial laundries, but management wanted no black laundry-truck drivers—white housewives, the companies argued, would not open the door to a black man making deliveries.

The same argument prevailed at Michigan Bell. "The company would say," as union activist Al Verhaeghe remembered, " 'We can't send a black man into a woman's house to install a phone.' So it [the company] was, I got to say, 99 percent white."

The advances made by blacks in Detroit's manufacturing plants were the exception rather than the rule in the 1940s. Even here, many of those advances would be checked and slowed by the sudden wave of plant closings sweeping Detroit after 1954.

The recession beginning in that year marked the beginning of the end for all of Detroit's independent automakers. As late as 1950, the largest of these companies, Packard and Hudson, together employed over 40,000 workers in their East Side plants (sites 14 and 30). But their modest sales and slim profits thereafter declined as the "Big Three"— GM, Ford, and Chrysler—poured billions of dollars into TV advertising and annual styling changes.

Unable to match these huge expen-

In 1952, Sam's Cut Rate department store was the downtown's first major retailer to integrate its sales staff. Occupying the old Detroit Opera House on lower Woodward, Sam's was distinguished from its competitors by its decidedly blue-collar clientele and its collective bargaining agreement with the Amalgamated Clothing Workers. Kern's and Hudson's, in contrast, resisted unionization. The Clothing Workers persuaded management at Sam's to make Joel Mays, a maintenance worker and union steward at the store, the downtown's first black salesman. (All three stores have since been closed, and all but Hudson's demolished.)

Supporting the Southern struggle: The Trade Union Leadership Council sent regular shipments of food to help sustain the Southern civil rights movement. Among those loading this particular shipment in front of TULC's Freedom House are John Conyers, Sr. and Buddy Battle, second and third from the left.

Detroit also sent organizers to support the Southern campaign. Among them were two white Detroiters who paid dearly for their commitment to civil rights: Walter Bergman, a teacher-union activist nearly beaten to death while trying to desegregate bus travel, and Viola Liuzzo, the wife of a Michigan Teamster official, who was murdered in Alabama by the Ku Klux Klan.

ditures, both Packard and Hudson closed in the wake of the 1954 recession. Hudson merged with Nash to become American Motors, closing its Detroit plants and moving to Kenosha, Wisconsin. Packard merged with Studebaker and moved to Indiana before folding in 1963.

Many of Detroit's supplier firms collapsed as well, swelling the city's unemployment and welfare roles still further. Motor Products closed its Mack Avenue plant in 1956, leaving 4,300 workers permanently laid off. Murray Body, once a major supplier of car bodies to Ford and Chrysler, closed its plant (site 29) the same year, idling 5,000 more UAW members. Both Ford and Chrysler were beginning to make all of their automobile bodies "in house," forcing suppliers like Murray Body and Motor Products to either close their plants or, like Briggs Manufacturing in 1953, sell their assets to Chrysler.

"From the standpoint of job security for Briggs workers, the Chrysler purchase was the best thing that could happen," said UAW Local 212 at the time

of the buyout. The union's early enthusiasm for the deal was soon tempered, however, as Chrysler, like Ford and GM, replaced many of its workers with automated machinery. Employment steadily declined in the former Briggs stamping plant on Mack Avenue, especially after Chrysler opened a new facility in Twinsburg, Ohio.

The new Ohio plant was, as the union saw it, an ominous move. Such "decentralization" of production could only partially be explained, according to the union, by the desire to build more efficient and modern plants closer to regional market areas. "In addition," concluded the *Voice of Local 212* in 1956, "it is clear that a major aim of these moves is to undermine the strength and militancy of the large pioneer local unions such as Local 212 UAW."

Whatever the motive, the Big Three's decentralization stategy did, in fact, cut heavily into UAW membership in Detroit's biggest and most militant factory locals. And many of these locals were in factories where blacks had made

their greatest strides in employment and upgrading. In 1941, Ford's giant Rouge complex in Dearborn employed 85,000 workers—nearly 15,000 of them blacks—making steel, glass, paint, tires, and finished cars. By 1957, after Ford automated many of its operations and moved others to places as close as Livonia and as far away as New York, the Rouge's workforce had fallen below 40,000.

Some Detroit industries disappeared altogether. By 1950, all but a handful of cigar manufacturers had abandoned the city, moving to locations in Ohio and the South where they were closer to the tobacco harvest—and further from Detroit's unions.

It was a fateful trend for the city's black population. For decades, factory work had been the first step most immigrant workers took in their difficult climb out of Detroit's slums. Now, as companies automated, moved to rural locations, or simply went bankrupt, that "ladder" of upward mobility lost many of its rungs. According to most estimates, black unemployment in the Detroit area was at least double the

Supporting the Southern struggle: Detroiters picketed the city's Woolworth stores in the spring of 1963, urging customers to boycott the company until it desegregated its lunch counters in Alabama and elsewhere.

average for whites in every recession of the 1950s. Over the same decade, the income gap between the races also widened dramatically. In 1950, according to the Detroit Commission on Community Relations, the median income of the city's black families averaged 76 percent of white income; by 1960, it had fallen to only 52 percent.

For everyone except Detroit's black community, the stagnating economy of the inner city was not a priority concern. Whites, after all, could move to the suburbs, and during the 1950s, over 350,000 did so. Many, including the white congregation of the North Woodward Avenue Congregational Church (site 72), left reluctantly. In 1952, when members first voted on whether to move the church-site to the suburbs, a slim majority (265-252) chose to stay in their racially changing neighborhood. But they soonafter changed their minds, and

in 1955, the congregation moved to a new church in suburban Southfield.

As the UAW's membership also shifted to the suburbs, the union lost none of its formal commitment to racial equality. But the campaign to desegregate the workplace faltered when it reached the most enduring color-line in the city's factories—the skilled trades. As late as 1960, Chrysler acknowledged that only 24 of its 7,400 skilled workers were black, and only one of its 350 apprentices. GM could identify only 67 black skilled tradesmen out of 11,000 in its Detroit plants. At Ford Rouge the figures were only somewhat better, with 250 skilled blacks in a workforce of 7,000 tradesmen.

Going slow on integration, as many whites now recommended, apparently meant going nowhere. "It is easy to be patient when you are not a Negro," declared Horace Sheffield, a Ford worker and UAW staff member, "for you are not suffering.... Patience

doesn't come so easily when you are at the bottom of the economic and social heap."

Sheffield's impatience was shared by millions of black people across the country, particularly after the Supreme Court ruled against racially segregated schools in 1954. Rosa Parks, the local Secretary of both the NAACP and the Brotherhood of Sleeping Car Porters in Montgomery, Alabama, was one of the first to take action. In December, 1955, she refused to move to the back of the bus when a white passenger demanded her seat. Her protest and subsequent arrest rallied Montgomery's black population behind a full-scale boycott of the city's bus system and downtown stores. One year later, the boycott, mounting public pressure, and the federal courts finally forced the city to abandon segregated bus seating.

The Montgomery victory galvanized a national movement. Following Parks' example, thousands of civil rights activists in the North and South launched boycotts, voter registration drives, court cases, Freedom Rides, sit-downs, sit-ins, and kneel-ins. The goals of these diverse strategies varied from case to case, but the overall aim was the same—to break down the discriminatory barriers that kept blacks in under-financed schools, dilapidated slum housing, and second-class public facilities.

When, in 1957, Rosa Parks and her family moved to Detroit to escape the repeated threats on her life, the city's black community had already joined the front ranks of this nationwide movement. Black Detroiters were well suited to this leadership role, for they had gained a degree of organizational power and experience in the city's union movement unmatched by any other urban concentration of blacks. The rights they had won on the job not only reinforced demands for full equality, but also strengthened the feelings of group pride essential to any mass movement. "In Detroit," as one black resident surveyed in the early 1950s put it, "I don't have to

Freedom's Beat

Even as Detroit's independent automakers closed their plants, the remaining factories of the Big Three—together with scores of supplier firms—provided the base for black America's largest concentration of industrial workers. In the three decades after World War II, that workforce not only produced one of the nation's most dynamic civil rights movements, but also a music as rollicking and distinctive as the Motor City itself.

John Lee Hooker, the Mississippi-born guitar player and blues singer, worked as a factory hand at both Ford and Chrysler before launching his recording career in 1948. A fellow bluesman, Bobo Jenkins, spent a quarter century of his life at Chrysler. Yusef Lateef, the internationally recognized jazz flutist and sax player, worked at Ford; so too did Earl Van Dyke, the jazz musician who later became the Motown Record Company's musical director. Motown's founder, Berry Gordy, Jr., worked at Ford's Wayne Assembly plant before embarking, in 1957, on the songwriting career that made Motown the national trend setter in Top 40 music.

For countless musicians who could not pay their bills on music alone, Detroit's auto plants were a meal ticket. "That's how the cats could make it," percussionist Roy Brooks later said of the 1950s jazz generation he admired as a teenager. "In the plants during the day to do music at night."

It was a jumping, fast-paced scene that drew these blue-collar musicians to Paradise Valley, the show-bar and vaudeville strip on the edge of the lower East Side slums. In the 1940s and 1950s, nightspots like Brown's Bar, the Valley Forest Club, and Club 606 (site 74), along with the Paradise Theater on Woodward (site 75) and the West Side's Blue Bird Inn, all drew a working class audience that made Detroit's music something special. "It was a remarkable sort of environment," recalled Pepper Adams, one of the many white musicians who came to Detroit to learn his craft. "The Blue Bird...was the kind of neighborhood club patronized largely by working people, with terrific jazz on a regular basis.... Many times you'd see the bar quite full of people, and at least half of them would have lunch pails in their hands."

John Lee Hooker.

'Uncle Tom' to white folks.''

The same generation of black leaders who had backed the CIO harnessed this race pride into a formidable new movement. "Having been union leaders for many years," Ford worker and local-union officer Robert "Buddy" Battle later put it, "we thought we had the know-how to change the situation. And after twenty years of existence, we didn't feel we had to wait any longer." In August, 1957, Battle and Horace Sheffield, both veteran union leaders in the foundry at Ford's Rouge plant, met with a dozen other black labor leaders, including Nelson Jack Edwards from Ford's Lincoln plant, Willie Baxter from the Amalgamated Clothing Workers, and Nadine Brown, labor correspondent for the *Detroit Courier*. Together, they formed the Trade Union Leadership Council (TULC).

"The labor movement is far in advance of the rest of the community in the fight against discrimination," TULC announced soon after its formation, "[but] there are still unions where the

"The music," according to Brooks, "developed out of those kind of people, the working class. It was a faster lifestyle than people had lived before, so the music became more like that."

Even national music trends gained something unique when handled by Detroit musicians. "Bebop," the musical seed planted by Charlie Parker and Dizzie Gillespie in the 1940s, produced a bumper crop of nationally known jazz artists in Detroit—including trumpeter Donald Byrd, drummer Elvin Jones, and guitarist Kenny Burrell, to name a few. Detroit's jazz reputation grew through the 1950s. "For a while," as jazz critic Kim Heron summed it up, "it seemed like you had to have a Detroiter or two in your band if you wanted to be taken seriously. Miles Davis had Paul Chambers. Horace Silver had Roy Brooks. John Coltrane had Elvin Jones. Charles Mingus had both Charles McPherson and Lonnie Hillyer."

Even if this jazz tradition had not made Detroit nationally known in the music world, Motown certainly would. From Diana Ross—who grew up in Detroit's Brewster Housing Project (site 66)—to Stevie Wonder and Smokey Robinson, Motown was black Detroit's cultural emblem in the 1960s. Steeped in romantic lyrics, gospel harmonies, and Afro-American rhythms, Motown's exuberant music and commercial success paralleled the heady political gains black Detroiters won in the opening years of that decade.

While the political and social undertones of Detroit life rarely found expression in the music's lyrics, the connection between the city's cultural and political ferment was always present. In the 1960s, Detroit had two Franklins: Aretha, the "Queen of Soul," who began her singing career in the choir of the New Bethel Baptist Church; and Reverend Clarence Franklin, her father, who played the leading role in organizing the city's mammoth civil rights march in 1963.

Above: Twenty years after Detroit's 1943 riot, 200,000 people marched down Woodward Avenue in July, 1963, protesting police violence in Birmingham, Alabama. In the rally that followed this "Walk To Freedom," Reverend Martin Luther King spoke of a dream—whites and blacks "walking together hand in hand, free at last, free at last." The following month, King's dream became the byword of the civil rights movement when he addressed another massive rally of 250,000 in Washington, D.C.

Within a year of these unprecedented demonstrations in Detroit and Washington, Congress would pass the Civil Rights Act of 1964 making discrimination illegal in hiring, promotions, and access to public places.

Inset: For these Detroit marchers, celebrating their "Walk To Freedom" meant listening to jazz at the Blue Bird Inn.

The old cliches, the syrupy sentiments are no longer saleable. The pious platitudes about patience and fortitude we leave to the Uncle Toms. . . . A man either has full equality or he doesn't—there is no satisfactory twilight zone between.

TULC Open Letter to George Meany,
The Vanguard, 1962.

fight is far from won, and some... where the fight has not even started." When TULC backed A. Philip Randolph, founder of the Brotherhood of Sleeping Car Porters, in demanding that AFL-CIO unions remove all color bars from their constitutions, President George Meany angrily denounced Randolph and TULC for "splitting" the labor movement. TULC coolly dismissed the charges, pointing out that neither the Jewish Labor Committee nor the Italian Chamber of Labor had been accused of splitting the labor movement, yet both "have been doing in their constituencies what the TULC shall do in its area of operation."

That included criticizing the UAW for failing to bring a sufficient number of blacks onto its staff or any blacks at all into top leadership positions. At the UAW's 1959 convention, Horace Sheffield drew attention to this lack of representation by nominating Willoughby Abner, a black UAW activist and TULC member from Chicago, for election to the UAW's 25-man Executive Board. Abner declined as planned, but the gesture had a lasting impact on the union's internal politics. As a prominent member of the UAW's pro-Reuther caucus, Sheffield's nomination speech for Abner raised issues largely ignored since the Addes-Thomas caucus first proposed a black Executive Board member in 1943. With this new impetus, it was only a matter of time before black autoworkers won leadership representation. In 1962, TULC's Nelson Jack Edwards had Walter Reuther's backing in his successful election campaign for a UAW Executive-Board seat.

By that year, TULC's membership had grown to 10,000, with prominent white supporters like Leonard Woodcock and UAW radio announcer Guy Nunn among its numbers. TULC launched a newspaper, *The Vanguard,* and began offering free classes in leadership training and job skills to hundreds of students in its new education center on Grand River. "Freedom House," as it was called (site 73), became the hub of

repeated campaigns to desegregate Detroit's breweries, construction trades, supermarkets, and racetracks.

Paralleling TULC's growth, hundreds of block clubs sprang up in Detroit's neighborhoods. Having gotten their start from the City Planning Commission's crime-prevention and neighborhood-preservation program, many of these clubs began challenging city officials over urban renewal policies, School Board decisions, and zoning requirements. The city tried to discourage this opposition by scuttling the program, but the genie was already out of the bottle. Block clubs and neighborhood councils, including homeowners of both races, became fixtures throughout Detroit.

Since many block-club members were blue-collar workers, they frequently defined their neighborhood problems directly in terms of their precarious job security. "One day you're working and the next you're not," as one West Side activist put it during the 1958 recession. "Most of the people around here are out of work. The rest are just waiting for it." With the recession taking its heaviest toll among autoworkers, Detroit's block clubs mounted a campaign to have Governor Williams declare a moratorium on home-mortgage payments for the unemployed.

It was the twin issues of crime and the police, however, that pushed both the block clubs and TULC to the center of Detroit's politics. Crushing poverty and permanently high levels of unemployment in Detroit's black neighborhoods generated a wave of assaults and robberies, most of them directed at blacks. (In one inner-city precinct, 78 percent of the offenders and 76 percent of the victims were black.) Yet in a city with a 25 percent minority population, 96 percent of the police officers were white. Some of these white patrolmen treated every black as a potential criminal, subject to arbitrary searches and, at the slightest provocation, violence.

The long-simmering resentment over police behavior rose to the boiling point in 1961. Following the curb-side murder of two nurses, Louis Miriani, Detroit's Mayor since Cobo's death in 1957, ordered a general "crackdown" on crime. Under the Mayor's order, police began massive dragnets in the city's black neighborhoods, sweeping up any "suspicious" looking people who happened to get in their way. In one five-day period, over 1,000 suspects were detained—most of them blacks. "Every

policeman with an axe to grind could bring anybody he wanted in," remembered Mackie Johnson, a black patrolman in the 13th precinct. "See, before, there was a certain restraint, you had to have a reason for arresting someone. But now, they [the police] were just turned loose.... Every black who had a tie or a suit on, who drove a big car or something like that—that would really set off a lot of racist police officers. He would be brought out, [put] against the wall, searched, then brought into the station. If his attitude was wrong, he might even stay a couple of days."

When Miriani refused to curb the police or even meet with black leaders, the die was cast for one of the major political upsets in Detroit's history. Opposing Miriani in the 1961 Mayoral election was Jerry Cavanagh, a little-known lawyer from the Irish-Catholic wing of the Democratic Party. Backed by TULC, neighborhood block clubs, the NAACP, municipal workers (particularly the firemen) and Detroit's black churches, Cavanagh had undeniable grass-roots support. But Miriani had the money and the near-unanimous backing of Detroit's businesses and unions—including the UAW.

After repeated disappointments in the mayoralty campaigns of 1937-1949, the UAW no longer wished to risk its political capital on long-shots, and Cavanagh was an obscure figure from an opposing wing of the Democratic Party. The UAW's political organizers worked hard for Miriani, but they could not overcome the deep-seated resentment many blacks felt towards the Mayor's divisive race-baiting.

"Miriani's record was so bad," George Crockett later recalled, "Negroes could not sit still for that.... It didn't mean they were falling out, for any future elections, with the UAW. It meant that, for this election, this was it." With 85 percent of the vote in Detroit's black precincts, Cavanagh won 56 percent of the city-wide total. TULC's slate of five city-council candidates—including block-club organizer Mel Ravitz and black lawyer William Patrick—were swept into office.

Ironically, one of Cavanaugh's first appointments made George Edwards, the CIO's mayoralty candidate of 1949, Commissioner of Police. "My job," recalled Edwards, who had served until then as a Michigan Supreme Court Justice, "was to teach the police they didn't have a constitutional right to beat up Negroes on arrest."

FREEDOM NOW!

Shortly before dawn on Sunday, July 23, 1967, Detroit's Vice Squad raided an illegal after-hours club on the corner of 12th Street and Clairmount (site 76). Having already crashed four such "blind pigs" that night, none of the arresting officers could have guessed this final raid would light the fuse on the most sustained and violent urban rebellion in modern American history.

Instead of the expected handful of late-night patrons, over 80 relatives and friends of two returned Vietnam veterans filled the club. The black celebrants protested the untimely arrival of the Vice Squad—whose ranks were predominantly white. As the police loaded their patrol cars with club patrons and pulled away from 12th Street, someone in the growing crowd of onlookers threw an empty bottle at a squad car.

Within three hours, the crowd had grown to 3,000, too large for the handful of police on the scene. A store window was broken, then another, and by 7 a.m., looting was in progress along 12th Street. At 8:30 a.m., a shoe store went up in flames; by mid-afternoon, rock-throwing crowds had forced Detroit's fire department to abandon a 100-square-block area on either side of 12th Street.

It would take over 10,000 state and federal troops and most of four days before the rioting was finally quelled. By the time the smoke cleared, 43 people were dead, another 347 were seriously injured, and over 7,000 were under arrest. Some 1,300 buildings lay in ruins.

January 7, 1967: The Moors, a black social group, holding their banquet at the Whittier Hotel. Many observers believed Detroit's black middle class was large enough and influential enough to discourage the mass rioting that plagued other major cities.

For many observers, the violence and fatal bloodshed of July, 1967, was all the more shocking for having happened in Detroit. As urban rioting had spread from Harlem, to Los Angeles, to Newark and dozens of other cities between 1964 and 1967, many saw Detroit as an oasis of relative calm.

"Of all the accomplishments in the recent history of the city," *Fortune* magazine commented during the boom year of 1965, "the most significant is the progress Detroit has made in race relations. The grim specter of the 1943 riots...has enabled the power structure to overcome tenacious prejudice and give the Negro community a role unparalleled in any major American city."

There was abundant and frequently cited evidence to back up this hopeful picture. By mid-decade, nearly 3,000 black students were enrolled at Wayne State University—more than the total black enrollment in the Big Ten and Ivy League combined. Detroit was the only city in the country with two black congressmen, and with blacks making up 40 percent of the city's population, the whole tenor of municipal politics was rapidly changing. In 1966, George Crockett, a black lawyer who had defended the civil rights of Communists

in the 1950s, overcame the racial slurs and Red-baiting directed at his candidacy and won election as Recorders Court Judge.

The visible progress made by these black politicians and professionals was matched, many believed, by the gains of black workers. Union wages and upgrading into higher-paid production jobs had made homeownership possible for 60 percent of Detroit's black families, and peaceful pressure, many hoped, would widen economic opportunities still further. In November, 1966, the Trade Union Leadership Council could look back over nine years of reform activity and see ample reason for hope. "While riots often attended the efforts in many cities to break the barriers of Race in the Building Trades," said TULC on the occasion of its annual Freedom Ball, "TULC was slowly but surely integrating the Trades in Detroit....

"Significantly," TULC said of this progress towards integration, "it was achieved without violence or open conflict."

When, just nine months later, street fighting and looting engulfed the

city, TULC, *Fortune* magazine, and many other commentators appeared to have been celebrating a mirage. Yet the progress they all saw in Detroit's race relations had been substantial: substantial enough, as it turned out, to generate the hope and expectation of full equality, but not substantial enough to satisfy those intense longings.

Even for the city's black elite, upward mobility bumped against the whites-only institutions of the power structure. Prominent whites were among the Detroit NAACP's 24,000 members, but blacks were conspicuously absent from the corporate boardrooms and private clubs where white businessmen planned the city's future. In 1967, posh watering holes like the Detroit Club still barred blacks, women, and Jews.

For poor and working-class blacks, the gains of the early 1960s seemed less tangible when set against the relative affluence of the surrounding society. Detroit's economy was booming in 1967, yet the inner city's declining manufacturing base left 11 percent of all black workers without jobs, more than triple the metro-area's white unemployment average of 3.2 percent. President Lyndon Johnson's War On Poverty promised to aid these longterm unemployed, but the money budgeted for welfare assistance fell far short of the inner city's needs. Of the 360,000 Detroiters living below the poverty line in 1967, only 70,000 actually received aid.

Unable to afford decent housing, the poor were packed into ghettos like the 12th Street area, where one-quarter of the housing was considered irreparably dilapidated. The population density along 12th Street was twice the city average, and so was the crime rate and the proportion of broken homes.

Getting an education was one route out of this economic purgatory. But even when black students surmounted the barriers of under-financed schools and impoverished households to get a diploma, they found their escape route partially blocked by racial discrimination. In 1967, a black high-school graduate in Detroit could expect to earn $1,600 less per year than his or her white counterpart. With a college degree, black Detroiters earned slightly less, on average, than whites with only a high school diploma. And many young blacks earned nothing at all — estimates of unemployment among blacks aged 25 or younger ranged between 30 and 40 percent in 1967.

Poverty and youthful unemployment were not exclusively black problems in

Detroit. Roughly 14 percent of the city's white families lived on less than $3,000 a year in 1967, well below the government-defined poverty level. But fully 34 percent, or one in three, of the city's black families lived below this poverty threshold. To many of these low-income Detroiters, the contrast between black poverty and white affluence must have seemed all the more extreme when watching TV images of white society—a world depicted in countless ads as brimming with late-model cars, lavishly furnished homes, and smartly dressed people.

Only a few blacks could buy into this world. For the great majority, access to the goods so highly prized by TV culture was more often a matter of installment buying, higher-than-average interest charges, and potential repossessions by furniture stores and appliance dealers—all reminders of how far blacks lagged behind the celebrated (and frequently exaggerated) affluence of whites.

Even cash itself was less valuable in Detroit's minority neighborhoods. Since fewer blacks owned cars, and public transportation to the suburbs was spotty at best, many black families had to shop at inner-city markets where price markups were as much as 50 percent higher than in the suburbs. In part, higher prices reflected the cost of doing a low-volume business with a high rate of shoplifting. But blatant price gouging also reflected the greed of some white storeowners, who simply exploited their "captive" shoppers. "Those who despised their Negro customers," the *Free Press* later commented, "showed it by the filth that lay in the grocery aisles, the sour smell of clotted milk and rotting meat that rose from their counter."

Faced with economic and social conditions like these, many blacks felt that winning equal access to lunch counters and bus seating was not enough. Even the political gains won after 1961 seemed inadequate. The Cavanagh administration did amend some of the city's Urban Renewal priorities to accommodate the black community—but the bulldozers kept rolling. Families forced out of Black Bottom in the 1950s again found themselves only one step ahead of the wrecking ball in the 1960s. Many were ordered to move out and make way for the Lodge Freeway, the Medical Center, Wayne State University, and other white-controlled institutions.

S ome refused to budge. When the city moved to evict families in the Hobart Street area, a near West Side neighborhood slated for university development (site 77), a group of families reoccupied their padlocked homes and defied the authorities. When the City turned off their water and removed the plumbing, the determined residents reinstalled the fixtures and turned the water back on themselves. Efforts to cut off electricity and gas were likewise foiled. In 1966, after police arrested two dozen protesters during one eviction-blocking confrontation, the city finally negotiated a compromise renewal plan with the West Central Organization, a coalition of 40 local community groups committed to self-determination for inner-city residents.

The white power structure, some blacks concluded, would only back off when confronted by its opposite: Black Power. In the eyes of younger blacks in particular, an integrated, reform-minded civil rights movement was no longer relevant. "We have got to do something else," the Rev. Albert Cleage Jr. declared in 1964. "We have got to mobilize the masses of Negro people into an independent political movement."

As Chairman of the Freedom Now Party, Cleage figured prominently in the rise of Black Power politics in Detroit. The belief that blacks should go it alone—a view long advocated in reli-

July 24, 1967: Looting on Harper Avenue at Seneca. Rising expectations, continued poverty, and racial discrimination ignited the violence in Detroit's slums.

Above: National Guardsmen on patrol near the Brewster housing project.

Inset: On this block, as on many others, arsonists firebombed the commercial strip and 25 m.p.h. winds carried the flames onto neighboring homes. Efforts by local residents to stem the fires with garden hoses proved futile.

gious terms by both Cleage and the Black Muslims—gained currency among a new generation of activists. The political writings of radical leaders like Stokely Carmichael and Malcolm X became popular. Some of the youthful rebels looked to Africa—even Cuba—for their political models, and many redefined themselves as Afro–Americans. The Rev. Cleage's Shrine of the Black Madonna, formed in

1954 as the nucleus of the Black Christian Nationalist Church, was only one of the many organizations that helped define this burgeoning black consciousness in the 1960s.

A half century before, the aspirations of Detroit's Poles for freedom, autonomy, and self-reliance had found expression in organizations like the Polish National Catholic Church. Most Poles had shunned this particular embodiment of

nationalist sentiment, fearing it would split the mother church and isolate Polish Catholics. In 1967, many blacks had a similar response to the separatist trend represented by the Reverend Cleage. "Cleage's view on whether blacks and whites could work together was diametrically in opposition to ours," recalled Horace Sheffield, Vice President of TULC. "He supported an all-black slate of candidates and, hell, we said, 'that's crazy.' We supported an integrated slate—we had a Polish candidate, we had a Jewish candidate. In that respect we were bound to be in conflict with Cleage."

But in 1964, TULC was also at war with itself. In the Congressional primary of that year, two black candidates, John Conyers Jr. and Richard Austin, fought for TULC support and split the organization. After Austin won the TULC endorsement, Nelson Jack Edwards and the UAW formed a rival group, the Metro Detroit Labor and Community Association (MDLCA). MDLCA later merged back into TULC, but for four years, the black labor movement in Detroit was bitterly divided.

This fragmentation of Detroit's black leadership was just one of many ingredients in 1967's recipe for disaster. Poverty-in-the-midst-of-plenty for blacks generally, high unemployment and restricted opportunities among black teens in particular, a "whites only" power structure impinging on the inner city, and the precedent-setting violence in other cities all contributed to the explosive situation.

A few individuals, notably George Edwards (who had resigned his post as Police Commissioner in 1963), warned that a single spark could ignite the volatile mixture. Few listened, and inevitably, the flinty underside of Detroit's police department touched off the explosion.

Despite the political changes in the city, the Police Department still reflected the values and racial attitudes of an older, whiter Detroit. In 1967, all but 214 of the city's 4,356 police officers were white, and many continued to behave as if nothing had happened since Miriani's defeat. In June, 1967, a young black Army veteran on a picnic with his wife was shot to death in Rouge Park by a white gang; his pregnant wife miscarried shortly after the murder. The police released all but one of the seven gang members involved. Blacks were incensed, charging that had the victims been white and the assailants black, there would have been a different outcome.

Just one month later, on July 23, the police Vice Squad made its ill-fated raid on one of 12th Street's after-hours clubs. In the pressure-cooker atmosphere of Detroit's inner city, the sparks from this minor confrontation ignited four days of unprecedented rioting.

Unlike 1943, the violence in July, 1967, was not a race riot. With few exceptions, there was no fighting between black and white citizens—in several sections of the city, whites even joined in the looting. The rioters were primarily poor people "shopping for free," as the saying went. Most were black and young, and according to subsequent surveys, 30 percent were unemployed. When these young men struck out in anger, they attacked the most available symbols of their frustration, pelting squad cars with stones and impetuously setting fire to grocery stores, appliance outlets, and loan offices. Wind-blown fires and fallen power lines killed at least four people. Police, National Guardsmen, and store owners killed all but a handful of the 39 others who died that week. Many of those killed were innocent bystanders felled by the panicked and random gunfire of the National Guard.

In the aftermath of the violence, the

While an Edison lineman repairs damaged power lines, his military escort watches for snipers. "What is probable," the U.S. Riot Commission later reported, "is that there was at least some sniping. What is certain is that the amount of sniping attributed to rioters . . . was highly exaggerated." In many cases, reported "sniper fire" actually originated from nearby police and Guard units.

Supporters of Alabama Governor George Wallace rallying at Detroit's Cobo Arena, October, 1968.

press labeled it all a senseless riot. Black militants, in contrast, called it a spontaneous uprising. There were elements of truth in both characterizations. There was also little doubt that the events of July, 1967, categorically changed Detroit.

Thousands of white families fled the city in the wake of the fighting. Some sold their homes at panic prices, while others simply shuttered their windows and walked away. By 1970, the forty-year decline in the city's white population had reached 670,000—the equivalent of a city the size of Milwaukee. Over 75 percent of the white population in metro Detroit lived in the suburbs, and the city they left behind was correspondingly drained of the commerce and cash that once supported many neighborhood businesses. Thousands of vacant storefronts dotted the city's landscape by the end of the decade, all stark reminders of this massive population shift.

Detroit's business and trade-union leaders searched for ways to stem the exodus and rebuild the city's economy.

The very day the rioting ended, a blue-ribbon panel, the New Detroit Committee, convened its first emergency meeting on the future of the city. "We're here because the white community has failed," observed Stanley Winkleman, President of Winkleman Stores. "We have a tremendous job to change attitudes and institutions. We must mobilize the resources of people." To that end, UAW President Walter Reuther, also a Committee member, promised that 600,000 union members would volunteer to help clean up the riot damage. "What we're talking about is facilitating peaceful social change," Reuther declared at one New Detroit meeting. "Only this way can we prevent violent social change."

GM, Ford, and Chrysler thereafter began special hiring programs in Detroit's inner city, eventually bringing some 10,000 new minority workers into the industry. But hiring was slow and the number of jobs was limited compared to the needs of the unemployed. The army of 600,000 union volunteers Reuther had promised to clean up the riot-torn city

never materialized. In the post-riot turmoil of 1967, Detroit's labor movement cancelled its Labor Day parade, ending a tradition revived in 1937. While many corporate executives committed themselves to New Detroit's revitalization campaign, their companies continued to abandon the city for suburban locales. Budd's automotive division and K–Mart both moved their headquarters from Detroit to suburban Troy after 1967. When the Michigan Automobile Club later moved its headquarters from downtown Detroit to suburban Dearborn, the city lost another 800 jobs.

As suburb and city became more economically and racially polarized, so too did the region's politics.

Thirty years before the 1967 riot, the explosive emergence of the CIO and the wartime hiring of blacks each produced a right-wing reaction. Now, in the late 1960s, whites who felt threatened by the rhetorical militancy of Black-Power advocates turned once again to right-wing political movements. The resentments that fueled this backlash focused on everything from the special hiring programs the auto industry launched in the inner city, to the "welfare cheats" and "looters" who allegedly won special favors from the government. As many whites saw it, blacks had only themselves to blame for their poverty—white immigrants had struggled out of the ghetto, "so why can't blacks?" Whites who held such views seldom acknowledged that racial discrimination was a barrier to black advancement, or that plant closings and the suburbanization of production had destroyed the job ladder out of the ghetto. Suburban whites knew only that their own taxes were too high, their own workday too long, and the return on both too meager.

In 1968, the Presidential campaign of Alabama's George Wallace galvanized their resentment. "Both national parties have kowtowed to every group of anarchists that have roamed the streets of Michigan," the pro-segregationist Governor announced to a packed house at Cobo Arena in October, 1968. "That day is over in our country!...Folks are sick and tired of the breakdown of law and order."

Backed by several maverick UAW locals in Flint and Livonia, Wallace's American Independent Party threatened to take 15 to 20 percent of Michigan's vote in the 1968 elections, insuring a Republican victory for Richard Nixon over Democrat Hubert Humphrey. Only a last-minute educational blitz by the UAW, the state AFL–CIO, and the Michigan Teamsters reduced the actual Wallace tally to 10 percent, allowing Humphrey to carry the state even as he lost nationally. "Once we got Wallace's anti-labor record known," UAW Executive Board member Doug Fraser commented after the election, "it turned out his support was a voice protest rather than a vote protest."

Voices of a far different sort were being heard on the other end of the union's political spectrum, particularly in those Detroit locals where black membership—boosted by the post-riot hiring programs of Chrysler—accounted for more than half the membership.

Conditions in these inner-city plants were generally regarded as the worst in the industry. As early as 1948, the half-century-old Dodge Main was declared a fire hazard. Twenty years later, each of the factory's two assembly lines was cranking out cars at a breakneck pace of 58 an hour, or nearly one car a minute. "Adding to the severity of conditions," claimed the *Inner City Voice*, a radical newspaper formed after the "Great

Rebellion," "are the white racist and bigoted foremen...snapping the whip over the backs of thousands of black workers." The UAW, as the *Voice* saw it, provided little solace—it was a "bogus bureaucracy" in the eyes of its editors, "unable...and in many cases unwilling to press the demands of black workers." Accordingly, they urged black workers to bypass the union and "strike and negotiate at the gates of industry."

In the spring of 1968, these were not idle words. That May, 4,000 Dodge Main workers—whites as well as blacks—walked off the job without the UAW's strike authorization. Out of that unexpected, largely unplanned protest over working conditions, activists associated with the *Inner City Voice* forged a new organization—the Dodge Revolutionary Union Movement, or DRUM.

Drawing its support from young, radicalized black workers inside the plant, DRUM assailed Chrysler for "going into the ghetto for common labor while going to the suburbs for supervision and skilled workers." Roughly 60 percent of the factory's workforce was black, yet according to DRUM, 95 per-

cent of the foremen, 100 percent of the superintendents, and 90 percent of the skilled-trades positions were still held by whites. "Have you ever wondered why," DRUM asked of its members, "all of the easier jobs are held by whites? [And] whenever whites are on harder jobs they have helpers?" Even seniority, said DRUM, was a racist concept, "since black workers were systematically denied employment for years at this plant."

Calling on its supporters to "damn the grievance procedure," DRUM organized a second wildcat of black workers in July, followed by demonstrations against Chrysler and the UAW that built DRUM's reputation citywide. "RUMs" soon began appearing in other workplaces: at Cadillac (CADRUM), United Parcel Service (UPRUM), and the Detroit News (NEWRUM), among others. Some of these groups were small and ineffectual, but the Eldon Avenue Revolutionary Union Movement (ELRUM), centered in Chrysler's Eldon Avenue Gear and Axle plant (site 78), grew larger than DRUM. Large and small, they all came together in 1969 to form the League of Revolutionary Black Workers, an organization dedicated, in

Shop newsletters.

Anti-STRESS demonstrators, circa 1971, marching from Masonic Temple to Kennedy Square.

its own words, "to waging a relentless struggle against racism, capitalism, and imperialism."

The rhetoric blew hot and hard on both sides. Some UAW officials condemned DRUM as a "handful of black fascists" and "a sinister attempt to split Dodge workers." The League declared that blacks and whites were already divided—DRUM and ELRUM simply gave black workers a voice. But in the plants, the League's supporters frequently widened the rift between the races by labeling white opponents "Polish Pigs" and "Peckerwood Honkies." Equally scalding remarks were aimed at black UAW leaders and TULC members. Characterizing the black-run Local 961 at Eldon Avenue as "Uncle Tom's Cabin," ELRUM attacked President Elroy Richardson as a "lard-belly" and a sell-out—"a jive of-

ficial who ran under the slogan of 'Vote Black'... [but who] only functions in the corporation's interests."

Such invective appealed to many younger black workers, but for older blacks and most whites, the abusive language isolated the League from potential supporters. Despite the fact that blacks were a solid majority at both Dodge and Eldon Avenue, League candidates were unable to win more than 30–40 percent of the vote in a series of controversial local-union elections. When the League's declining fortunes led to internal faction fighting in 1971, the organization collapsed.

But even as their organizational existence came to an end, DRUM, ELRUM, and the League left a permanent imprint on Detroit's labor movement. "I was one who fought DRUM," recalled Joe Elliot, an officer of UAW

Dodge Local 3, "but they were sincere in their motives. They couldn't be bought. That's why I respected them." Because of League pressure, Chrysler hired more black foremen, the UAW hired more black staff, and the whole tenor of internal-union politics was transformed in many locals. By the early 1970s, UAW members in Chrysler's five East Side plants (Dodge, Plymouth, Chrysler, Eldon Avenue, and Mack Avenue) had elected black presidents, several of them prominent militants. Among these was Jordan Sims, a former union Committeeman at Eldon Avenue who led several wildcat strikes in 1970 over deteriorating safety conditions. Three years after being fired for his role in these strikes, Sims won election as President of Local 961.

During these same years, Detroit's racial and political polarization came to a head. The 1970s began with Detroit's police killing more civilians than any other police force in the nation—seven civilian deaths for every 1,000 police officers on the force in 1971; Houston was second with a rate of five per 1,000. The 100-man "STRESS" unit formed that year (STRESS stood for "Stop The Robberies, Enjoy Safe Streets") added 22 more civilians to the death toll—21 of them black—while conducting over 500 provocative and frequently illegal raids in black neighborhoods. Far from stopping crime, STRESS added to the growing violence. In 1973, the number of homicide victims in Detroit was three times higher than the death toll in Northern Ireland's civil war.

STRESS certainly had its supporters, especially among those whites who believed crime was simply a "black" phenomenon. In 1972, this constituency was large enough to make George Wallace the winner in Michigan's Democratic Party presidential primary.

The following year, it was Black Detroit's turn to flex its political muscle. Since 1971, the anti-STRESS campaign had brought together a unified and broad-based protest movement, marked by demonstrations, petition campaigns, and court suits. The anti-STRESS court suit was especially representative of the movement's emerging united front. Prepared by lawyers previously associated with the League of Revolutionary Black Workers, the suit was backed by the NAACP, UAW Local 600 (Ford Rouge), and AFSCME Local 26 (sanitation workers).

The mayoral election in November,

1973, finally decided the issue. The white candidate, police commissioner John Nichols, defended STRESS and promised to preserve the unit. The black candidate, State Senator Coleman Young, denounced STRESS and promised to abolish it. When Young narrowly defeated Nichols, STRESS's violent mandate came to an end. So too did decades of racial discrimination and anti-black violence in the city's police department.

The following year, the first black mayor in Detroit's history was inaugurated.

The Mayor Comes in From the Cold

Detroit's first black mayor spent most of his life on the outside looking in. At age 13 he could not accompany his Scout troop on the Bob Lo boat —even cruising the river was "whites-only" entertainment. Being a black worker and union supporter at Ford Rouge later meant frequent run-ins with the notorious Service Department —until Young was fired for reportedly decking one of Bennett's goons during an in-plant confrontation.

His stint in the armed forces during World War II also ended in controversy. In 1945, Young was one of 100 black Air Force officers jailed for entering and refusing to leave the whites-only officers club at Freeman Field in Indiana.

Out of the frying pan and into the fire, Young returned to Detroit and became an organizer for the ill-fated United Public Workers, soon to be destroyed in the Red-scare. Elected Director of Organization for the Wayne County CIO Council in 1947, he was immediately embroiled in the faction fighting then coming to a head in the UAW and CIO. Young was backed by the UAW's Addes–Thomas caucus, and as that wing of the union went down to defeat in 1947–1948, he and Council President Tracy Doll were ousted from their posts by the Reuther-caucus slate of Mike Nowak and Al Barbour.

Five years later, Young's long association with civil rights and trade union organizing landed him in the hot seat before the House Un-American Activities Committee. Hounded by the FBI and his "subversive" reputation, he found it nearly impossible to get a decent job in these years.

Things began to turn around in the late 1950s when Gus Scholle, head of the Michigan AFL–CIO, hired Young onto the state federation's staff. But it was at the polls that Young won complete vindication, beginning with his election to the state Constitutional Convention in 1961 and the Michigan Senate in 1964.

Coleman Young, fourth from left, and John Conyers Jr., far right, in an early TULC demonstration.

PRIDE AGAINST PREJUDICE

Militancy, struggle, change— these were the bywords of Black Detroit after 1967. Even among those who rejected radical confrontation, "We Shall Overcome" was the favored hymn.

"I subscribe wholeheartedly to the rhetoric of black nationalism," said Marcellius Ivory in 1968, shortly after UAW convention delegates elected him the union's Regional Director of West Detroit and nearby suburbs. "I disagree with their conclusions. I don't believe in separatism. I don't believe in not voting.... [But] one of the things I give the Black Nationalists credit for is that they have awakened the Black Consciousness and created pride in Blackness."

After 1967, that black pride collided with a stubborn, institutionalized, and sometimes unconscious white prejudice. In dozens of Detroit industries, black job applicants found that despite the equal-opportunity provisions of the 1964 Civil Rights Act, whites still got a disproportionate share of the better jobs in higher paying industries. Yet many employers had repudiated, at least publicly, the discriminatory practices of

past generations. Where racial imbalance occurred, managers now insisted, it was only because "objective" hiring tests and "neutral" seniority agreements favored the more qualified and experienced whites.

In the late 1960s and early 1970s, such claims came under increasing attack in a wide range of companies. From the Association for the Betterment of Black Edison Employees, founded by laborers and janitors at Detroit Edison, to the Afro–American Association, formed by white-collar workers at the Automobile Club of Michigan, these groups vigorously challenged the notion that hiring exams and seniority provisions were "neutral" and color blind. How could they be, blacks argued, when centuries of racial discrimination gave whites an undeniable head start in education and job experience? Hiring exams and seniority simply institutionalized this past inequality, insuring that whites could still get first pick of jobs without using explicitly racist stereotypes.

Equal opportunity, according to civil rights advocates, could only be achieved when society took positive steps to

eradicate the legacy of past discrimination. In practice, this could only be achieved, they argued, by "affirmative action" programs to hire, train and promote minority workers. Once these programs put blacks on equal footing with whites, then—and only then—could seniority and hiring exams be considered fair.

Eradicating "institutional" racism, however, would prove to be a long, hard, and bitter campaign. "We were not a militant organization," remembered David Adams, a data processor for the Automobile Club and one-time Chairman of the Afro–American Association. "We met with management to give them recommendations on how they could improve things. Unfortunately, they didn't change anything." Having exhausted the options for voluntary change, Adams and 100 black co-workers sued the Automobile Club for denying them equal opportunity in promotions and pay. "The rest," said Adams of the 11-year court battle that finally ended in victory, "is history."

For **Willie Stamps**, a black janitor at Detroit Edison, history was also a slow-moving affair. Hired into the utility's Buildings and Properties Department, Stamps won election in 1968 as one of 28 Division Chairmen in Local 223 of the Utility Workers of America—making him the first black officer in the local's 30-year existence. Because, as he later put it, "we recognized that blacks constituted only two to three percent of the Edison workforce in a city which was approximately 50 percent black," Stamps and his supporters soon after formed the Association for the Betterment of Black Edison Employees (ABBEE). In 1969, they asked management to inaugurate an affirmative action plan of minority hiring.

The company flatly denied there was racial discrimination in its employment and promotion policies. Recently expanded hiring of blacks into clerical positions was sufficient evidence, Edison added, that race played no part in the company's employment decisions.

But Detroit's courts found otherwise when Stamps and the ABBEE brought a lawsuit against Edison in 1971. "It is the conclusion of the Court," wrote District Judge Damon Keith in 1973, "that the company is refusing to acknowledge the obvious." Noting that, in 1966, only 300 of Edison's 9,500 employees—and only 4 of its 1,700 managers and officials—were black, the Court ruled that the company's discrimination "has been deliberate and by design." With few exceptions, the Court found that Edison only hired blacks into "low-opportunity jobs such as...Building Cleaner, Janitor, Porter, Wall Washer, Elevator Operator, and Attendant," and that once trapped in these low-wage jobs, blacks were discouraged from transferring to better-paying departments by a web of discriminatory practices.

When, for example, openings for cable splicer, fireman, brickmason, and other skilled jobs in high-wage departments were announced, Edison initially notified only the junior employees already working in those particular departments. And since those departments were exclusively or predominantly white, so too were most of the applicants who sought promotions and training. The same network of inside references gave whites an advantage when they first applied for work at Edison. Over half the white workers interviewed by federal investigators said they had been steered to Edison by word-of-mouth referrals from friends and relatives already working for the company. In the meantime, Edison failed to list job openings with

the Michigan Employment Security Commission until required to do so by law in 1971.

Even when blacks knew of and applied for openings in high-wage jobs, they had to pass a battery of tests which were not, in the Court's view, "valid predictors of job performance." For those who passed this obstacle, personal interviews and unfavorable evaluations by white managers frequently ended their job search. The few who survived even this hurdle then confronted a bitter irony: to transfer from the top of a low-wage department like Buildings and Properties to the bottom of a high-wage department like Transmission or Maintenance, applicants usually had to accept a new "starting wage" that was lower than their previous rate. In addition, none of the seniority protection against layoffs they had accumulated in their

old job could be transferred to the new department. To venture a new career, Edison's blacks had to risk throwing away whatever wage increases and job security they had won in their old positions.

The evidence, concluded the Court, made it clear that "a substantial number of black employees held in low-opportunity jobs had qualifications ...superior to a substantial number of whites who had been selected for skilled trades jobs." Judge Keith therefore ordered Edison to increase minority hiring and promotions until 30 percent of the company's overall workforce, and 25 percent of its skilled trades, were minority workers. Though a subsequent Appeals-Court ruling in 1975 reduced the back-pay damages assessed by Detroit's District Court, Judge Keith's ruling was upheld in its basic conclu-

UAW skilled tradesman and apprentice.
Opposite: The Wall of Dignity, Saint Bernard's Church.

Among the 81 apprenticeship graduates (60 pictured here) who began their four-year training program with Electrical Workers Local 58 in 1975, 15 were minorities—nearly equal to the number called for under the affirmative action guidelines of the Detroit Plan. In Detroit's depressed economy, however, there was no guarantee they could find steady work.

sions and remedies.

The Court also found that Local 223 of the Utility Workers, together with Local 17 of the International Brotherhood of Electrical Workers (representing linemen), had "negotiated and acquiesced in procedures which lock blacks into low opportunity jobs." Both unions had therefore neglected their legal duty to fully represent all their members, though Local 17 had not, in the Court's view, "acted with the requisite malice of the Company or Local 223."

Local 223 was not the only union in Detroit that acquiesced in, or actively promoted, the discriminatory policies of employers. The Edison local simply did it more consistently and, after the ABBEE court suit, more publicly than most. According to court testimony, the union negotiated job-bidding procedures and seniority restrictions with the deliberate aim of deterring black promotion. As management then enforced these restrictions, white union officers discouraged black members from pressing grievances against the discriminatory results of such practices. The Utility Workers union did question Edison's use of testing procedures on union members as a whole, but Local 223 never questioned the blatantly discriminatory impact of these tests on *black* applicants for hiring and promotion.

Local 223, no less so than Detroit Edison, was under tremendous pressure to change after 1971. As the Court moved to implement its affirmative-

action ruling, the local's President, who cast the only vote on the union's national executive board opposing a Human Rights Committee, lost his post to more tolerant leadership. As the number of black Edison workers rose above 1,500 under the Court's affirmative-action order, the union also had to respond to the numbers—and the votes—of this growing black membership.

So too did the labor movement in general. Black workers were the fastest growing constituency in many Detroit unions, and in a significant number of autoworker and public-employee locals, they achieved majority status. The trend towards black leadership in such local unions eventually worked its way to the top of the city's labor movement. In 1968, Tom Turner, a former steelworker and the then-current President of the Detroit NAACP, became the first black President of Detroit's AFL–CIO.

With legal backing from the 1964 Civil Rights Act—and with prodding from militant groups like DRUM—Turner, Marcellius Ivory, and other black trade-union leaders pressured employers and the labor movement to widen access to skilled and better-paying jobs. The response was usually positive, though always slow moving. In time, union and management negotiators in the auto industry substantially overhauled their jointly run apprenticeship programs, reducing the number of tests and lowering the minimum cut-off scores for black *and* white applicants to the skilled trades. A 15-week remedial training program was also established for applicants of both races who failed the tests. And those who passed and

transferred to apprenticeship programs were guaranteed their pay would not be cut to entry-level wages.

In the construction industry, it took more than three years of negotiation before a comprehensive affirmative-action program—the Detroit Plan—was implemented in 1971. Since the construction industry was one of the few where craft unions, rather than employers, controlled access to basic skills and job opportunities, the Plan hinged upon the unions' pledge to expand their minority training and placement until each craft union had at least 15–20 percent minority membership.

Black trade-union leaders were generally pleased with the Plan's results, at least initially. "In the life of the Detroit Plan," recalled Tom Turner, "over 700 blacks, Latinos, and women got journeymen cards in the Building Trades unions. And the vast majority were able to get cards without going through the normal four-year apprenticeship program. That was a significant breakthrough."

But in this and other affirmative action plans, results varied widely by craft and by company. While the electricians' union made measurable strides in opening its ranks to minority workers, some crafts showed considerably less enthusiasm for the Detroit Plan's ambitious goals. By 1971, 25 percent of Chrysler's skilled-trades apprentices were minority workers, while at GM the proportion of minority apprentices rose to only 17 percent. A court suit against GM promised to force additional progress on the company, but the future of affirmative action dimmed appreciably in the mid-1970s when the federal government cut back its financial commitment to such legal challenges. Indeed, federal cutbacks in funding for affirmative action played a key role in undermining the Detroit Plan in 1975.

From its inception, however, the Plan was shadowed by an even more troublesome flaw. According to the terms of the Plan, affirmative action in the construction industry would be implemented only "when economic conditions permit." In the boom years of the early 1970s, this condition posed little immediate problem. But if history was any kind of guide, Detroit's economy would eventually slump into yet another recession, with layoffs and decreased job opportunities significantly narrowing the options for minority hiring. Then, and only then, would the durability of affirmative action be truly tested.

V: New Workers, New Work

Buick workers, Flint, Michigan.

BUCKING THE LINE

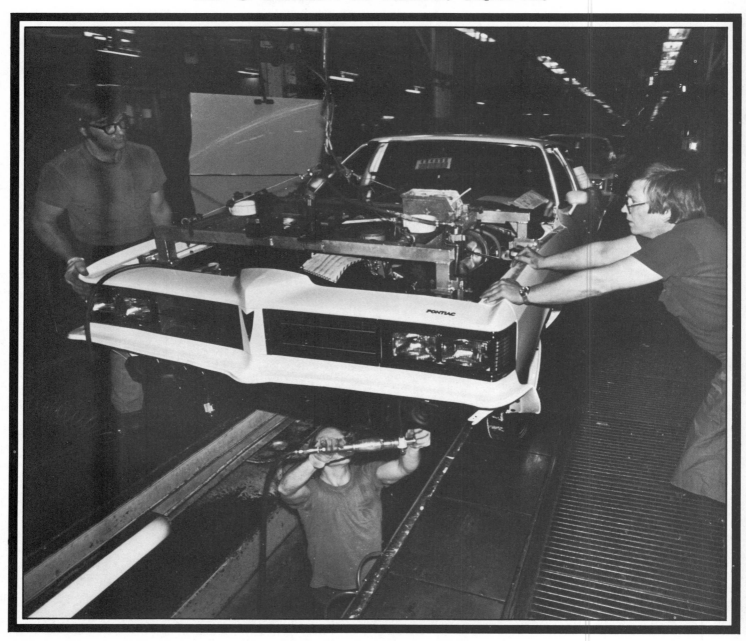

In matters of human relations, Detroit's factories had not changed much since Henry Ford's time.

Physically, the plants were more automated than in Ford's day, and, with mechanization, there were fewer "bull-work" jobs requiring continuous heavy lifting. But in terms of workplace organization, the same principles of top-down management prevailed in the 1960s and 1970s. Most jobs were still sub-divided and pigeon-holed into detailed, repetitive tasks requiring little or no training. Workers were still expected to follow orders and obey rules like soldiers in an industrial army.

Factory command structures remained as authoritarian as ever, but in the boom years after 1961, the industrial army working in the plants changed dramatically. The new recruits were younger than the workers they replaced, more educated, and less inclined—or as many managers saw it, less equipped—to tolerate the boot-camp regimen of factory life. "Nowadays," as Ford's Vice President of industrial relations, Malcolm Denise, remarked in 1969, "employees are less willing to put up with dirty and uncomfortable working conditions. [They are] less likely to accept the unvarying pace and functions on moving assembly lines.... Large numbers of those we hire find factory life so distasteful that they quit after only a brief exposure."

The shift in generational attitudes was no less evident to union leaders. "There is a new breed of worker in the plant," acknowledged UAW President Walter Reuther shortly before his death in a 1970 plane crash. "[He is] less willing to accept the discipline of the work place. He is unwilling to accept corporate decisions that pre-empt his own decisions....

"There is a different kind of worker than we had 25 or 35 years ago."

Thirty-five years before, workers had not been so tolerant of factory management either. In the 1930s, their generation had occupied factories, marched in labor demonstrations, and built the CIO into a mass movement of considerable daring and combativeness —experiences that were indelibly stamped in the memories of middle-aged Detroiters.

For members of this older generation, the social and political contours of blue-collar Detroit had thereafter remained relatively fixed. Their reference points included, with varying degrees of emphasis and credibility, the Great Depression, the Union, the Democratic Party, and the Job. For veteran union members, these events and institutions had enduring and supposedly self-evident meanings.

The Depression experience underscored the obvious value of a regular paycheck. Job security became a priority concern of older Detroiters, and the periodic and severe recessions of the 1950s only reinforced their commitment to secure employment. For most members of this generation, the Union and the Democratic Party were the only credible advocates of a full-employment economy. This remained true even if, as some complained, these two champions of the "workingman" had grown more cautious over time.

For the "baby-boom" generation born immediately after World War II, the world looked very different when they came of age in the 1960s. Unlike their parents, most of these younger workers did not have to face the prospect of long-term joblessness: the twelve-year boom in production and employment between 1961 and 1973, broken only by a mild recession in 1970, was one of the longest periods of economic growth in American history. In Michigan, the official unemployment rate fell from 10 percent in 1961 to 4 percent by 1966. Jobs were more plentiful than at any time since World War II.

Most new industrial recruits entered the plants with little or no experience of working in a non-union factory. They tended to take the union for granted; understandably, since membership was automatic for new hires and most companies deducted union dues from workers' paychecks. The Democratic Party had no automatic relevance for the young either. For that matter, after

1964, voters of all ages found fault with President Lyndon Johnson for doing too little—or too much—to subdue Vietnam, eliminate domestic poverty, and eradicate discrimination.

If the generational shift inside Detroit's factories had been a gradual changing of the guard, the discordant views of younger workers might have been moderated or rechanneled by the more numerous presence of older workers. But generational turnover occurred in a series of sudden shifts, set against a background of social crisis.

This rapid turnover resulted from two complementary factors. On the one hand, union-negotiated benefit plans provided strong incentives for older workers to retire after 1958, when special early-retirement benefits became available to Big-Three autoworkers. Over the next six years, the UAW won a $400-a-month early retirement program, full funding of medical insurance for retirees, and a near doubling in regular pension benefits. Thousands of older workers retired between 1958 and 1961, with expanded benefits for early retirement prompting another wave of departures in mid-decade.

Simultaneously, companies which had not hired new employees in the recession years 1958–1961 began hiring thousands

of new workers in the boom years after 1962. Many were young blacks, hired under federally sponsored "Plans For Progress" or through company-initiated, post-riot hiring programs. Many were young whites hiring into suburban plants and, less frequently, into inner-city factories. White or black, these younger workers were concentrated in less-skilled, entry-level jobs, often on the afternoon shifts that employers added after 1961. By 1968, half of the UAW's membership at Chrysler had less than five years' seniority.

Once inside the plant, these newcomers confronted a world where education and individual initiative, virtues younger workers had been told to value, counted for little. They faced, instead, the unrelenting tedium of factory labor: feeding materials into the same machine all day long; grinding the same small parts, one after another, for hours on end; bolting the same part on each car as it passed on the assembly line, 55–70 cars an hour—hour after hour after hour.

All the while, close at hand or just around the corner, was the ever-present foreman. As the "front line of management," foremen were usually older than the workers they supervised. Whatever their individual personality, they were still the enforcers of a potentially inflexible discipline. Workers risked immediate

Shift change at Chrysler's Jefferson Avenue plant, 1967. Shift change meant generational change in many plants: as these older men left the factory, a far younger workforce would replace them on the afternoon shift.

Opposite: Pontiac's final assembly line.

suspension or firing if they refused to obey orders, even when such orders violated the work rules negotiated by the union. It was "do it my way or hit the highway," and the only recognized recourse for countering such management authority was the grievance procedure—frequently effective, but often slow-moving.

Workers, like obedient children, were supposed to be seen and not heard. Most managers had little interest in consulting them about production problems or improving quality. Some supervisors were actually contemptuous of their blue-collar subordinates, while others, aware that hourly employees possessed a wealth of production knowledge, refused to tap this resource for fear it would undermine their role as "Boss."

Working under these conditions for eight hours a day was bad enough. But in the boom years of the 1960s and early 1970s, cost-conscious plant managers frequently forced workers to stay on the job for 10 or more hours a day, 6–7 days a week. Workers got premium pay for the additional hours, but the company still saved by avoiding added benefit and social-security costs for a new hire. For the worker on mandatory overtime, it meant that the world of the factory—with its clouds of welding gas and dust, its continuous clanging of metal on metal, its ever-present supervisors—became the dominant environment of their waking lives.

The response of autoworkers to that world was described by contemporary observers in varying terms: the blue-collar blues, worker alienation, the generation gap. Whatever the title, few doubted that factory workers in general, and Detroit's in particular, were becoming increasingly unhappy with their jobs. Even where workers expressed overall satisfaction, they generally applied this favorable description to their pay, their on-the-job friends, and the advantages of factory work compared to low-wage alternatives. The work itself, most agreed, was boring, exhausting, and frequently degrading, and the younger the worker or the more unskilled the job, the greater the dissatisfaction.

Researchers had found evidence of such negative feelings in the 1950s, particularly as Detroit's car companies automated many of the remaining non-assembly-line jobs in their foundries, engine plants, and metal-bending operations. As automated machines, conveyor lines, and self-loading processes were installed, the machine operators became machine watchers. Instead of pulling levers and hand-loading materials, they were reduced to gazing at lights and reading meters. Many welcomed the corresponding reduction in physical lifting and shoving of heavy metal parts, but engine-plant workers surveyed in the mid-1950s also complained that the fast-moving machines reduced their individual control over the work pace. The non-stop operations, by requiring unbroken concentration to monitor the machinery, created more stress and mental fatigue. Machine tenders reported that with fewer people required to operate the automated machinery, the work became more solitary. "There are not so many people around," said one engine-plant worker interviewed in Detroit in 1957. "That's why it is more boring and lonesome."

In the 1960s, the longer hours on the job and the shorter tempers of many jobholders produced a measurable jump

Above: Anti-war demonstrators in Detroit's Kennedy Square, November, 1971.
Inset: UAW Secretary-Treasurer Emil Mazey at the microphone.

War and Dissent

Students predominated in the demonstrations against U.S. military intervention in Vietnam, but opinion polls consistently found the greatest anti-war sentiment in blue-collar and low-income households. In 1968, when 57 percent of Dearborn's voters backed a referendum calling for withdrawal of U.S. troops, the heaviest anti-war vote came from those who did not have a college degree or earned less than $15,000 a year.

While the AFL–CIO backed the war effort, trade unionists led by UAW Secretary-Treasurer Emil Mazey publicly condemned it. The UAW's switch to an anti-war stand was a major reason the union left the AFL–CIO in 1968 and remained independent for the next 15 years.

in such expressions of worker dissatisfaction. Daily absenteeism in Detroit's factories doubled during the decade to 5 percent of the workforce, with as many as 20 percent skipping work in some plants on Mondays and Fridays. Growing numbers of these workers simply did not return to their jobs at all. Between 1960 and 1965, the auto industry had to hire upwards of 1.5 million persons to fill just 250,000 new jobs. Throughout the rest of the decade, the majority of unskilled new hires quit within one year.

The decade also saw a rising number of workers ensnared in the tight mesh of the factory's disciplinary code. Younger workers were more likely to talk back to their foremen, take a few extra minutes during their lunch break, or join in horse play around the job area. Drinking and drug abuse, each a form of in-plant absenteeism, both increased over the decade. And union-initiated grievances over health and safety, work assignments, discipline, and countless other issues all steadily multiplied, rising from 106,000 a year at GM in 1960, to 250,000 by 1969.

Of all the issues at stake in these frequent tangles with management, none was more important to blue-collar union members than workplace health and safety. They had ample cause for worry. In the 1960s, America's factories were becoming measurably and irrefutably more dangerous.

There was, most visibly, the 30 percent increase in reported workplace accidents between 1958 and 1970. By decade's end, 14,000 Americans were dying on the job each year, while another two million suffered disabling injuries. Workplace accidents felled more Americans every year than the war in Vietnam. More ominous still was the mounting toll taken by industrial diseases, the silent, usually unseen chemical and dust-born killers that struck an estimated 400,000 workers a year. According to the Public Health Service, these killers annually claimed upwards of 100,000 lives.

After decades of officially-celebrated improvement in industrial health and safety statistics, the "bad old days" of lethal hazards and maiming accidents were making a comeback. None of these hazards had entirely left the workplace, but the coincidence of several long- and short-term trends brought them back with a vengence in the 1960s.

At the most basic level, American industry was developing ever more powerful, numerous, and potentially dangerous machines. There were bigger stamping presses and boring mills to puncture and shape metal; bigger trucks, conveyors, and hoists to carry materials; faster printing presses to publish newspapers and books; and new machines producing everything from xerox copies to X-rays. Even as some of these innovations reduced the potentially dangerous lifting and pushing that plagued workers in older plants, others brought with them new or augmented hazards—including noise, vibration, heat, radiation, or the whirling clash of exposed parts.

Perhaps more dangerous than the new machines was the generation of industrial chemicals entering the workplace. Between 1958 and 1970, the number of solvents, acids, degreasers, oils, and other agents catalogued by *Chemical Sources* magazine soared from 17,000 to 41,000, and only a handful of these potentially toxic substances had

Metal-bending machinery at Kelsey-Hayes Wheel.

been tested for their long-term health effects on workers. High-speed machinery spewed more oils, gases, and fumes into the air, and the more powerful the machinery, the more completely those pollutants were pulverized into tiny particles. The resulting mist was all the more likely to penetrate skin and lungs.

While new machines and chemicals created hazards in their own right, those dangers multiplied dramatically in combination with poor supervision.

At McLouth Steel in suburban Trenton, this deadly combination became all too characteristic when the company installed the first Basic Oxygen Furnaces (BOFs) built in America. Unlike older furnaces, which took upwards of four hours to "cook" iron into steel, the new BOFs produced the same amount of metal in a half hour. Unfortunately, they also produced a record wave of accidents in the late 1950s as McLouth rushed to bring the new furnaces on line. "We had some terrific explosions," recalled Harry Lester, then a local union officer at McLouth, "and a lot of burn victims just learning the new process. We knew little about it, and the supervisors at that time were really pushy. It

was go, go, go.... It seemed [some days] like we had an ambulance run every two or three hours out of the plant."

It was go, go, go throughout the economy for most of the next 15 years. "Output per manhour"—the government's measure of how much an average worker produced in one hour—soared after 1958. And with each upward tick in productivity, the annual number of job-related injuries and illnesses jumped as well: from 11 of every 100 manufacturing workers in the late 1950s, to 16 of every 100 by 1972. Certain occupations were well above this national average, others well below. Among Michigan's auto and construction workers, 19 of every 100 would be injured on the job in 1972; among foundry workers, 40 of every 100; among truck drivers and warehousemen, 22 of every 100; among insurance agents, only 1 of every 100.

Rising output meant rising injuries because, under the prolonged boom conditions of the 1960s and early 1970s, managers tended to push both humans

and machines to the limits of their capacities. Workers on mandatory overtime, particularly if they used drugs or booze to blur the long hours, became prone to accidents. Machines operating at full tilt for much of the day also became more dangerous, particularly as plant managers cut back inspections and preventive maintenance to meet tight production schedules. A loose guard rail, an erratically timed stamping press, a malfunctioning ventilation system were "non-essential" repairs that did not contribute to production. They were therefore postponed until, in many cases, the rail gave way during an accident, the stamping press suddenly amputated a finger, or the ventilation failed to remove or dilute the clouds of metal dust and fumes.

Harry Englebrecht, plant manager at Chrysler's Eldon Avenue Gear and Axle plant (site 78), later described working conditions during the boom years of the 1960s. "We had to produce axles for the entire corporation," he said of the inner-city factory employing 4,000 workers, "and there was an interim period when the corporation demanded more axles than the plant could efficiently produce. As a result, the conditions became more crowded, with more equipment than normally you would put into this plant.... It became difficult then to maintain some of the standards you would like to maintain."

It became difficult, in fact, to keep machines and skid boxes full of parts from completely blocking the factory's aisles, or oil from the constantly running machines from coating the entire plant. "Oil on the stairs to the johns," remembered a union steward who worked at Eldon Avenue, "oil seeping up from the floors, oil coming around on the floors from the machines, oil on the racks you have to stand on while you're operating the machines."

Accidents were common in this environment. According to former company attorneys, upwards of 3,000 workers at Eldon Avenue were injured seriously enough every year to warrant examination by Chrysler's workmen's-compensation lawyers. That 75 percent injury rate far exceeded the officially reported rate of "lost-time" accidents for the plant. Chrysler, like other major employers, minimized official accident figures by keeping many of these injured workers on the payroll and avoiding lost-time accident reports to the state. Joseph Baltimore, a former compensation adjuster for the company, later acknowledged to writer Rachel Scott that "we had a number of cases where

Connecting dashboard wiring in a 1965 Chrysler. This worker would crawl in and out of moving cars on the assembly line for 9–10 hours a day, 6–7 days a week.

people had operations, fingers cut off, and they brought them [the workers] back the same day."

Injured workers either got assigned to light-duty tasks while they recovered, or struggled through their regular job assignments as best they could. They might gain in the short. run, since the present wages or temporary medical benefits paid by the company were higher and more assured than disability benefits. But because the accident went unreported, they lost their claim to future compensation for injury-related disabilities. When back strains, welding "flash," or other apparently small injuries were aggravated or repeated, these disabled workers could not claim long-term compensation.

The company, in the meantime, retained its safety record for reported accidents, thereby reducing its long-term cost of compensating disabled workers.

Whether the real number of serious workplace accidents was two million a year, as reported by employers, or 25 million a year, as some analysts claimed in the early 1970s, the question remained: whose fault?

Who was to blame, for example, when Gary Thompson, a jitney driver at Chrysler's Eldon Avenue plant, was crushed to death on May 26, 1970 by a hopper loaded with 3,000 pounds of steel scrap? A jitney driver for less than three months, this young, black Vietnam veteran had never loaded scrap before the day his supervisor assigned him that task at the start of his shift. No one saw the accident which killed him ten minutes later, but it may well have resulted from carelessness on Thompson's part. Worker carelessness, said the National Association of Manufacturers, accounted for 75–85 percent of all accidents like the one that killed Gary Thompson.

But whose fault was it that Thompson was ordered to perform, without adequate training, a job he had never done before? Equally important, who was responsible for the state of his equipment? "I found the emergency brake to be broken," said UAW safety director Lloyd Utter, after inspecting Thompson's jitney. "As a matter of fact, it was not even connected. The shift lever to the transmission was loose and sloppy. . . . It seems to be a practice of foremen, when equipment is needed, to pull the tags off the equipment in the repair area that badly need corrective maintenance, and put them back into service on the floor."

James Johnson under arrest.

At the Breaking Point

On a hot July day in 1970, James Johnson, a 35-year-old conveyor loader at Chrysler's Eldon Avenue Gear and Axle plant, walked into the factory with an M–1 carbine and shot three men to death—one a white foreman, another a black foreman.

The son of a Mississippi sharecropper, Johnson had been a quiet, brooding, Bible-reading man who had never participated in an organized protest. Yet the conditions that drove him to murder were not uncommon features of factory life in Detroit.

In May, he was injured in an auto accident, but was threatened with dismissal unless he returned to work. In June, after making the required arrangements to go on vacation, he was mistakenly fired for being absent. In July, after getting his job back, his foreman promoted a white man to a job Johnson had long been seeking.

Finally, on July 15, when Johnson refused to work in an oven area without protective gloves, his foreman fired him again. Beleaguered, enraged, out of control, Johnson returned to the plant that afternoon and began shooting.

Defense attorney Ken Cockrel, a spokesman for the League of Revolutionary Black Workers, promised to "put Chrysler on trial for damages to this man caused by these working conditions." A jury of Johnson's peers was sympathetic: at the close of his 1971 trial, they found that management abuse and deteriorating working conditions had driven Johnson to the breaking point. Instead of sending him to Jackson Prison, the court turned him over to the Ionia State Hospital for the Criminally Insane. Chrysler was later ordered to pay Johnson workers' compensation benefits of $75 a week.

Many of Thompson's co-workers had little doubt where to lay the blame for his death. Unwilling to wait for strike authorization from the union, they struck Chrysler the next morning, shutting down Eldon Avenue for the third time that year with an unauthorized wildcat. Sixteen workers, most of them union stewards, were fired for leading these walkouts in defiance of the contract's grievance and arbitration procedure.

Protests like these rocked many Detroit auto plants in the 1960s and early 1970s. Harsh working conditions and disciplinary firings triggered most of the wildcats, which took their leadership from radical groups like DRUM or from in-plant union representatives impatient with the grievance procedure. Union-sanctioned walkouts also protested working conditions and discipline, but most official strikes in these years, as in the past, focused on wages and benefits. In either case, 1968's combined total of 354 strikes in all industries set a post-war record for Michigan. Two years later, some 400,000 UAW members struck GM for 67 days to win a pension plan, called "30-and-out," allowing early retirement at full benefits after thirty years in the plants. Strike-related production losses of that year surpassed anything in Michigan's history.

For most union members, the new pension plan was a welcome escape hatch from the plants. But the prospects of an early retirement in the future could not alleviate the harsh working conditions in the present. Neither could such benefit plans pacify the growing turmoil in union ranks. In 1973, the UAW reported that power-press accidents in Michigan killed four workers and injured 621, with over 300 of those injuries

One Union, Two Picket Lines

In the 1960s, the UAW—already fractured by racial, political, and generational conflict—was further divided by renewed tension between skilled and less-skilled workers. Encouraged by a craft-union revival that began in the late 1950s, a sizable minority of UAW skilled tradesmen concluded they could win higher wages and stronger work-rule protections if they negotiated separately from production workers and voted on their own contract language.

Some of these dissidents urged fellow tradesmen to break away from the UAW and join the craft-oriented International Society of Skilled Tradesmen (ISST). When the National Labor Relations Board ruled the ISST could not raid UAW members one plant at a time, but would have to win a company-wide majority among all skilled tradesmen, the craft-union revival floundered for lack of such a majority.

Above: Dissident skilled tradesmen picketing the UAW's headquarters in 1967.

Below: UAW members picketing in Dearborn the same year. The eight-week Ford strike of 1967 won wage increases and improved Supplemental Unemployment Benefits.

involving amputations. That August, after the machinery at Chrysler's Detroit Forge (site 50) tore the arm off one worker and crushed the finger of another, most of the plant's 1,100 workers walked off the job without UAW strike authorization. It was one of three spontaneous and unauthorized wildcat strikes that summer in Chrysler's East-Side factories, the last of which produced bitter street confrontations between union loyalists and dissidents in front of the Mack Avenue stamping plant (site 27).

In an unprecedented response to the mounting discontent, the UAW suspended its national negotiations with Chrysler in 1973 and sent staff members into the company's 21 Detroit-area plants to survey conditions. They found, among other things, that a majority of the workers at Detroit Forge had been working mandatory overtime, seven days a week, for the past six months; that such heavy overtime was frequently assigned throughout the company; and that no fewer than 59 "distressingly bad" safety hazards plagued workers in Chrysler's Detroit-area plants.

The national contracts the UAW subsequently negotiated that year with Chrysler, Ford, and GM took the first steps towards addressing, if not eliminating, these problems. The new contracts gave workers with a perfect attendance record during the week the right to refuse overtime on Sundays, on every third Saturday, and on any day they had already worked nine hours. The UAW also won an expedited grievance procedure and a new structure of in-plant union representatives to monitor health and safety conditions. National Safety Committees were established for each company, and union health and safety representatives—selected by the union but paid by the companies—inspected plants on a weekly or bi-weekly basis. In addition to challenging unsafe practices, these representatives reviewed company records on chemicals and other physical agents used in the plants, tested for gas and noise levels within the workplace, and monitored employee exposure to hazardous substances.

T he UAW's 1973 contract negotiations capped an unusually dramatic and highly visible conflict within Detroit's leading union. But automobile manufacturing was not the only industry where a new generation of workers brought new attitudes and new demands to workplace issues.

"When it came to safety, the older

Members of Pontiac Local 653 line up for picket duty during the 1970 GM strike.

guys would say 'If you die, you die,' " recalled former construction worker Rich Julin, a one-time officer in the Lathers' Union and, in 1964, Michigan's first Construction–Safety inspector. " 'I don't care what kind of ladder the boss sends over,' you'd hear them say. 'I don't want to tie up with a safety line. I'll just do the job.' But younger guys were smarter. They wanted to go home at the end of the day. The macho thing didn't mean as much to them."

It also did not mean as much to the new generation of linemen who built and repaired power lines for Michigan's electric utilities. Their predecessors, by comparison, had been largely indifferent to the hazards of the job. Pete McManus, President of Electrical Workers' Local 17, described the men he learned his craft from in the 1940s as "roustabouts, a tough bunch. Back in their day, they

used to hit a job, and then they'd leave. They lived in camps.... For them it was a macho-type thing to go up and work live wires with just your leather gloves. And the fatality rate back in those days was something like, oh my God, it was horrendous—two men a month. Not just on the Edison property."

"And then they started to settle in," McManus recalled. After World War II, suburban construction and union-negotiated benefits encouraged many linemen to settle down earlier and raise families. "They weren't bumming all over the country," and they also were not willing to take the unwarranted risks accepted by previous generations of roustabouts. "Young men," the union observed in 1968, "are not anxious to enter a trade which requires a man to lay his life on the line nearly every time he

Above: Chrysler's Huber Avenue foundry. "You can see the little particles floatin' in the air," said former foundryman Al Stevenson of the air workers breathed on the job. "When a doctor looks at your X-ray, he can tell you work in a foundry."

Inset: Climbing iron. Over 1,000 Michigan construction workers died in job-site accidents in the 1960s and 1970s. One third lost their lives in fatal falls.

performs a job." Paid $4.50 an hour to handle lines carrying more voltage than the electric chair, the linemen at Detroit Edison struck for four months in 1968 to win a 50¢ raise. An underlying issue in this sometimes violent confrontation was management's assertion that workers could safely handle 13,000-volt lines with gloves rather than "hot-sticks."

Conflict over working conditions became three-sided in 1970, when Congress passed the Occupational Safety and Health Act (OSHA). Pushed by the union movement as the workplace equivalent of the Environmental Protection Agency, OSHA empowered the federal government to establish health and safety standards for 57 million American workers in private industry. At the request of workers or unions in particular workplaces, federal inspectors could now enter factories, inspect conditions, and fine employers who violated OSHA's minimum standards.

Hobbled as it was by inadequate funding and Washington's shifting political priorities, OSHA nevertheless gave a substantial boost to Detroit's burgeoning health and safety movement. If nothing else, workers and unions were becoming increasingly aware of the hazards around them. "We didn't have the knowledge years ago," remembered Charles Younglove, President of the Steelworkers local at Great Lakes Steel and later District Director of the union. "Like asbestos—we didn't know using asbestos [as machine insulation] was dangerous. Or tetrachloride—we didn't know tetrachloride [an industrial solvent] was dangerous to peoples' health, and how it could permanently injure their liver."

Alerting workers to these dangers and giving them the legal right to call for inspections, OSHA helped dispel the fatalism many held toward industrial disease. "When I got into the trade," David Jacobs remembered of his early years as a printing pressman, "if you got bi-chromate poisoning, you were simply told 'this isn't your industry.' " Owners and most workers assumed the skin ulcers and lung disorders caused by the printing fluids were unavoidable and irreversible. When men who had worked twenty years in the printing trades gradually lost their tolerance to the chemicals, they tried to hide the tell-tale skin lesions that marked the disease. "Their hands were something out of a horror movie. You know, bending their hands actually would open the sores and cause bleeding."

The occupational safety movement, backed by OSHA, decisively changed the pressmen's outlook. "Finally," Jacobs recalled, "we said to the employers, 'Hey, we're not going to get out of the industry. We're going to demand that you change, that you eliminate these dangerous chemicals.' Which to a degree, they did."

They did by finding substitute chemicals that would do the job without poisoning the job-holders. In other industries and other workplaces, similar innovations dramatically improved health and safety conditions. In the auto industry, new ventilation systems removed many of the chemical fumes that plagued die-casting workers, while

An automatic Letter Sorting Machine (LSM) in Detroit's Post Office.

Express Mail

First introduced in the 1960s, Letter Sorting Machines marked a dramatic shift away from the traditional hand-sorting of mail. As the LSM mechanically fed letters to its twelve consoles, each clerk was expected to keypunch routing instructions at the rate of one letter per second.

"It's not a bad job," said Al Fouche of the American Postal Workers' Union (APWU), "but it's not a preferred job because of the mental problem with it. Once you're on it, the concentration, the sitting there, the confinement, and so forth...make employees want to get away from it after a number of years."

The union negotiated job rotation for LSM clerks (twenty minutes per hour doing other tasks), plus a $1,000 raise in annual pay grade and retraining programs for the growing number of maintenance and technical positions in the Post Office. But even as automation increased these skilled jobs somewhat, the more rapid decline in clerking positions reduced the overall number of postal workers. A union-negotiated no-layoff clause protected most clerks, but retirements cut the APWU's membership by 12 percent in the 1970s.

The number of supervisors, however, did not decline. Reflecting a pattern evident in the auto industry as well, the proportion of management personnel to blue-collar union members rose significantly with automation. "More now than ever before in my life," observed Fouche after ten years of mechanization and computerization. "I've never seen so many supervisors."

in stamping plants, machine guards and safety gates curtailed the number of serious accidents. On construction sites, new regulations for digging excavations helped prevent cave-ins, while above ground, safety lines on swing scaffolds reduced the number of fatal falls. Improved maintenance procedures and better "housekeeping," both mandated by OSHA, also helped cut the accident rate in these and dozens of other industries.

But while exposure to hazards could be reduced, it could not be entirely eliminated. New and potentially noxious chemicals found their way into in-

News of the New

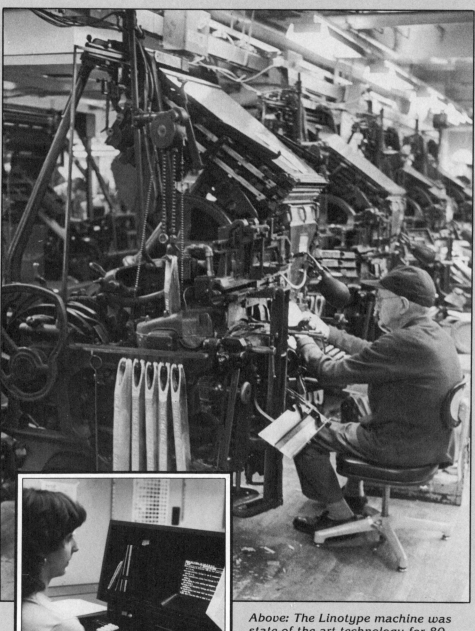

Above: The Linotype machine was state-of-the-art technology for 80 years when it came to setting type in the printing industry.

Inset: In the 1960s and 1970s, the venerable Linotype gave way to computerized typesetting machines that were faster, cheaper to operate, and easier to use.

Years ago, any one craft could shut a newspaper down. Today, the system is so automated that it becomes very difficult for any one union to do it.

Don Kummer,
Council of Newspaper Unions

For many of the 13 different craft unions in newspaper publishing, new production technologies meant a steady narrowing of skills or an equally steady loss of jobs—or both. For some trades, new methods even meant extinction.

The rapid and spectacular changes in newspaper technology that brought this about were all the more remarkable given the industry's relative stability between the 1890s and 1960s. For three-quarters of a century, printing techniques for big-city dailies remained more or less fixed. Skilled typesetters used enormous, one-ton "linotype" machines—each equipped with its own caldron of molten lead—to cast a reporter's story in raised metal letters. Photoengravers then chemically etched photographs onto metal plates, to be combined with the type. "Stereotypers" made molds reproducing the typeset plates on curved metal, and pressmen bolted the curved plates onto huge printing presses. With paperhandlers feeding half-ton rolls of paper to each press, the newspapers would fly off at 42,000 copies an hour, leaving mailers and drivers a mounting stack of bundled papers to load and deliver.

It was a dirty business. "On a Saturday night you could walk in the *News'* old Lafayette building," Kummer recalled, "and you couldn't see from one end of the pressroom to the other, that's how thick the ink mist was. When you finished a shift, you spit black." With the presses roaring like a locomotive in a tunnel, few pressmen retired without significant hearing loss.

dustrial use at an estimated rate of one every twenty minutes, and new machinery and new production methods appeared in the workplace with ever-increasing frequency. Under these constantly changing conditions, the only way to completely eliminate human exposure to potential hazards would be to fully automate the factory and eliminate the need for human labor.

But this solution would only aggravate another long-standing "hazard" for Detroit's workers—the threat of unemployment and worker obsolescence.

When the *News* and the *Free Press* finally installed new machines and methods, the unions and the federal government pressured the publishers to reduce some of the hazards. Sound proofing, improved ventilation, and enclosed control booths cut exposure to noise and ink mist: unfortunately, new technologies also cut the number of workers in the old mechanical trades, especially in typesetting.

By the mid-1970s the linotype machines and their operators had disappeared altogether. Reporters now wrote their first draft on a Video Display Terminal (VDTs)—a television screen and keyboard connected to a computer—and editors hooked into the same system did revisions and corrections on their desk-side VDTs. When the article was ready for typesetting, the computer automatically spaced the type into columns with straight margins on both sides, producing copy at speeds of anywhere from 450 to 1500 lines a minute. The ageing linotype machines could not top 14 lines a minute.

The old printing presses, using raised letters to press ink against the paper, were also phased out. The new "offset" presses used smooth printing plates, made automatically by machines which photographed the computer copy and chemically transferred it to aluminum sheets. Once on the presses, these sheets rolled the images onto paper by chemically attracting ink to certain areas and repelling it from others. At full speed, the new presses could each turn out 70,000 copies an hour, with a computerized system of conveyors, carts, and chutes automatically sliding the papers into waiting trucks.

As forerunners of this new technology began to appear in the mid-1950s, each piecemeal change sparked a bitter fight between management and Detroit's allied craft unions. The Stereotypers, supported by all the other trades, struck for six weeks in 1955 to prevent the industry from using pre-cast color plates. New mailing machines caused considerable turmoil and a brief strike at the *News* in the late 1950s, and the Pressmen, backed by

The 1967-1968 strike of the *Free Press* and the *News* was the longest press strike in American history.

the other crafts, struck for four months in 1964 to maintain crew sizes on the ever-larger presses at both papers. The bad blood generated in these strikes was an important factor in 1967-1968, when a wage dispute between management and the drivers in Teamster Local 372 sparked a 267-day strike of all crafts at the *News* and *Free Press*. It was the longest big-city press strike in American history.

By the late 1970s, the stereotypers had disappeared: there were no more raised plates to cast. The Typographers, Detroit's oldest union, lost the bulk of its membership at the *News* and the *Free Press* as linotyping became obsolete. Mailers, paperhandlers, and pressmen meanwhile saw their numbers decline and their skills rapidly change.

"Progress," as the Typographers' Union *Review* reported in 1967, "refuses to be sidetracked. . . . It is imperative that members learn the intricacies of electronics." In the meantime, the union tried to soften the impact of the new technology. "We knew it was coming," recalled David Grey, a former linotype operator at the *Detroit News*, "but it came at a very rapid pace. But through collective bargaining between the employer and the union, we were able to negotiate life-time jobs for all the printers involved." Guaranteeing them work on the new computerized typesetting process, or in other departments of the paper, the negotiated arrangement insured that these skilled tradesmen wouldn't be dumped on the same scrap heap as their linotype machines.

GOING PUBLIC

It was clear to everyone involved that the sitdown strike would end the fourth day of the occupation. The strikers would either win union representation or be evicted and carted off to jail by the Hamtramck police.

The 60 occupiers had many friends. On the sidewalks outside, supporters from nearby auto plants and union activists from all over metro Detroit maintained a spirited picket line. The Hotel and Restaurant Employees delivered food and the Musicians' union provided entertainment for the strikers. Management's efforts to reopen several unoccupied buildings had collapsed the day before when a third of the strikebreakers recruited for the occasion refused to cross the union's picket lines.

Now, management had only two re-

maining choices: either settle on compromise terms favorable to the union, or order the police into the building. They would announce their decision that afternoon in the court house where injunction proceedings were already under way. A union car caravan had meanwhile transported hundreds of members, relatives, and sympathizers downtown, where they now packed the court's hearing room and hallways.

The scene had all the elements of the organizing drives of 1937, when thousands of Hamtramck's autoworkers seized Dodge Main and its surrounding supplier plants. But this was not the 1930s and the strikers were not members of the UAW. They were members of the American Federation of Teachers, and they were striking in April, 1965.

The teachers' unprecedented action was the first spark of an explosive movement for union recognition among public employees. Throughout the 1960s and well into the 1970s, public-worker unions were unquestionably the fastest growing sector of Detroit's labor movement.

In fact, union or non-union, the number of public employees was growing faster than any other occupational group in the labor force. They were teachers, police officers, fire fighters, public-health workers, garbage collectors, bus drivers, clericals, life guards, postal workers, engineers, prison guards, and air traffic controllers, to name a few. In 1950, their numbers represented 14 percent of the nation's employed workforce but only 3 percent of metro-Detroit workers, a proportion little changed from the 1930s. By 1970, however, the proliferation of suburban towns and the expanding educational, regulatory, and welfare needs of our industrial society had together boosted the number of government workers in the Detroit area from 40,000 to 190,000. Detroit's local, state, and federal government workers totaled 12 percent of all metro-area employees in that year.

Growing numbers, however, did not mean growing prestige. For many government workers, the opposite was the case. As "public servants," they were still treated as just that: servants.

Traditionally, their underpaid and frequently servile status was compensated for by a secure tenure, a modest pension, and, in some cases, paid vacations and sick leave. Before 1950, these benefits made government work relatively attractive. But as private-sector unions won superior benefits and considerably higher wages after 1950, public employment lost much of its appeal.

What remained seemed increasingly intolerable to workers influenced, directly or indirectly, by the social activism of the Civil Rights movement. For it was civil and workplace rights that public employees sorely lacked. Even when carrying a gun, a government worker could be reduced to the most demeaning "step-and-fetch-it" status. "A Sergeant in a far East Side precinct," recalled Dave Watroba, President of the Detroit Police Officers Association, "could call a patrolman over and say, 'Smitty, we expect you to take my cleaning and get it cleaned'—at Smitty's expense. When Smitty rebelled one day against that..., the next day the Sergeant comes up and asks 'What are you doing here?' 'Well, I work here.' 'No you don't [said the Sergeant], you work on the far West Side and you're walking a beat by yourself at midnight.'"

It was the same in countless public-sector workplaces in the years before 1965. No matter what occupation—white collar, blue collar, uniform collar—work assignments and promotions for public employees depended all too frequently on the petty favoritism of supervisors and top management. For many public administrators at the state and municipal level, seniority and experience carried less weight in evaluating candidates for promotion than whether the applicants were Masons, members of the Knights of Columbus, or contributors to the "right" political campaign. The "favors" demanded of Smitty were

common, and so were complaints about managers taking cash kickbacks in return for jobs and promotions.

For many public workers, their seniority also didn't count for much when it came to management policy on pay raises. Letter carriers and postal clerks had to work for 21 years to reach their top pay grade of roughly $4 an hour; even then, some had to take a second job to make ends meet. Martin Forgash was one of many such "moonlighters" who clocked into a second job after finishing his shift as a postal clerk in the Detroit Post Office.

"I had another job for 13 years," Forgash later recalled. "But it got too much for me. I developed ulcers and had to quit." With three children to feed and clothe, Forgash's wife took a paid job to

supplement her husband's government paycheck.

Many Detroit-area teachers also relied on spouses or a second job to help pay the bills. Summer vacation, without pay, often meant a round of low-wage temporary jobs tutoring students, cutting grass, or tarring the School's new roof. When teachers, like postal workers, joined unions to lobby for better pay and working conditions, their pleas generally fell on deaf ears. Even when they won clear-cut victories in union-representation elections, as Detroit's teacher union did in 1964 (see box), management still refused to bargain.

The state's Hutchinson Act, passed in 1947 (Part III), imposed no obligation on public administrators to negotiate with unionized employees. But the Act

Detroit firemen in the 1980s (above) and the 1960s (opposite).

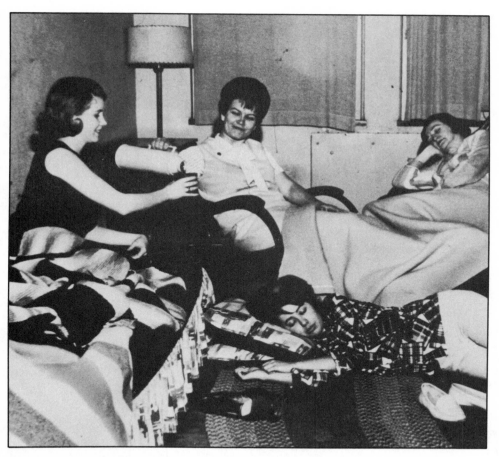

Hamtramck teachers during the 1965 occupation of Copernicus Junior High School. (Halina Zegota, Connie Andrews, Sandra Kulczycki, and Dana Wall.)

did impose severe and mandatory penalties, including immediate dismissal, if public employees dared withhold their labor and demand face-to-face negotiations.

"The Hutchinson Act," recalled June Fieger of the American Federation of Teachers (AFT), "held Michigan's teachers in terrified silence for 18 years."

It was no coincidence that when teacher protest finally erupted, the first call to arms came from the factory town of Hamtramck. Few cities in the state could boast a more union-conscious population. And few, if any, could match the self-serving corruption of Hamtramck's School Board.

In years past, jobs and promotions in the city's schools had been sold to the highest bidder—a practice exposed in 1946 when Judge George Murphy (brother of the former Governor) indicted four Board members for taking bribes. Over the next 20 years, the School Board had been more discreet, but no less self-serving, in distributing non-teaching jobs to political cronies. By 1965, Hamtramck ranked second among Detroit-area school systems in

the proportion of money spent on janitorial and maintenance services; that same year, it ranked 55th—dead last—in the proportion of money budgeted for instruction.

Payrolls in non-teaching jobs were 50 percent higher than necessary according to consultants from Wayne State University, putting the school system in chronic debt. Characteristically, the Board financed the deficit by keeping a tight lid on teacher salaries. "We were paid about $1,000 below what other metropolitan areas paid," one Hamtramck teacher estimated in 1965. At a starting salary of $5,500, many teachers were below the $7,500 paid to Hamtramck's school bus drivers.

The city's 150 public-school teachers were less inclined than most to accept such shabby treatment. However much these white-collar professionals took pride in their teaching skills and their apparent middle-class status, a large number had also grown up in union families. Fighting for job rights and better working conditions was a routine way of life, and joining the Hamtramck Federation of Teachers (HFT) seemed only natural. Seasoned leadership was therefore available. Teacher-union President Robert Kulczycki's father was

an active member of UAW Local 3, centered in Hamtramck's huge Dodge Main plant. Cornelius Quinn, another HFT leader, was the son of Local 3's former President, Pat Quinn.

For Quinn and the majority of HFT members, an already strained relationship with the Hamtramck School Board finally reached an unbearable impasse in the spring of 1965. "Collective Begging," as many described their futile lobbying for improved working conditions, had gotten them nowhere. Their delegations to the Board were ignored and their requests for decent pay routinely dismissed. Things appeared no different in March when the HFT appeared before the Board and asked for future meetings to discuss the union's salary requests. In response, the Board's President summarily adjourned the proceedings and refused to schedule any additional meetings.

"The roof leaks, desks need to be replaced, and these take precedence over teacher raises," said Superintendent Tishuck in early April. The city, he declared, could not be expected to raise teacher salaries for the next five years.

With these remarks fresh in their minds, HFT members met in secret on Friday, April 23, and voted 133 to 23 to strike if negotiations with the School Board could not be initiated. When Superintendent Tishuck purposefully avoided their scheduled meeting at Copernicus Junior High the following Monday morning, the die was cast. "The progeny of former immigrants," as The Detroit Teacher later described the sitdowners, "these first- and second-generation Poles, Ukrainians, and Russians borrowed a page from the current struggle for civil rights and held a 'sit-in.'"

Their four day occupation of Copernicus Junior High—a "prolonged teachers' meeting" as they called it, hoping to circumvent the anti-strike provisions of the Hutchinson Act—ended in victory on April 29 when State Superintendent of Education Lyn Bartlett helped arrange an eleventh-hour settlement. Hamtramck's School Board agreed to negotiate a written and legally binding collective bargaining contract with the HFT. As the first teachers' union contract in Michigan's history, it was a stunning achievement. Its raises and benefits totalled as much as $1,400 per teacher, and with increased spending on supplies and other teacher expenditures, the instructional portion of Hamtramck's school budget rose from 64 to 70 percent, equal to the state average.

"**W**hen Hamtramck's teachers 'sat down,'" wrote Sophie McGloin in the AFT's Detroit paper, "the whole teacher union movement stood up." In 1965, the whole public employee union movement was on its feet, pushing the state Legislature for a new public-sector collective bargaining law. As it happened, recent events made such a new law possible for the first time in nearly two decades.

The legislature that passed the Hutchinson Act in 1947 had drawn a disproportionate number of its Senate and House members from Michigan's rural districts. The state's 1850 Constitution, as amended in 1908, gave these less populated areas additional representation to counter the political weight of a rapidly growing Detroit. With this advantage, rural-based Republicans and conservatives exerted a far greater political influence than their actual constituent base warranted, and Michigan's

Legislature had been correspondingly unwilling to reconsider the Hutchinson Act before 1965.

Things began to change in 1959 when Gus Scholle, President of the newly merged Michigan AFL–CIO, filed a court suit claiming the over-representation of rural districts diluted his voting rights in Detroit's suburban Oakland County. When the U.S. Supreme Court, acting on a similar case from another state, ruled favorably on population-based representation, the Michigan Supreme Court declared in favor of Scholle's suit in 1962. Two years later, with metro-Detroit counties given their full weight in the elections, the Democrats captured control of the State Legislature for the first time since 1936. Their victory was amplified by the landslide turnout that gave Democrat Lyndon Johnson a runaway victory over Republican Barry Goldwater in the Presidential elections that year.

Events then moved quickly. Five

months after the election, Hamtramck's teachers collectively defied the Hutchinson Act; the following July, Michigan's recently installed Legislature enacted a new law that guaranteed bargaining rights for public workers and required good-faith negotiating by public employers. Though public employee strikes were still illegal, many of the Hutchinson Act's mandatory punishments for public-sector strikes were stricken from the books.

The pace of organizing immediately quickened. Newly active workers were forming unions where there had been none before. Others were forming professional associations and turning them into unions. And some, where unions already existed, were pushing their organizations in new and militant directions.

This led to strikes in many cases. Public workers, heartened by their newly won rights and visibility, were not always willing to wait for piecemeal

Striking letter carriers in Detroit during the 1970 strike.

Detroit's McKenny Elementary School.

A Union of Professionals

Trade unions are legitimate and valuable in their proper sphere, but they are distinctly class organizations. . . . The public school teachers of this city will gain nothing by class entanglement that they will not, in due time, acquire if they retain their status of a free profession.

**Detroit Free Press,
March 1, 1920**

In 1920, editorials like this were enough to persuade the founding members of Detroit's first teacher union to disband. "In view of the universal sentiment, in which teachers concur, that the teaching body must serve the entire public," the Detroit Federation of Teachers (DFT) announced they were severing their ties with the American Federation of Labor and dissolving their organization.

Forty-four years later, the majority of Detroit's teachers no longer believed their status as professionals and public servants would, "in due time," gain them nearly as much as collective bargaining. On the contrary, professionalism, as defined by the School Board and the anti-union

Detroit Education Association (DEA), seemed to require teachers' acquiescence to stagnating pay, arbitrary rule changes, and blatant favoritism. As the activist members of the revived DFT saw it, the teachers who benefitted most from "professionalism" were the DEA leaders who, having opposed the more militant demands of the DFT, frequently won speedy promotions into management.

"The issue that they [the DEA] raised," recalled DFT President Mary Ellen Riordan, "was that 'Professional people' don't belong to unions. 'Teachers are professionals,' they'd say, 'and we should not lower ourselves to the blue-collar, dirty fingernail kind of thing.' That's how they saw unions."

It was not how most Detroit teachers saw unions. When the DFT pressured the city for an election in May, 1964, to determine which organization teachers wanted as their exclusive representative, the outcome was decisive: 5,740 (60 percent) voted for the DFT, 3,848 for the DEA.

"We were the legal collective bargaining agent for our teachers," Riordan said of the outcome, "and with that, the Michigan Education Association [parent body to the defeated DEA] began to also move as a union—and has done so increasingly ever since."

deliberation of their long-standing grievances. Public administrators, in turn, were not always willing to shed the authoritarian habits they had cultivated before 1965. In Detroit and nationally, the resulting clashes were numerous and bitter. In the previous six-year period, 1960–1965, public-sector walkouts averaged barely 30 a year nationwide, with less than 20,000 employees walking picket lines in the entire country. Between 1965 and 1973, the average soared to over 300 strikes and nearly 180,000 strikers a year. With few exceptions, Michigan's public workers led all other states in this escalating strike activity, accounting for 20 percent of the national total in some years.

The nature and outcome of these walkouts varied as widely as the workers who launched them.

When protesting letter carriers in New York City refused to deliver the mail on March 18, 1970, their illegal strike challenged every level of public authority—postal management, the President, Congress, and top leaders of their own union. Within two days, 200,000 angry postal workers had nevertheless joined the "wildcat," spreading the strike from New York, to Detroit, to Dallas. "We didn't want this kind of action," said one local officer of the Dearborn Letter Carriers, picketing in the early morning rain on March 20. "But it's time to stop begging. Some of our members live on less than $100 a week."

After six days of picketing—during which time President Nixon mobilized 30,000 troops to move the mail in New York City—the walkout ended. A week later, Congress agreed to raise postal wages 14 percent and establish collective bargaining with seven major postal unions. (That June, a long-awaited Postal Reorganization Act separated the Post Office from congressional control and established an independent corporation to carry the mail.)

Unlike the postal walkout, most public employee strikes were local conflicts, pitting teachers against the school board, garbage collectors against the sanitation department, or bus drivers against the transit authority. Some were not strikes at all, at least not technically.

After the city of Detroit refused to reopen its 1966–1967 budget and consider the police union's proposal for a new salary scale, members of the Detroit Police Officer's Association (DPOA) all stayed on the job. But many officers stopped writing traffic tickets. When the Police Department, in an effort to break the slowdown, suspended 185 officers in the spring of 1967, "a strange illness then began sweeping the membership," as DPOA leader Carl Parsell later described it. "There was coughing and sneezing. Eyes began to water. The media called it 'Blue Flu.'" Whatever it was, the job-related ailment kept half the city's officers at home.

Many were apparently sickened by their low pay. At a maximum of $8,300 a year, Detroit's police officers were paid "about what a plumber's helper gets," as one DPOA member put it. When a Citizens Committee diagnosed the same ailment and recommended a raise to $10,000 a year, the city "took the cure" and raised salaries accordingly.

Most cures were not as spectacular. Sickouts, sitdowns, and strikes were dramatic episodes in public employee organizing, but they were also the exceptional cases. Particularly in the white-collar bureaucracies of state and local government, union organizing was more often a slow, methodical campaign to win over the fearful, the hesitant, and the indifferent.

Flo Walker, a typist in Detroit's Department of Buildings and Safety, recalled the response of many of her co-workers when the American Federation of State, County, and Municipal Employees (AFSCME) began organizing clericals in 1966. "They would say, you know, 'well, we don't want to pay union dues, we don't want to be in [the same union] with garbage workers. We're professionals.'

"So I would ask them, 'Are you going to have *this* supervisor evaluate you for promotions?'" It proved to be a telling question in a department where seniority and Civil Service requirements were routinely ignored, where applications for upgrading were filed away and test scores withheld, and where promotions often went to the supervisor's relatives and cronies.

When 30 percent of the clericals in Walker's department signed cards asking for a union representation election, management unwittingly gave an added incentive for voting pro union. "They became very tight on rules where they had not been before," Walker remembered. "You couldn't drink coffee at your desk, you couldn't have a personal phone call, you couldn't leave your desk without permission. Naturally then, people were upset. So they helped us get the vote for the union."

After AFSCME won the state-supervised election, "the rules," Walker recalled, "went back to being relaxed."

Whether it was by slowdowns, campaigns for friendly public officials, sickouts, union-representation elections, and, when all else failed, strikes, Detroit's public-employee unions gradually transformed government sector working conditions. Teachers won raises and increased funding for education. Clerical workers eliminated much of the previous favoritism in promotions. Police officers won strong contract protections on transfers, job assignments, and seniority. And firefighters successfully lobbied for a state law requiring outside arbitration between municipalities and their uniformed (police and fire) employees if contract negotiations broke down.

Postal workers won a new salary schedule requiring only eight years of seniority (instead of the previous 21) to reach the top of any particular pay grade. AFSCME members negotiated a unique package of benefits, including automatic cost-of-living raises for those on the job, and Supplemental Unemployment Benefits for those the city had to lay off during budget cutbacks.

There was much in all of this that private sector workers supported, and much that they did not.

Parents could readily endorse the class-size limitations that teachers won in their contracts, but above a certain point, paying for higher teacher salaries was another matter. Much of the local school budget came out of property taxes, and for those parents and non-parents who owned homes, increasing millage rates for *any* reason was usually an unwelcome event.

Public tolerance for government sector strikes also cut both ways. When workers withheld their labor in the public sector, it was more often their

Garbage collectors (below, late 1940s) were among the first city workers to join trade unions. By the late 1970s, the majority of non-uniformed city workers had joined the American Federation of State, County and Municipal Employees.

In 1976, when the Crestwood School District in western Wayne County hired strikebreakers to replace its 180 striking teachers, Detroit-area unions responded with mass picketing. The Michigan Education Association went to District Court and delayed the mass firing of its members, but the Crestwood Board of Education ultimately prevailed when the State Supreme Court ruled in its favor.

clients, not public administrators, who bore the brunt of the ensuing disruption. And many of these clients were considerably worse off than even the most underpaid public employee. Social workers and public health nurses, however exploited and overworked, were generally in much better shape than the destitute people they served. Striking for increased staff and more manageable caseloads might improve service in the long run, but during any strike, society's poorest citizens might go without health care and emergency income. Had Detroit's woefully underpaid postal workers continued their 1970 strike another week, they would have risked alienating 440,000 metro-area people waiting for their monthly Social Security checks.

Public-employee unionism could become controversial when the rights of workers clashed with the rights and aspirations of either the public as a whole, or a significant portion of it. Nowhere was this potential conflict more evident than in the strained relations between Detroit's police union and the city's black population.

The seniority system the DPOA sought to protect after 1966 was designed to prevent management from arbitrarily transferring, demoting, or otherwise abusing the rights of police officers. Seniority, by making length of experience at least a major determinant of promotions and benefits, prevented such divisive favoritism. If seniority also prevented the newly hired black officer from moving into positions long dominated by whites, that was not, according to the DPOA, the union's fault. Management, after all, was responsible for the discriminatory, whites-only hiring policy of past years, not police officers.

But in practice, most white police officers had endorsed such policies and tried to strengthen them. When Conrad Mallet, one of the handful of black patrolmen on the force in 1952, went to work in the lower East Side's 3rd precinct, "a lieutenant had just made the mistake of assigning a white officer and a black officer to work together. The decision was later rescinded, but for the next 18 months, the white officers would not speak to the black officers, even to say hello." The only white who broke this "wall of silence," Mallet remembered, "was a guy named Joe Ortakowski. He liked to play a card game named tonk, and it was only played by blacks."

Police administrators were no less inclined to pigeon-hole blacks into segregated duties and lower-wage jobs. Jesse Stewart, a police Sergeant for 22 years when he retired in 1966, was one of the many victims of this deliberate policy. "I was denied promotion to Lieutenant because I was black," he later recalled. "They could not deny me seniority, they could not deny me my written exams. I always had the best scores in the department, time after time."

There was little support within the police department for men like Stewart until 1963, when black patrolmen from the 13th precinct (Woodward near Wayne State) decided to transform their after-hours social organization, the Shields Club, into the nucleus of a pressure group for black officers—known as the Guardians. More often than not, the white-dominated DPOA, led by Carl Parsell, was as much or more an adversary than the police department's hierarchy. "Just about on most political positions, we were on the opposite side from the DPOA," recalled Mackie Johnson, a co-founder of the Guardians. "We fought them on the use of the Stoner Rifle, and we fought them when they tried to lead an impeachment of Judge Crockett. And we were definitely opposed to STRESS."

The discriminatory posture of the DPOA and the Detroit police department was not the norm for all public-sector workplaces. In some cases it was the opposite. While private trucking companies, for example, had a workforce in 1968 that was 90 percent white, 43 of the Detroit Post Office's 49 tractor-trailer drivers were black.

In 1968, minorities made up 40 percent of Detroit's school teachers. "That's why we say Detroit is no New York," remarked DFT leader Zeline Richards in 1969, referring to the bitter opposition of New York's teacher union (with only an 11 percent black membership) to community-controlled schools. "You can see the difference. If the union moves in Detroit against the community, a great percentage of the teachers who would be moving would have to be black, and we [black teachers] aren't about to buy that.''

Eleven years later, when Mary Ellen Riordan retired as leader of Detroit's teacher union, all three candidates for President, including eventual winner John Elliot, were black teachers.

By then, Detroit's police union was beginning a similar process of integration and readjustment. Throughout the 1970s and into the 1980s, the DPOA continued to pursue a court suit against Mayor Coleman Young's affirmative action plan, particularly its partial dismantling of rank-order promotions to compensate for past discrimination. But as black membership rose during the decade after Young's 1973 election, the tenor of internal politics within the DPOA also began to shift. By 1979, there were 1400 black officers on the police force, representing 38 percent of the department's uniformed workforce —a sevenfold increase from the 5 percent minority representation of 1967. ''Times have changed in the Detroit Police Department,'' David Watroba, the DPOA's new President, observed in 1982. ''As minorities achieve the numbers in the units where they are, they get to elect representatives who have full voice in the organization. Our Board of Directors is approximately one-third minority, and I think there is a tendency now that our union will become more socially involved.''

Some black officers, on the other hand, were not entirely convinced the DPOA had turned the corner on race. ''The real power is still concentrated,'' as Mackie Johnson saw it in the early 1980s. ''Blacks have virtually no input. They are stewards, and the Board has a sprinkling of blacks...but the real power committees within that organization have no blacks on them.''

Even so, change for the better was visible to everyone. With a black police chief and 6 of 13 precincts under black commanders, Detroit's police no longer represented an alien, predominantly white force occupying the city's predominantly black neighborhoods. That alone was a tangible measure of progress. Ten years before, between 1970 and 1974, civilian gunfire had killed 26 patrolmen. After the election of Coleman Young in 1973 and the inauguration of affirmative action the following year, anti-police violence tapered off dramatically. Between 1975 and 1982, not a single officer was fatally wounded.

That seven year period marked the longest stretch of ''peaceful coexistence'' between Detroit's police and community in a century.

Detroit police in the 1980s (above) and a union picket line in the 1960s (inset).

A Long Way, Sister

For Dolores Dunlap, women had "come a long way" indeed. It was not, however, the kind of progress depicted in high-gloss ads for "feminine" cigarettes. Advertisers might congratulate fashionable women for coming "a long way, baby" from the days when they were not supposed to smoke in public, but Dunlap marked her progress in far different terms.

"When I started at Chrysler Tank in 1973, there were only about a dozen women," she recalled, six years after becoming a parts clerk in the Warren, Michigan, defense factory. "Now there are more than 200 of us. Families can't survive today unless two people are pulling in wages."

In 1980, there were three-quarters of a million women like Dunlap working for wages in the Detroit area. They represented one-half of the metro area's adult women and 41 percent of the region's total workforce. More important, they represented the future of Detroit's labor movement.

In years past, the mothers and grandmothers of Dunlap's co-workers took jobs outside the home when and if they could. But nothing compared with the dramatic upturn in the number of women wage earners after 1960. The one woman in three who worked for wages in that year became, by 1980, one of every two women in the paid labor force.

Mary Ellen Servitto, a clerical worker and mother of three, was among the thousands of women entering or re-entering the labor market. Servitto had tried to hold "small jobs" after she married in the early 1960s, "but then I got pregnant again and again." Childcare and housework kept her home until the early 1970s, "when I began thinking about going back to work because the economy got really tough. And by this time, my kids were in grammar school and headed for Catholic high school, and we knew what that was going to involve financially."

With inflation eroding her husband's salary as an IRS systems analyst, Servitto began working part time, first as a publicist for her local church, then as a temporary clerical for Kelly Girl Services.

Her decision to re-enter the paid

workforce was not, of itself, a break with tradition: in previous generations, married women had, once their children grew older, sought paid jobs to supplement their family's income. But in the 1960s and 1970s, there were added reasons for married women to become wage earners, particularly when inflation pushed the price of goods valued at $100 in 1967 to $250 by 1980.

Like Servitto, many women worked part time to accommodate full work schedules at home. But the nature of household commitments also changed after 1960. Opinion surveys of Detroit-area wives reported a steadily declining priority placed on childrearing as the most valuable aspect of marriage. By 1971, 60 percent of the wives surveyed saw companionship with their husband as most important, compared to 13 percent who valued childrearing most highly. The growing acceptance of contraceptives and abortion made such priorities possible, and smaller family sizes and reduced childcare were the inevitable result of the 40 percent decline in Michigan's birthrate between 1960 and 1980.

New appliances and convenience foods also redistributed the burden of household labor. As more elaborate furnishings, clothing, and personal hygiene became customary, the related tasks of cleaning and washing did expand. But other chores now took less time. Refrigerators and freezers, as they became more widely available, eliminated the need for daily food shopping. Packaged and frozen foods also reduced food preparation time, and vacuum cleaners, washing machines, and laundromats all marked significant improvements on older hand-washing methods. Housework was still done primarily by women, but wives who could take advantage of these homecare innovations had more time to seek social contacts outside the home.

A growing minority of women were postponing or ending their marriages altogether. The doubling of Michigan's divorce rate between 1960 and 1980, combined with increased use of contraceptives, contributed to a steady growth in the proportion of single women in the Detroit area. Whether they were divorced, separated, widowed, or never married, the majority of these single women were, like their male counterparts, working or looking for work outside the home.

Most women were finding it in the growing number of white-collar jobs opening up in Detroit and nationally. In fact, rapid changes in the scope and technology of corporate expansion were shifting the entire job market towards white-collar work—a shift that depended upon, as well as encouraged, the growth in women wage earners.

After World War II, Detroit's major banks, retailers, and car companies expanded across North America and around the world, and as long-distance marketing grew, company managers called on an ever-growing clerical workforce to help monitor and coordinate these far-flung operations. The increasingly powerful computers developed to sort and manipulate the necessary information required data processors and keyboard operators to feed the machines. Marketing operations, home offices, and Detroit-based branches of out-state corporations all needed receptionists, personal secretaries, typists, stenographers, and file clerks to sort accounts, answer phones, handle correspondence, and route billings through the expanding corporate maze. Clerical jobs in metro Detroit multiplied accordingly, and to fill the mushrooming demand for clerical labor, employers turned to the most readily available—and, by tradition, underpaid—supply of workers: women.

New technology gave an added boost to women's employment, even as it undercut many of the blue-collar jobs held by men. Inside Detroit's factories, computerized machines could operate with far fewer workers, but the new machinery often required additional keyboard operators and programmers to produce computerized work instructions. Expanding medical technology, instead of reducing the number of health-care workers in the hospital industry, usually expanded the number of intensive-care nurses, machine technicians, and other support workers performing new medical procedures.

Changing technology, growing population, and the demands of a complex, science-based economy also buoyed employment in education after 1960, where women held the majority of teaching positions in elementary and secondary schools. The health-care industry grew even faster, bankrolled by new federal insurance programs and the pension-plans and medical benefits unions had won in Detroit's manufacturing industries.

The net result of these multiple trends

Chrysler Corporation clerical workers in the 1960s. Between 1960 and 1980, metro-Detroit employers added 110,000 clerical workers to their payrolls— 98 percent of these new positions were filled by women.

Opposite: Shift changes in a small electric parts plant, 1976.

was a significant shift in the Detroit-area workforce. In the twenty years after 1960, the number of jobs for machine operators and fabricators in manufacturing grew imperceptibly as mechanization and automation cancelled out the gains of a growing metro economy. But the number of jobs in clerical occupations, food-service trades, the medical professions, and elementary and secondary education all grew rapidly, adding 230,000 jobs to the Detroit-area economy by 1980. And women held four out of five of these new positions. Whether full- or part-time, working women could no longer be considered exceptional among adult females. They were fast becoming the majority among women.

As their numbers grew, women workers became increasingly aware of the stereotypes and prejudices that restricted their options outside the home. Where only scattered voices in the union movement and the professions had previously called public attention to this workplace bias against women, now a social movement—the Women's Movement—emerged in the 1960s and 1970s to challenge sexism in all its forms.

Much of that movement's initial inspiration, and most of its legal grounding, grew out of the peculiar legislative history of the 1964 Civil Rights Act. When Congressional opponents of racial desegregation sought to delay the Act's passage, they did so by extending the bill's equal-opportunity guarantees to include women. Equality for women, they reasoned, was a joke, a novelty that no one would take seriously, and their amendment would therefore embarrass supporters of civil rights for blacks. When the bill nevertheless passed both houses of Congress, it still included this unintended "joker" of sexual equality.

Many women failed to see the humor, however, in the federal government's failure to put sexual discrimination on its regulatory agenda. In 1966, a group of prominent writers, educators, and other professionals formed the National Organization for Women (NOW) and publicly called for "affirmative action" programs in both government and industry.

NOW's founders included trade-union women, like Caroline Davis and Dorothy Haener of the UAW, who had focused their concerns for many years on the practical problems and unequal treatment that working women experienced. For a younger generation of women activists, however, these concerns no longer went far enough. The heart of the matter, particularly as many campus-based women saw it in the 1960s and early 1970s, was the subordination of women in every facet of social and personal life, from the bedroom to the boardroom. Genuine liberation, they argued, required a complete reappraisal of all male-female relations, marriage included.

Among the majority of women who still defined themselves primarily as wives and mothers (even when they held jobs outside the home), such ideas generated considerable anxiety and hostility. To many of these family-oriented women, childrearing and household labor were socially valued tasks even if men refused to share the work or acknowledge its equal worth. As they saw it, rejecting those roles altogether meant rejecting their families, their lovers, their socially-defined skills—their whole self-conception.

Feminist politics, as sensationalized by the media, alienated these potential supporters of the movement in its early years. Even so, more and more women—including those identifying themselves as feminists, and those who did not—were pushing against the cultural and institutional barriers that restricted their choices in life.

"I had no interest in the women's movement," Susan Susselman recalled of her first months in the University of Michigan's Personnel Office.

Student nurses in Detroit. Of 37,000 jobs created between 1960 and 1980 in Detroit's health-care professions, women held four out of five of the new positions.

"And I was raised in an anti-union family. My father had been a union member, and had had very disastrous experiences with the union that he belonged to. So I personally had no interest whatsoever in a union.

"On the other hand," she remembered, "I was angry." Her anger focused on a starting salary for clericals of barely $6,000 in 1974; the "brown-nosing" expected in return for small merit raises; and "the visible injustice that was passing my desk [in personnel] every day. For instance, four women would be hired on the same day at the same salary grade, and be receiving four different starting salaries."

These were oft-repeated complaints after the mid-1960s. "Before 1975, we had 176 different job classifications for 250 people," remembered Ruth Eberle, a clerical worker at Oakland University in Pontiac Township. The individual job titles given each worker were "as vague as they were numerous," allowing management to assign work and set salaries "indiscriminately," as Eberle saw it. "Pay was all over the map," but with the abundance of different job titles, it was hard to compare salaries or know how such pay differentials were justified.

Since working women were frequently separated from men by occupational stereotyping and job segregation, there was also no direct means, in such cases, of comparing their pay and working conditions with those of their male counterparts. At Henry Ford Hospital, where all but a handful of the nurses were women, Monique Pittman and her co-workers could only compare their salaries to the paychecks men received in some of the surrounding male occupations. Job descriptions for elevator repairmen, Pittman recalled, required "a high school education and then on-the-job training. They needed no licensing from the state, and were only responsible for their elevators and their tools."

Nurses, by comparison, had to finish at least two years of education beyond high school. "They are also licensed by the state, [and] are responsible for hundreds of thousands of dollars' worth of equipment.... Patients would not live if there were no nurses." But, Pittman and her co-workers concluded, "by the time elevator repairmen reached their maximum [pay], they were making about three dollars an hour more than nurses."

Practices like these had short-changed women for years, and after 1960, the income gap between the sexes widened still

Chrysler's truck plant in suburban Warren, 1982. While the number of men in less-skilled factory jobs declined between 1960 and 1980, the number of women in such jobs (machine tenders, assemblers, fabricators, inspectors) jumped 49 percent in the metro area—from 35,000 to 52,000.

further. In 1956, a woman working full time earned 63¢ for each dollar a man earned; by 1976, with the dramatic expansion of low-wage clerical and service jobs, her comparative wage had fallen to only 57¢.

Low wages did not deter women from seeking self-esteem in their work. "I knew I was smart enough to get into medical school," Dottie Deremo remembered of her decision to become a nurse. "But I wanted to provide a different kind of care than physicians provided.... Doctors are into the curing aspects of health care and nurses are into the caring aspects. And both are

Lunch hour, Chrysler's Warren Truck plant.

Running the Gauntlet

One woman in three had been propositioned. "They figure if you work in a factory, you're an easy pickup."

One woman in four had been verbally taunted. "The name calling, it happens a lot.... 'Whore, slut, bitch....'"

One woman in seven had been physically attacked. "This [drunk] guy came up on my platform, grabbed me from behind.... I tried to get off the platform. Three other guys came over and grabbed the guy. The line was stopped...."

The circumstances varied from case to case, but they added up to the same thing: sexual harassment. For working women, it was all too common an occurrence. In 1981, researchers from the University of Michigan found that 36 percent of the women they interviewed in a Detroit-area auto plant had been pestered or molested on the job. Such harassment, they found, was not simply a matter of men aggressively acting out their sexual impulses. More often than not, the harassers were trying to assert or preserve male dominance—the general dominance of males in the factory, and the particular dominance of male supervisors over female workers.

The role of foremen was especially prominent in the Detroit study. While they represented only 5 percent of the men on the shop floor, foremen were the harassers in 27 percent of the cases reported. As a rule, they used their power to influence promotions and transfers as a lever in forcing sexual submission. "When I first hired in," one woman recalled, "I had a general foreman approach me and tell me if I'd go out with him, I'd have a good job. Well, I didn't go out with him, and I still have the same shit job."

Harassment from male co-workers also underlined the power relationships in the plant. When women were either a small minority in a department or a large majority, sexual harassment from male co-workers was relatively rare. But when the number of women in a predominantly male department began to approach equality, men often responded by harassing the growing number of women. In such cases, said researchers, women were more visible and more threatening, and sexual harassment was one way men tried to preserve male authority in a changing workplace.

necessary in the health-care system."

But in the health-care system where Deremo worked, doctors were "income generators" and nurses were "costs." Salaries for Detroit's nurses averaged barely $14,000 a year in 1979, and acute understaffing and heavy patient loads were business-as-usual. In this setting, occupational pride could take a beating. "I remember one day," nurse Diane Havaich recalled of the neurological unit where she once worked, "we had 12 patients, [including] five new surgeries, one girl who had just broken her neck in a car accident, and three patients who were having active seizures on and off. There were only two of us staffed for the floor. When patients wanted to talk, we had to say, 'I'm sorry honey, we're only doing what's absolutely necessary.'"

"The stress is so bad in nursing," Havaich added, "you can't understand it unless you're there." Stress was built into many of the jobs women chose, and teachers and social workers, no less so than nurses, felt it when they worked with people struggling to stay alive, keep their families together, or get through school.

Stress could enter the office as well, particularly as high speed machines paced and monitored more and more of the work.

"The job itself was very stressful because you were on the phone all day," Elisa Lopez said of the position she took in 1979 at Blue Cross, Detroit's major health-insurance company. "We were plugged into an outlet which plugged us into a computer. And the phone calls came in from subscribers and they just fell in at a clip, you had no control over the number of calls you got.... [Management] had this 'Star Time,' they called it. These computer-issued reports on your performance, of how many calls you took in, how long it took you to go through the call—they called that 'talk time'—and then they had 'after hang-up time' from the time you hung up and went back in [to the computer], showing you were open. And they ranked your performance on these things, and your promotions, and your raises, and your reviews."

To Lopez and many of her co-workers, the rankings seemed biased. "I had sat there and watched them [management] promote their in-group, harass people, issue all sorts of strange computer reports on people who were damned good workers, who really knew their stuff, and really worked hard, and yet they got consistently screwed. Then I decided this was totally unfair.'' A slim majority of Lopez's co-workers agreed. In January, 1981, they voted by a 1630–1360 margin to join the United Automobile Workers, hoping a UAW–negotiated contract would standardize promotion policies and improve pay.

The frustrations that motivated these women and men to join a predominantly blue collar union were shared, in varying degrees, by most working women in the metro area's white collar workforce. But unlike Lopez and the workers at Blue Cross, the majority of Detroit's clerical and service workers stopped short of joining a union.

Some simply quit their jobs rather than endure arbitrary treatment and low pay. In Detroit's hospitals, health-care analysts estimated that 10–20 percent of all nursing positions were vacant in the late 1970s, largely because three of every ten nurses quit each year. Surveys sponsored by Professional Secretaries International found that two-thirds of the clericals they polled believed their jobs were underpaid, low status, and dead end, and two of every three secretaries under 30 planned to abandon clerical work altogether.

Of those remaining, many chose temporary jobs or part-time work. Short tenure could minimize the stress of a particularly unpleasant job, and short hours left time for family commitments. ''When I once worked a full-time job for six weeks,'' Mary Ellen Servitto recalled of her years as a Kelly temporary secretary, ''I finally got to see what women have to put up with who work full time. And I didn't like it. It was hard to keep up with the house and the family. . . . All that leaves you no time for yourself.''

If family demands impinged on some women, so too did the more immediate presence of their boss in the workplace. Many office managers and doctors worked in the same areas of the building as their white-collar subordinates, and personal secretaries and head nurses in particular felt personally loyal to (or dependent upon) the administrator or doctor they worked with. For some of these women, professional associations, not unions, were the preferred vehicle for pursuing career goals. Groups like the Michigan Nurses Association focused their energies on state licensing procedures and nursing education, while downplaying or neglecting collective bargaining and grievance handling. Professional Secretaries International (PSI), with a small 300-member branch in Detroit, sought to enhance the status of clerical workers by sponsoring National

Sexual enticement by waitresses in Detroit's Playboy Club was not only a required practice in 1963, it was also the only means to a paycheck. When the Club opened that year, the 62 ''Bunnies'' serving tables received no wages—just tips.

The Hotel and Restaurant Employees picketed the Club from the day it began hiring. Charging that ''Playboy's no-wage policy makes the Bunny beholden to the customer for her livelihood,'' the union called upon the state to deny a liquor license to ''an employer who believes femininity is a commodity to be sold.'' When Michigan's Legislature passed a union-sponsored minimum-wage act the following year, Playboy was finally forced to pay $1.00 an hour. After several months of picketing, the Club also agreed to recognize the union as the waitresses' bargaining agent.

Fifteen years later, femininity was still a commodity to be sold in the cocktail lounges and hotel restaurant at Metropolitan Airport. In 1973, Michigan Host, operator of the airport facilities, ordered its waitresses to wear costumes featuring a plunging V-neck, a skating style skirt, ruffled underwear, and two-inch heels. The company hoped to attract more male customers with the provocative outfits, but for waitresses, the new costumes also attracted taunts, propositions, and physical harassment.

In 1978, thirty-two waitresses filed suit against the company for enforcing the dress code even when managers knew it invited harassment. A grievance filed by the Hotel and Restaurant Employees also protested the Host Corporation's costume policy. Faced with a possible court injunction and unfavorable arbitration ruling, the company withdrew the outfits—but continued to insist that management alone should determine how the women dressed. The com-

Above: Yvonne Tiffany, a secretary for the Hotel and Restaurant Employees Union, picketing the Playboy Club in 1963.

pany, management said, had no intention of forcing its waitresses into provocative and demeaning roles.

The women who protested the dress code saw it differently. They vividly recalled the response of one female executive to their complaints about the doll-like costumes. ''Dolls you are,'' the manager reportedly told the waitresses, ''and dolls you shall remain.''

Secretaries' Day every year since 1952.

Ruth Stephens, President of Detroit's PSI chapter and personal secretary to Hudson's Chairman of the Board, saw career advancement as more of a personal project than a collective issue. "You have to look ahead and set goals," she counseled individual clerical workers. "Many companies will assist secretaries who want to progress to supervisory jobs in word processing, accounting, or personnel. These avenues are open, but you have to seek them out."

When such individual striving encountered management favoritism or discriminatory wage policies, women could also turn to the law as an alternative to collective bargaining. Monique Pittman and her co-workers at Henry Ford Hospital had no union to back up their complaints about unequal and inadequate pay. But Pittman and her colleagues could, and did, file a suit against the hospital with the Equal Employment Opportunity Commission, the federal agency established to enforce the 1964 Civil Rights Act.

For the majority of women, the alternatives to a union—court suits, professional associations, temporary work, or quitting—seemed more palatable than the relative unknowns of collective bargaining. But for a steadily growing minority of working women, these non-union alternatives just did not go far enough.

"There is the idea that on Secretaries' Day the boss will take you out to lunch and maybe give you a rose," said Wanda Brown, a clerical worker at Harper

Sending a Message

Their gathering announced a new agenda for the labor movement.

"We have a message for George Meany," Detroit's Myra Wolfgang, waitress-union leader for 40 years, told the founding convention of the Coalition of Labor Union Women (CLUW). "We didn't come here to swap recipes! ...Men aren't going to resign their posts. They're just going to have to make room for more people on the boards."

In March, 1974, three thousand women gathered in Chicago—many of them half the age of the 60-year-old Wolfgang—and readily endorsed the aging leader's call for female representation on union executive boards. The need for affirmative action was obvious to most. With more than four million women in U.S. unions, representing over a quarter of the labor movement's membership, the AFL-CIO did not have a single woman on its Executive Council. None of its member unions had significant female representation on their international staffs, and only a handful had women in top policy positions.

Among the exceptions was Myra Komaroff Wolfgang, Vice President of the Hotel and Restaurant Employees International Union and Secretary Treasurer of its affiliated locals in Detroit. Together with Olga Madar, the former Chrysler employee and bomber-plant worker elected to the UAW's Executive Board in 1966, Wolfgang and members of her generation had long advocated the reforms which CLUW now endorsed: maternity leave and childcare assistance, affirmative action for women on the job

and in the union hall, and concerted organizing efforts among unorganized workers.

CLUW's endorsement of these principles, broadcast to the labor movement and the general public, vindicated years of solitary advocacy by women like Wolfgang. Yet there was one CLUW endorsement which Wolfgang could not second. When the delegates voted overwhelmingly to back ratification of the Equal Rights Amendment (ERA), they rejected Wolfgang's advocacy of "protective" legislation for women.

First passed by liberal reformers in the opening decades of the twentieth century, protective laws like Michigan's 1909 statute prevented companies from forcing—or allowing—their women employees to lift more than 35 pounds at a time, or work more than 10 hours a day and 54 hours a week. Without such protective laws, argued Wolfgang, employers could more readily force women out of their jobs, since women's smaller size made heavy lifting difficult, and their home obligations made heavy overtime impossible. Unless husbands shared housework and communities provided childcare—measures she desired, but despaired of achieving in the near future—Wolfgang saw protective legislation limiting overtime as the only way to guarantee equal opportunity for women in the workplace.

Since the ERA, if ratified, would prohibit such sex-based distinctions in any legislation, Wolfgang denounced the amendment as "a negative law with no positive provisions to combat discrimination.... The dual role of

women in our society [mother and worker] makes protection for them a necessity." Echoing the initial reaction of the AFL-CIO, which also opposed the ERA during congressional debates, Wolfgang saw a class bias operating among ERA supporters. The ERA, she declared, guaranteed the "emancipation of business and professional women at the expense of working women," since only the wealthy could afford maids and work long hours away from the family. As a trade unionist, Wolfgang could not help but ask why ERA proponents did not push to broaden, not eliminate, protective legislation so that it limited overtime for men as well as women.

Wolfgang's opponents in the labor movement had a ready answer. As trade unionists, they favored limitations on mandatory overtime for all workers—but as women, they had little to gain from one-sided laws that either discouraged employers from hiring women, or prevented women workers from getting their share of overtime when they wanted it. "If they worked 11 hours a day," remembered Phoebe Nowaczewski, a Chrysler worker and local union leader, "I had to give up my job to the man next to me.... I was a breadwinner in my home, and I was denied that money because I was a woman."

Because sex-specific protective legislation violated the 1964 Civil Rights Act, Michigan's Attorney General had already declared the state's 10-hour-day limitation on women workers null and void in 1969.

Hospital before joining the Service Employees International Union as an organizer. "Well roses are nice. But we want a little recognition on the job, too."

Barbara Fletcher and her fellow nurses at Metropolitan Hospital found no such recognition through the Michigan Nurses Association. "They [the MNA] were effective on the professional issues. But as far as negotiating economic issues, they did not have the expertise.... And with all their staff in Lansing, we lost a lot of grievances because of time lapses. MNA just sort of cream-puffed through our negotiations from 1971 on.... Basically, our contract was just xeroxed year after year." After nine years of "spinning our wheels," as Fletcher put it, she and 150 registered nurses at Metropolitan's two hospitals voted to leave the MNA and affiliate with the UAW.

Here and there, in workplaces across the Detroit area, groups of white collar women were drawing the same conclusions during the 1970s. Their fledgling unions did not spring from the same dramatic mold of sitdown strikes and mass demonstrations that characterized the 1930s, and the slow and unspectacular growth of their organizations did not command as much public attention. It was, more often, a war of words rather than picket lines.

For Gloria Williams, a Red Cross nurse who led her MNA chapter into the Michigan Health Care Workers union, the key words were those linking unionism and professionalism. "We try to tell people that you can be dedicated and be a professional, and still get a de-

During the founding convention of the Coalition of Labor Union Women (CLUW), delegates from the Farm Workers Union and the Teamsters could embrace even as their respective unions fought over representation of California harvest hands. On the left is UAW staffer Edie Van Horn, a former Chief Steward at Dodge Main. On the right is Olga Madar, member of the UAW Executive Board and first CLUW President.

Legal limits on what women could lift were voided at the same time.

But in the 1970s, many men still applied these protective standards in the workplace, often with the intention of "protecting" jobs against affirmative-action hiring and promotion of women. "For those of us women who made it through the exam," recalled Diane Hyde, an apprentice pipefitter at Ford's Sterling Heights axle plant,

"the consensus of foremen and supervisors is that we can't hack it.... When they realize we're serious, they get a little nervous. There's always the strength test: 'Can you lift that, honey?'

"So I say, 'Let's see *you* lift it.' Most of the time they can't. Men use power lifts just like we do."

By 1974, these arguments on behalf of equal rights prevailed over the reasoning behind protective legislation.

The year before, the AFL–CIO dropped its opposition to the ERA, clearing the way for CLUW's enthusiastic endorsement of the Constitutional amendment. Union women, CLUW announced in its message to the labor movement, could now "take aggressive steps to address ourselves to the critical needs of 30 million unorganized sisters, and to make our unions more responsive to the needs of women."

cent wage. Being organized and having a union contract doesn't change how you take care of patients."

But it changed how women dealt with management, and the potential for open conflict alarmed some who liked their immediate boss. Others, especially nurses, feared strikes would continually disrupt their work. "I know a lot of nurses, and that's one of their biggest hang-ups," observed Barbara Fletcher, local union President of Metropolitan Hospital's nurses. " 'Trade unions—they're always on strike.' That's not true. We tell them a strike is the very last thing you use.

"But you know, before [the UAW replaced the MNA]...what did you do? I mean, you asked for something, and management said 'no.' And you couldn't say, 'then we're going to set a target date [for a strike].' You said 'OK'.... So now, just hearing the threat of a strike [can] many times resolve negotiations."

It took more than the threat of a strike at Wayne State University. Two years after voting to merge their independent Staff Association with the UAW in 1978, most of the 1,000 clericals and technicians represented by Local 2071 walked out in protest when the university delayed its response to their bargaining proposals. Four days of picketing dispelled any doubts about the fledgling union's staying power in a strike, especially after the local chapter of the American Association of University Professors (AAUP) joined the walkout. With the backing of the biggest AAUP local in the country, the clerical and technical workers won modest salary improvements and substantial innovations in upgrading and redefining job classifications.

"A committee of our members wrote up descriptions of what they do on their jobs," Local 2071 President Laura Paige said of the classification-review process. "After reviewing them, we told management, 'This is what we do and this is what we should be called.' Little by little we have been establishing fair job descriptions and/or salary grades." In a major improvement on the sparse and ineffective organization of their old Staff Association, Local 2071's members also elected 36 stewards, in worksites around the campus, to handle grievances on a day-to-day basis and protect the members' newly won contract rights.

Clerical workers and technicians in Chrysler's plant-production offices had established such protections twenty-five years earlier, when UAW Local 889 won recognition rights for the company's white-collar workers in the Detroit area. After 1970, this older generation of white collar trade unionists was joined by new groups of workers from Detroit-area colleges and universities, from smaller hospitals like Metropolitan and Detroit Osteopathic, and from insurance companies like Blue Cross and the American Automobile Association.

But most of the white collar workers in Detroit's Medical Center hospitals, in the city's major banks, and in the auto industry's corporate headquarters remained non-union. General Motors hoped to keep it that way by automatically paying its non-union clericals and technicians the same wage increases and benefits the UAW negotiated for blue-collar workers. Able to take home the rewards of collective bargaining without having to take on the responsibilities of union membership, most of these white-collar workers remained indifferent, if not hostile, towards unions.

Just the same, attitudes were changing in many workplaces. "I attended a union meeting only because I was very concerned," recalled Susan Susselman of her first encounter with the UAW. "I felt we were getting a raw deal, and I better see what's happening. I wanted to know, and that was all. And it was just gradually, through meeting these other women and relating to them as people, that I decided they were likeable and sincere. It was at that point that I overcame my [anti-union] bias.

"Anyway, gradually I began to understand the relationship between individual concerns and concerns of the group, and then how that meshes in with the larger society around it....

"What happened to me," concluded Susselman, who later left her job as a university clerical and became a union organizer, "is I got an education. That was my education, in both the labor movement and, I guess, a world view."

Union members at Detroit's Blue Cross—Blue Shield study their first proposed contract in 1981.

VI: AT THE CROSSROADS

Demolishing Dodge Main

END OF THE LINE?

"The blacks and the whites just get along," according to Frank Weaver, a black welder with 17 years seniority at GM's Detroit Fleetwood plant. "Basically, you've really got the same worries, the same problems. You're in the same economic situation."

Fleetwood, like Detroit, had changed dramatically over the years. "We've got blacks in just about every area, every department that exists in the plant," President Joe Gaston of UAW Local 15 could boast. Gaston, serving his third term since 1971, was the first black to be elected President of Local 15. The plant manager, Thomas Clifford, was also black. So too were 28 percent of the plant's foremen, nearly equal to the proportion of minority workers in Fleetwood's workforce.

Black citizens represented 63 percent of the surrounding city's population, nearly twice the proportion of minority workers at Fleetwood. Nevertheless, the progress made in integrating the aging automobile plant was impressive. Change had not occurred overnight. When management appointed Wilburn Wheeler the plant's first black foreman in 1962, some white workers greeted him with racial slurs and refused to follow his orders. Twenty years later, Jim Buck, a black foreman in the plant's body shop, reported a far different attitude. "I'm accepted. It's just like you forget you are black."

It took decades to turn things around at Fleetwood. Unfortunately, it would take only a day or two to undo it all—a day in which management confirmed the many rumors the half-century old plant

would close.

After 1979, it was the same throughout Detroit as plant closings and layoffs became all too common. Along with the jobs, wages, and hard-earned seniority workers had struggled to win, economic catastrophe destroyed the future.

"Who's going to hire a 56-year-old woman with a bad back?," worried Beatrice Mullins after Ferro Manufacturing laid her off in the winter of 1981–1982. Fifteen months after the company closed its Detroit plant, Mullins and nearly 80 percent of the former Ferro workers interviewed by the Detroit *Free Press* had not been able to find work. Most found only long lines of jobseekers chasing every notice in the help-wanted ads. Employers, as Mullins observed, ''can pick and choose now,'' and most of the aging ex-Ferro workers found themselves shunted aside.

Their plight was shared by thousands of others. In Wayne County alone, 42 auto-related companies closed their factories between 1978 and 1981, and employment in this vital industrial sector fell by over 100,000. By the end of 1982, Detroit Edison's partial survey of southeastern Michigan listed over 100 plant closings and liquidations since 1978—plants that once produced everything from automobiles, to chemicals, to retail drugs.

The litany of disaster included big factories and small, old plants and new. Chrysler's Dodge Main and Uniroyal's East Jefferson tire plant were both over 70 years old and already partially abandoned when management terminated their remaining operations in 1980. Chrysler's Huber Foundry in Detroit and Ford's Michigan Casting Center in suburban Flat Rock were, in contrast, relatively modern structures when management shuttered both facilities in 1981. And as these large plants went down, they took scores of parts supply plants with them: companies like Omega Stamping in Hamtramck, Machine Tool and Gear in Dearborn, and Webb Forging in Belleville, each employing between 25 and 125 workers.

By the fall of 1982, half the auto industry's total factory capacity and two-thirds of the nation's steel-making operations were idle. The padlocked gates and empty plants were silent testimony to the worst economic downturn since the 1930s. ''It's hard to take,'' observed 51-year-old Simmon Blackmon when Guardian Industries closed its Detroit windshield plant. Blackmon worked 30 years in the plant as a laborer and boilertender before the company decided to fill its dwindling orders from a non-union facility in Ohio. ''Who'll talk to you about a job at my age? I'm too old to find work and too young to retire.''

E ven in Detroit, a city long accustomed to sharp downturns in production, a slump of this magnitude seemed unimaginable in the 1960s and early 1970s. Between 1965 and 1974, metro-Detroit's bustling auto plants produced over two million cars a year, 30 percent more than production averages of the previous decade. As late as 1977, when total U.S. output surpassed 9 million automobiles for the second time that decade, the Detroit area still

turned out 2.1 million Chrysler, Ford, and GM cars.

But even in these boom years, there was an ongoing and ominous shift in worldwide production. During the very decade when autoworkers like Beatrice Mullins and Simmon Blackmon were setting new production records, American companies were losing the virtual monopoly in auto production they had enjoyed since World War II.

After 1945, the war-shattered industries of Europe and Asia were no match for American competition. U.S. and Canadian factories produced nearly 80 percent of all cars and trucks sold in the world in 1950, a year in which Japan's tiny auto industry built fewer than 5,000 passenger cars. North America, as the world's biggest and wealthiest market for automobiles, was the exclusive hunting ground of U.S. car manufacturers. They had little to fear from outside poachers.

This worldwide dominance could not go on forever. But while the U.S. monopoly lasted, America's Big Three automakers were free to focus their entire production and sales strategy on high-powered (and high-priced) automobiles. So long as gasoline was cheap and there was little foreign competition, Americans bought these cars—if they

Signs of the times. Above: Detroit, 1982.

Inset: Detroit, circa 1932.

could afford them. When the UAW, in a 1949 article called ''A Small Car Named Desire,'' advocated a fuel-efficient compact for low-income buyers, the industry scoffed. Even when Germany's Volkswagen ''Beetle'' found a market in the

U.S. in the late 1950s, American manufacturers were unimpressed. The VW, said Ford designer George Walker, was "just a bathtub.... Europeans may like it, but it doesn't have American style."

For U.S. auto companies, compact cars also lacked the American-style profits they were accustomed to. "Smaller cars," *Business Week* observed in 1974, "produce smaller profits," and maximizing profits was, after all, the goal of capitalist enterprise. Since the basic labor and overhead costs of production were roughly the same for any size automobile, "you'd just put a few bucks into a car to enlarge it," admitted Leonard Piconke of Chrysler, "and then sell it for a lot more money."

All the while, Europe and Japan were rebuilding and retooling their economies. Their car factories, steel mills, and electronics plants were brand new. Their machinery was often state-of-the-art, and their workers, by American standards, were underpaid. While America's Big Three automakers continued to rely on aging but still profitable technologies, foreign carmakers broke into the U.S. market by investing in innovative production techniques and high-mileage car designs.

When gasoline prices suddenly skyrocketed after the 1973 Arab–Israeli war, American companies found themselves on the short end of the global auto industry. Foreign imports, already 15 percent of the U.S. market in 1971, rose to 20 percent during the recession of 1974–1975. The situation only grew worse after 1979, when the Iranian revolution drove gasoline prices still higher. The escalating cost of fuel, together with rising interest rates in the U.S. and the rippling effects of the 1980 and 1981 recessions, cut heavily into sales of high-priced, low-mileage cars built in North America. By 1980, imports had taken nearly 30 percent of the U.S. market, and, for the first time in post-war history, Japan's production of cars and trucks surpassed America's faltering output. U.S. and Canadian factories produced only 22 percent of the world's motor vehicles that year, and Detroit-area factories turned out fewer than one million cars—the lowest figure in more than two decades.

"The area where I worked had a whole industrial park," remembered George Williams, a former production worker at Chrysler's Lynch Road complex. "But they closed the whole thing down, three factories. It's almost like a ghost town, like a gold town from the prospecting days. It's pathetic."

By the fall of 1982, Michigan's "gold rush" was over for 730,000 unemployed workers. According to official statistics, 17 percent of the state's workforce was unemployed and looking for work, but with thousands of discouraged job-seekers dropping out of the labor force and turning to relatives and friends for support, the real rate of joblessness in any one month was well over 20 percent. Roughly one in three of Michigan's workers, when they looked back over the year, could count some period of unemployment.

The physical traces of this catastrophe were etched in Detroit's crisis-pocked landscape. In nearly every neighborhood of the city and its blue-collar suburbs, there was at least one abandoned factory—a single or multi-story shell vacated within the last year or the last decade. From each abandoned workplace, the ripple effect of its closing left shuttered restaurants, deserted gas stations, half-empty bars, "for-sale" signs, and boarded-up homes.

A tour through any section of the city found equally vivid evidence of Detroit's changing human landscape.

In the downtown City–County building, a deputy sheriff stood in the lobby every weekday of 1982 and auctioned off foreclosed homes. Most of the 300 homeowners who lost their property every month in that year (up 80 percent from 1980) got only enough from the

The partially demolished Anderson Brass plant in southwest Detroit. After 1980, the company moved its production of valves and auto parts to South Carolina.

Job Wars

In 1981, Bill Davidson, principal owner of the Detroit Pistons, owned two factories making windshield glass. One factory was non-union, with a young, virtually all-white workforce. It was in Sandusky, Ohio. The other factory was a UAW plant, with an older, multi-racial workforce. It was in Detroit.

In the summer of 1981, Davidson told the 200 workers in his Detroit plant they would have to take wage cuts. As the only unionized workforce in the 20 factories owned by his Guardian Industries, Davidson said they were too expensive compared to non-union workers in his Ohio plant.

"We never ruled out concessions," recalled Sam Loiacano, local union leader in the Detroit plant. "But they had to show us. All they said was the plant was making money, but not enough. Hell, what's 'enough?' We could never find out. Their books stayed shut."

When union members struck against the company's take-back demands, Davidson permanently closed the factory. Even when the union agreed to accept the concessions three days later, Davidson remained unmoved. The jobs, he announced, had already been moved to Sandusky.

Union pickets demonstrated at a Detroit Pistons game to protest the "runaway" move to Ohio, and union lawyers began legal proceedings against the company for withholding financial information during bargaining. Davidson, the union charged, had planned to close the Detroit plant no matter what the union did, and had expanded his Ohio factory accordingly. His concession demands were intentionally provocative, said the union,

Above: One of several hundred UAW members leafleting the fans at a Detroit Pistons game.

Inset: The former Guardian plant in Detroit.

and the resulting strike only made it easier to close the Detroit plant.

The jobs were gone. But under mounting pressure from the legal rulings and wide publicity won by the union, Davidson finally agreed to pay each worker in Detroit a severance check of $300 per year of service (up from his initial offer of only $70), plus lifetime health and life insurance for retirees. The $2–3 million settlement was, according to the union, several times more expensive than the wage concessions originally demanded.

public auction to pay their debts. They walked away with nothing.

On the city's Northeast side, Solomon's Temple Church announced in November, 1982, that it would distribute free Thanksgiving provisions to the needy. On the appointed day, over 10,000 people waited in the rain for hours to collect the donated food.

On the Northwest side, during August of that year, police patrolled the 22-square mile 14th precinct with just five squad cars. Because of extensive layoffs, a clerk and computer operator had to pair up in one police cruiser to meet minimum patrolling schedules. A local court bailiff, attempting to repossess a car, found neighbors forcibly blocking the driveway. His emergency call to the precinct headquarters brought only apologies—there were no available squad cars to help out. Neither were there enough officers to investigate the rising number of reported

burglaries in the precinct.

"It's like the frontier out here," commented one officer. "The people aren't getting the service they want, and we aren't getting the support we need. . . . Too many people don't have jobs."

Far from the 14th precinct, *New York Times* columnist William Safire evaluated the impact of unemployment in far more upbeat terms. The recession, he argued, was just the sort of "discipline therapy" needed to cure inflation. It would only harm the inefficient. "Timid managers and lazy workers will suffer, while the go-getters can go and get.... The work ethic," Safire happily concluded, "is renewed."

Such Hooveresque commentary was not the media norm. Unlike the scolding press coverage directed at the unemployed a half-century earlier, TV and print coverage of jobless workers in the 1980s was generally sympathetic, if spotty.

Unlike the early years of the 1930s, Detroit's jobless were not left to shift for themselves. For thousands, the welfare "safety net" first established during the New Deal provided emergency income and food subsidies that significantly cushioned the blow of long-term unemployment. By 1981, over half the city's population depended on some form of public assistance, principally unemployment insurance, training allowances, food stamps, trade-adjustment benefits, or, when all else failed, welfare.

Yet just as the need for such income protection became most acute, the federal government cut these social-service programs and raised military spending instead. Most Detroit-area congressional representatives voted against the social-service cuts, but prominent leaders of both major parties backed the shift towards military priorities. The impact on Michigan was disastrous. In 1981, with 8,000 jobless workers running out of unemployment benefits every *month* in Detroit, the federal government cut $420 million from the state's social-service subsidies.

To qualify for welfare benefits after these massive cutbacks, a family had to liquidate all but $1,000 of its savings and property—not counting their home or their car if it was valued below $1,500. "In Pontiac," George Covintree of the Southeastern Michigan Emergency Food Coalition pointed out, "a lot of the workers at the plant bought a Pontiac car to help with the big campaign to buy what they build. Now they're unemployed, [but]...that Pontiac puts them over the limit for eligibility."

Even after selling off their few remaining assets, families had to wait months—sometimes a year—before they could collect benefits. The anguish and uncertainty of such a wait made the paltry benefits all the more humiliating. After federal and state budget cuts in social services, the *maximum* welfare benefit for a quarter-million Michigan families in 1981 was only $35 a week per family member. Many refused, as a matter of self respect, to apply for welfare under these terms. Others had little choice when hunger began to wear down their pride.

Hank Wallace said he would stick it out as long as he could without turning to public assistance. "I am a very proud person," said the unemployed autoworker, two years after his plant closed in 1981. Without a family to support, the 43-year-old former maintenance man took up residence in his rusted automobile, parking it under the lights of a 24-hour diner to ward off prowlers while he slept. "I only wear what I can wash in public washing machines," Wallace told a news reporter. He washed himself in gas station restrooms.

There were thousands of homeless people in Detroit like Wallace, living in cars, emergency shelters, or abandoned buildings. For the many other poor and unemployed who managed to hold onto their homes or find alternative shelter, life was only marginally better. In 1980, 414,000 people in metropolitan Detroit lived below the federally defined poverty level; by the end of 1982, the number had jumped past 600,000. Unemployment among the city's blacks reached 37 percent by the end of 1982—68 percent among black teenagers. Unfortunately, many blamed themselves, not the economy, for their misfortune. As unemployment climbed between 1980 and 1982, the suicide rate rose by 20 percent in Detroit and Michigan. The number of suburban whites seeking counseling for heroin addiction jumped dramatically in these same years, while deaths by drug overdose more than doubled in the metro area.

Detroit's desperate plight drew international comparisons and international aid. In the city's most impoverished neighborhoods, the infant mortality rate rose to 33 deaths per 1,000 live births, equaling the death rate in Honduras, Central America's poorest country. Cutbacks in government health programs, inadequate nutrition, and low birth weight accounted for most of the increase.

Autoworkers and civic organizations in West Germany, prodded by the grim news from Detroit, were moved to action. In 1982, they began sending canned goods and clothing to aid the hard-pressed citizens of America's sixth-largest city.

The poor, unemployed, and elderly of Detroit's Poletown line up for surplus food distributed by the city. In 1937, when the building was owned by the Mazer–Cressman Cigar Company, it was the site of a sitdown strike by 400 women cigar workers (site 42).

"**D**etroit faces a winter of crisis," announced Mayor Young in December, 1982, as thousands of city residents fell through the tattered mesh of the welfare safety net. "It is the task of government and the responsibility of a concerned citizenry to see that no one starves and no one freezes."

The city, however, could do little on its own to meet the needs of an estimated 400,000 ill-nourished and impoverished Detroiters. The same crisis that forced thousands to seek public assistance also left many of the city's property owners delinquent on their tax bills. As crime rates rose, the city had to pare 1,500 officers off its police force, reducing neighborhood protection and undermining affirmative action. Even after voting to increase their income taxes in 1981, the city's residents could only look forward to further cutbacks in trash collection, public transportation, and other essential services.

Much of the burden of feeding and housing the unemployed fell to the souplines, shelters, and emergency food pantries set up by private charities and self-help organizations. From the Salvation Army's Harbor Light center in the inner city, to UAW Local 735's emergency food program in suburban Ypsilanti, these 200 metro-area food providers were feeding upwards of 50,000 people a week in the closing months of 1982. "A year ago we maybe helped 50 to 75 families with food," reported the Reverend Wayne Pohl of St. Paul's church in suburban Trenton. "Now it's twice that number and more."

At the Capuchin Community Center on Detroit's East Side, the number of needy applying for food packages and meals rose with stunning abruptness. "Four years ago, we fed less than 500 daily, mostly men in their fifties," manager Lewis Hickson reported in November, 1982. "This last week, we have served on the average 2,000 people a day, men and women, most of them in their 30s."

Donations of food and money from unions, restaurants, caterers, farmers, and corporations usually provided enough to feed only the penniless. Applicants with even the smallest income were generally refused aid. "If we didn't have criteria, we'd have a line from here to Belle Isle," as Hickson put it. "There's absolutely no way we can pick up the slack that the federal government has created."

"They said it wasn't an emergency. Well what's an emergency?" asked one

Members and staff of the Service Employees International Union serving soup in 1982. Their downtown soupline was part of a protest demonstration against government economic policies.

Souplines Revisited

"We have not seen as many people in need of food since 1929," said Lewis Hickson, manager of the Capuchin Monastery's soup kitchen.

By 1982, the Capuchin friars had been serving donated food to the poor for 53 years. Their soupline, opened within days of the stock market crash of 1929, had been a landmark for the city's unemployed throughout the Great Depression. A half-century later, with widespread hunger once again a publicly acknowledged problem, the Capuchins and the Salvation Army were joined by dozens of more recently organized groups.

The Gleaners, formed in 1977, collected nearly 4 million pounds of donated food in 1982 for distribution to emergency food centers. Focus:

HOPE, a civil rights organization formed in 1968, distributed surplus federal food to 50,000 mothers and infant children that same year. The men and women who managed Manna Meals at St. Peter's Episcopal Church had only been at it for five years in 1982. But as members of Day House, a Catholic Worker shelter opened in 1976, they traced their spiritual roots to the Worker-run souplines and shelters of the 1930s.

"In 1977, serving 75 meals would have been a big day," observed Day House member Tom Lumpkin. Not so in 1982. "A lot of the people we now serve are scrimping by on Veterans benefits, social security, or welfare. When those checks run out at the end of the month, the number of people we feed rises to 400 daily."

tearful woman turned away by the Center because she and her family got $372 a month in welfare. Her husband, a laid-off Chrysler worker, had exhausted his unemployment benefits the year before. "We're hungry.... . We didn't ask to be in this situation. My husband wants to work."

There was little chance, however, that laid-off Chrysler workers would soon be going back to work, and no

chance they would be earning the same high wages that prevailed before 1979.

When Chrysler lost $1 billion that year, it appeared that all the company's 80,000 Detroit-area workers would lose their jobs. Sales of Chrysler's big-car models had slowed to a crawl, and the company only averted bankruptcy by halving employment and appealing to the federal government for loan guarantees. Under federally-imposed bailout plans, workers, suppliers, creditors, and cities where Chrysler

Above: Striking teachers in Woodhaven, Michigan, being led to jail in handcuffs and chains, April, 1980. That spring, over 1,000 members of the Michigan Education Association (MEA) struck four south-suburban school boards that failed to negotiate new contracts. After six weeks of picketing, during which nine Woodhaven teachers and two MEA staffers were jailed for violating the Circuit Court's no-strike injunction, the teachers and the school boards agreed to binding arbitration of unresolved issues—with no reprisals against striking teachers.

Inset: A member of the Detroit Federation of Teachers protests proposed cuts in teacher salaries and benefits.

plants were located all took cuts to save the company. UAW members shouldered the lion's share of the burden: $720 million in wage and benefit concessions, or roughly $15,000 per worker over three years.

Chrysler, like GM and Ford, thereafter promised to bring more competitive car models into production. But as Detroit's auto manufacturers downsized and redesigned their cars to meet foreign competition, they also downsized employment levels and moved some of their parts production overseas.

"The expressed objective of our engineering staff," according to a Chrysler memo leaked to the press in 1982, "is to increase the foreign content of our vehicles from the current 7 percent [2 percent Japanese] to as much as 25 percent by 1990." Company officials later characterized this policy as only a threat aimed at domestic parts suppliers and workers, but UAW researchers predicted an overall increase from 5 percent foreign-made components in all U.S.-assembled cars in 1982, to 20 percent by the end of the decade. Overseas plants supplying U.S. companies with engines and transmissions were already located as far away as Japan and as close as Mexico.

"It's not hard to see why American companies like to make parts in these places," *Ford Facts*, the monthly paper of UAW Local 600, observed in 1981. "Last year, Mexican autoworkers earned one third what UAW members make. In Japan, autoworkers made just $7.20 an hour. In South Korea (where GM owns half of Saehan Motors) unions are outlawed and the typical autoworker earns a meager $2 an hour."

At $11.62 an hour in 1982 wages, Detroit's autoworkers, according to U.S. car companies, were simply too expensive, particularly with the added cost of pensions, health insurance, and union-negotiated work rules. If U.S. operations could not be made "cost effective," as Ford's Vice President for North American operations put it, "I'll move to the place where I can get the product at a competitive cost."

Ford, in fact, was prepared to actually buy the competition. In 1979, the company purchased 25 percent of Toyo Kogyo, maker of Mazda, and began importing trucks and front-wheel-drive axles from the Japanese car builder. GM already owned 34 percent of Isuzu and bought 5 percent of Suzuki in 1981, enabling the company to import engines, transmissions, and finished cars from its partners' Japanese plants. Chrysler had owned 15 percent of Mitsubishi, maker of the Dodge Colt, since 1970, and acquired 14 percent of the French automaker, Peugeot, after selling its other foreign assets in 1980.

For Detroit's autoworkers, the threat of additional "outsourcing" of work to these overseas sites marked a fundamental shift in their bargaining position. For forty years, their union had been able to win continuous improvements in wages and benefits. Now, for the first time in the industry's history, the benchmark for wages in U.S. auto plants—particularly for parts manufacturing—was no longer the productivity or living standards of American workers, but the far lower labor costs American companies paid in their expanding overseas operations.

Among corporate leaders and economists, there was little doubt how American workers should respond to the threat posed by such low-wage competition. "It's time for U.S. autoworkers to stop moaning about our economic plight," said economist Robert Dunn in the December, 1980, *Detroit News*, "and do something about it. Like take a sizable wage cut." The UAW, Dunn declared, "had priced itself and its employers out of the market."

UAW President Doug Fraser saw things in distinctly different terms. "No one," he declared in public rebuttals to Dunn and other critics, "has a bigger stake in the fight to remain competitive with foreign producers than the worker." The problem, he argued, was not that American wages were too high, but that foreign wages were generally too low—to the point where many Asian and Latin American autoworkers rode bicycles to jobs producing cars they couldn't afford.

"Competing on wages with countries that share only minimally the benefits of productivity with their workers can hardly be an appropriate national goal for America." Such a policy, according to Fraser, would only undermine purchasing power in the United States and reduce economic activity still further. Far wiser, he argued, if the government first lowered interest rates from their artificially high levels, and then required both foreign and U.S. carmakers to build their cars where they sold them. Companies could then compete on the basis of design, engineering, and quality, but not on the price of human labor.

The price of human labor, as many Detroit workers saw it, was not high enough in any case, particularly as the

Former employees of Cunningham Drug Stores protest the conversion of the chain to non-union Apex Drugs, a move which cost them their jobs.

price of everything else kept rising after 1979. Non-union workers and the unemployed saw their income and savings steadily eroded by this continuing inflation, but union members could negotiate and, if necessary, go on strike to protect their wage and working standards. In the fall of 1982, 5,000 UAW members struck the General Dynamics tank plant in suburban Center Line for two weeks to restore previous cuts in pay and benefits. In December of the same year, unionized musicians of the Detroit Symphony Orchestra also walked off their jobs to win higher salaries and a continued role in selecting their conductor.

Other unions meanwhile fought just to keep what they had. Detroit's teachers waged a three-week strike to block the School Board's wage-cut proposals in 1982. Municipal workers, after voting down one set of concession proposals in 1981, finally forced the city to accept a two-year freeze on layoffs in return for the union's agreement to freeze wages.

In these particular confrontations, the job security of most union members was not directly at stake. Detroit had already laid off 20 percent of its municipal workers by the end of 1982, but the city's School Board could not move to South Carolina to escape the union; neither could the Detroit Symphony Orchestra. General Dynamics, as one of the nation's leading military contrac-

Breadwinners and Roses

A summer evening in 1980. Leona Ruffin left the health clinic where she worked as a medical secretary on Detroit's West Side, talking and joking with her co-workers as they walked to their cars. Married and mother of a baby girl, Ruffin did not rush home to care for her daughter and feed her husband. She lingered instead with the other women in the parking lot, hashing over the day's small emergencies and disrupted routines.

Finally, she and several friends piled into a car and drove to Clark Park, stopping to pick up beer for the softball game they would play that night. Leona's husband Eddie—laid off for nearly a year by Great Lakes Steel—would take care of the baby and fix dinner.

Tonight, Leona would play second base.

Fifty years before, such a reversal in traditional roles would have been dismissed as a rare, even freakish situation. But not after 1979, when economic catastrophe made women breadwinners all the more crucial to their families.

Even before the economy slumped, the traditional role of man as sole breadwinner had become the exception rather than the rule in Detroit-area households. By the late 1970s, over half the families in the metro area relied on paychecks from two family members, usually the husband and wife. In one of every five families with children, a woman was the sole parent and head of household; within the city limits of Detroit, women were the sole parent in 42 percent of all families with children. Whether single or married, a paycheck to support their families was the primary reason many of these metro-area mothers sought wage work.

The heavy layoffs that began in 1979 accelerated these trends. The industries hardest hit by the economy's downturn—auto, steel, trucking, construction—employed a predominantly male workforce. Yet even as the Detroit area lost 130,000 of these blue-collar jobs in 1980, the number of clerical jobs—most of them held by women—remained virtually unchanged.

The net result in many households was that women became sole breadwinners and men became unemployed "house husbands." This sudden change in roles, forced upon the family by outside events, created stress and conflict for both wife and husband as they tried to adjust to their new relationship.

For James Leija, a production foreman laid off by Chrysler in 1980, the prospect of taking over domestic duties in his St. Clair Shores home filled him with dread. "I resented very much having to stay home.... I felt slighted. I would pray and beg God to give me a job." But there were no jobs for Leija, and when the family's savings ran out, his wife returned to work as an attorney. Leija, ignoring the ribbing of friends who called him "Betty Crocker," learned to plan meals, clean the house, care for his infant son, and still make time for classes in computerized information systems.

For Leona and Eddie Ruffin, the change in roles was especially difficult. "Eddie felt like he'd failed us," said Leona, whose $140-a-week salary barely covered food, car payments, and medical expenses for their ailing baby. No longer able to afford their five-room apartment, they had to crowd into a single room of her mother-in-law's house. "We went through a stage of him drinking—like four- and five-day binges. He only stopped this last Christmas after the baby had a seizure and he couldn't even get out of bed to help take her to the hospital."

For Fran Marchone, a full-time barmaid working in Detroit for $3.50 an hour plus tips, the transition to sole breadwinner became all the harder when her husband, after losing his trucking job, refused to do either housework or childcare. "I told him, 'Hey, I just only have so many hours in the day. I can only do so much.'" After considerable wrangling, he took on most of the cooking, much of the laundry, and some of the childcare and shopping.

Men who agreed to take on these tasks often did so as a temporary expedient. They either expected to find work again in Detroit, or planned to look elsewhere if nothing turned up. Jean Carter's husband, an unemployed driver for a carhauling firm, wanted to look for work in the South, while she, a press operator in a Livonia auto-parts plant, wanted to stay in Detroit. As a woman and a black, she did not look forward to surrendering ten years of hard-won seniority. "It'd be tough leaving my job, the situation I've set up, being a union officer, my friends and things. It would be a little hard for me to go down there and try and get a job. I don't feel like I could just sit at home and do nothing."

tors, was one of the few Detroit manufacturers in a growth industry: it could clearly afford to raise wages from the depressed levels that prevailed when Chrysler owned the tank plant before 1982.

But other employers who could not or would not raise wages often could—and did—leave the state. National Twist Drill, for example, not only could move south to escape the UAW, but had the incentive to do so when sales to Detroit's car companies slumped after 1979. The company had already used profits made in Michigan to build a plant in non-union North Carolina during the mid-1970s. In 1981, it opened another new factory in South Carolina. After gradually shifting work south and reducing employment in its Rochester, Michigan, plant from 1800 to 250, National Twist Drill asked the remaining workers to take steep cuts in wages and benefits. The workers refused when the company would not guarantee their jobs, and in November, 1982, management announced plans to close the suburban facility altogether.

Such episodes were not limited to industrial settings. Non-manufacturing employers, prodded by declining profit margins and the precedent-setting Chrysler concessions, also demanded cutbacks in wages to keep their businesses open. Some even switched to non-union labor without leaving

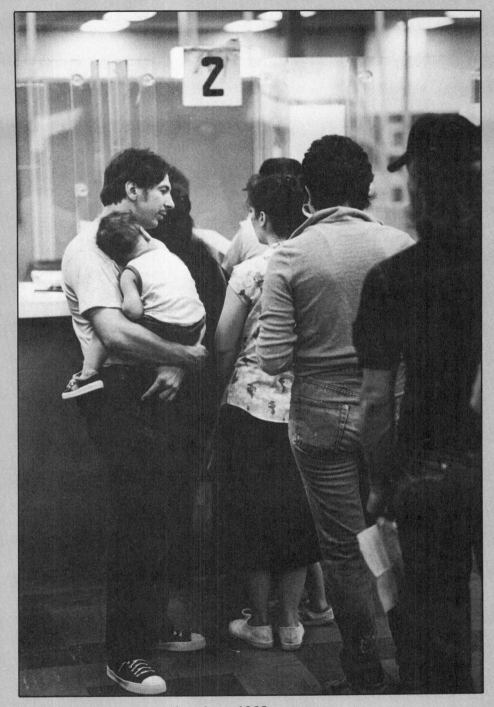

A Detroit unemployment line, June, 1982.

Helen Mauer's role as sole breadwinner also had an air of impermanence. "I realize that we can't continue like this," she said of the secretarial job she took when Chrysler laid off her husband. "I don't make enough money.... My husband plans to get in his car and drive south and call me on the phone and say, 'Helen, I got a job.' But for now, I enjoy our life, him being at home, taking over some of my responsibilities, learning to be closer to his children, and my going to work and coming home and my dinner being ready. It's nice."

For Rex Gray, a former machine operator at GM's Detroit Diesel plant, a job would come "someday when things pick up." In the meantime, his wife worked both as a cashier at Montgomery Ward and as a part-time clerk at West Dearborn Vision. Rex worked fulltime at home, raising three boys, washing diapers, cooking meals, cleaning the house. When he could find a job again outside the home, the housework would "definitely be a two-party thing," Gray promised. "I just don't see how she ever went through it alone."

For Gray and others like him, the crucible of unemployment recast all the norms of family life. Under the intense pressure, some families became more unified, while others fell to pieces. In no case, however, could the boundaries of traditional male-female roles remain unchallenged. "I don't want to raise my children with this idea that 'this is man's work and this is women's work,'" Helen Mauer explained. "I've come too far to go backwards."

Detroit. In 1982, two Directors of CD Holding Company, after buying 29 Cunningham Drug Stores from their own firm, summarily fired the unionized workforce and reopened the chain as Apex Drugs. Collective bargaining agreements with Local 876 of the United Food and Commercial Workers and Local 337 of the Teamsters were ignored, and 400 clerks who had previously earned $6.17 an hour plus benefits suddenly found themselves on the street.

"The only thing the manager told us was they were going to pay $3.57 an hour," recalled one female clerk with seven years seniority. "No insurance, no full-time work. We were not told a place to apply." Apex turned instead to the long lines of unemployed jobseekers willing to work for these near-minimum wages.

Peaceful picketing by Local 876 and Local 337 turned many customers away from Apex. But while the unions, in a series of lengthy legal proceedings, pressed charges against the company for breach of contract, the picket lines gradually thinned, the customers slowly returned, and Apex's owners ultimately reaped the harvest of their union-busting strategy.

Neither Ford nor GM was about to drive the UAW out of their U.S.-based operations. The future of those

and Ford rising above 200,000, the UAW's elected Bargaining Councils at both companies voted in January, 1982, to discuss contract changes with management. "The situation in the industry," UAW President Fraser told union members, "has changed considerably since we last discussed this question. You have to review your policy in light of the circumstances."

The new contracts negotiated with GM and Ford over the next several months reduced labor costs by between $1 billion and $2 billion at each company, spread over 2½ years. Union negotiators agreed to give up some holidays, to delay several cost-of-living allowances, and to drop a scheduled 3 percent raise for the 420,000 UAW members still working at Ford and GM. In return, the companies agreed to reconsider plans for foreign sourcing of parts, to share a portion of future profits with union members, and to guarantee another job or income-to-retirement for those high-seniority employees who suffered future layoffs.

This latter benefit, called the Guaranteed Income Stream, represented an historic step forward in the union's campaign for secure employment. But the wage concessions the union granted in return marked an equally historic turnabout. For the first time since World War II, the UAW's negotiations with GM and Ford had not focused on what union members would gain, but on what they would lose. This, in turn, provoked the most embittered debate within the union since the faction fighting of the 1940s.

The outcome of this infighting, as it continued throughout 1982, varied company by company, plant by plant. At Ford, where financial losses were the most serious, 73 percent of the UAW's voting membership favored the new contract. At GM, a majority also backed the proposed agreement—but only a slim majority of 52 percent. In many of the company's body and parts plants, members voted heavily for the new contract in the hope it would keep their factories open. But in major car-assembly operations, where the potential for foreign "outsourcing" by GM was not so immediate a threat, the contract was often defeated. Opponents resented having to freeze their wages when the company was making profits again in 1981 (even if reduced), and when GM's top 55 executives paid themselves salaries averaging $500,000 apiece—400 percent higher than the average $100,000 salary for Toyota executives.

The contract was narrowly ratified

The former Whitehead & Kales plant in suburban River Rouge. In the 1970s, 800 members of the United Steel Workers built automobile-carrying rail cars for this 80-year-old firm. Company owners decided to close the plant in 1982, two years after receiving a tax break to upgrade the facility.

operations, however, was very much in doubt in 1980 and 1981, particularly at Ford. Led by huge losses in its North American division, the number-two automaker lost $2.5 billion in the two-year period. Even GM, which had weathered the Great Depression of the 1930s without a single year in the red, lost $760 million in 1980.

Seeking the most immediate solution to their financial crisis, both companies called on the UAW to extend to them the same concessions granted Chrysler. Otherwise, predicted GM Chairman Roger Smith, "there will be more plants shutting down and more auto-industry jobs going offshore."

With laid-off union members at GM

despite these resentments, and the debate over union concessions at GM and Ford immediately shifted to the local level. Here, plant managers had long sought to amend locally negotiated work rules that defined job responsibilities, work schedules, transfer procedures, overtime, and seniority rights. Some UAW locals, under direct threat of plant closings or promises of future work, agreed to far-reaching amendments in these work rules. But many other locals either refused to alter the day-to-day job rights and protections they had won over the years, or agreed to only minor concessions.

The year-long turmoil that accompanied these concession debates ended with an especially bitter confrontation at Chrysler. After working nearly three years under contract terms that paid $3-an-hour less than GM and Ford, union members expected substantial improvement in their sub-par wages in 1982. When the contract negotiated in the fall of that year fell short of their expectations, workers voted by a 70 to 30 percent margin to reject the proposed agreement. Their lopsided ''no'' vote was the first contract rejection in the history of the UAW's Big-Three negotiations.

Another precedent was set in November, when Canadian UAW members struck Chrysler without the backing of their American co-workers. Canadian inflation was even higher than in the United States, and after three years without compensating wage increases, Canadian workers had run out of patience. Five weeks after the walkout began, the company agreed to raise hourly wages $1.15 in Canada and 75¢ in the United States. Union members on both sides of the Detroit River voted heavily in favor of the compromise settlement.

That same December, the UAW and GM agreed to divert $30 million from a union-negotiated education fund to unemployed GM workers. Each would receive $300. ''With this $300, my 9-year-old daughter will have a Christmas,'' said Lida Belcher, a former worker at GM's Ypsilanti plant. In every other respect, the future looked as bleak as before. ''I got my last unemployment check on November 22 and will be sign-ing up for welfare next month. I have looked everywhere for a job but nobody's hiring.''

The long months of unemployment would be harsh indeed for thousands of jobless workers who had exhausted their savings, their unemployment benefits, and their hopes of finding work. Some families pulled together through the crisis; others were pulled apart.

''The pressure is bad,'' explained George Azzopardi, one year after Ford laid him off and the Hyatt Hotel cut back his wife's laundry job. ''My stomach is all nerved up. Sometimes we go a day or two without eating. When I got a minimum-wage job cutting grass for the city, they cut off our food stamps. We're losing weight, hungry, nervous all the time. We don't even feel like husband and wife anymore.''

For the Azzopardis and thousands of unemployed workers in the Detroit area, it appeared to be the end of the line for the region's economy. Many, like the unemployed of the 1930s, would decide to leave Detroit behind, to pack their belongings and set out on the highway—headed for Dallas, Houston, or wherever else jobs were rumored to be.

Detroit, Woodward Avenue and Six Mile, 1981.

REMAKING DETROIT

I think it is really more difficult to lead now. There are so few victories.

**Doug Fraser,
past President, UAW**

A half century after the Great Depression, Doug Fraser, the last representative of the UAW's founding generation, retired from the union's Presidency. His departure in May, 1983, marked the end of an era.

Virtually all of his contemporaries in Detroit's labor movement had already left office. Some had died before their time: Walter and May Reuther in a small plane crash in 1970; former Teamster President Jimmy Hoffa in a 1975 gangland killing; Myra Wolfgang, head of Detroit's Hotel and Restaurant Employees, after surgery in 1976. Most, however, had retired. In the UAW alone, 13 of 18 regional directors and 5 of 7 vice presidents left office between 1979 and 1983, clearing the way for a new generation of leaders.

Owen Bieber, Fraser's successor as UAW President, was acutely aware of this change in generations. "I was but eight years old," he told union convention delegates in his inaugural address, "when our brave brothers and sisters put their lives on the line and won the General Motors strike in Flint. Like many of you, I was not around for the birth of the union."

Bieber, the son of a UAW member and father of three more, could nevertheless claim to be "a product, heart and soul, of what was created in those difficult struggles." Many of his listeners could make the same claim, for the labor movement's collective-bargaining victories and legislative achievements, born of the Great Depression, had shaped the lives of Michigan's workers in crucial ways. The world was a better place to live in, and the labor movement, by challenging the worst abuses of a boom-bust, segregated, and profit-maximizing economy, had done much to make it so.

Yet now, as the union's founding generation retired, that world was apparently coming unglued. Fifty years after the stock market crash of 1929, another severe depression had settled upon the city and the region where the UAW, and much of the modern labor and civil rights movement, had originated. Plant closings, layoffs, wage freezes, and wage cuts had once again become commonplace.

Victories for working people were now few indeed.

Detroit's labor movement was at a crossroads, and charting the new road ahead was no simple matter.

The path to recovery would have been easier to define if the catastrophic slump beginning in 1979 had been a mere repeat of the 1930s. If such had been the case, the tactics and strategies that worked in the 1930s might work again in the 1980s. But beyond the double-digit unemployment and the human misery evident in both, the two eras had little in common.

The Great Depression of the 1930s followed decades of intensive urbanization and concentration of production, symbolized in Detroit by Ford's gigantic River Rouge plant. Few doubted that the Rouge, or Dodge Main, or GM's Flint factories were the most productive manufacturing facilities in the world, unrivaled by foreign or domestic competitors. These massive production centers apparently needed just one thing to make them profitable again—more customers. Spurring consumer spending was therefore seen by many trade unionists and public planners as the key to reviving underutilized factories. To create this new purchasing power, they called for more government jobs programs to boost employment, more trade-union militancy to raise wages, and more social reforms to aid the poor and unemployed. Once the New Deal's spending policies and the union movement's negotiated wage increases had "primed the pump" of consumer spending, business, it was argued, would expand both production and employment to meet the rising demand.

For much of the post-World War II era, government programs to aid the poor and spur consumer demand helped underwrite a buoyant national economy. By 1979, however, this economic formula had lost much of its relevance. Simple "pump priming" was no longer enough to keep Detroit afloat, for the city's economic "pump" had fallen into serious disrepair. Since the 1930s, suburbanization and decentralization of production had drained the city of

The Three Things Needed

Above: *In this 1945 cartoon from the **United Automobile Worker**, government job programs are "priming the pump" of purchasing power and creating full employment. Some 40 years later, the pump carried less of that purchasing power to Detroit, and more of it to Sunbelt states and overseas.*

Opposite: *Dodge Main being demolished in 1981.*

population and capital, and Detroit's aging factories were no longer models of efficiency. Many employers had moved some or all of their production to rural Michigan, to the Sunbelt, to Mexico, or other regions, and unlike the 1930s, lower-wage foreign competition from Japan and elsewhere was capturing much of the North American market for automobiles and parts.

Under these circumstances, government programs to spur consumer demand could still revive car sales, but unlike the 1930s, many of those cars would be made in the overseas plants of Nissan, Toyota, and GM. The militant union tactics of the 1930s might forestall the "takeaway" demands of some employers, but they could not prevent other companies from shifting production to low-wage areas at home and abroad. Neither could militancy alone prevent foreign competitors from undermining U.S. wage and working standards with low-cost imports.

The economy had changed dramatically since the 1930s. So too had the constituency of Detroit's unions.

In 1937, the city's workers were drawn together by their shared experience of job insecurity, low pay, and harsh workplace discipline. Autoworkers did get higher wages than cigar workers, but during the Great Depression both hardly got enough to make ends meet, and neither could count themselves far removed from the poverty and unemployment that afflicted their neighbors. Under these uniformly depressed conditions, many workers readily endorsed the militancy of their counterparts in other industries, and the labor movement that grew on this solidarity called itself the champion of all working people.

Ironically, by 1979, the movement's very success in collective bargaining had partially undermined its claim to speak for all workers. The labor movement still championed the general interests of

Above: Toyota cars being loaded for export in Nagoya Port, Japan.

Inset: In 1934, a cargo of automobiles bound for England represented the world-wide dominance of Detroit's car companies—a dominance that Japanese manufacturers captured in the 1970s.

working people—for social security, unemployment insurance, and a safe workplace—but a gulf now separated its relatively high-wage, dues-paying constituency from the growing number of lower-wage, non-union workers in service and clerical jobs. Fast-food workers making $3.60 an hour, with no union, no benefits, and no guarantee of full-time work, often had a hard time sympathizing with the militancy of auto-workers making $11.50 an hour plus benefits. For many workers in occupations and industries where unions had failed to organize, the labor movement was just another interest group, out to protect the privileged position of blue-collar union members.

In the boom years before 1979, some unions had not only lost touch with this growing non-union workforce, but also with their own members. "When times were good and there were lots of dues rolling in, people got lazy," said union leader Florence Farr of her own organization, the Hotel and Restaurant Employees. "They [union representatives] got isolated from the people. They got out of the shops. They handled grievances, but didn't really go in and say 'Hi, how are you, and how's your kids.' And that built a wall."

It was, in many cases, a wall of mistrust. "Union Presidents—and I'll include myself—are too often called 'bosses' rather than leaders by our own members," observed the late Jerry Wurf, President of the American Federation of State, County, and Municipal Employees. "And there is some accuracy to that perception," he told a Michigan AFL–CIO gathering in 1981. "We tend to make our grand decisions and then hand them down expecting to be followed. So what happens? The members go out and vote for Reagan."

In 1980, blue-collar and minority voters in Detroit actually rejected Ronald Reagan by a wide margin. But statewide, the Republican Presidential candidate won enough votes from union members to carry Michigan and defeat the union-endorsed candidate, incumbent Jimmy Carter. The conservative victory was a critical setback for the labor movement. It also marked yet another contrast with the 1930s.

Fifty years before, Detroit's unions looked to Washington for support as they struggled to overcome the determined—and frequently illegal—resistance of employers. The New Deal administration of President Roosevelt did not always deliver on its promised aid to the labor movement, but the government did pass a multitude of job bills, social-service programs, and labor laws that benefited unions.

After 1980, a decidedly different atmosphere prevailed in Washington. Detroit's labor movement, already beset by the worst economic crisis since the Great Depression, now faced an ad-ministration that promised to reward profit making and return the government to the pre-New Deal policies of unregulated "free enterprise." Stable growth, President Reagan argued, would not be achieved by policies that boosted consumer demand through high wages and government spending. Instead, the President backed measures favoring the "supply side" of the economic equation, such as deregulation of industry, lower taxes on profits, and other incentives that might encourage business expansion.

Detroit's labor movement did not expect to benefit from these policies. Indeed, after 1980, more employers were closing factories in Detroit and moving production out of the region. Foreign imports of autos, steel, and other products were on the rise, and federal support for the poor and unemployed was on the decline. Public opinion, in the meantime, did not seem to favor a militant response to the takeaway demands of employers. Caught in this bind, Detroit's unions traded concessions in wages and work rules for whatever they could win in the way of job security. It was not a happy compromise.

"This industry is a God-damn shambles," Doug Fraser said of the city's carmakers in 1982, shortly after renegotiating UAW contracts at Ford and GM. "All of management's mistakes are catching up with them, and there's certainly controversy in our union as to whether or not we did the right thing [renegotiating]." The concessions granted in the new contracts would, Fraser hoped, forestall further plant closings. The profit sharing and guaranteed employment-or-income for senior employees might also break ground for future gains. But as Fraser himself acknowledged, these concession contracts were, at best, holding actions.

A lasting and equitable recovery for Detroit's workers required much more. Confronted by an unprecedented crisis, Detroit's labor movement had to devise new initiatives in organizing, political action, and economic policy. Above all, if the movement was to survive as a vital, democratic force, it would have to reinvigorate its own membership and reach out to allies beyond the workplace.

Detroit's corporate leaders also had reason to re-evaluate their past and ponder their future.

As owners and managers of billions of dollars worth of assets, they wielded a domineering influence over the city's economy. That economy was now in crisis, and many observers blamed these "Captains of Industry" for steering the wrong course. Some executives hardly cared—they could move their business elsewhere and leave Detroit's troubles behind. But others had already, by the mid-1970s, committed themselves to a modest program of rehabilitating the city's economic base.

The most visible symbol of this corporate initiative was the $357 million, multi-tower Renaissance Center on Detroit's downtown waterfront—the single most expensive private building project in the nation's history. Heavily promoted by Henry Ford II, Mayor Coleman Young, and the newly formed Detroit Renaissance coalition, the "Ren Cen" was not the kind of profit-maximizing investment businessmen were accustomed to make. Few of the 51 Detroit-area corporations who bankrolled the project expected it to return

End of the Beaten Path

As its auto industry floundered, Detroit's factories no longer attracted migrant workers from around the world. Yet Arab and Hispanic immigrants continued to arrive in the city, seeking relatives and job referrals among previously established compatriots.

By 1980, the Detroit area's Arab-American population numbered about 200,000. The majority were Lebanese Christians and Iraqi-Chaldeans—the latter group especially visible as owners of over 400 grocery stores—living in North Central Detroit, North Dearborn, and nearby suburbs. The fastest growing Arab population, however, was Muslim, principally Palestinian and Yemeni, driven by poverty and Arab-Israeli conflict to Dearborn's Southend and Wayne County's western suburbs.

Hispanic Detroit was also divided by old and new immigration: the city's 90,000 Mexican-Americans were more established and more likely to hold jobs at nearby Ford and Great Lakes Steel than the city's 20,000 Puerto Ricans, who arrived later and found it more difficult to get a job in Detroit's depressed economy.

Above: West Vernor, main artery of Detroit's Hispanic barrio.

Inset: Dearborn's Arab–American enclave, next to the Ford Rouge plant.

Rather than bring foreign labor to Detroit, as Ford had in the early years of the auto industry, car manufacturers moved work around the world in the 1970s and 1980s. The computer pictured above linked Ford's Engineering Center in Dearborn with the company's computer center in Dunton, England, allowing Ford to tap a worldwide supply of engineering labor as it designed its new models.

substantial or immediate profits when it opened in 1977. For companies like K-Mart, the *Detroit News*, Kelsey-Hayes, and others that had already moved production and office facilities to the suburbs, investing in the Ren Cen was belated recognition that, as metro-area employers, the viability of their operations depended on a minimally healthy downtown.

"Suppose we didn't put up that money and the town closed," said Ford executive Wayne Doran the year after the Ren Cen opened. "That could have cost us a lot more.... . The Rouge plant investment, the downriver investments that we have—they all depend on Detroit making it."

According to the Renaissance Center's backers, the project's 70-story hotel and surrounding office buildings would anchor Detroit's downtown revival and serve as a symbol of the core

city's future vitality. That future, they promised, would see Detroit established as a regional convention center, communications hub, and bedroom community for high-income professionals and executives. New office towers, apartment buildings, and a giant stadium, Joe Louis Arena, heralded this new beginning. Construction jobs and service-sector employment in the downtown grew apace.

But it was the auto industry, more than the downtown, that attracted the attention of corporate planners after 1979. The precipitous drop in production, employment, and profits that began in that year dramatically underlined the need to restructure Detroit's bread-and-butter industry. New cars, new factories, new machines, and new labor policies followed in short order.

There was even a new model of industrial success to guide this automotive

"renaissance." Seventy years before, Detroit's employers had launched a campaign to Americanize the city's immigrant and migrant workforce, but now the shoe was on the other foot. "If we hope to compete with Japan," said GM vice president Alex Mair in January of 1983, "we have to become like them."

"Becoming like them," as Mair and other executives saw it, meant adopting Japan's fuel-efficient, front-wheel-drive automobile designs. It meant older factories making rear-wheel-drive components had to be closed or converted to front-wheel-drive technologies. It meant that engine plants building gas-guzzling V-8s would give way to newer plants, here and abroad, building four- and six-cylinder engines. It meant that metal parts made in die-casting and stamping plants would, in many cases, be replaced by lighter, corrosion-resistant parts made of plastic, fiberglass, or carbon fiber.

Factory closings were inevitable, particularly as the "downsized" Chrysler Corporation closed iron foundries, stamping plants, and other parts suppliers in the Detroit area. But even as these supplier plants were closing, Ford and especially GM were rebuilding their assembly operations in the Midwest. In fact, with imports (mostly Japanese) accounting for 51 percent of California's automobile sales by 1982, Ford and GM reversed their previous policy of decentralized assembly in the North American market. Between 1979 and 1982, these two companies closed all but one of their five assembly plants on the West Coast and began a partial retreat to their traditional base in the Midwest.

The new assembly plants that GM began building in Michigan were entirely unlike the older factories they replaced. Where before, separate Fisher Body plants shipped car bodies to nearby assembly plants, now GM built huge factories in Detroit, Flint, and the Pontiac suburb of Orion Township that consolidated these separate operations under one roof. Each factory covered three million square feet, the equivalent of 342 football fields. In Detroit's Poletown, the city, state, and federal governments spent $200 million in taxpayers' money to make way for the new Cadillac facility, clearing away 1,500 home and businesses. In Flint, the new "Buick City" plant required demolition of 400 homes.

Buick City, the company promised, would rival Japan's Toyota City in its production efficiencies. There was even a Japanese word to describe the streamlined operations planned at this and other new factories: "Kanban," or "just-in-time" delivery.

Under Kanban, instead of spending billions of dollars a year to ship, handle and stockpile a 35- or 60-day supply of parts in factory warehouses, "just-in-time" delivery allowed plant managers to order parts only as they needed them, cutting inventories to something approaching the two-day supply maintained by Japanese automakers. Some components—engines and transmissions especially—would be imported in growing numbers from factories in Mexico and Japan. But for Kanban to work, the car companies had to favor parts suppliers in and around Michigan. Instead of taking shipments by the trainload from these suppliers, automakers increased their small-batch deliveries by truck, reducing the need for storage space and handling. "The less shipping time," noted Robert Rennard, regional operations manager for Ford, "the less money you have tied up in inventory and shipping."

Ironically, the Japanese had learned this simple rule by copying the original Ford and GM operations in Dearborn and Flint. "The entire Buick operation in Flint in the 1920s was set up for 'just-in-time,'" acknowledged GM's Alex Mair. But in the post World War II boom, "efficiency became less important, and we began to erect assembly plants all over the country."

By 1981, the Japanese were teaching the Americans. Ford Rouge, once the world leader with GM in combining parts-manufacturing and car-assembly operations in one coordinated production complex, now looked to Japan for the capital and know-how to modernize its operations. When Ford sought a buyer to take over and upgrade the aging steel mills on the Rouge site, the company initially turned to Nippon Kokan, one of Japan's largest steelmakers.

Japanese precedent was no less compelling when it came to labor relations.

"The real difference between us and the Japanese," said Ford vice president Peter Pestillo, shortly after the company's 1982 negotiations with the UAW, "is that our labor-relations system is law driven, and the Japanese is human-relations driven.... [And] their system," he added, "is working better than ours."

As some executives belatedly recognized in the 1970s, the "law-driven" nature of American labor relations was a product of the top-down decision-making process established in American industry after 1900. "At the dawn of the twentieth century," noted Ted Mills, management consultant and advisor to GM, "Frederick Taylor urged dividing human and machine labor down into the smallest and easiest functions: to create dumb, foolproof jobs for dumb human beings, whom he characterized as essentially lazy, greedy, and demanding of discipline."

When workers rebelled against management's authoritarian "laws" in the 1930s, they did so by pushing for union work rules and a grievance procedure. In union workplaces, conflicts were to be resolved according to the "common law" precedents established by this grievance and arbitration process. Compared to management's one-sided rule, it was an equitable system for resolving disputes. It was a workable system at least until the 1960s, when rising discontent with factory discipline clogged the grievance procedure and periodically paralyzed the production process.

In Japanese automobile factories, on

The General Motors Poletown plant (site 32) under construction in the foreground, and the Renaissance Center four miles distant in the background. The continued slide in auto sales delayed construction of the Poletown plant and forced the Renaissance Center to default on its taxes and mortgage in 1982.

Clericals, engineers, and other white-collar workers often viewed computerized operations with mixed feelings. A desk-top terminal and keyboard could dramatically improve information retrieval, work speed, and problem-solving capacities. But computer terminals could also replace or de-skill bank tellers, typists, and engineering draftsmen—with no guarantee managers would upgrade displaced workers to new jobs.

the other hand, a "human relations approach," as Pestillo called it, sought to minimize conflict in the first place by incorporating workers into the decision-making process. Workers, instead of being pigeon-holed into narrow tasks, could learn new skills and be paid for their added knowledge. "Quality Circles," made up of blue- and white-collar workers, jointly discussed production problems and implemented solutions on their own authority. Instead of 11 to 15 levels of management separating the shop floor from the front office, as in American auto plants, there were only 5 or 6 management levels in most Japanese auto factories.

Beginning in 1973 and with a growing sense of urgency after 1979, Ford and GM worked with the UAW to implement similar innovations in their U.S. factories. Dubbed Employee Involvement (EI) at Ford and Quality of Work Life (QWL) at GM, both programs had the same official goal: to give blue-collar workers more responsibility for creating a satisfactory work environment and producing a better-quality car. Neither EI or QWL was to replace collective bargaining or the grievance procedure,

but both, it was hoped, would improve worker morale and initiative. "Labor and management really have to find a way for getting along," argued Pestillo, "because the price of not getting along is to have us both lose our jobs."

But some jobs would be lost in any case as the industry adopted yet another innovation employed by the Japanese: robots.

Here again, robot technology, like Kanban, actually had an American pedigree. Unimation, a Connecticut-based company, built the first industrial robot and sold it to General Motors in 1961, but the company decided the machine had little future in the industry and bought fewer than 70 Unimates over the next ten years. It was left to Japan to adopt this American-made technology and become the eventual world leader in "robotics."

Their innovations marked a dramatic departure from the "hard" automation that had characterized auto production since Henry Ford's day. Previously, the automated machines and conveyor lines in a factory could do one job only—they had a single specialized function that could only be modified by lengthy and

costly retooling.

The development of "microprocessors" in the 1960s and 1970s made possible an entirely different sort of automation. Using a tiny, $5 computer chip with more computing power than older room-size computers, robots could be built and programmed to perform a variety of functions with varying tools. Their crucial advantage over "hard" automation was their capacity to be reprogrammed, quickly and cheaply, to perform new operations.

Their advantage over humans was price. Working three shifts a day, a robot cost about $6 an hour in 1980, roughly one-third the cost in wages and benefits of an autoworker. During those shifts, robots could be programmed to weld bodies, spray paint, machine parts, move engine blocks, assemble components, retrieve inventory, load and unload machines, or inspect their own work—and all without taking coffee breaks or filing grievances.

By 1980, GM had installed only 400 robots, but as the company began to rebuild and modernize its factories in earnest, it rapidly expanded its robot workforce. By 1982, there were 1,600 robots installed or on order in GM's factories. By the end of the decade, the company planned to have 14,000 in use, many of them built under a joint production arrangement with Japan's leading robotics firm, Fujitsu Fanuc.

Ford and Chrysler were also committed to the new technology. Ford planned to install over 5,000 robots in its North American car and truck plants during the 1980s. In 1982, robots and automated machinery in Chrysler's Jefferson Avenue plant (site 22) already performed 98 percent of the welds in the company's K-car—compared to 97 percent in Nissan's most advanced Japanese plants.

By the end of 1983, Detroit's automotive "renaissance" appeared to be in early bloom.

Rising production of cars and trucks brought more than 100,000 autoworkers back to work nationwide. Output was still 25 percent below pre-1979 levels, but the industry's cost-cutting and the UAW's wage concessions produced record profits at Ford, Chrysler, and GM. Cutbacks in capacity and union wage concessions also made Great Lakes Steel one of the few mills in the country to operate at a profit in 1983.

Chrysler's turnaround was especially encouraging. Nearly bankrupted during the crisis years of 1979-81, the company had not only survived with government-backed loans and union sacrifices, but had posted record profits and embarked on an $8 billion, five-year program to develop new product lines. Chrysler had closed ten Detroit-area factories between 1980 and 1982, but in 1983 the company began planning for a new assembly plant in suburban Sterling Heights. It even repaid its government loans seven years ahead of schedule, while also negotiating wage increases that brought its workers back within $1 of hourly wages at Ford and GM.

There were signs that the Detroit area was also well on its way to the high-tech, service-economy future promised by corporate planners. "It's generally understood that Michigan is becoming a center for robotics," the director of the state's Commerce Department claimed in 1982. Tapping the state's large supply of unemployed machinists and toolmakers, 15 robotics firms had already located their operations in Michigan—more than in any other state. In 1983, Automatix Incorporated, the nation's largest manufacturer of robot vision systems, added its name to the list by announcing plans for a robot assembly plant in suburban Detroit. "The reason we chose Michigan," said company President Philippe Villers, "is [that] the Michigan and Detroit area, in particular, is by far the largest user of robots in the country."

These were encouraging signs for a working population accustomed to uniformly bad news since 1979. But for many, it was too little too late, and for others, the economy's promised renaissance contained pitfalls and costs that significantly dampened their enthusiasm.

Expanding auto production was bringing thousands back to work, but as sales and profits boomed, employment lagged well behind. Great Lakes Steel had 5,000 people on its payroll by the end of 1983, but most of the 2,500 steelworkers still on layoff would never be recalled. Neither would many of the 125,000 Detroit-area members the UAW had lost since 1979 (40 percent of its metro-wide membership). Factory managers, by scheduling an average six hours a week overtime in the fall of 1983, were avoiding recall of 95,000 autoworkers nationally, according to the UAW. Had the plants operated without overtime, new machines were just as likely to fill out future production increases as unemployed workers. *Automotive Industries*, commenting in

But They Don't Buy Cars . . .

"They never get drunk and their wives don't have babies." As suggested by this advertising slogan of a robot leasing firm, factory managers in the early 1980s viewed robots as the perfect worker: tireless, obedient, never absent. The one pictured above in GM's Pontiac truck plant applied waterproofing sealant to windshields, lifted the finished windshield with a suction cup beneath its arm, and placed it on a storage rack.

Factory workers viewed the new technology with mixed feelings. Few

doubted that robots could improve quality and reduce human exposure to work hazards. But computer-controlled devices also increased worker anxiety about job loss and skill dilution. In response, unions called for advance notice of changes in technology, a shorter workweek, improved early retirement benefits, and other measures that cushioned the impact of labor-saving innovations and shared productivity gains with workers.

1981, predicted that the 14,000 robots GM planned to install by the end of the decade would take the jobs of at least 42,000 hourly employees on a three-shift basis.

Even the high-tech assembly lines producing these new machines were subject to job-cutting automation. "A human assembler might be able to put in 200 to 240 parts in an hour," observed the owner of ADCO Circuits, a manufacturer of computer circuit boards in suburban Troy. In 1983, each of the automatic machines he was installing on his assembly line was capable of inserting 10,000 electronic components an hour. "It can do the work of 48 assemblers on an eight-hour shift."

The job loss from these manufacturing innovations would be offset, many hoped, by the new job openings in the

steadily expanding technical and service trades. But these white-collar occupations were not growing fast enough to absorb the unemployed, and skill requirements in the better-paying technical jobs (medicine, computer software, etc.) disqualified most blue-collar workers. The unemployed autoworker, truck driver or construction worker who previously earned $9 an hour or more, plus benefits, usually found the available job openings were for service and clerical positions paying as little as $3.50 an hour and seldom more than $8—with few if any benefits. Many of these were also part-time jobs. "Do you think anyone can survive on 16 to 20 hours a week?" one K Mart worker asked in a 1983 letter to the Detroit *Free Press*. "No wonder so many give up and go on welfare. . . ."

Even in low-wage growth sectors, jobs were not so easy to find. In 1983, Tom Bell, an unemployed autoworker, was living in a mobile home in suburban Ypsilanti and trying to support his family of five on a $700-a-month welfare check. When he applied for a service job delivering pizzas, the employer told him he was "too old and too overqualified" for the minimum-wage job. "They just want kids," Bell had to conclude.

Bell and thousands like him hoped the auto industry, as it re-concentrated its assembly operations in the Midwest, would one day call him back to work. But it was a longshot hope, for company plans to retool domestic plants only went so far. Major components like engines and transaxles were slated for production overseas. And while GM's new Michigan plants might assemble these components for large and mid-size cars, the company planned to import 300,000 subcompacts a year from its Japanese partners, Isuzu and Suzuki. Ford and Chrysler had similar plans.

These trends only reinforced a widespread cynicism among UAW members. "Our auto manufacturers aren't fighting the foreign imports," toolmaker Harold Hamric told a UAW skilled-trades conference in 1982. "They *are* the foreign imports!"

The price tag for rebuilding the auto industry's Detroit-area base also drew angry criticism. The cost of persuading GM to build its new Cadillac plant in Detroit seemed especially high to many. The $200 million in taxpayers' money the city spent to condemn and clear the 500-acre plant site would not bring a single new job to Detroit. The new Poletown plant (site 32) would simply replace the aging Clark Avenue assembly and Fleetwood body plants on the city's West Side (sites 21 and 35).

Eddie Niedbala, a Poletown grocer for thirty years, was among those who

QWL: The Quality of Work Life

QWL is an extension of the age-old thrust of unionism: to bring democratic values into the workplace.

Irving Bluestone,
retired UAW Vice President

If, in the early 1980s, a factory manager from the Model-T era could have returned from the grave and wandered through Plant 55 of Pontiac Motors, the setting before him would have seemed alien beyond imagining. Accustomed to the authoritarian, top-down command structures in the factories of his day, the visitor from the past would have been wholly unprepared for the cooperative work relations inside Plant 55.

The plant had not been designed by engineers alone, but with input from blue-collar workers on everything from machine layout to the design of an in-plant restaurant for hourly and salaried employees. Instead of foremen barking orders at workers, hourly and salaried employees in each department jointly discussed work issues in weekly "Participation-Group" meetings. Membership in the groups was voluntary, and group leaders were chosen by the participants; they might choose an hourly worker to lead their group, or a salaried employee.

In either case, salaried personnel were not expected to dominate a Participation Group. In discussions of how to improve work procedures and working conditions, how to reduce absenteeism, or how to rotate jobs, group members, according to Fred Wilder, a union participant, could "let that salary person know, 'are you in here to try to be the boss? Because if you are, then you're in the wrong place.'"

In Henry Ford's day, such "back talk" to a foreman would have been grounds for immediate dismissal. But in Plant 55, there were no foremen in the engine-testing department, in final repair, or in the dock areas. There were line foremen in the machining and assembly departments, but no General Foreman.

To the observer from Henry Ford's era, such arrangements could only have produced anarchy and inefficiency. In the 1980s, however, they produced results of a far different sort. The previous decade, when QWL had not been effectively established at Pontiac Motors, the 15,000 workers in the Division filed as many as 5,000 grievances a year. In 1982, the 500 workers in Plant 55 had no pending grievances. Able to hash out many of their problems in Participation Group meetings, they were also able to improve quality: only 4 of every 5,000 engines produced in Plant 55 had to be pulled for repairs once they were bolted into a finished Pontiac—the lowest "pull rate" for any GM engine plant.

I f the ghostly plant manager visiting from the past found QWL difficult to digest, his adversaries from the Industrial Workers of the World—the revolutionary union of the pre-World-War-I era—would probably have found it poisonous.

The IWW's "Wobblies" would have approved of only one thing in Plant 55: the absence of foremen in some departments and their reduced number in others. They would have choked on the rest. How could the union cooperate with management, they would ask, when the company was simultaneously pushing for wage concessions and moving some production overseas? QWL would turn out to be a Trojan Horse, the Wobblies would warn—a management ploy for promoting speed up, undermining the union's authority and work rules, and encouraging workers to snitch on each other in their Participation Groups. The Wobblies would expect management to exploit the notion of "one big family" in each plant, thereby encouraging local unions to make concessions and compete with each other for scarce jobs.

There were trade unionists in the 1980s who voiced the same fears. Supporters of QWL also recognized the potential for abuse, but they believed that despite the risks, the union should not reject or abstain from QWL. Whether the union liked it or not, they argued, companies like GM that faced growing world competition would promote *some* version of QWL to boost worker morale and efficiency. As QWL advocates in the union saw it, only by intervening at the start could

thought the price of moving to make way for the plant was too high. "Hell, I'm too old to start over.... Detroit needs that plant, but they could make it smaller. GM is getting it for nothing, so they take what they can get."

Despite the high cost, most Detroiters—especially those living outside the area slated for condemnation—believed the new Poletown plant was worth the price in neighborhood disruption and public expense. Detroit, they agreed, needed to hold onto its remaining industrial jobs if Tom Bell and others were ever to return to work. Without the Poletown site, GM said it would probably move Cadillac production to Canada.

Most Detroiters also agreed that Michigan's "business climate" had to be improved before businessmen would bring new employment to the region. People could not always agree, however, on who should bear the cost of the called-for business incentives. An Economic Alliance for Michigan, founded in September, 1982, did unite top labor leaders and corporate executives behind a program to eliminate the state's huge budget deficits—a program requiring painful cuts in social services and equally painful tax hikes. When Michigan's debt-ridden unemployment fund needed an overhaul, union leaders also found they could work with several business groups to fashion a compromise bail-out.

But there was no compromise when it came to reforming the state's workers' compensation system. Everyone agreed there was a problem, but no one agreed on its causes. Michigan's program, supporting 85,000 disabled workers plus the dependents of those killed on the job, cost more than workers' compensation in any surrounding state. Yet the max-

An "Awareness Training" class for QWL participants from Pontiac Motors' skilled trades.

the union hope to make QWL a genuine process of democratization, and not a manipulative gimmick for speeding up work and undermining the collective-bargaining agreement.

At Pontiac Motors, the union shaped the QWL process from its inception in 1978, a year when worker resentment over management's authoritarian style came to a head. Conflicts over foremen who were "treating people like dirt on the floor," as one union representative claimed, culminated in confrontations where the union's entire Shop Committee surrounded offending foremen and verbally castigated their behavior. After a series of such incidents disrupted production in the assembly plant, management agreed to negotiate new work procedures throughout the Division.

"That's what kicked off QWL,"

Shop-Committee Chairman Ted Creason recalled. "Management can tell you it was their idea, but that is really how it began here at Pontiac Motors." The QWL program that followed established Operating Committees of union and management representatives to oversee the process in each of the Division's plants. Under pre-established guidelines, management agreed that QWL should not speed up work, should not result in lay-offs, and should avoid interfering with the local-union contract and collective bargaining. Both sides also agreed that either the union or the company could veto the QWL program if they found it ran counter to their interests.

QWL did not mean the union and the company "lived happily ever after" at Pontiac Motors. There were simply too many points of conflict. Should seniority protections be amended, as the company suggested, to keep new-hires in certain skilled occupations, even when long-term employees were laid off? Should foremen with an "It's-my-way-or-hit-the-highway" attitude be reprimanded by top management, as the union advocated? Did the new technology and team concepts being introduced in the plants mean the existing skilled-trade classifications should be modified? Or should these job classifications be preserved and training expanded for skilled-trades workers? These and other conflict-laden questions deadlocked local-union negotiations in 1982 and later forced union shop committees in Pontiac's Warehouse and Fiero-assembly plants to withdraw temporarily from QWL.

But in Plant 55 and the other Pontiac engine plants, foundries, and assembly operations where QWL was initially successful, many union activists believed that Quality of Work Life was the only viable route. Shop-Committee Chairman Ted Creason, who admitted to questioning "many times, in my mind, if we are being used by the QWL process," still saw the democratization of the workplace as the way of the future. "We're involved in an industrial revolution," said Creason. "It's a fact of life. It's here. Henceforth, the employee is going to have a say as to what his job is going to be."

imum benefit of only $210 a week was lower than in 31 other states. The high cost and low benefits were the result, unions claimed, of rate gouging and profit-taking by the private firms selling compensation insurance to employers. Business leaders, on the other hand, said government-established benefit standards were too high, and thousands of unwarranted recipients were driving up costs and discouraging employers from investing in Michigan.

Following a bitter political battle, business lobbyists won support for a bill that cut benefits, tightened standards, and required disabled workers to take whatever job "reasonably" fit their physical limitations. The bill, said James Barrett of the state's Chamber of Commerce, would go "a long way toward making Michigan more competitive with other states."

For 54-year-old Hershel Scroggins, crippled by a foundry accident in 1963, the benefit cuts that followed the bill's passage went a long way toward impoverishing him. "It really put a change in my life," he reflected in the fall of 1982, after GM cut his benefits from $168 a week to $19. With that and his $122-a-week pension, Scroggins could not see how he would pay his gas bills, his $200-a-month mortgage, and his food expenses. "I call the people I owe and tell 'em I can't meet the full payment.... . I'm so doggone nervous from my obligations."

The cost of making Michigan competitive—and profitable—was higher than people like Scroggins had ever imagined. Indeed, "unless you can cut costs to where Korea's are," business consultant James Mateyka said of Detroit's auto parts industry in 1983, "you're out."

Many workers felt that if Scroggins and others had to lower their standard of living so dramatically, so should management. GM and other companies had, in fact, agreed to "Equality of Sacrifice" when the UAW accepted wage concessions in 1982. The very month the contract was signed, however, GM announced sharply higher bonuses for its top executives. The union's leaders, outraged at this turn of events, convinced management it should delay the bonuses, but the episode soured many who supported the concession contracts. "We the workers have made GM and all the companies what they are," said local 653 president Bob Kinkade. "The pencil-pushing executives have not. The workers have sacrificed—now GM, it's your turn."

Sacrifice, many Detroit-area workers

believed, could only go so far in any case. "We are unable to get 'contract concessions' from the mortgage company, the finance company, the tax collector, and other agencies," complained Budd Wheel worker Bob McCarty in the winter of 1983, one year after he and his co-workers agreed to wage concessions. When the company said a second round of concessions was needed to keep the plant open, Budd workers rejected their local union's advice and voted 863 to 66 against the cuts. "We simply cannot af-

ford an annual pay reduction of $4,000," McCarty insisted.

Top union officials were acutely aware that the membership's tolerance for concessions only went so far. "We've made our sacrifices," said Owen Bieber the following spring, addressing his inaugural remarks to the auto industry in general. "We've helped the industry survive. Don't confuse the UAW's approach to collective bargaining when you're losing millions with our approach at the table when you're earn-

Fast-Food future (left) and High-Tech hopes (right). The student on the right is studying computer language in the Detroit public schools. The young men on the left joined a union organizing campaign led by the independent Detroit Fastfood Workers. In 1983, after losing a bid to organize several McDonalds outlets, the union won a contract, 12 percent pay raises, and a grievance procedure for its members at Burger King in the downtown Greyhound station.

ing millions in profits.... We've given all we're going to give.... I'm deadly serious when I say it's their [the companies'] turn to do some giving.''

The actual outcome of future bargaining would depend on the state of the economy, the relative strength and resolve of union and management, and the political climate surrounding negotiations. In the volatile, unchartered conditions of the 1980s, few observers

wished to predict that outcome. There was little doubt, however, that whatever happened, the future would be full of change and uncertainty.

It was a future many hoped to forestall by attacking the most visible symbol of Detroit's distress. "Toyota, Datsun, Honda—Pearl Harbor!'' After 1979, bumper stickers bearing such anti-import slogans were a common sight in factory parking lots across southeastern Michigan. Calls for trade barriers to exclude foreign competition were accom-

panied by "Buy American" campaigns that gained considerable support among blue-collar workers. In 1982, import sales in Michigan were only 12 percent of the state's total car sales, the lowest percentage of any state in the country.

Detroit's workers were understandably committed to buying what they built. But the potential for encouraging violent scapegoating was always present in sloganeering that portrayed the Japanese as mortal enemies. The UAW officially discouraged such ''Jap Baiting'' by stressing the import strategies of U.S. car companies, and by having the head of the Japanese Auto Workers Union address UAW conventions. Nevertheless, some union leaders and many members saw the issue in starkly nationalistic terms. Anti-Japanese sentiment ran deep, and a few Detroiters vented their frustration by physically attacking Asian–Americans—in one case, beating their victim to death during a barroom brawl.

These violent incidents underlined the need for an alternative strategy that avoided nationalistic scapegoating on the one hand, and free-trade decline on the other. As trade unionists searched for such an alternative, they began by redefining the respective roles of public planning and private profit.

Public planning, as most trade unionists saw it, was the only way to insure a lasting and equitable recovery. ''We must not engage in wishful thinking about an orderly transition from an industrial to a service economy,'' the monthly newspaper of UAW Local 600 editorialized in the spring of 1982. ''Business won't solve the problem, thus, we must reject a public-sector role limited to creating a context in which private business, if it wants to, may invest. We, the citizenry, through government, can choose the rewards we want and use public resources to achieve them.''

Profits, in turn, would be redefined by this public planning process. ''There's nothing wrong with basing an economic decision on 'profits and losses,' '' the UAW argued in a 1983 position paper. ''It's just a matter of who profits and who loses.'' When a company closed a viable factory because it could maximize profits elsewhere, stockholders and executives certainly gained by the decision. But according to the UAW, ''the rest of us lose—workers their jobs, communities their tax base, taxpayers their payout for higher welfare and unemployment, and the country much of its industrial base.... Such social costs,'' the UAW concluded,

All in the Family?

It's working, it's efficient, and we've got the satisfaction of building something that somebody else had been supplying in the past.

Frank Czuj,
Ford Motor Company Worker

As a millwright, Frank Czuj had installed a lot of machinery in his 40 years at the Ford Motor Company. But the 80-foot-long oven that he and 180 skilled workers built in the Rouge Glass Plant had a special significance. After years of turning to outside suppliers for such machinery, Ford management had, in 1982, given the UAW members the chance to build the oven in-house.

The lowest bid from an outside contractor for supplying the huge oven—used to produce laminated windshield glass—was $900,000. Outside contractors said it would take seven to nine months to install. Ford, cash-starved and pressed for time, could not afford to pay so much or wait so long. The company turned to its workers.

Millwrights, tinsmiths, electricians and other skilled tradesmen in the plant set to work designing and installing the equipment in January, 1982. "There were the least amount of engineers on this job," reported Wally Kniceley, a tinsmith and UAW Employee Involvement coordinator. "They helped us. They advised us. But they let us have a free hand in construction."

Three months later, the new equipment was in operation. The worker-designed electric oven, replacing older gas-fired designs, produced better-quality glass with less scrap. It cost only $400,000—less than half the price offered by outside suppliers. "They

wanted something modern," said Czuj. "They got it."

Getting it "in-house" was not, however, the first choice of every employer. "The building contractor bids a [construction] job at union scale, then sublets to his non-union arm," said Stan Arnold, head of the Michigan Building Trades Council, during legislative hearings in 1983. "Our union wage package is about 33 percent fringes, and they [the companies] save that with their non-union subsidiary. They make a pretty healthy profit that way." So did trucking companies like Consolidated Freightways and Leaseway, who both formed non-union subsidiaries after 1980 to compete with their own unionized divisions.

New technology further widened the opportunities for such non-union subcontracting, particularly as management began to rely more on robots and computers in their manufacturing operations. In some cases, warranty and servicing contracts with robot makers, computer manufacturers, and outside engineering firms simply bypassed the skilled, blue-collar workers who traditionally installed, maintained, and retooled factory machinery in unionized plants. When management turned to its foremen and non-union technicians to program the new machines, the role of union tradesmen in operating this latest generation of computerized equipment was diminished all the more.

Maintenance work that remained for union tradesmen also required fewer skills, in many cases, than those associated with older technologies. "Many of the computer systems now are designed to do a lot of their own

trouble shooting," observed Bob King, an electrician at the Ford Rouge plant and President of Local 600. "If something's wrong, you can ask the computer a question and it will tell you an answer, whereas before, you would have had to use your own brain to figure it out." Instead of repairing relays or changing wires to correct the malfunction, the maintenance worker would, in some cases, just "go in and pull a whole computer board out and plug another one in."

At Ford Rouge, the trend towards deskilling and outsourcing of work took a dramatic turn in 1979, when the company began sending its computer circuit boards to an outside contractor for testing and repair. The firm, Service Engineering and Research Facilities (SERF), employed non-union workers hired from trade schools and the military to perform work which UAW electricians inside the plant would otherwise have done.

In this case, however, the on-the-job knowledge of UAW workers gave them the edge over Ford's non-union "SERFs." While the union filed grievances against the company's subcontracting arrangement with the outside firm, UAW members—on their own initiative—devised testing rigs and repair procedures that proved to be more efficient than the work done by the lower-paid and less-experienced SERFs.

The union's pressure eventually turned Ford's head. Instead of sending the circuit boards out for testing and repair at $100 to $500 apiece, the company built dust-free "white rooms" in its stamping plants where union electricians did the work in-house. And with further prodding from the union, the company significantly expanded its

"outweigh the private gains."

From this "social accounting" perspective, the first priority in protecting Detroit's economic "balance sheet" was to restrain the globetrotting mobility of U.S. and foreign corporations. Trade unionists were unanimous in arguing that employers should at least

be required, by law, to give a six- or twelve-month notice of plans to close a factory. If the employer and the local community could not arrive at a mutually agreeable strategy for keeping the plant open, the logic of social accounting, as union advocates saw it, required that the departing company bear some of the social cost of its action—paying, for example, into a community develop-

ment fund.

By the same logic of social accounting, companies that profited from selling goods to American consumers should reinvest a portion of that revenue in American production. The UAW's proposed "Content Law" promised to achieve that end by requiring both American and foreign automakers to include some proportion of U.S. labor and

Skilled tradesmen with the windshield oven they built "in house" at the Ford glass plant in Dearborn.

training of UAW tradesmen in programming and maintaining computerized machinery.

The incident highlighted the central issue of new technology for skilled workers in the union. "Like the assembly line before," Gary Horn, a Chevrolet worker, wrote in his local union newspaper, "the computerization of work is ushering in a whole new economic era, one that will disrupt past customs established over decades of labor relations.... To consider new technology, therefore, is to consider not only jobs, but power.... If labor does not find a way to control technology, then management will use technology to control labor."

parts in the cars they sold here. The proportion ranged from only 10 percent U.S. content for companies selling 100,000 cars a year, up to 90 percent for companies selling 900,000 cars or more in the U.S. Unlike the trade barriers that European and Latin American countries used to exclude Japanese competition, the UAW said its Content Law would allow Japan's automakers to compete in the U.S.—but it would also require both American and foreign companies to create or preserve, by the union's estimate, 700,000 jobs that would otherwise be located offshore.

Union backers insisted the Content Law, if enacted, would put fewer restrictions on world trade than the rigid import barriers already in place in Europe and Japan. The *Wall Street Journal*, on the other hand, believed the bill would promote the further spread of trade restrictions, "throwing Americans and foreigners alike out of work." In similar terms, the Michigan Manufacturers Association argued that regulations on plant closings would only create "another disincentive for doing business in Michigan," thereby driving away corporate investment.

To fill the void left by private investors, union leaders therefore called on the federal government to adopt a new "Industrial Policy," one that would reindustrialize Detroit and re-employ its jobless citizens. The union blueprint for this program borrowed ideas from as far away as Japan, and as close as Ohio.

Drawing on precedents established by America's industrial rivals, planning advocates in Detroit's labor movement called for representatives from business, labor, government, and public-interest groups to come together on a National Planning Board. In both Western Europe and Japan, similar bodies had played crucial roles in establishing overall economic goals and targeting industries that needed a boost. By tailoring their trade policies, tax rates, research subsidies, and training programs to meet these publicly defined goals, the governments of Europe and Japan had promoted consistently higher growth rates than America's sputtering economy.

The labor movement believed the United States could benefit from such a planning process, so long as it avoided the potential for bureaucratic decision making. "Not only is top-down planning by a private or public elite undemocratic," the UAW argued in its call for public planning, "but it won't work well. We need democratic decision making."

To insure "democratic input," the UAW proposed a decentralized, industry-by-industry planning process, with "Strategy Committees" in each industry composed of workers, management, and public representatives. Instead of a top-down plan developed in Washington, these Strategy Committees would establish their own agendas for retooling obsolete plants, diversifying into socially useful product lines, and retraining the workforce. The National Planning Board would then evaluate these plans in light of national priorities—including environmental protection and affirmative action—and recommend changes or approval accordingly.

To finance reindustrialization, trade unionists took another cue from America's trade rivals and called for the creation of public development banks. In Japan and Europe, such publicly owned banks, by making the long-term loans and investments that private investors often shunned, had helped new companies get off the ground and old companies stay afloat. By tying financial support to social-accounting standards,

Blueprint for Change

Reflecting the changed circumstances of the 1980s, the UAW's *Blueprint for a Working America* was considerably more elaborate than the union's pump-priming metaphor of 1945 (page 223).

Just as management borrowed from Japan in devising its revitalization strategy, the labor movement also looked to overseas precedents in developing its economic alternative. "We don't have to reinvent the wheel," declared the UAW, the Steel Workers, and the Machinists in a joint proposal for public planning. "Other industrialized nations have extensive policies and programs relating to economic dislocation," and such

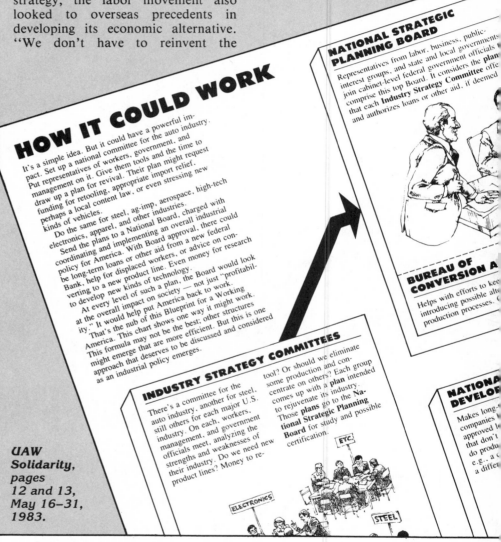

HOW IT COULD WORK

It's a simple idea. But it could have a powerful impact. Set up a national committee for the auto industry. Put representatives of workers, government, and management on it. Give them tools and the time to draw up a plan for revival. Their plan might request funding for retooling, appropriate import relief, perhaps a local content law, or even stressing new kinds of vehicles.

Do the same for steel, ag-imp, aerospace, high-tech electronics, apparel, and other industries. Send the plans to a National Board, charged with coordinating and implementing an overall industrial policy for America. With Board approval, there could be long-term loans or other aid from a new federal Bank, help for displaced workers, or advice on converting to a new product line. Even money for research to develop new kinds of technology.

At every level of such a plan, the Board would look at the overall impact on society — not just "profitability." It would help put America back to work. That's the nub of this Blueprint for a Working America. This chart shows one way it might work. This formula may not be the best; other structures might emerge that are more efficient. But this is one approach that deserves to be discussed and considered as an industrial policy emerges.

NATIONAL STRATEGIC PLANNING BOARD

Representatives from labor, business, public-interest groups, and state and local governments join cabinet-level federal government officials comprise this top Board. It considers the plan that each **Industry Strategy Committee** offe and authorizes loans or other aid, if deemed

BUREAU OF CONVERSION A

Helps with efforts to kee introducing possible alt production processes. C

INDUSTRY STRATEGY COMMITTEES

There's a committee for the auto industry, another for steel, still others for each major U.S. industry. On each, workers, management, and government officials meet, analyzing the strengths and weaknesses of their industry. Do we need new product lines? Money to re- tool? Or should we eliminate some production and concentrate on others? Each group comes up with a **plan** intended to rejuvenate its industry. Those **plans** go to the National **Strategic Planning Board** for study and possible certification.

ELECTRONICS   ETC.   STEEL

NATIONA DEVELOP

Makes long- companies approved t that don't do produ e.g... a c a differe

UAW Solidarity, pages 12 and 13, May 16–31, 1983.

they had, in many cases, made the recipient companies improve their pollution control, workplace safety, or employee training.

Public resources, the labor movement argued, could also be used to improve Michigan's business climate without cutting workers' benefits and undermining the general standard of living. In Ohio, the UAW pointed out, the state's government-owned, non-profit insurance company already paid disabled workers higher benefits than in Michigan, but at half the cost (per benefit dollar) that Michigan's private, profit-making insurance companies charged employers. Canada's system of government health insurance and regulated fees also meant employers paid less for medical benefits than in Michigan. Publicly owned insurance companies and community-administered health-care centers could, the labor movement argued, provide the same

planning policies "found in Sweden, West Germany, and the United Kingdom, had not deterred U.S. corporations from investing, locating, and operating profitably there."

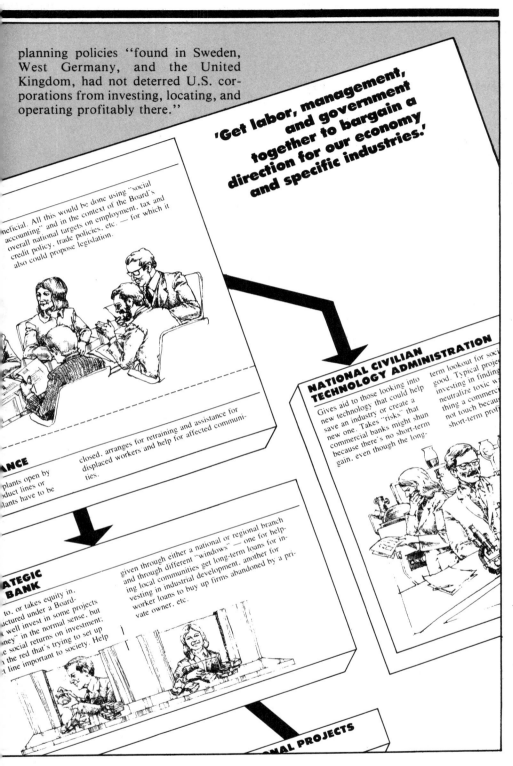

'Get labor, management, and government together to bargain a direction for our economy and specific industries.'

...neficial. All this would be done using "social accounting" and in the context of the Board's overall national targets on employment, tax and credit policy, trade policies, etc. — for which it also could propose legislation.

...closed, arranges for retraining and assistance for displaced workers and help for affected communities.

...ANCE

...plants open by ...oduct lines or ...lants have to be

NATIONAL CIVILIAN TECHNOLOGY ADMINISTRATION

Gives aid to those looking into new technology that could help save an industry or create a new one. Takes "risks" that commercial banks might shun because there's no short-term gain, even though the long...term lookout for soci... good. Typical proje... investing in finding... neutralize toxic w... thing a commerc... not touch becau... short-term prof...

...ATEGIC BANK

...to, or takes equity in. ...uctured under a Board- ...well invest in some projects ...ney" in the normal sense, but ...e social returns on investment; ...the red that's trying to set up ...t line important to society. Help

...given through either a national or regional branch and through different "windows" — one for helping local communities get long-term loans for investing in industrial development, another for worker loans to buy up firms abandoned by a private owner, etc.

...NAL PROJECTS

---

low-cost benefits for Detroit's workers.

The range of public initiatives the labor movement presented was quite broad. Outright nationalization of stagnant industries or failing companies had relatively few advocates—though some pointed to successful European precedents like Renault, owned by the French government, as evidence that even this extreme solution could work. But more often, union planning advocates called for mixed enterprises—

much like Germany's Volkswagen—that combined government backing with some mixture of private investment, worker participation, and community ownership.

The UAW called its planning proposal a *Blueprint for a Working America*. In 1983, when the union first articulated its proposal, the *Blueprint* was still only a sketch. "It is not a perfect vision," the

UAW acknowledged. "It is a working document that will evolve."

The *Blueprint*, in fact, raised as many questions as it answered. How, for example, would disagreements between the groups represented on the National Planning Board be resolved? Could a majority of the Board prevail on a dissenting minority, or would each group have veto power? What kinds of guarantees would insure that better organized groups and bigger companies did not dominate a Strategy Committee at the expense of less organized groups and smaller firms? What kind of wage and work-rule concessions would be expected of workers in return for potentially greater job security? And how would public representatives be chosen for the various planning bodies?

More important, how much public support was there for implementing any kind of Industrial Policy? In recession-ravaged Detroit, there was considerable cynicism among wage earners and the poor about any plan, public or corporate, Democratic or Republican, being able to reverse years of industrial decline and business failure. When it came to improving their individual lot, many Detroiters had more confidence in the Lottery than in politicians from either major party.

There was also considerable opposition to any government program that promised to raise taxes. Planning advocates believed that with money transferred from the military budget to the civilian sector, and with funds generated by government loans and investments, Industrial Policy programs could be implemented without a significant tax increase. But particularly in outlying suburbs where anti-tax sentiment ran deepest, many people were likely to dismiss such claims and vote against advocates of public planning.

This distrust of "Big Government" was perhaps the single biggest obstacle to implementing the labor movement's planning proposals. There was little likelihood that it would be neutralized unless voters saw Industrial Policy as a cooperative, people-oriented program to save jobs.

Union workers at McLouth Steel in suburban Trenton, for example, did win community support for government loan guarantees to keep their plant open. People believed the plant's closing would devastate the local economy, and the workers won substantial backing for their offer to buy the plant and run it themselves if no other investor stepped forward.

Government investment programs

could also win popular support when the benefits were obviously higher than the costs. When the state invested $2 million in Synthetic Vision Systems of Ann Arbor, it did not cost taxpayers a cent—the funds came from Michigan's public-employee pension system, which expected a substantial return on the investment.

It cost Detroit only $10 to buy three factories abandoned by Chrysler in 1982 (including sites 27a and 48). According to planning advocates, rehabilitating these plants and reopening them as community-owned enterprises would be at least as good an investment as the $200 million in taxpayers' money spent to subsidize GM's Poletown plant. The reopened plants could, they argued, produce both jobs and continuing revenue as they retooled to build such things as

Rebuilding the Union

What has happened in the last few weeks reminds us of the Spirit of 1937. We again see thousands of frustrated members who don't want to see their union die.

Floyd Loew,
Waiter and Strike Organizer

In June, 1982, Floyd Loew, leader of sitdown strikes in Detroit's hotels a half century before, believed he had seen the dawn of a new day in Local 24 of the Hotel and Restaurant Employees. "After years of no meetings, raises of dues, and loss of membership," the 80-year-old former waiter reported, "the members said 'Enough is enough.'" That month, an insurgent slate of union reformers finally won control of the 12,000 member local, once headed by the nationally recognized Myra Wolfgang.

For more than 30 years, the outspoken Wolfgang had allied her organization with a succession of progressive causes, from the anti-war movement to the Farmworkers' grape boycott. But in Wolfgang's waning years, and especially after her death in 1976, the union had fallen under the control of a self-serving, incompetent group of leaders.

Efforts to organize new members tapered off, and servicing of existing members suffered. In 60 smaller workplaces that once had union agreements, the contracts were allowed to lapse with no effort to reopen negotiations. Membership grievances were ignored. Employers who wanted "sweetheart" deals got special arrangements that allowed them to pay less than union scale. In some restaurants, management personnel actually served as union stewards, with no fear of censure from Local 24's top officers.

In the mid-1970s, opposition leaders who questioned these practices were turned back by beatings and threats. Membership apathy, nurtured and encouraged by years of top-down decision making, also cut the ground from under reform-minded activists.

But by 1982, membership dissatisfaction was so widespread that intimidation could no longer carry the day. That year, a rank-and-file movement led by two dissident members of the local's staff, Florence Farr and Dan Spinks, organized an election challenge that promised to "turn the local around."

Farr, a waitress for 15 years at Stouffer's in suburban Southfield, made racial unity a key element in her campaign to replace Herb Triplet as Secretary Treasurer. "Dan [who ran for President] and I wanted to get the message across that I'm a white lady and he's a black man, but we're one. And the people came together—people who worked Clubs, who are out in the suburbs, and people who worked the downtown Hotels, who are definitely city. We saw a gorgeous blending that was so needed."

The incumbent slate countered by firing Farr's campaign manager from the union staff, turning the union newspaper into a campaign sheet for the top incumbent, and maneuvering to prevent the nomination of Farr and Spinks. All of these moves backfired. When the election was finally held, the reform slate won with 62 percent of the vote.

Farr and Spinks could not promise immediate success in organizing Detroit's non-union motels and restaurants. But by beginning new organizing drives, by renegotiating lapsed contracts, by reforming union finances, and by putting union staffers "back in the shops" to handle grievances, they could rehabilitate a faltering union. "A clean, fresh breeze," the local's revamped newspaper promised, "is reviving the union from a torpid sleep."

The women and men who reawakened Local 24 had their counterparts in other Detroit-area unions. Few were more visible than the activists in Teamster Local 299, the 10,000-member local of general freight drivers, carhaulers, and warehousemen once headed by Jimmy Hoffa.

In the 1960s and 1970s, this pivotal local—home base for the Teamsters' national leadership for a quarter century—had been dominated by a small clique of rough-house leaders. When union members complained about sell-out contracts, negligent grievance handling, or the multiple salaries union officers paid themselves, they were physically intimidated and sometimes beaten. Dissident groups that ran opposition candidates found their offices ransacked and the homes of their members dynamited or firebombed.

By 1974, the incumbent leaders had solidified their control so thoroughly that no opposition candidates bothered to contest their hold on the local. With only incumbents running for office, the elections were cancelled.

By the late 1970s, however, things had changed dramatically. Teamsters for a Democratic Union (TDU), formed after a 1976 wildcat strike in Detroit's Local 299, helped galvanize a union-wide reform movement against sell-out contracts and corrupt leadership. Inside Local 299, independent reformers established a new group, Concerned Teamsters, and began laying the groundwork for challenging the

solar collectors, mass transit, or oil-drilling equipment.

Framed in this way, democratic planning was an option that the labor movement believed people would support.

Mobilizing that support would be difficult nevertheless. Detroit's union leaders believed some form of industrial planning was inevitable—but they feared that without a grassroots movement on behalf of democratic input, planning would be tailored to suit corporate needs and little else. "Only a collective effort on a par with the winning of industrial unions in the 1930s can give us real hope," the UAW argued, "that the coming reindustrialization of America will be rational, humane, and creative for all of us who work for our living."

There were some who doubted wheth-

Dan Spinks and Florence Farr (standing, second and third from left) with kitchen workers at the Sheraton Hotel in suburban Southfield.

local's incumbent leadership.

Peter Karagozian, a Concerned Teamster and former freight driver, finally became the first successful reform candidate for Local 299's Presidency in 1980, when he won 53 percent of the vote in a government-supervised election. Following his victory, Karagozian cracked down on local staff who failed to service their members, and prohibited the previous practice of eating lunch with the boss. While repudiating the gangsterism of top union officials, he also established a more tolerant, democratic atmosphere within the local.

By the time Karagozian won re-election in 1982, some union reformers felt he still had not done enough to rid the local of corrupt and self-serving elements. But few doubted that Local 299 had come a long way from the violent days of the 1960s and 1970s. "We have managed to make people in the union politically sensitive," said carhauler and TDU activist Jim Carothers, one of 49 candidates running for the local's seven executive posts. "They know now this union doesn't have to be a dictatorship."

Some of the several thousand steel workers and supporters who protested the threatened closing of McLouth Steel (in background) in 1982.

Save Our Steel Mill

When McLouth Steel filed for bankruptcy in December, 1981, company officials cited two major problems plaguing their modern mill in suburban Trenton: the auto industry's slumping demand for steel, and the union's $26-an-hour wage and benefit package.

United Steelworkers Local 2659 cited a different and longer list: poor investments by management in trucking companies and out-of-state coke ovens; failure to reduce the company's near-total dependence on sales to GM; heavy reliance on expensive outside contractors; and a top-heavy ratio of one supervisor for every four workers, compared to the 1-to-15 ratio the union proposed.

To save the ailing firm, the union immediately agreed to concessions in return for a hefty cut in supervisors. Even so, as conditions worsened, management announced it would close the plant in March, 1982. In the

meantime, with no buyer interested in purchasing the mill, banks with loans to McLouth began to favor a complete liquidation and sell-off of company assets to recover their money—a move that would eliminate jobs and destroy much of the workers' hard-earned pension credits.

Seeking to avert a permanent shut down and liquidation, the union developed an employee buyout proposal with the aid of local mayors, utilities, and other suppliers who wished to preserve McLouth as an on-going customer and employer. Their joint proposal, by preventing court approval of liquidation, kept the mill operating as a going concern until Tang Industries of Chicago bought the company. The union thereafter negotiated a new contract that lowered wage and benefit costs to $18 an hour—but preserved the jobs and pensions of McLouth workers.

er Detroit's unions could inspire or lead such a collective effort. The labor movement, they claimed, had grown too bureaucratic to lead a grassroots campaign, and too self-centered to work with groups outside the union fold. Some critics argued that unions had become "obsolete," and would eventually be reduced to isolated pockets of membership in an otherwise non-union economy.

There was little doubt that unions were on the defensive, besieged on all sides by a multitude of problems. The decay of basic industry, the emergence of international trade rivalries, the rise of new technology, the increase in union busting, the escalation of arms spending, and the deterioration of social services—all directly impinged on unions and working people, and most required responses that went well beyond collective bargaining.

There was, however, nothing new in this. "In the modern world," historian Charles Beard wrote in the *Detroit Labor News,* five years after World War I, "crises are forced upon the labor movement by circumstances not of its own making, and it is compelled to make momentous decisions on matters unrelated to collective bargaining.... Can we doubt," Beard predicted in 1923, "that in the future, labor will have to make decisions and take actions more fraught with destiny than any thus far taken?"

Whether the labor movement would shape that destiny—or be overwhelmed by it—was as much a question in the 1980s as in Beard's day. In both eras, there were those who doubted the union movement could meet the challenge of changing times.

"American trade unionism is slowly being limited by changes which destroy the basis on which it was erected.... I see no reason to believe that American trade unionism will so revolutionize itself within a short period of time as to become in the next decade a more potent social influence than it has been in the past decade."

George Barnett, a noted economist, made this observation in 1933. Four years later, the CIO, the Flint sitdown, and the extraordinary wave of plant occupations that followed fundamentally "revolutionized" the labor movement, and with it, America's industrial society.

George Barnett was not the first critic to declare the labor movement obsolete. Neither was he the last to be proven wrong.

Labor Day in Detroit, 1983. The annual parade, discontinued after the violence of 1967, was revived after the slump of 1979. In 1983, thousands of union members once again paraded down Woodward Avenue.

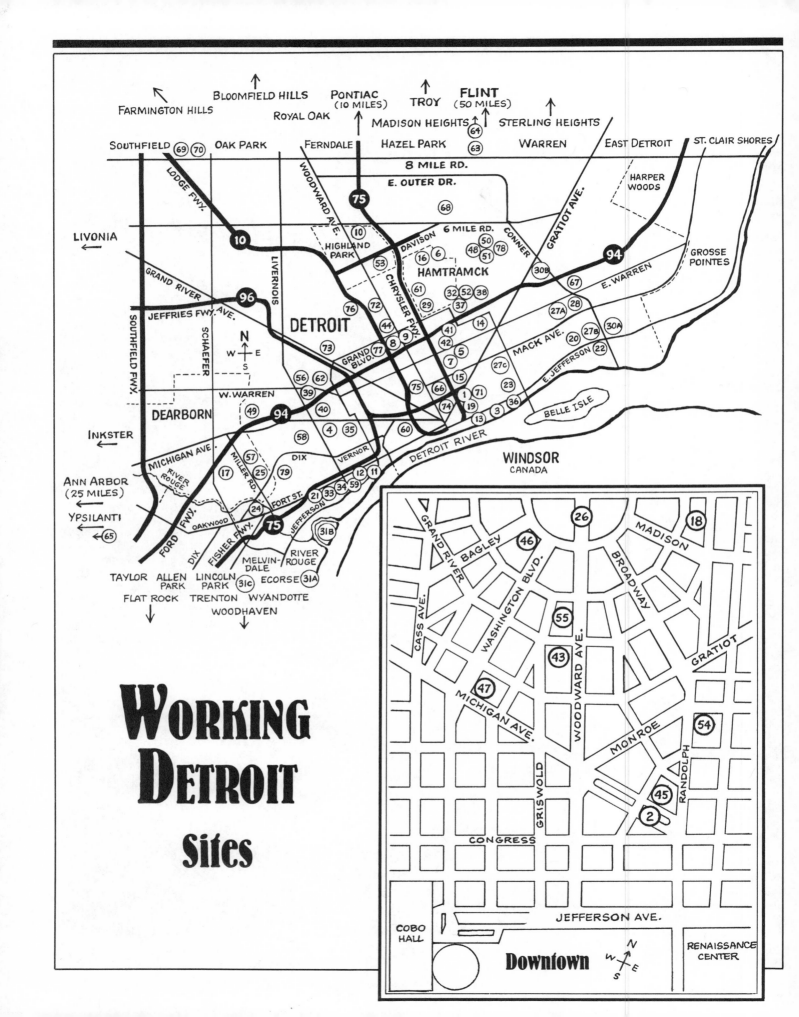

Working Detroit Sites

Sites

1) **Stroh Brewery**, One Stroh Drive, north of Gratiot, west of Rivard. Present brewhouse was built in 1912.

2) **Cadillac Square.** The city's Central Market in the 19th century and frequent locale for labor rallies in the 20th.

3) **Engine Works of the Detroit Shipbuilding Company**, 1801 Atwater at Orleans. Between the 1850s and 1920s, this firm was one of the leading shipbuilders on the Great Lakes. The present structure, built in 1901, is now occupied by the Globe Trading Company.

4) **Dom Polski**, West Side, 3432 Junction, between Otis and Kopernick. Meeting place for Polish clubs and trade unionists.

5) **Dom Polski**, East Side, 2281 East Forest, between Chene and Dubois.

6) **International Workers Home**, 3014 Yemans near Joseph Campau. The leftwing mutual-aid society once housed here collapsed during the Red Scare of the 1950s.

7) **Saint Albertus Church**, St. Aubin and Canfield. Detroit's first Polish church. The present structure was built in 1884.

8) **Cadillac Motors**, 450 Amsterdam at Cass. Built in 1905, this three-story factory housed the Cadillac Company's main operations until 1921, when General Motors (which bought Cadillac in 1908) built the Clark Street plant (site 35).

9) **Ford Piquette plant**, Piquette Avenue at Brush. Ford built this plant in 1904 and later began production here of the Model T. After Ford moved to Highland Park (site 10), Studebaker bought the plant in 1911 and expanded its operations eastward. The nearby Plant 10 at Piquette and Beaubien served as a shelter for the unemployed in the 1930s.

10) **Ford Highland Park plant**, Manchester Avenue east of Woodward. Only two main buildings survive of the original complex, where Ford developed the auto industry's first moving assembly line between 1910 and 1913. After Ford moved production to Dearborn in the 1920s (site 17), Briggs Manufacturing leased part of the complex to build auto bodies for Ford.

11) **Studebaker**, West Jefferson at Clark Street. The few remaining buildings of this complex were the site in 1913 of the auto industry's first major strike, led by the IWW.

12) **Timken Axle**, Clark Street between Oak and Wabash. A major parts supplier in the early years of the auto industry.

13) **Studebaker Corporation Plant #5**, 1938 Franklin Street near St. Aubin.

14) **Packard Motor Car Company**, 1580 East Grand Boulevard near Mt. Elliott. Built between 1903 and 1911, this plant produced high-priced cars and aircraft engines until Packard closed it in 1954. It is now sub-divided into lofts for small-scale industry.

15) **House of the Masses**, 2101 Gratiot at St. Aubin. Detroit's Socialists bought this hall during World War I from a German fraternal organization and made it their headquarters. Closed by the Palmer Raids of 1920, it served in the 1930s as union headquarters for the Mechanics Educational Society of America.

16) **Detroit Workmen's Co-Operative Restaurant**, 2934 Yemans east of Joseph Campau. Organized to serve single men working in Detroit's auto industry, the Co-op's upstairs hall was a frequent meeting place for unions, ethnic groups and socialists. The Polonia Restaurant occupies this site today.

17) **Ford River Rouge complex**, Miller Road and Dix. The Rouge was the largest auto production center in the world when completed in the 1920s.

18) **The Detroit Athletic Club**, Madison Avenue at John R.

19) **Hastings Street**, presently the Chrysler Freeway. What is now I-375 was once the center of Detroit's black community.

20) **The Ossian Sweet home**, 2905 Garland at Charlevoix. Clarence Darrow defended Sweet and his brother for shooting into a white mob attacking their home in 1925.

21) **Fisher Fleetwood plant**, Fort Street at West End Avenue. This plant built LaSalle bodies until 1940 and Cadillac bodies thereafter. Fleetwood was one of two Detroit GM plants occupied during the 1937 sitdown.

22) **Chrysler Jefferson Avenue plant**, East Jefferson near Conner. In 1937, UAW sitdowners occupied the plant on the south side of the street and the Kercheval plant on the north side. In the 1980s, Chrysler began producing K-cars here.

23) **Capuchin Monastery**, 1740 Mt. Elliott north of Lafayette. The soup kitchen that opened here in 1929 is still feeding the poor and unemployed.

24) **West Fort and Oakwood.** The Hunger March of 1932 assembled at this intersection.

25) **Gate 3 at Ford River Rouge.** In 1932, an overpass (since torn down) crossed Miller Road near the powerhouse. The Hunger March massacre began here.

26) **Grand Circus Park**, downtown. Detroit's Unemployed Councils rallied here in the 1930s. The Hazen Pingree monument is on the Park's southern edge.

27) **Briggs Manufacturing**, later Chrysler:
A) Mack Avenue stamping plant, now owned by the city.
B) Vernor Tool and Die.
C) Waterloo (3100 Meldrum) custom body plant.

28) **Motor Products**, Mack Avenue near Hart. After this parts maker closed in the 1950s, Chrysler built an extension of 27a over the site.

29) **Murray Body**, 7700 Russell at Clay. Now the Russell Industrial Center.

30) **Hudson Motors.** Before merging into AMC in the 1950s, this independent automaker (founded by the department store family) had two main plants: A) at East Jefferson and Conner, now a parking lot, and B) the stamping plant on Conner south of Gratiot, later a GM plant, now closed.

31) **Great Lakes Steel**, Ecorse and River Rouge: A) The main complex on Tecumseh and West Jefferson. B) The Zug Island blast furnaces. C) The

original buildings on Mill and West Jefferson.

32) Dodge Main. Employing 35,000 workers at its peak in World War II, Dodge Main closed in 1980. The city demolished the plant and surrounding residential areas for GM's new Poletown plant.

33) Kroger Warehouse, 120 South Green Street near Fort. Site of the first strike for Jimmy Hoffa, then 18.

34) Ternstedt General Motors, Fort Street at Livernois.

35) Clark Street Cadillac plant, south of Michigan Avenue. One of two Detroit GM plants occupied in the 1937 sitdown.

36) Parke Davis and Company, Joseph Campau Avenue at the Detroit River. An innovator in producing "ready made" drugs, Parke Davis had moved production out of Detroit by the 1980s and sold its headquarters plant to Stroh Brewery.

37) Midland Steel, 6660 Mt. Elliott at Strong. The first sitdown in Detroit began here in November, 1936.

38) Slovak Hall, 7151 Strong Avenue at Carrie. Meeting hall for the Midland Steel strikers.

39) Kelsey-Hayes Wheel, McGraw Avenue at Livernois. Site of the second sitdown in Detroit and first for Walter Reuther, December, 1936.

40) Polish Falcons Hall, 4132 Junction north of Michigan Avenue. Meeting hall for the Kelsey-Hayes strikers.

Cigar Plant Sitdowns, 1937

41) Webster-Eisenholer Cigar, 5545 Grandy near Ferry, now empty.

42) Mazer-Cressman Cigar, 5031 Grandy at Theodore, now owned by the city's Neighborhood Services Department.

Downtown Sitdowns, 1937

43) Woolworth's Store, 1249 Woodward at Grand River.

44) Woolworth's Store (New Center), 6565 Woodward at Grand Boulevard.

45) Barlum Hotel, 111 Cadillac Square.

46) Statler Hotel, corner of Park Avenue, Washington Boulevard, and Bagley Avenue.

47) Book Cadillac Hotel, corner of Washington Boulevard and Michigan.

Chrysler Sitdowns, 1937

48) Plymouth Assembly, Lynch Road at Mt. Elliott, now owned by the city.

49) DeSoto, 6000 Wyoming at McGraw.

50) Dodge Forge, Lynch Road.

51) Dodge Truck, Lynch Road.

52) Amplex Engine, Conant north of Dunn (since demolished).

53) Chrysler Highland Park, Oakland Avenue south of the Davison Freeway.

★ ★ ★

54) Sam's Cut Rate, 1056 Randolph at Monroe and 15 Campus Martius (since demolished). Until the 1950s, Sam's was Detroit's major blue-collar clothing and drug store.

55) Frank and Seder Department Store, 1437 Woodward Avenue near Grand River. Police evicted sitdowners on March 17, 1937, amid charges of gangsterism. Presently Albert's.

56) Ford Lincoln plant, West Warren and Livernois. Presently owned by Detroit Edison.

57) Gate 4, Ford Rouge, Miller Road. Site of the Battle of the Overpass in May, 1937. Present overpass is a new structure.

58) Federal Screw, Martin Street at Otis. Here and at site 59, employers tried to break the union in 1938.

59) American Brass, 174 South Clark at West Jefferson.

60) St. Martha's House, 1818 Leverette, west of Trumbull. Former shelter run by the Catholic Worker.

61) Chevrolet Gear and Axle, 1840 Holbrook west of St. Aubin. A key site in the 1939 tool and die strike.

62) Hartford Avenue Baptist Church, 6300 Hartford at Milford. Rev. Charles Hill was among the few black ministers who opened his doors to union meetings during the UAW's Ford organizing campaign.

63) Hudson Naval Armory, Mound Road north of 9 Mile Road. GM's Hydromatic Division now occupies this former defense plant.

64) Chrysler Tank Arsenal, Van Dyke north of 11 Mile Road. General Dynamics bought the facility in 1982.

65) Willow Run Bomber plant, Ypsilanti. Ford built B-24 bombers here during World War II. GM's Hydromatic Division now occupies the site.

66) Brewster Public Housing, between Mack Avenue, Beaubien, and I-75. Construction began in the late 1930s on this first public housing project in Detroit. It opened as segregated black housing.

67) Parkside Public Housing, East Warren and Conner. Begun shortly after Brewster (site 66), Parkside was initially a whites-only project.

68) Sojourner Truth Public Housing, Nevada at Fenelon. Neighborhood whites rioted when this segregated, all-black project opened in 1942.

69) Northland Shopping Center, Greenfield and 8 Mile Road.

70) Richard's Drive In, Greenfield and 8 Mile Road.

71) Lafayette Park Redevelopment Area, formerly the "Black Bottom" ghetto.

72) North Woodward Avenue Congregational Church, 8715 Woodward Avenue at Blaine.

73) Freedom House, the activities center of the Trade Union Leadership Council, 8670 Grand River north of West Grand Boulevard.

74) 606 Horse Shoe Lounge, St. Antoine near Madison. The last survivor of the Paradise Valley entertainment district.

75) Paradise Theater, Woodward Avenue at Parsons. In the 1940s, the Paradise was a nationally known center for Big-Band jazz. Now Orchestra Hall.

76) 12th Street and Clairmount. This intersection was the flashpoint for the 1967 riot/rebellion.

77) Research Park, 5500 Trumbull north of I-94. In the 1960s, urban renewal pitted the residents of the former Hobart Street area against developers allied with neighboring Wayne State University.

78) Eldon Avenue Gear and Axle, Lynch Road at Eldon. This Chrysler plant was the site of bitter disputes over working conditions in the 1960s and early 1970s.

79) Woodmere Cemetery, West Fort and Woodmere Streets. In the Northeast section, Fernwood, Block 18, Graves 20–24, UAW Local 600 retirees placed headstones in 1979 to mark the graves of four victims of the 1932 Ford Hunger March massacre.

Readings & Sources

Working Detroit draws heavily on the published and unpublished work of many historians. A partial list of books follows, together with a brief description of their contents where the title is not indicative. No editorial recommendation is associated with this list: some of the titles adopt an overtly neutral perspective, some are avowedly pro-union, and some are openly critical of the labor movement.

Space does not permit a list of the articles and unpublished essays used to research this book. Those interested in sampling the growing literature of labor and urban history can review back issues of *The Journal of American History, Labor History, Michigan History, The Journal of Negro History, Detroit in Perspective,* and other relevant journals. Students who wish to dig deeper can consult the unpublished essays and dissertations collected by university libraries and history departments in Michigan, as well as the oral histories, special collections, and official documents housed in the Walter P. Reuther Library at Wayne State University, the Burton Historical Collection at the Detroit Public Library, and the archives of the Henry Ford Museum. The Michigan Labor History Society has also published a 400-entry bibliography of labor-history sources, available at the Reuther Library.

Among the many historians whose research informed the writing of *Working Detroit,* certain individuals stand out. Richard Oestreicher's published articles and unpublished dissertation on Detroit's nineteenth-century labor movement were especially valuable resources. Chris Johnson's soon-to-be published biography of Maurice Sugar and Tom Klug's unpublished essays on the Employers' Association of Detroit were equally helpful. So too was Jack Russell's unpublished essay on the Ford Highland Park assembly line; Lois Rankin's extended essay (*Michigan History,* 1939) on ethnic Detroit; Thaddeus Radzialowski's articles on Detroit's Poles; Joyce Shaw Peterson's published work on black autoworkers; George Coleman's unpublished study of Detroit's steelworkers; Richard Thomas's dissertation on Detroit's black workers; Joe Fardella's unpublished essay on the Catholic Church and the labor movement in the 1930s; Ray Boryczka's published articles on factionalism in the UAW, 1935–1941; Ruth Milkman's, Judy Rosen's, and Nancy Gabin's studies of women workers during World War II; the Rosie-the-Riveter project's compilation of research papers and oral histories on this same topic; and Joe Davis's case history of the Hamtramck teachers' strike of 1965.

Individual recollections quoted in *Working Detroit* come from four major sources: the oral histories housed in the above-named libraries; published histories; daily and union newspapers; and over 85 interviews (listed below) conducted by members and associates of Detroit Labor History Tours. Steve Babson, Ron Alpern, Jane Dobija, Dave Elsila, and John Revitte conducted the bulk of the interviews. Bill Bryce, Peter Friedlander, Jim Jacobs, and Dave Riddle contributed the balance.

Abrams, Charles. *Forbidden Neighbors: A Study of Prejudice in Housing* (1955).

Baba, Marietta, and Abonyi, Malvina. *Mexicans in Detroit* (1979).

Bernstein, Irving. *The Lean Years: A History of the American Worker, 1920–1933* (1960). *The Turbulent Years: A History of the American Worker, 1933–1941* (1969).

Burton, Clarence. *The City of Detroit, Michigan, 1701–1922,* 5 Volumes (1922).

Calkins, Fay. *The CIO and the Democratic Party* (1952).

Catlin, George. *The Story of Detroit* (1926).

Caute, David. *The Great Fear: The Anti-Communist Purge Under Truman and Eisenhower* (1978).

Clive, Alan. *State of War: Michigan in World War II* (1979).

Cochran, Bert. *Labor and Communism: The Conflict That Shaped American Unions* (1977).

Conot, Robert. *American Odyssey* (1974). A history of Detroit from 1800 to the 1970s.

Denby, Charles. *Indignant Heart: A Black Worker's Journal* (1978).

Detroit Free Press. *Blacks in Detroit* (1980).

Deskins, Donald Jr. *Residential Mobility of Negroes in Detroit, 1837–1965* (1972).

Dunn, Robert. *Labor and Automobiles* (1929).

Farmer, Silas. *The History of Detroit and Michigan,* 2 Volumes (1889).

Fenton, John. *Midwest Politics* (1966).

Fine, Sidney. *The Automobile Under the Blue Eagle* (1963). *Frank Murphy: The Detroit Years* (1975). *Sit-Down: The General Motors Strike of 1936–1937* (1969).

Foster, James. *The Union Politic: The CIO Political Action Committee* (1975).

Fountain, Clayton. *Union Guy* (1949). The autobiography of a left-wing autoworker.

Freidlander, Peter. *The Emergence of a UAW Local, 1936–1939* (1975).

Georgakas, Dan, and Surkin, Marvin. *Detroit I Do Mind Dying: A Study In Urban Revolution* (1975). A history of Black Power politics in the workplace and community between 1967 and 1973.

Geschwender, James. *Class, Race, and Worker Insurgency: The League of Revolutionary Black Workers* (1977).

Glaberman, Martin. *Wartime Strikes* (1980).

Gould, William. *Black Workers in White Unions.* (1977).

Greene, Victor. *For God and Country: The Rise of Polish and Lithuanian Ethnic Consciousness in America, 1860–1910* (1975).

Gutman, Herbert. *Work, Culture and Society in Industrializing America* (1966).

Haber, William. *Industrial Relations in the Building Industry* (1930).

Hardman, J.B.S., ed. *American Labor Dynamics* (1928/1969).

Hoffa, James, as told to Fraley, Oscar. *Hoffa: The Real Story* (1975).

Hollander, Jacob, and Barnett, George. *Studies in American Trade Unionism* (1912/1969).

Holli, Melvin. *Reform in Detroit* (1969). A political biography of Hazen Pingree.

Humphrey, Judy Stamp. *Segregation and Integration: A Geography of People in Metropolitan Detroit* (1972).

Hyde, Charles. *Detroit: An Industrial History Guide* (1980).

James, Ralph and Estelle. *Hoffa and the Teamsters* (1965).

Katzman, David. *Before the Ghetto: Black Detroit in the Nineteenth Century* (1973).

Keeran, Roger. *The Communist Party and the Auto Workers Unions* (1980).

Kefauver, Estes. *Crime in America* (1951). Chapter 14 focuses on underworld-business ties in Detroit.

Kornhauser, Arthur. *Detroit as the People See It: A Survey of Attitudes in an Industrial City* (1952).

Laslett, John. *Labor and the Left: A Study of Socialist and Radical Influences in the American Labor Movement, 1881-1924* (1970).

Leggett, John. *Class, Race, and Labor: Working Class Consciousness in Detroit* (1968).

Levine, David. *Internal Combustion: The Races in Detroit, 1915-1926* (1976).

Lichtenstein, Nelson. *Labor's War At Home: The CIO in World War II* (1982).

Luria, Dan, and Russell, Jack. *Rational Reindustrialization: An Economic Development Agenda for Detroit* (1981).

Marquart, Frank. *An Autoworker's Journal* (1975).

McLaughlin, Doris. *Michigan Labor: A Brief History from 1818 to the Present* (1970).

Meier, August, and Rudwick, Elliott. *Black Detroit and the Rise of the UAW* (1979).

Meyer, Stephen. *The Five Dollar Day: Labor Management and Social Control in the Ford Motor Company, 1908-1921* (1981).

Moldea, Dan. *The Hoffa Wars: Teamsters, Rebels, Politicians, and the Mob* (1978).

Montgomery, David. *Workers' Control in America: Studies in the History of Work, Technology, and Labor Struggles* (1979).

Mortimer, Wyndham. *Organize! My Life as A Union Man* (1971).

Mowitz, Robert. *Profile of a Metropolis: A Case Book* (1962). A case study of urban renewal politics in Detroit.

Nevins, Alan, and Hill, Frank. *Ford*, 3 Volumes. (1954-1963). The definitive history of the Ford Motor Company and its founder.

Northrup, Herbert. *The Negro in the Automobile Industry* (1970).

Pflug, Warner. *The UAW in Pictures* (1971).

Pitrone, Jean Maddern. *Myra: The Life and Times of Myra Wolfgang, Trade-Union Leader* (1980).

Reuther, Victor. *The Brothers Reuther and the Story of the UAW: A Memoir* (1976).

Sarasohn, Stephen and Vera. *Political Party Patterns in Michigan* (1957).

Schneider, John. *Detroit and the Problem of Order, 1830-1880. A Geography of Crime, Riot, and Policing* (1980).

Scott, Rachel. *Muscle and Blood* (1974). Two chapters cover health and safety hazards in Detroit's auto plants.

Seaton, Doug. *Catholics and Radicals* (1981).

Serrin, William. *The Company and the Union: The "Civilized Relationship" of the General Motors Corporation and the United Automobile Workers* (1974).

Starobin, Joseph. *American Communism in Crisis, 1943-1957* (1972).

Stieber, Carolyn. *The Politics of Change in Michigan* (1970).

Sugar, Maurice. *The Ford Hunger March* (1980).

Sward, Keith. *The Legend of Henry Ford* (1948).

Tentler, Leslie Woodcock. *Wage-Earning Women: Industrial Work and Family Life in the United States, 1900-1930* (1979).

Tull, Charles. *Father Coughlin and the New Deal* (1965).

Weinstein, James. *The Decline of Socialism in the United States, 1912-1925* (1967). *The Corporate Ideal in the Liberal State: 1900-1918* (1968).

Widick, B.J. *Labor Today: The Triumphs and Failures of Unionism in the United States* (1964). *Detroit: City of Race and Class Violence* (1972). Ed., *Autowork and Its Discontents* (1976). With Irving Howe, *The UAW and Walter Reuther* (1949).

Wood, Arthur. *Hamtramck* (1974).

Zunz, Olivier. *The Changing Face of Inequality: Urbanization, Industrial Development, and Immigrants in Detroit, 1880-1920* (1982).

Interviews

Alfaro, Jose
Alpert, Bob
Astel, Madeline
Battle, Robert "Buddy"
Beber, Lavina
Beltram, Olga
Berthelot, Helen
Bertram, Walter
Bluestone, Irving
Boatin, Paul
Bowers, Helen
Brown, June Tolan
Brown, Wanda
Carter, Jean
Cassily, Estelle Gornie
Cook, Louis
Covintree, George*
Creason, Ted
Deremo, Dottie
Duda, Walter
Dewey, Charles
Farr, Florence
Fletcher, Barbara
Fouche, Alton
Fraser, Doug
Gazen, Max
Gelles, Catherine "Bebe"
Grey, David
Haggerty, Martin

Hewgley, Charles
Hickson, Lewis
Jacobs, David
Johnson, Mackie
Julin, Rich
Kapuscinski, Ted
Kaystead, Mary
Kern, Fr. Clement
King, Bob
Kummer, Don
Langston, Clay*
Lester, Harry
Llewellyn, Percy
Loew, Floyd
Lopez, Elisa
Lumpkin, Tom*
Marchone, Fran
Marshall, Bill
Mason, Hodges
Mauer, Helen**
McManus, Pete
Merrelli, George
Milleski, Bill
Moore, Dave
Murphy, Justine
Murphy, Lou
Nowaczewski, Phoebe
Nowak, Margaret
Nowak, Stanley

Oreste, Marie
Paige, Laura
Parmen, Audrey
Piwkowski, Helen
Pittman, Monique
Riordan, Mary Ellen
Ruffin, Leona**
Sarrach, Willard
Servitto, Mary Ellen
Sheffield, Horace
Silver, Paul
Spinks, Dan
Stamps, Willie
Susselman, Susan
Sweeney, Florence
Tappes, Shelton
Turner, Tom
Van Horn, Edie
Verhaeghe, Al
Walker, Flora
Watroba, David
Westphall, Charles
Wilder, Fred
Williams, Gloria
Worley, Doyle
Yochim, Elizabeth
Younglove, Charles
Zellar, Jack
Zipser, Ernie

* Phone interview.
** Interviewee wished to use a fictional name.

BUNKER HILL COMMUNITY COLLEGE

3 6189 00010 1716

LIBRARY
BUNKER HILL COMMUNITY COLLEGE
CHARLESTOWN, MASS. 02129

#10777172